LONDON AND THE OUTBREAK OF THE PURITAN REVOLUTION:

City Government and National Politics, 1625-43

Oxford University Press, Amen House, London E.C.4

GLASGOW NEW YORK TORONTO MELBOURNE WELLINGTON
BOMBAY CALCUTTA MADRAS KARACHI LAHORE DACCA
CAPE TOWN SALISBURY NAIROBI IBADAN ACCRA
KUALA LUMPUR HONG KONG

First edition set and printed by The Camelot Press Ltd.
London & Southampton, published 1961

Second impression reprinted lithographically
at the University Press, Oxford
from corrected sheets of the first edition
1964

London
and the Outbreak
of the Puritan Revolution

CITY GOVERNMENT AND
NATIONAL POLITICS, 1625–43

Valerie Pearl

OXFORD UNIVERSITY PRESS

PREFACE

I WISH to thank the Principals and Fellows of St. Anne's and St. Hugh's Colleges, Oxford, the Trustees of the Eileen Power Studentship, and the Worshipful Company of Fishmongers, for the research studentships and awards which made it possible to undertake this work at Oxford.

Much of the research was done at the Guildhall Library and Record Office of the City of London, and I am grateful for the patient help and advice of Mr. P. E. Jones, Deputy Keeper of the Records, Dr. A. E. J. Hollaender, Assistant Librarian, and other members of the staff. I must also thank the many other libraries in Oxford and London from whom I have received help. I have benefited from discussions with Mr. T. F. Reddaway, Mr. J. Safford, Dr. C. V. Wedgwood, Professor C. M. Williams, and Miss D. Williams. Professor R. H. Tawney read an earlier draft of the work; like so many students, I am indebted to him and also to Professor W. Notestein for advice and suggestions arising in both from a lifetime of scholarship devoted to the period. I am most grateful to Mr. Christopher Hill for his invaluable help from the earliest days of this work and for reading the typescript. I am also greatly indebted to Professor H. R. Trevor-Roper, who made valuable suggestions about the plan of the book. I have benefited very much, as have many others, from his encouragement and his generosity in sharing ideas and suggesting sources. Above all, my greatest debt is to my husband. The interpretation which I present in this book and any errors in it which remain are my own.

I have modernized the spelling, punctuation, and capitalization of quotations, but not of titles of books and pamphlets.

V. P.

October 1959

To my Mother
and Father

ABBREVIATIONS

Add. MSS.	Additional manuscripts.
Am. H.R.	*American Historical Review.*
C.C.C.	*Calendar of the Committee for Compounding.*
C.C. for A.M.	*Calendar of the Committee for Advance of Money.*
Chamb.Acc.	Chamberlain's Accounts.
Co.H.Bk.	Common Hall Book.
C.J.	*Journal of the House of Commons.*
C.S.P.	*Clarendon State Papers.*
C.S.P.Col.	*Calendar State Papers, Colonial.*
C.S.P.D.	*Calendar State Papers, Domestic.*
D.N.B.	*Dictionary of National Biography.*
E.H.R.	*English Historical Review.*
Ec.H.R.	*Economic History Review.*
Harg.MSS.	Hargraves manuscripts.
Harl.MSS.	Harleian manuscripts.
H.M.C.	*Historical Manuscripts Commission.*
J.Co.Co.	Journal of Common Council.
Lans.MSS.	Lansdowne manuscripts.
L.Bk.	Letter Book.
L.J.	*Journal of the House of Lords.*
P.C.C.	Prerogative Court of Canterbury.
P.C.R.	Privy Council Register.
P.R.O.	Public Record Office.
Rem.	Remembrancia.
Rep.	Repertories of the aldermanic Bench.
S.P.Dom.	State Papers Domestic.
V.C.H.	*Victoria County History.*
V.M.Bk.	Vestry Minute Book.
V.S.P.	*Calendar State Papers, Venetian.*

CONTENTS

INTRODUCTION   1

I. THE GROWTH OF LONDON: A PROBLEM IN
    GOVERNMENT   9
    The effects of London's growth   13
    *The problem of new buildings and the policy of the
        City*   17
    The problems of the liberties and outparishes   23
    *The powers of the municipal Justices of the Peace
        over the liberties and outparishes*   30
    The Incorporation of the Suburbs   31
    The impending crisis: the problem re-stated   37

II. THE CONSTITUTION OF THE CITY OF
     LONDON   45
    Common Hall   50
    Court of Common Council   53
    Court of Aldermen   59
    Leading Officers of the municipality   62

III. THE CITY GOVERNMENT AND THE CROWN,
      1625-40   69
    1625-30   72
    1631-8   79
    The crisis of 1639 and 1640   91

IV. THE CONSTITUTIONAL CRISIS, 1640-2   107

V. THE CITY PARLIAMENTARY PURITANS
    BEFORE THE LONG PARLIAMENT   160
    The City Members of Parliament   176
    The representation of the municipality in Parliament   193

VI. THE CITY MEMBERS OF PARLIAMENT AND
         THE CITIZENS, 1640-2   197
      *The City Members and the problem of financing the
         Long Parliament*   197
      *The City Members, church reform, and the citizens'
         petitions*   210
      How the citizens were organized   228

VII. THE NEW COURSE, 1642-3   237
      The New Men   240
      The municipality and constitutional reform, 1642-3 246
      The municipality and Parliament, 1642-3   250

CONCLUSION   276

APPENDIX I. THE ALDERMEN, OCTOBER
         1640-DECEMBER 1641   285

APPENDIX II. THE NEW MEN   309

APPENDIX III. THE CHAMBER OF LONDON   332

BIBLIOGRAPHICAL NOTE I. MANUSCRIPT
         SOURCES   339

BIBLIOGRAPHICAL NOTE II. COMMON
         COUNCIL ELECTION RETURNS   344

INDEX   347

Introduction

SEVENTEENTH-CENTURY historians and letter-writers, especially those of Royalist sympathies, frequently described the City of London as the instigator of the troubles of the Civil War. What Clarendon called 'the sink of the ill-humours of this kingdom'[1] was the subject of abuse for its rebellious activities by a host of less eminent commentators. 'Could Saye or Pym and their beggarly confederates', wrote one of them, 'have found money to levy an army against their liege lord, that had not money to pay their own debts, had not London . . . furnished them? . . . If . . . posterity shall ask . . . who would have pulled the crown from the King's head, taken the government off the hinges, dissolved Monarchy, enslaved the laws, and ruined their country; say, 'twas the proud, unthankful, schismatical, rebellious, bloody City of London . . .'[2] A few seventeenth-century historians hinted at more complex struggles, taking place amid a clash of groups and interests in London and preventing the City from speaking with a single voice; John Nalson,[3] for instance, was eager to assert that the respectable, wealthy citizens, including the Lord Mayor and Aldermen, supported the crown, while the allies of Parliament were to be found amongst the 'mechanic citizens' and the 'rabble'. But, nevertheless, the more characteristic account to appear in contemporary writers described the City, in alliance with Pym, as the King's main antagonist—the villain, in fact, in a Stuart melodrama.

Nineteenth-century historians, influenced by the Whig interpretation of history, were eager to assume that the City of London under the impact of its growing commercial hegemony, had allied itself in the seventeenth century with the side of progress, and adopted the same *simpliste* view of the City's part in the early years of the Long Parliament. J. Forster, in his

[1] W. D. Macray, ed. *History of the Rebellion and Civil Wars in England*, Oxford, 1888, Bk. iii. 57.

[2] *A Letter from Mercurius Civicus to Mercurius Rusticus: Or London's Confession, but not Repentance* . . . 1643, in Somers Tracts, 1748-52, i, p. 419.

[3] *An Impartial Collection of the Great Affairs of State, from the beginning of the Scotch Rebellion in the year 1639 to the murder of King Charles I*, 1682, passim.

Arrest of the Five Members, put the accepted view in a characteristic way: 'when the cause of public freedom was in peril, the City of London cast in its fortunes unreservedly with the opposition to the Court'.[4] R. R. Sharpe in *London and the Kingdom*[5] assumed that the municipality[6] sided with Parliament from 1640; this underlay his representation of events. Thus, he did not draw a distinction between the declarations of the citizens and those of the municipal government. His failure to make this distinction led him to refer to the citizens' declaration of November 12 1641 against the Bishops retaining their seats in the House of Lords, as though it came from the City government.[7] S. R. Gardiner in *The History of England, 1603-1642* had also failed to make this distinction in some parts of his narrative and had called this declaration against the Bishops, 'the turning point in the struggle'[8], as though the municipality had supported the declaration. Nevertheless, both Gardiner and Sharpe recognized that towards the end of 1641 there was an influential section of the aldermanic Bench that was sympathetic to the crown, even though they did not substantiate their statement fully. For this view, they had the support of Leopold von Ranke in *A History of England* . . . a lone voice for his time, who had recognized that royalism was strong in the municipality towards the end of 1641. Gardiner and Sharpe, however, did not adopt his further suggestion that these events in the City 'would be worth a searching investigation'.[9]

More recent historians, however, who have treated the problem, have neglected these hints and have accepted completely the Whiggish view of the part played by the City in this period. A German historian, Emil Andler, in *Die Beteiligung der stadt London am streit zwischen Karl I und dem Langen Parliament* . . . *1640-1644*[10] concluded that not only the citizens, but the City government including a majority of the Aldermen

4 *Arrest of the Five Members*, 1860, p. 256.

5 1894-5, 3 vols.

6 I have avoided the term "corporation" since the City of London, owing its status to immemorial custom, was never granted a charter of incorporation.

7 Sharpe, op. cit., ii, p. 147.

8 1883-4, x, p. 71.

9 *A History of England principally in the seventeenth century*, Oxford, 1875, ii, p. 308.

10 Ravensburg, 1906, *passim*.

supported Parliament throughout 1641. C. H. Firth in his article 'London during the Civil War'[11] stated that 'all classes in London manifested their hostility to the crown' in 1641. Melvin. C. Wren in his article 'The Disputed Elections in London in 1641'[12] attacked Gardiner for falling into the assumption that the Aldermen as a body would side with Charles and the Peers. 'The Court of Aldermen', he wrote, 'as a body, of course, cast their lot with Parliament.' He asserted that the City's attitude towards Charles I changed gradually to opposition from 1625 onwards, and concluded, '. . . the City, like the Kingdom, could not in January 1649, point back to any one time when its attitude towards its King had changed. . . . For that reason, the student who looks for violent or radical change in 1641 must be disappointed.' One of the purposes of this work is to show that on the contrary Charles I enjoyed throughout his reign[13] a small but powerful nucleus of support in the City government, that in particular the most influential section of the aldermanic Bench and probably of the Court of Common Council, although unwilling to commit themselves to support Charles in 1640, preferred to back the crown by the autumn of 1641 and that substantial changes in the City government were needed to give power to the supporters of Parliament.

It might appear at first that what seems to be a grave difference of opinion between historians on the attitude of the municipality towards King and Parliament in 1641 and 1642, might be resolved to some extent by a clearer definition of terms. The failure to draw a distinction between the acts and declarations of the citizens, and of the municipality, has considerably confused the issues, as we have seen; indeed, the editor of the *Calendar of State Papers* (vol. 1641-1643)[14] has rashly stated in his introduction that the questions dividing the nation in 1641

[11] *History*, 1926, xi, p. 26.

[12] *E.H.R.*, vol. lxiv, p. 35, n. 1. Wren's assumption that the municipality supported Parliament in 1641 appears clearly and without ambiguity in his unpublished Ph.D. thesis, 'London in the Revolution of 1648', Iowa Univ., U.S.A., 1941, *passim*.

[13] In this work, the years from Charles' accession to 1640 have been treated in outline, the years from 1640 to 1643 in detail. The evidence suggests that after 1643, in spite of the changes in City government, Charles still had a small body of supporters in the municipality.

[14] W. D. Hamilton, 1887, p. x.

were first thrashed out in the Court of Common Council, a statement for which there is no evidence in the municipal journals or elsewhere and which was presumably based on the assumption that the citizens' petitions (that abound in this volume) must have originated in the municipal councils. More is involved here, however, than confusion in terminology. Moreover, since both Emil Andler and Melvin C. Wren have asserted that the municipality gave its support to Parliament in 1641 and since they have used only a small part of the available evidence, their assumptions need to be examined again by a close study of the municipal archives in conjunction with the parliamentary diaries and journals of the time.

The general importance in the history of this period of determining the attitude of the City government to the breach between King and Parliament needs little elaboration. The attitude of the City government impinges directly on the central problems of the time: the politics of the Long Parliament, the party conflicts within it and the relations between the King and Parliament. J. H. Hexter in *The Reign of King Pym* has stated that, 'any writer on the politics of the Long Parliament will eventually feel the lack of a reputable and thorough study of London during the Rebellion. One political problem after another remains insoluble because of our ignorance of what actually went on in the councils of the City. Neither R. R. Sharpe's *London and the Kingdom* nor C. H. Firth's article, "London during the Civil War" . . . even approach the problems.'[15] This subject also impinges on the broader question of the attitude of the City mercantile community towards the King and Parliament and therefore colours our view of their relationship with Charles I during the 'eleven years tyranny', and with Parliament after 1641. The investigation of this problem throws light on our understanding of the governmental problems and privileges of the City, and the extent to which its favoured position drew it into dependence on the crown.

The problem of discovering the 'politics' of the City at this time is not a straightforward affair. The Journals of the Court of Aldermen and Common Council, like most official records of corporate bodies, can be annoyingly brief. The compilers of the records were concerned mainly with those decisions of

15 J. H. Hexter, *The Reign of King Pym*, Harvard Univ. Press, 1941, p. 95, n. 76.

the Court, to which reference would have to be made in the course of day to day administration. The debates that led up to these decisions, although so vastly interesting to historians, might only prove embarrassing to the City and the leading citizens if recorded in detail. Such was the feeling of the Court of Common Council in 1660 when it ceremoniously cancelled its entire proceedings for the Civil War years, so as to expunge the guilty record of its association after 1642 with the parliamentary cause. Fortunately for the historian, this cancellation was made by striking a line through the relevant pages, not by their removal and destruction, a wilful desire, perhaps, in this case, for some record to remain. Mingled with the welcome to the crown in 1660 and the fervent expressions of loyalty, there may well have been a desire to preserve some relics of London's independence and power.

In order to fill out the picture of City politics in these early years of the Long Parliament, a many-sided approach is needed. It is important to examine not only the official acts of the City government and the constitutional disputes of these years, which are recorded in the City journals, but the personnel of the City government and their connexions with the court and later with Parliament. At the same time, it is necessary to trace in the City and in the City government, the growth of an opposition party that finally took control of the City government in January 1642. This opposition I have called the 'parliamentary puritan' party. To have called them Puritan would have been inadequate, as some of the citizens who supported the parliamentary opposition did so for what were obviously political reasons. Those City merchants, like Samuel Vassall, Richard Chambers and John Fowke, who opposed tonnage and poundage and Ship Money, did so for the constitutional principles involved; many of these men were Puritans, but their opposition to Charles expressed itself in political terms rather than religious. Even the word 'Puritan' can be ambiguous at this time. Although it was still sometimes used in its original precise sense, of someone opposed to the hierarchy of the Church, it was also beginning to assume political overtones and the exact emphasis of the word was not always clear even to contemporaries. Since it is impossible in the case of most citizens to separate religious from political motivations (and contemporaries would have denied that any such clear distinctions existed), I have used the expression 'parliamentary puritan' as a general term for all those citizens who supported the parliamentary opposition from 1625 until the outbreak of the Civil War: the men denounced by their opponents as 'the Faction' or the 'Puritan Faction'. Similar difficulties arise in describing the politics and religion of the leading citizens in and after 1643. I have therefore used the controversial terms 'Presbyterian' and 'Independent' in their religious sense, and 'political presbyterians' and 'political independents' where political attitudes are being described. By 'political presbyterians', I refer to those who were later prepared to accept the King's third reply to the Newcastle propositions in May 1647, and who opposed the policy and the claims of the Army. By 'political independents', I mean those who did not wish to restore the King except on terms accepted by the Army.

One of the difficult but fascinating problems that this subject has raised is how the City parliamentary puritans were organized in these days before political parties as we know them had taken shape. The parliamentary puritans had no properly constituted political organization or fully responsible leaders in our present sense—and no formal records of their activities. Therefore, the historian has to look for evidence in the ordinary everyday associations of London citizens, their parishes, trading organizations and their centres of social activity. It was also in the nature of things that at a time when the crown suppressed organized groups that wished to reform any aspect of government and refused to countenance political or religious petitions, much activity had to be carried on by backstairs methods, leaving little trace for the historian. A saying attributed to John Preston, a leading figure in the Puritan movement in the sixteen-twenties, is almost too plain spoken and blunt for one of his sharp and subtle thought: 'when we would have any great things to be accomplished, the best policy is to work by an engine which the world sees nothing of.' Yet this is not an unfair description of the tactics forced on a movement that found no favour or expression in government policy, and which, with increasing repression, existed in a world of semi-legality. After the calling of the Long Parliament, the task is easier. The parliamentary puritan organization is carried on much more openly, now that it has the backing of Pym and the leaders of the House, and their work is visible in Parliament and in the City parishes and wards.

Another problem has been to define the politics of the Aldermen and wealthy citizens, who as merchants often found it unwise to commit themselves, and needed, more than any other class, to trim their sails to the winds. Even declared Royalists among the citizens found it difficult to leave London in 1642 to join the King. The financial sacrifice was too great. As leaders of trading companies, financiers, wholesale dealers and retailers, their world was the City and by leaving London they would lose their entire living. For men like Sir Nicholas Crispe with vast landed estates and industrial interests in other parts of the country, the sacrifice could be made. Most, however, stayed and suffered imprisonment rather than flee. Fortunately, contemporary comments in newsletters and in records of parliamentary committees for raising loans and assessments, and the Committee for Compounding, usually pinpoint the political attitude of the leading merchants and Aldermen in the City.

A problem that has always faced historians of the early years of the Civil War has been that of distinguishing fact from political bias in the books, pamphlets and newsbooks of the time. Some of the most well-known Royalist histories of the Civil War were written as late as the sixteen-eighties (such as the works of John Nalson, Sir William Dugdale and Anthony à Wood) and therefore their evidence can only be accepted if corroborated by reliable contemporary sources. Contemporaries who wrote of these events have always to be examined for exaggerations and prejudice, born of political passions and hatred. There was a small group of writers, of whom Peter Heylin is perhaps the best known, who attributed all responsibility for the Civil War to the factious Puritan citizens of London. These assertions, particularly those of two anonymous pamphlets in the Thomason Tracts, have been checked by an examination of the City's records and other sources, and have been found much more reliable than might at first have been expected. If checked in this way, a vast mine of information, hitherto inadequately used, still lies buried in the Thomason Tracts.

The theme of revolution in the City in 1642 inevitably arouses questions of wider historical interest. What was the nature of political power at this time when landowners with private armed retainers no longer existed and in the days before public police forces? What political consequences followed from the fact that governments had to rely on citizen militias for their defence? Or again, was this a class revolution? (Where, if not in London, would one expect to find evidence of the 'bourgeois revolution'?) Or was it just a matter of the 'court party' against 'the country party', the 'ins' versus the 'outs', those who monopolized offices in the City against those who sought them? Obviously such questions cannot be answered from a study of these years alone. Clearly, greater changes took place in 1649 than in 1642 in the City government and in the liveries and trading companies. Furthermore, a study of the economic interests of leading citizens throughout this period would be needed for definite answers to these questions. However, an understanding of the politics of the City from 1640 to 1643 throws some light into dark corners and goes a little way to suggest tentative answers to these problems. Such conclusions as emerge, derive, I hope, from the detailed analysis of what actually happened in the City in these years. The complex picture that results warns us against any facile use of historical categories for the history of the Civil War, but not, of course, against using these categories as hypotheses to be proved or rejected. The questions must be posed before they can be answered, and can only be answered at first in a piecemeal way. When the entire record of City politics between 1640 and 1660 has been uncovered, an admirable vantage-point will be gained from which to view the political struggles of the Interregnum, which may add immeasurably to our understanding of its character and its significance in English history.

CHAPTER I

The Growth of London: a Problem in Government

THE expansion of London within and beyond the walls is the most salient feature of the City's history in the sixteenth and seventeenth centuries. The rapidity with which buildings were shooting up and the speedy increase of population are chronicled in the literature of the time and in the works of contemporary historians; they are also delineated in the unrivalled series of maps which, beginning with Wyngaerde in the 1550s, continue to appear for the whole of this period. The panoramas of Visscher (1616) and Merian (1638) reveal the atmosphere of a thronging commercial city and a comparison of the maps of Speed and Norden with the mid-seventeenth century work of Wenceslaus Hollar, Richard Newcourt and William Faithorne, although an expert and difficult task, provides detailed information on the directions in which London was extending.[1]

For the purposes of the historian, however, who seeks to know the causes of this growth and the problems to which it gave rise, the famous 'Surveys of London', starting with John Stow, provide the most informative material. Stow, a working tailor, first conceived the idea of making a Survey of London from the example of the contemporary topographers, John Norden and William Camden, and particularly from William Lambarde's *Perambulation of Kent*.[2] The result of his work is a faithful account of the most characteristic features of the City as he knew it. The interest of the work does not stop at this, for the Survey was conscientiously extended, first by Anthony Munday, the official City chronologer, and by Humphrey

---

[1] For the caution which is necessary in comparing these early maps, see the discussion on the subject by W. Martin, *Transactions of the London and Middlesex Archeological Society*, 1917, N.S., vol. iii, pp. 255-86. An authoritative account of these maps is contained in *Panoramic Views of London, 1600-1666*, Irene Scouloudi, 1953. (Corporation of London, multilith.)

[2] John Stow, *A Survey of London*, 1603, ed. C. L. Kingsford, 1908, Oxford, i, p. xxxvi.

Dyson in 1618, by Munday again in the fourth edition of 1633, and finally by John Strype's fifth edition of 1720. *The Annales of England*, first published by Stow in 1592, also went through a series of editions in 1601 and 1605, and was continued by his literary executor, Edmund Howes, in 1614 and 1631. Although, as its sub-title shows, this work was designed to be 'A General Chronicle of England', both Stow and Howes could not refrain from making London the pivot of events and adding particular references to the City throughout their work.

The *Survay* and the *Annales*, in their successive editions, date the beginning of the real expansion of the City in the decades following the dissolution of the monasteries, although for two centuries previously there had been a steady overflow of poor craftsmen from the City into the suburbs[3] as well as 'foreigners' from other parts of the country. But the greatest impetus was given to the growth of the outparishes and the overcrowding of the suburbs when the pressure upon space created by the growing industry and trade of the metropolis filled up the empty places left by the dissolution within and outside the walls. Moreover, around this time London was attracting immigrants from the rest of England and from a continent distracted by religious wars. Howes, in 1631, gives us a view which is unusually sympathetic to alien residents. The houses which had stood empty since the dissolution, he writes, soon became filled with refugees from France and the Netherlands. This, together with the 'increase of our own nation', the growth of commerce, and intermarriage with foreigners, he saw as '. . . the main cause of our increase of wealth and great ships, the undiscernable and new building of goodly houses, shops, sheds and lodgings within the City in many vacant places, with the converting of the City bulwarks into houses of pleasure'. He ends his description of the enlarging of the suburbs with a list of these newly inhabited areas, '. . . namely, Ratcliff, Limehouse, Rederiffe [Rotherhithe], and St. Katherine's, the new buildings about the Tower Ditch, Houndsditch, Petty France, Long lane, Great St. Bartholomew's, Holborn, Chancery lane,

[3] In the seventeenth century, the term 'suburbs' in respect of London was used to denote all the areas adjoining the territory under City jurisdiction, including often those liberties outside the walls. I have used the word in this general sense where it is applicable. But where a more exact description is needed, I have used the terms 'outparishes' and 'liberties'.

and the Strand, Drury lane, now called the Prince's street, the west side of St. Martin's lane, the building about St. James' Park with other new increase of infinite buildings in Tothill Field, and on the south side of Westminster Abbey . . .'.[4]

From the various editions of the 'Surveys of London', it is possible to trace the early years of this expansion in some detail. It is clear, as Howes suggests, that some of the earliest expansion of building took place on monastic precincts in the decades immediately following the dissolution. In his first edition of the *Survay*, Stow describes the development to the north of the City walls where there was a cluster of monastic sites and liberties to attract builders: the precincts of the Priory of St. Bartholomew the Great, and St. Bartholomew's Hospital, Charterhouse, St. John's Priory and Clerkenwell Priory. To the north-east of the City, the Priory of St. Mary Spital had once stood secluded in green fields, where the citizens used to walk for recreation. Stow, *laudator temporis acti*, laments the changes that had overtaken them: 'This Hog [later Brick] lane stretcheth north toward St. Mary Spital without Bishopsgate, and within these forty years had on both sides fair hedgerows of elm trees, with bridges and easy stiles to pass over into the pleasant fields, very commodious for citizens therein to walk, shoot, and otherwise to recreate and refresh their dulled spirits in the sweet and wholesome air, which is now within [a] few years made a continual building throughout, of garden houses and small cottages; and the fields on either side be turned into garden plots, tenter yards,[5] bowling alleys, and such like, from Houndsditch in the west, so far as Whitechapel and further towards the east.'[6]

To the east of the Tower and of Aldersgate, there had been continual building that was already linking the City with the manors of Shadwell, Limehouse and Wapping. From Shadwell, according to Stow, 'there hath been of late, in place of elm trees, many small tenements raised, towards Ratcliff'.[7] The

---

[4] *The Annales, or Generall Chronicle of England*, augmented by Edmund Howes, 1615, p. 868.

[5] Tenteryards were open spaces used for the drying and stretching of cloth. Houndsditch had attracted gunfounders, another example of industry settling in the outparishes.

[6] Stow, *Survay*, i, p. 127.

[7] Ibid. ii, p. 71.

growth of commerce and overseas expansion brought into existence a seafaring and shipbuilding community to the east of the
City, and a new dock, the East India Company's at Blackwall,
built in 1614,[8] added to its importance: Stepney, with its har-
bours of Blackwall and Ratcliff, became, with Deptford, the
cradle of the Royal Navy. Stow remarks on the predominance of
seamen amongst the population, the houses of the sailors stretching from Ratcliff down to Poplar and beyond to Blackwall.[9]

Development westward of the City walls dates in the main
from the beginning of the Stuart period, although a fashionable area had already arisen north of the Strand around Drury
lane and Chancery lane where aristocrats and lawyers were
beginning to buy town houses. Under Charles I, a building
mania raged amongst the aristocracy and at court. Already,
Lincoln's Inn Fields, Long Acre, Great Queen street (named
after Henrietta Maria) and Covent Garden were being planned,
under the guidance of Inigo Jones, into commodious, brick-
fronted residences set amongst spacious squares. Edmund
Howes, writing before Inigo Jones had begun his most ambitious housing scheme in Lincoln's Inn Fields, tells us of the
earlier development in '. . . the west part of Holborn and
Bloomsbury, and the parts on that side . . . and from thence,
the new fair buildings called Queen's street leading unto Drury
lane, and then on the other side, the highway in the great field
anciently called Long Acre, with the south side of the street
called Covent Garden, that leadeth unto St. Martin's lane,
which is newly made a fair street . . .'.[10] But in these western
suburbs, there were slums intermingled with the new fashionable
districts. The Fleet river, now little more than an open

---

[8] N. G. Brett-James, *The Growth of Stuart London*, 1935, pp. 196-7.

[9] It should not be imagined that the east end of London was already a slum
quarter by the early seventeenth century. Other evidence suggests that the monastic sites surrounding the City walls and the liberties were becoming by far the
most populous areas. See the returns made to the Commissioners of New Buildings,
quoted below. In 1605, it was still possible for Edward Reynolds to write to a
friend, Thomas Rawlins, Sheriff of Essex, recommending him to convalesce after
an illness in the pure air of Limehouse. Brett-James, op. cit., p. 191. But by the
Restoration, Stepney, Wapping, Poplar and Ratcliff were becoming noted for
their slums, and the plague of 1665 took its greatest toll in Stepney. The customs
of the manors of Stepney and Hackney, by which copyholders were forbidden to
make leases for longer than thirty-one years, did not conduce to strong permanent
building. J. Strype, *Survay of London*, 1720, Bk. iv, p. 87.

[10] Edmund Howes, *The Annales*, p. 1048.

sewer,[11] contaminated the parishes on its banks. St. Bride's, St. Sepulchre's, St. Andrew's, Holborn, and St. Giles', Cripplegate, were already scarred with pestilential slum dwellings. The environs of Westminster were still mainly marshland, while it was from the slum quarters of St. Martin-in-the-Fields that the great plague was said to have started.[12]

Charles I's proclamations forbidding building on new foundations did not cause a slackening in the rate of expansion. A list prepared by the Lord Mayor for the Building Commissioners in 1638 of 'such as have compounded for buildings erected contrary to the proclamations', revealed that 1,361 houses had been compounded for since 1603.[13] Of these, 618 had been built to the west of the City, mainly in Drury lane and Long Acre in the parishes of St. Giles' and St. Martin-in-the-Fields, 404 had been built to the north, mainly in Clerkenwell, Bishopsgate Without, and St. Giles', Cripplegate, and to the east there were 282 houses newly built in and around Wapping. South of the river in Southwark, only fifty-seven buildings were recorded.[14] This list shows that the main area of building for the well-to-do was moving from the monastic sites of the north to the fields of St. Martin and St. Giles', linking the City to Westminster. Although the northern and eastern districts were developing less rapidly as residential areas, they were still expanding at a considerable rate. More houses in these areas were probably being built, especially for the poor, than is shown in this list, since new houses on which composition was not paid, were usually demolished by the Commissioners. There are many complaints in the State papers of houses being pulled down in this way in the northern and eastern suburbs.

THE EFFECTS OF LONDON'S GROWTH

All authorities agree that the relative growth of population in London was of a remarkable order, although the absolute figures are almost impossible to determine. Various estimates

[11] W. G. Bell, *The Great Plague of London in 1665*, 1924, p. 9.
[12] Ibid. p. 41.
[13] S.P.Dom. 16/408/65.
[14] As Southwark was within the City's jurisdiction, the activities of the City Sheriffs may well have led to many houses being demolished there. This may account for the small number of new houses mentioned in the list. Other evidence suggests that building south of the river was proceeding much faster than suggested here.

have been made, often mere guesses; some contemporaries as well as later writers calculated that the population had nearly doubled in the first sixty years of the seventeenth century, rising from a quarter of a million or rather less, at the beginning of the century to nearly half a million at the Restoration. It is probable that these figures were exaggerated, although the predominance of the metropolis and its phenomenal growth are not in doubt. Gregory King, one of the most acceptable of the early demographers, calculated, a generation later, at the end of the century, that Greater London's population was around half a million, a figure which modern scholarship has suggested should be reduced by about one-fifth. But in 1695, at the time of King's survey, Norwich, which had long contested with Bristol the honour of being the second city of the kingdom, is believed to have had about 29,000 inhabitants, and Bristol 20,000.[15]

The social and political effects of the expansion presented a host of new problems both to the Privy Council and the City government. The new concentrations of population were occurring in many areas where the jurisdiction of the City did not reach. John Strype describes such areas occupied by aliens: '. . . the streets and places where they ["strangers"] chiefly inhabited, were either in the suburbs, or in privileged places, as St. Martin's le Grand, Blackfriars, Clerkenwell, Turnmill street, St. John's street, High Holborn, the Duchy of Lancaster without Temple Bar, St. Katherine's, Holywell, Holywell street, Norton Folgate, Shoreditch, Hoxton, Whitechapel, Wapping and Southwark'.[16] Strype, in an antiquarian's aside, tells us that one of these places in the liberty of St. Katherine's, was known as Hangman's Gains, a 'strange corruption' of Hames and Guines, two French towns whose 'poor trades people' had been evacuated with the English when Calais fell.[17] There were various 'Returns of Aliens'[18] made at

[15] P. E. Jones and A. V. Judges, 'London Population in the late Seventeenth Century', *Ec.H.R.*, vi, 1935-6, pp. 45-65; D. V. Glass, 'Gregory King's Estimate of the Population of England and Wales, 1695', *Population Studies*, iii, 1949-50, pp. 338-75.

[16] Strype, op. cit., Bk. v, p. 299.

[17] Ibid.

[18] R. E. G. Kirk and E. F. Kirk, *Returns of Aliens dwelling in the city and suburbs of London*, Huguenot Soc. Pub. x (1900-1908), Parts 1-4, *passim*.

intervals throughout the sixteenth and early seventeenth centuries by the Lord Mayor or the Justices at the request of the Privy Council, sometimes prompted by popular xenophobia and stimulated by discontent caused by political and economic insecurity. From these returns it appears that the largest number of immigrants were weavers, tailors, silk throwsters and dyers, occupations which were subject to the economic vagaries and depressions of the cloth trade. Returns made in 1635 by the Lord Mayor reported 2,547 aliens in the City of London.[19] Another return made in 1639 by the Justices reported a total of 2,006 outside the City: 838 in Westminster, 830 'near the City of London' in Middlesex, and 338 in Southwark.[20] The returns of 1635 show that the districts on the edge of the City spilling into the suburbs had a special attraction for the immigrants. Over half of the foreigners were concentrated into three northern and eastern wards mostly outside the walls. Bishopsgate alone, merging into Spitalfields, had about one-third of all the aliens in the City. Here, as frequently found elsewhere in London, the great majority were weavers employed in domestic industry.[21]

From at least the early sixteenth century, partly as a result of the laxer imposition of apprenticeship regulations and the absence of municipal taxation, there had been a tendency for domestic industry to establish itself in the suburbs where it was often possible to escape the powers and penalties of the Livery Companies. By 1600, nearly all the leatherworkers and makers of felt hats had left the City and were living in Bermondsey, Southwark and Lambeth. By 1619 there were said to be only forty persons concerned in the leather industry working in the City, while there were over three thousand living outside the walls.[22] Many of the newer industries of the period were being attracted to the liberties and outparishes: sugar-refining and glassmaking around Stepney and Islington, alum and dye works

[19] S.P.Dom. 16/294/11; 16/302/35; 16/305/11.

[20] C.S.P.D. 1638-1639, vols. 414/96, 97, 139. The returns illustrate the familiar tendency for minorities to congregate in particular areas. It is necessary to be cautious, however, about the too-ready acceptance of over-all figures, where heads of families, complete families and even Englishmen working for foreigners were sometimes indiscriminately jumbled together.

[21] S.P.Dom. 16/305/11.

[22] G. Unwin, *Industrial Organisation in the Sixteenth and Seventeenth Centuries*, 1904, p. 128.

to the north and east of the City, and copper and brass mills at Isleworth. Large-scale industrial enterprises, such as ship-building at Rotherhithe and Deptford, and brewing in Clerken-well and Holborn, were also migrating to the suburbs. There were older industries too: brick- and tile-making in the northern outskirts (Islington with its brick kilns and its lawless popula-tion was notorious in Elizabeth's reign);[23] clock-making in Holborn and Westminster; bell-founding in Whitechapel; paper-making in Middlesex, while St. Giles', Cripplegate, was crowded with artisans of the weaving, printing and paper-making trades.[24] Thomas Mun, writing in the sixteen-twenties, described the concentration of workers in the silk industry and recalled how in the past thirty-five years, the winding and twisting of imported raw silk, which previously had employed not more than 300 people in the City and suburbs, had now 'set on work above fourteen thousand souls'.[25] The great majority of these would have been workers in the outskirts of London.

The concentration of population and the ever-present threat of unemployment, particularly amongst cloth-workers, brought with them social evils, such as famine in times of high prices, overcrowding, rack-renting and plague, which frequently led to disturbances and riots. The City had evolved methods of dealing with the poor and with vagrants within its own juris-diction, which were considerably advanced compared with the rest of the country. In 1570,[26] two Marshals, each with six beadles, had been appointed by order of the Privy Council to keep strict watch over the gates of the City from three o'clock to seven o'clock in the morning and from seven o'clock to eleven at night, to prevent the influx of beggars; infirm beggars found within the City were to be taken to St. Bar-tholomew's or St. Thomas's Hospitals, beggar children were to go to Christ's Hospital, sturdy beggars to Bridewell to be

[23] C. T. Onions, ed., *Shakespeare's England*, 1916, ii, p. 179.

[24] W. Page, ed., *V.C.H. Middlesex*, 1911, ii, pp. 128 seq.

[25] T. Mun, *England's Treasure by Forraign Trade*, 1664. Reprinted Oxford, 1928, p. 11. B. E. Supple, *Bulletin of the Institute of Historical Research*, xxvii, 1954, pp. 91 seq. But industry had not entirely migrated to the suburbs. See John Evelyn's account of limeburners, dyers, etc., who were still working in the City: *Fumi-fugium, or the inconvenience of the aer and smoak of London dissipated*, 1661, *passim*.

[26] Strype, op. cit., Bk. vi, pp. 431-3.

set on work, and lunatics to Bedlam. In contrast, the county of Middlesex did not acquire a House of Correction or a Prison House until 1614, when Hicks's Hall[27] was built in St. John's street, Clerkenwell. Moreover, the policing system in Middlesex, where parishes were far larger than in the City, was entirely inadequate; the City, on the other hand, could rely, to some extent, on its Trained Bands to suppress serious riots. The City's system of poor relief was also more highly organized. It provided for stocks of 'sea-coals'[28] to be sold at cheap rates in the winter for the benefit of the poor and obliged the Livery Companies, since the middle of the sixteenth century, to lay up stores of corn to be sold at cheap prices in times of scarcity and famine.[29] The Justices of Peace for Middlesex and Surrey could not deal similarly with their problems: they lacked the municipal organization and privileges of the City. The City magistrates were already alarmed by the situation in Elizabeth's reign; they realized that no amount of efficient organization within their jurisdiction would isolate them from their neighbours, and that vagrancy, overcrowding and plague[30] were bound to spill over into the City.

THE PROBLEM OF NEW BUILDINGS AND THE POLICY OF THE CITY

The problem which most immediately presented itself to the magistrates of the City was that concerned with the rapid growth of new building in and around London. The erection of cheap, shoddy dwellings, the conversion of great houses into

[27] The building was mostly financed by Sir Baptist Hickes, himself a Middlesex Justice of the Peace. It was to serve as a Sessions House and for the punishment of rogues and vagabonds. J. C. Jeaffreson, ed. *Middlesex County Records*, 1887, ii, pp. xxiii-xxiv.

[28] The City government was allowed to buy 4,000 chaldrons of coal at Newcastle-on-Tyne free of duty and tolls for this purpose. W. H. and H. C. Overall, ed., *Analytical Index to the Remembrancia*, 1878, p. 84. The Lord Mayors also frequently petitioned the Council to prevent the coal-owners of Newcastle from keeping up prices artificially. Ibid. pp. 78 seq.

[29] Ibid. pp. 383, 387-90. The Privy Council also kept close check on the Lord Mayor to see that he carried out his duty of modifying food prices.

[30] Outbreaks of plague usually started in the suburbs particularly in the marshy fenland to the north-west of the walls and from the parishes bordering on the Fleet river. Apart from overcrowding, the City's practice of burying its dead outside the walls exacerbated the insanitary conditions of the suburbs.

tenements, and the extortion of rack-rents, inevitably accompanied the increase in population. Stow does not hide his horror
at the practices of the greedy 'landlords and leasemongers' and
describes a row of almshouses in Russell's Row, Shoreditch,
originally the property of the Prior of the Hospital of St. Mary
Spital, where each tenant '. . . paid one penny rent by the
year at Christmas, and dined with the Prior on Christmas
Day'.[31] After the suppression of the Hospital, he tells of a
lamentable change: 'these houses for want of reparations, in
[a] few years were so decayed, that it was called Rotten Row,
and the poor worn out . . . houses, for a small portion of
money, were sold from Goddard to Russell, a Draper, who
new builded them and let them out for rent enough, taking
also large fines of the tenants, near as much as the houses cost
him purchase and building; for he made his bargains so hardly
with all men that . . . carpenter, bricklayer and plasterer were,
by that work, undone; and yet in honour of his name, it is
now called Russell's Row'.[32] Stow gives many examples of the
conversion of mansions, houses and palaces into tenements
and pleasure gardens, amongst them Oxford Place, Worcester
Place and 'The Garland' in Little Eastcheap. The gardens of
Northumberland House had been turned into bowling alleys
and dicing houses.[33] His complaints against profiteers who put
up shoddy buildings for gain were echoed in a tract denouncing housing speculators and the exorbitant rents they imposed. 'The desire of profit greatly increaseth buildings', wrote
the anonymous author, 'and so much the more, for that this
great concourse of all sorts of people drawing near unto the
City, every man seeketh out places, high-ways, lanes and covert
corners to build upon, if it be but sheds, cottages, and small
tenements for people to lodge in. . . . These sort of covetous
builders exact great rents, and daily do increase them in so much
that a poor handicraftsman is not able by his painful labours to
pay the rent of a small tenement and feed his family. . . .'[34]
    In 1580, the Lord Mayor drew up a remonstrance on new

[31] Survay, ed. Kingsford, ii, p. 74.
[32] Ibid. ii, pp. 74-75.
[33] Ibid. i, p. 149.
[34] 'A brief Discoverie of the great purpresture of newe Buyldinges neere to the
Cittie with the meanes howe to restraine the same . . .' Lansdowne MSS. 160,
fol. 90. Printed, Archaeologia 1831, vol. 23, pp. 121-9.

buildings and sent it to the Privy Council. He stated that the continual increase of new buildings in and around the City, the growing number of tenants, and the converting of large houses into tenements were becoming a danger not only to the metropolis, but to the kingdom at large. The Privy Council therefore issued a Proclamation against any building on new foundations, and for the next half-century the policy of the municipality and the Privy Council towards the growth of London was partly contained in legislation and proclamations against new building.

The Proclamation of 1580 set forth the evils that were likely to follow from excessive building; it prohibited, within three miles of the City gates, the erection of any new house or tenement on sites vacant within living memory; it also prohibited any increase in the number of families already inhabiting houses.[35] Although the City supported these orders, such hasty legislation may have made conditions worse rather than better: one consequence was the patching up of old buildings which might otherwise have been rebuilt in healthier surroundings. The Proclamation was followed by a Statute to which was added the proviso that the prohibition was not to apply to houses 'for the better sort of men', a clause which was dropped in some of the later legislation, to the dismay of the municipality. Neither the Act nor the Proclamation made it clear whether the Lord Mayor and his officials had power to operate in the liberties and outparishes; but it is plain from the precepts which the Lord Mayor issued in pursuance of the Proclamation that the City magistrates were to be responsible for enforcing its terms only within their own jurisdiction, and had no power to operate in the liberties and outparishes. In 1583, the Lord Mayor, in answer to a letter from Burghley asking for a schedule of new buildings, answered, '. . . They understood from his Lordship, that they were not to include any [houses] erected in the dissolved monasteries and other such places pretending exemption from the City's liberties, but that the same should rather be done by the Justices of Middlesex as parcel of that county'.[36] This ruling remained a grievance

[35] R. R. Steele, ed., *Bibliotheca Lindesiana. A bibliography of royal proclamations of the Tudor and Stuart sovereigns*, Oxford, 1910, i, no. 749.

[36] *Index to Remembrancia*, op. cit., p. 43.

with the municipality for the next fifty years. The terms of the original Proclamation were repeated in the Act of 1593, but they were to be in force for a period of seven years only.

No further Act was passed under James I, but during his reign eight proclamations were issued dealing with the subject of new buildings. New matters were now introduced which made the crown's policy even less acceptable to the City authorities. Commissioners especially chosen by the crown, in place of the Lord Mayor and senior Aldermen, were to be responsible for enforcing the proclamations and prosecuting the offenders in Star Chamber; the proclamations were to apply to all inhabitants, rich and poor alike (the City magistrates protested against this in a petition to the King in 1621); and a system was initiated by which offenders against the proclamations could compound for their offence on payment of a large fine. The King's letter to the Attorney-General in 1615, after stating the inconveniences of the new buildings and his determination not to let the offenders go unpunished, continued with a command for a Commission to be appointed to 'treat and compound' for fines with any who had broken the law by building in the City or within seven miles of it, 'since the first year' of his reign.[37] This policy was to prove most unpopular with the City magistrates, who realized that the principle of compounding or selling of licences would entirely undermine the efficacy of the proclamations. Later, in the sixteen-thirties, the City discovered that the activities of the Commissioners for Buildings who were appointed to issue licences and collect compositions were to give rise to an attack on certain of the City's chartered privileges.

The Privy Council's new policy was a financial expediency; its manner of operation brought it few friends and many enemies. These aspects of the proclamations became more pronounced and oppressive during the years of Charles I's rule without Parliament. In February 1634, George Garrard, soon to occupy the post of Master of Charterhouse, wrote to Strafford saying that it was expected that the Commission for Buildings, together with one appointed for licensing the sale of tobacco in and around London, would bring in 'a great sum of money

[37] *Acts of the Privy Council in England, 1615-1616*, pp. 121-2.

to his Majesty'.[38] It is not surprising that such Commissioners
themselves were heartily disliked. Writing again in October
1637, at a time of mounting political tension, Garrard spoke
of another Commission charged under an Elizabethan enactment against cottages without four acres of ground, the
enforcement of which particularly affected suburban cottage-
dwellers. It was looked upon by the poor as 'far more
burdensome than Ship Money', it benefited only courtiers; and
the 'mean and needy . . . men of no fame', even prisoners in
the Fleet, 'are used as principal Commissioners to call people
before them and compound with them'.[39] As part of the Stuart
policy of reviving royal claims to ancient feudal rights, an
attack was made at the same time on the City's traditional
claim to exact fines for building on the streets, wastes and
public places within the area of the City's jurisdiction.
This attack was closely linked with the crown's policy of compounding for new building, and was probably suggested by it.
The possibilities of profit from this privilege and from widen-
ing the sphere of activities of the Building Commissioners were
expressed in a paper sent by Christopher Vernon to the
Attorney-General, Sir John Bankes, in October 1635. It was
entitled 'Mr. Vernon's observations touching the Greenwax[40]
and the wastes and purprestures within the City with some
other encroachments without warrant'. Vernon pointed out
that there was a legal flaw in the City's grant, since the Charter
of 23 Henry VI, by which the City claimed its right, had been
declared void by a statute passed in 28 Henry VI.[41] The potential value of the privilege was considerable, he claimed. Upon
'a superficial estimate', it was worth £4,000 a year, but if the
rents were raised, the return would be at least £40,000. He
warned the King not to give the City 'a firm grant', since
without it they had lately exacted a penny a foot from those
who had enlarged their foundations or otherwise extended
their buildings in accordance with the proclamations. The City
had also extended its claim to the new building on Tower Hill.

[38] W. Knowler, ed., *The Earl of Strafforde's Letters and Dispatches*, 1739, i, p. 206.
[39] Ibid. ii, p. 117.
[40] See Chapter III, p. 84, n. 64.

[41] George Norton, *Commentaries on the History, Constitution and Chartered Franchises
of the City of London*, 1869, p. 372, n. 2.

C

'What would they do', asked Vernon, 'if they had a firm grant from the crown?'[42]

Although the City's grant of 23 Henry VI, which was cancelled five years later, had been confirmed again by charter in Parliament in 1507, and by subsequent charters, Charles I followed the policy of his predecessor[43] and declared the City's title void. The value which the City placed on this privilege emerges, as will be shown later, from the negotiations with the crown between 1635 and 1638 concerning the City's title to the Irish Estates. In June 1636, the City offered to give Charles £100,000 spread over five years, in return for the renewal of certain privileges, amongst which was the desire 'that they may have the waste grounds and buildings thereupon within the City and liberties'.[44] These negotiations fell through but, in 1638 when the crown was faced with the financial crisis caused by the Scottish war, the City in return for a grant of £12,000 to the King, was permitted to draw up a list of 'Things desired . . . for strengthening of Government'[45] as a basis for the grant of a new charter. Clauses 16 and 17 again stated the City claim, and the Charter of 1638 confirmed the privilege to the City in full.[46]

Although this Charter settled the dispute concerning the City wastes and purprestures, it by no means reconciled the City to Charles' policy of compounding for houses built on new foundations. In January 1639, the Court of Aldermen ordered the Remembrancer to petition the King 'for restraint of the buildings now erecting in Lincoln's Inn Fields'.[47] In June 1640, the Court of Aldermen agreed to pay half the fine of Edward Brooke, whose shop, a City property, had been pulled down by the Building Commissioners because it adjoined the east end of the Church of St. Michael, Queen street.[48] After the opening of the Long Parliament, the first

[42] Bankes Papers, MSS. 50/50.
[43] James I had also attacked the City's claim. Rem. iv, fol. 126.
[44] J.Co.Co. 37, fols. 202-2v.
[45] Ibid. 38, fols. 103-7. The Bankes Papers contain an identical list, with a note appended that the Attorney-General has been ordered to prepare a Bill to be presented to the King for his signature. MS. 48/9. See Chapter III, p. 86n.
[46] W. de Grey Birch, *The Historical Charters and Constitutional Documents of the City of London*, 1884, pp. 159 seq.
[47] Rep. 53, fol. 59v.
[48] Rep. 54, fol. 196v.

Bill mentioned in the Chamberlain's Accounts as preferred to the House of Commons on behalf of the City was one 'for preventing the erection of new buildings in and about this City and for the provision of the poor in cottages new erected'.[49] There is no detailed record of the further stages of the Bill,[50] but from the clause of the Grand Remonstrance which complains of 'the sale of pretended nuisances in and about London', it is clear that the municipality's principal objection was to the policy of compounding.

THE PROBLEMS OF THE LIBERTIES AND OUTPARISHES

Even if the City government's policy towards building had been carried out, it could not have proved a panacea for the complicated political, social and economic problems that arose from London's rapid expansion. More far-reaching remedies were, however, vitiated by anomalies in the functioning of City government, and by the conflict of political, industrial and commercial interests within the City.

The weakest link of City government, long before the Reformation, had been the exclusion of City jurisdiction from the liberties, that is to say, from the private franchises within the walls and bars of the City which were in the hands of lay or ecclesiastical owners.[51] The majority of the twenty-three religious houses in and around the City before the dissolution of the monasteries formed a ring around the City walls and within the bars, stretching from the Hospital of St. Katherine's by Thames-side, east of the Tower and the Minories to a cluster of priories and nunneries in Clerkenwell, from there to St. Bartholomew's Hospital and Priory, then west to Whitefriars, and across the river to St. Mary Overies in Southwark. Within the walls, there were Blackfriars, the Royal Free Chapel and Sanctuary of St. Martin's le Grand, the Priory of Holy Trinity

[49] Chamberlain's Accounts, 1640-1, fol. 51.

[50] On June 14 1642, Common Council petitioned Parliament to make an order, while their Bill was in preparation, that no houses be built on new foundations within three miles of the City, and that no houses either in the City or without be built of timber or be subdivided, i.e. a reiteration of royal policy, except on the subject of compounding. J.Co.Co. 40, fol. 33.

[51] E. J. Davies, 'The Transformation of London', *Tudor Studies presented to A. F. Pollard*, ed. R. W. Seton-Watson, 1924, pp. 299 seq.

Aldgate, the Grey Friars, the Priory of the Austin Friars, the Crutched Friars and the Priory of Elsing Spital. Beyond the walls and the bars there were also the non-monastic liberties and precincts: the Duchy of Lancaster in the Savoy, the liberty of the Rolls, Ely House or Rents, and Norton Folgate. Within the City limits there were St. Paul's and the Inns of Court. The inhabitants of all these precincts were in some important respects exempt from the jurisdiction of the Lord Mayor and from the legislation of Common Council.

The dissolution of the monasteries brought about the transference to the King of the franchises and temporal jurisdictions of the religious houses. The City was not unaware of the opportunity to extend its jurisdiction in these areas, and it made a series of offers to the crown to purchase the lands, houses and churches of the Friars. Henry VIII dismissed the offers and denounced the City as 'pinchpence'.[52] Efforts to secure from Henry VIII and Edward VI the possession and re-establishment of the former monastic hospitals were more successful.[53] Meanwhile, many of the liberties with the houses and lands of the previous monastic owners had been sold to lay owners. Eight churches were converted to secular uses.[54] Stow voices his indignation at one such conversion of the Austin Friars. Sir William Paulet used the steeple and choir 'for stowage of corn, coal and other things'; his son, the Marquis of Winchester, sold the monuments and turned part of the buildings into stables.[55] Ultimately Austin Friars and four other religious houses became for a time splendid mansions: Charterhouse, St. Bartholomew's Priory, Christ Church, Aldgate, and Crutched Friars. Some of them were made into storehouses or factories. Glassworks were established at the Black, White and Crutched Friars, the Minories became an armoury, St. John's, Clerkenwell, was turned into a storehouse for the King's hunting-nets and tents, while St. Mary Graces was used as a depot for naval stores.[56]

[52] R. R. Sharpe, op. cit., i, p. 406.

[53] E. J. Davies, op. cit., p. 302. See also *John Howes' MS., 1582*, ed. William Lempriere, 1904, *passim*.

[54] Holy Trinity Aldgate, St. Martin's le Grand, Bethlehem Hospital, St. Mary Spital, St. Mary Graces, and the Black, White and Crutched Friars.

[55] *Survay*, ed. Kingsford, i, pp. 176-7.

[56] E. J. Davies, op. cit., p. 305.

The City did not get another opportunity of acquiring the spoils until the reign of James I. Before then, the crown's alienation to private owners of many of the precincts had seriously exacerbated the problem of governing the City. Prior to the Reformation, the immunities of the precincts had made them centres of 'foreign' and alien craftsmen and traders. As we have seen, the immigrants of Elizabeth's reign were also attracted to these areas, where the concentration of population and the ensuing social evils of overcrowding, bad sanitation, vagrancy and disorder became notorious.

In the precinct of St. Martin's le Grand in the time of Elizabeth, the inhabitants of the liberty were chiefly French, German, Dutch and Scotch, while the trades carried on were those of shoemakers, tailors, button and button-mould-makers, goldsmiths, pouch-makers, stationers, silk-weavers and throwsters.[57] According to Stow, the precinct was being built over at a great rate to provide houses at high rents for these foreigners.[58] Its government belonged to the Dean and Chapter of Westminster, who were engaged in frequent disputes with the City over the limits of their respective jurisdictions. In 1593, the inhabitants petitioned Burghley against the 'search' by officers of the Cordwainers' Company who had inspected wares without calling the 'officer of the liberty', or even deigning to inform him and who, when reproved, had asserted that they would do the same again. Burghley's lawyers upheld the right of the Livery Company to enter the liberty 'and search alone', but they replied in diplomatic tones: it would be 'convenient' for the officer of the liberty to accompany the 'search' and this could be obtained by writing to the Lord Mayor.[59] The parishes neighbouring on St. Martin's frequently found themselves inconvenienced by its immunities. A neighbouring wardmote complained in 1614 that St. Martin's was sweeping its 'filth and soil' into other parishes; a further complaint was made about the new building in St. Martin's lane, the southern end of which was outside the precinct in Aldersgate Ward:

[57] Strype, op. cit., Bk. iii, p. 111.

[58] Survay, ed. Kingsford, i, p. 306.

[59] A. J. Kempe, *Historical Notices of the Collegiate Church or Royal Free Chapel and Sanctuary of St. Martin-le-Grand*, 1825, p. 169, quoting Lansdowne MSS., no. 74, article 32.

this enabled all men to 'buy and sell' as if they were in St. Martin's to the violation 'of the liberties of this City'.[60]

The same general features were reproduced in the history of the other precincts: a population of 'foreigners' and aliens attracted by its immunities, rapid house and tenement building, and frequent disputes with the City over jurisdiction. The Royal Hospital and Collegiate Church of St. Katherine near the Tower was engaged in the fifteen-sixties in a dispute with the inhabitants of the precinct, when Dr. Wilson, the Master, lent a favourable ear to the City's proposal that he should sell them the Hospital's right to hold a fair. The inhabitants protested angrily against this proposal because they did not want to become subject to the regulations and taxes of the City.[61] According to Maitland, 425 aliens were living in this precinct in 1567.[62] In the Minories, the Ironmongers' and Cutlers' Companies, in a petition that 'foreigners' might be forced to bring iron wares into Guildhall, jointly complained that 'houses or chambers' had been taken 'in the Minories (a privileged place)' for the sale of their products 'to the deceit of his Majesty's subjects'.[63] On at least two occasions in the early seventeenth century, the inhabitants of the Minories had asserted their independence of the City, and under James II they were formally declared to be part of the Tower Liberties.[64]

The disputes between the City and the Rich family, the owners of the Priory, West Smithfield, were frequent and prolonged.[65] The remunerative tolls accruing from the fair of St. Bartholomew's were the subject of conflict between the City and the owner in 1596. In the following year, the inhabitants of the liberty refused to obey the Lord Mayor's precept for the levy of soldiers, but were answered by the Privy Council in a letter to Lord Robert Rich that 'in these public services the liberty gave no such exemptions'.[66] It had been the custom

---

[60] William Mcmurray, ed., *The Records of two City Parishes . . . SS. Anne and Agnes Aldersgate, and St. John Zachary*, London, 1925, pp. 83-84, quoting Guildhall MSS. 1502.

[61] F. S. Lea, *The Royal Hospital and Collegiate Church of Saint Katherine near the Tower*, 1878, pp. 56-57.

[62] W. Maitland, *The History of London . . .*, 1756, i, p. 257.

[63] Rem. vol. vi. fol. 24.

[64] E. M. Tomlinson, *A History of the Minories*, London, 1907, pp. 176 seq.

[65] E. A. Webb, *The Records of St. Bartholomew's Priory*, 1921, ii, pp. 209-10.

[66] *Acts of the Privy Council*, vol. 27, p. 128.

for the crown to authorize the City to collect subsidies and raise the militia in the liberties, and this duty was specifically imposed on the City by James I's second charter in 1608.[67] But the crown never countenanced the City's intrusion in these areas for any other purpose.[68] In 1624, the Privy Council ordered the Lord Mayor not to encroach on the franchises of Henry Rich, Earl of Holland, in the liberty of St. Bartholomew the Great, while the owner was in France negotiating the marriage treaty with Henrietta Maria.[69] In 1630, the Council dismissed the dispute between the City and the Earl of Holland over St. Bartholomew's by reason of the Earl's absence.[70]

In addition to the liberties that had a monastic origin, there were problems connected with the other lay and ecclesiastical franchises within and surrounding the City. Conflicts with the Tower Liberties had a very early origin, based on the natural fears of the City at the proximity of an impregnable royal fortress. The questions concerned with the Lieutenant's claims for his officers, of freedom of arrest in the City, and the right to ignore writs of habeas corpus, were decided against him by a judgment of 1585.[71] But the endless disputes over boundaries continued for a century, until the privileged status of the Tower Hamlets was again confirmed by James II.[72] The problems of the other liberties were, in comparison, minor ones for the City government. There were the Inns of Court and Chancery which were all locally included within the boundaries of the City, but which were nevertheless outside City jurisdiction and excluded from its franchises. The Duchy of Lancaster in the Savoy was governed on a manorial basis by a Court Leet, which was conducted by a Bailiff, four Burgesses and four Assistants who were chosen by it for life.

Adjacent to the City there was, of course, the City of

---

[67] W. de G. Birch, op. cit., pp. 139 seq.

[68] Except in the case of the particular grants made to the City by the Charter of 1608. See below p. 30.

[69] E. A. Webb, op. cit., ii, p. 209.

[70] C.S.P.D., 1629-1631, vol. 167/6.

[71] Index to Remembrancia, op. cit., p. 426.

[72] In 1644, the City government petitioned Parliament for the right to appoint the Lieutenant of the Tower and the officers of the Tower liberties, but its proposals never became law. J.Co.Co. 40, fol. 109v.

Westminister, whose authority in no way rivalled that of London. It was governed by a High Steward, chosen by the Dean and Chapter of Weŝtminster who, in turn, in accordance with Burghley's constitution of 1585, chose twelve Burgesses and twelve Assistants for Westminster's twelve wards. The powers of the Burgesses and the Assistants, however, had been strictly limited, for Burghley had taken care not to establish another powerful independent municipality at the gates of the royal palace.[73] The jurisdiction of the City of London in the Borough of Southwark presented special problems of its own. From the time of Edward III, the City had had vague powers of Bailiff over what was known as the gildable manor of Southwark. By the charters of 1406, 1443 and 1462, the City's jurisdictional powers were increased; the charter of Edward IV gave to the City full powers of the view of frankpledge, of treasure trove, escheats, forfeitures, and all the liberties which had belonged to the crown in the Borough, excluding those in the tenure of the Archbishop of Canterbury.[74] In 1550, the City purchased the full rights of the crown in Southwark, including the King's manor, the Great Liberty manor, and the lands of the Duke of Suffolk and of the Archbishop for the sum of £647. 2s. 1d., but with the exclusion of Suffolk Place, the Clink Liberty and Paris Garden.[75] Although Southwark was subsequently created the twenty-sixth ward of Bridge Without, it retained its manorial status, and was denied representation in the Court of Common Council or the power of electing its own Alderman. In 1558, an earlier Act allowing the inhabitants to choose their Alderman was repealed. The inhabitants of Southwark considered their position oppressive, and their discontent became politically significant in 1647 when they opened the gates of the Bridge to Fairfax's army. The City's purchase did not prevent disputes between the Justices of Peace for Surrey and the City government about responsibility for holding musters and their respective spheres of duty as Justices.[76] The City was engaged in further disputes arising from the

[73] The authority of the Middlesex J.P.s was expressly preserved over Westminster. A separate commission of the peace was not issued until the Restoration. S. and B. Webb, *English Local Government* . . . , 1906, i, pp. 213 seq.

[74] H. E. Malden, ed. *V.C.H., Surrey*, 1912, p. 137.

[75] Norton, op. cit., pp. 386 seq.

[76] Rem. i, fols. 545, 569, 571, 579.

government of Southwark, over the excluded area of Suffolk Place or the liberty of the Mint,[77] and from the anomalous status of Paris Garden[78] and the Clink.

The government of the outparishes did not present such immediate problems to the municipality as the liberties, although the housing conditions and lawlessness in these 'suburban areas' were troublesome enough, even if less disturbing than in the liberties. The outparishes did not lie so close to the municipality's jurisdiction. In the parishes north of the Thames, the Justices of the Peace for Middlesex were responsible for preserving law and order; in the late sixteenth and early seventeenth centuries, particularly, the Privy Council took some pains to see that the Middlesex Bench was efficient; as far as can be judged from the frequency of their prosecutions, they were reasonably active, and their authority and prestige were increased by the building of Hicks's Hall as a Sessions House. But the ancient system of vestry officials and constables could hardly have satisfied the needs of this rapidly expanding area, and the powers of local government were little exercised, particularly in the large parishes to the east, Stepney and beyond. South of the Thames, the Justices of the Peace for Surrey appear to have been less well organized than in Middlesex; but the river, which could be crossed on foot only by London Bridge, acted as a barrier between the populations of Lambeth, Southwark and Bermondsey, and the inhabitants of the City, although there was, of course, a large water traffic. The problems of the outparishes could not be confined within county borders, and the municipality, although less disturbed by the problems here than in the liberties which surrounded the City, was nevertheless increasingly forced to consider the government of the outparishes.

[77] This liberty was sold for £1,700 in 1636 to Alderman Edward Bromfield, the soap monopolist and later Royalist. He was said to have acquired a great bargain. Rents were twice as high in the 'Mint' as it was called, as elsewhere, owing to its immunities from arrest by the City Sheriffs. *V.C.H., Surrey*, p. 144.

[78] Paris Garden became notorious as a house of ill-fame, managed by the infamous Mrs. Holland. It was known subsequently as 'Holland's Leaguer'. Ibid. pp. 150-1.

THE POWERS OF THE MUNICIPAL JUSTICES OF THE PEACE OVER THE LIBERTIES AND OUTPARISHES

From the sixteenth century, the Privy Council, aware of the contrast between the well-organized City and the weaker manorial government of the liberties and outparishes, appears to have expected the City magistrates to accept some responsibility for ensuring that royal proclamations and statutes were observed in these areas. At first, they found it more convenient to put pressure on the Lord Mayor and the Recorder for this purpose than to strengthen the jurisdiction of the highly privileged City (although increased powers were conferred on the municipality by charter in the seventeenth century). Under Elizabeth, Burghley employed the Recorder, William Fleetwood, to carry instructions from the Privy Council and to spur neighbouring manorial and parochial officials to take action in times of crisis.[79] The Recorder had exercised some influence amongst the Justices of the neighbouring counties for more than a century, as he was himself a Justice for Middlesex and Southwark, and the chief official at the sessions of Oyer and Terminer and Gaol Delivery which were issued jointly for London and Middlesex.[80] Together with the Lord Mayor and Aldermen who had passed the chair, he had long exercised concurrent jurisdiction in Southwark with the Justices of Surrey.[81] The City government was content to exercise supervisory power over these areas, which would prevent the escape of criminals from their own territory, without involving City magistrates in heavy administrative duties. This is evident from the charters which they purchased from the crown under James I and Charles I. In the second charter of James I, the Lord Mayor, the Recorder, and those Aldermen who had held the mayoralty were given the powers of Justices of the Peace in the precincts of Duke's Place, the two Bartholomews, Blackfriars, Whitefriars and Coldharbour.[82] In the charter which the City bought

[79] The diary of William Fleetwood and his letters to Lord Burghley are printed in *Queen Elizabeth and her Times* . . . , ed. Thomas Wright, 1838. Entries in his diary in 1577 and 1584 describe how he was accustomed to consult the J.P.s of Middlesex and Surrey and the Dean of Westminster, and to survey the Duchy of Lancaster in the Savoy, as part of his weekly routine, ii, p. 185.

[80] W. de G. Birch, op. cit., p. 75.

[81] Ibid. See Charters 1 Edward III, 23 Henry VI, and 4 Edward IV.

[82] Ibid. 6 James I, September 20 1608.

from Charles I in 1638, it gained the right to increase the number of aldermanic Justices by adding to their number the three
Aldermen next in succession to the mayoralty. It also gained
power to nominate two Aldermen to act as Justices for Middlesex and Surrey, respectively. These provisions did not mean,
however, that the City government was anxious to gain complete responsibility as a magistracy for the liberties and outparishes. This would have involved it, to an overwhelming
extent, in problems of administration, a burden which it declined to assume. So, in 1637, when the crown ordered that
all the Aldermen of London should be placed on a special
commission of the peace for the parishes within and without
the liberties '. . . and in the parishes of Lambeth, St. Mary
Newington, Redriffe [Rotherhithe], St. Mary Islington, Stepney, and Hackney in the counties of Middlesex and Surrey',
(because of the great need for magistrates in these places in
time of plague), the Court of Aldermen protested to the Privy
Council that they would never have time to fulfil such heavy
duties, and the order was revoked.[83] As will also be seen from
the City government's attitude towards Incorporation, its desire to act as a magistracy in the liberties with some supervisory
control over the outparishes did not imply a desire to exercise
complete responsibility for preserving law and order there.
After the victory of Parliament, when the City was invited to
put forward suggestions for strengthening its government, it
followed the same policy:[84] concentrating on securing increased
jurisdiction in those areas for which it was directly responsible
and in those liberties over which it had gained jurisdiction in
the Charter of 1608, and claiming a nominal supervisory power
in the adjoining counties to prevent the escape of criminals.

THE INCORPORATION OF THE SUBURBS

The attempt of the City government to extend the powers
and numbers of its Justices of the Peace within the main area
of its jurisdiction, with a supervisory power only over the outparishes, could not have afforded a satisfactory solution to the
problem of preserving good government in the suburbs. From
the point of view of efficient administration, the logical solution was for the City to absorb these areas into its system of

[83] P.C.R., 2/48, fols. 125, 150.   [84] J.Co.Co. 40, fols. 108-10.

government, as it had done in medieval times when it had absorbed Portsoken, Farringdon Without, Bishopsgate and Cripplegate Wards. The swiftly spreading suburbs of the sixteenth and seventeenth centuries presented vastly different problems: political absorption involved closer connexions with suburban industry and a possible alteration in the social composition of the Court of Common Council.[85] The first step that the City made towards extending its area of jurisdiction occurred in connexion with the liberties in 1608. The second Charter of James I extended the jurisdiction of the City through the liberties of Duke's Place in Trinity parish near Aldgate, and through Great and Little St. Bartholomew's near Smithfield, and Blackfriars, Whitefriars and Coldharbour. Yet even these areas were far from being entirely absorbed into City government. Although their inhabitants were to be under '. . . the rule, government, jurisdiction, oversight, search, correction, punishment, precepts and arrests of the said Mayor and commonalty and citizens of our City of London for the time being, and their officers and ministers for ever . . .', as the Charter expressed it with legal precision and emphasis, they were to be exempt from the fifteenths of Common Council taxation, from the burdens of scot, and from watch and ward.[86] Blackfriars and Whitefriars were to pay the charges for keeping and cleaning the public ways in their areas, but their inhabitants were to be exempt from serving as constable, scavenger and other minor offices within the City wards and precincts; at the same time, they were to be 'chargeable and eligible' to the offices of Lord Mayor, Sheriff and Alderman, as well as to all Livery Company offices.[87] But no provision was made for these precincts to send members to Common Council or for them to take part in Common Council elections. Their relationship with the neighbouring wards remained anomalous, and although the City now clearly possessed the right of maintaining law and order there, the crown was able to take advantage of the grant to dispute some aspects of the City's claims.

Evidence abounds in the repertories and journals of the City

[85] Even in the Civil War, the municipality laid no claim to absorb the suburbs into its political government, but solved the immediate problems by claiming control over the militias of the outparishes. See Chapter VII, pp. 268-9.

[86] W. de G. Birch, op. cit., p. 144.

[87] Ibid. p. 145.

to show that this Charter led to frequent disputes. This was particularly the case after the establishment of the 'new Incorporation of the Suburbs'. The idea of incorporating the suburbs and the City was under discussion in different forms from the beginning of the century. 'The Incorporation of Westminster', as it was styled, was the final scheme of Charles I and his Privy Council for dealing with the problem, and although it reflected some of the crown's concern about the unregulated conditions of employment among suburban workers, like most of Charles' proposals of this nature, it was largely influenced by the need to increase royal revenues. The New Incorporation was elaborated by Sir John Coke, Secretary of State, in answer to a petition from the Lord Mayor and Aldermen. In February 1632, the Court of Aldermen had appointed a Committee to consider the state of the suburbs;[88] and in the following April, two of the Committee had been deputed to discuss the problem with the Bishop of London.[89] As a result, the City petitioned the Privy Council, complaining of the extraordinary enlargement of the suburbs, which caused the freedom of the City to be of little worth, drew multitudes of the 'meaner' sort of people to London, particularly as a result of the 'new erected buildings', caused markets to be forestalled and prices to be raised, and covered with buildings the pipes that conveyed water into the City.[90] The Privy Council in reply asked the City government whether 'they would accept . . . part of the suburbs into their jurisdiction and liberty for better government',[91] and a series of conferences sat to discuss the matter.

It soon became clear in the discussions that the terms of incorporation were to be laid down by the crown and not by the City. The initiative was taken by Secretary Coke who, as we shall see, was responsible for promoting a number of other attacks on the privileges of London. Coke proposed that the liberties and outparishes should be divided up into four wards to form a new incorporation of tradesmen and artificers, independent of the municipality. The City disliked this proposal as much as the earlier suggestion that it should absorb the suburbs into its jurisdiction, and it refused to pursue the

[88] Rep. 46, fol. 101v.   [89] Ibid. fols. 169, 189, 346v.
[90] S.P.Dom. 16/225/71.   [91] Rep. 47, fol. 422.

negotiations further. The crown therefore acted without the
City. On April 8 1636, Letters Patent were issued for 'An
Incorporation granted to the tradesmen and artificers inhabiting as well within the Cities of London and Westminster
exempt from the freedom thereof, as without the said City,
and within three miles of the same who have served apprenticeship . . .'.[92] The sealing of the Patent was delayed on the
petition of the Lord Mayor and Aldermen, but it was finally
passed on June 2nd and was followed by a Proclamation re-
affirming the terms of the Letters Patent and reasserting that
no one was to trade in the liberties and suburbs without seven
years' apprenticeship and enrolment by the New Incorporation. A large organization was planned for the new body.
Headed by Peter Heywood, a Westminster Justice, as Governor,
there were also two Chamberlains, Christopher Lewkenor ·and
John Reading, as well as one Warden and ten Assistants for
each of the four wards.[93]

The City government could hardly be expected to welcome
the creation of· a rival jurisdiction on its own doorstep, particularly since its terms offered a direct challenge to the privileges of the City. When the Privy Council had approached
the municipality in 1610, about high prices and the lax enforcement of apprenticeship laws in the suburbs, the City
government had answered that the best solution was to extend
the jurisdiction of the Livery Companies to the suburbs, if
necessary to a radius of five miles around the City, which
would be adequate to enforce these laws and regulate the
quality and price of manufactured goods.[94] The advantage of
this scheme from the point of view of the City magistrates,
was that it provided a closer check on the obligation of those
who traded in the City to take up the 'freedom' and did not
involve the setting up of a rival jurisdiction. There was now

[92] S.P.Dom. 16/318/44.
[93] Bankes Papers 12/46. A draft of the terms of the Incorporation from which
a Bill was to be prepared for the King's signature.
[94] Lansdowne MSS. 92, fols. 26, 27. Throughout the first half of the seventeenth
century, the City government was anxious to strengthen the supervision of the
Livery Companies over the crafts; and an Act of Common Council in 1634 laid
it down that the custom of following one occupation after being apprenticed to
another, applied to 'merchandising and trade but not [to] manufactures and
handicrafts'. 'The location and organization of London industry, 1603-1640',
J. Archer, M.A. thesis, London Univ., 1934, pp. 148 seq.

an implicit threat, and a foreboding, that the new body with its much greater area might develop into a serious political rival. There may have been some substance in this fear, since the seven senior officers were to be appointed Justices.[95] But the origins and purposes of the incorporation were mainly economic and social, and it is unrealistic to imagine that a new body politic rivalling the City could arise from such beginnings.[96] After the establishment of the Incorporation, the King and Privy Council ordered the Aldermen of the City to act as Justices for the liberties and outparishes, a duty which, as we have seen, they refused; but the proposal indicates that a lack of political government was still felt in these areas and that the New Incorporation had not been able to fill the part.

The City's opposition to the scheme was at least twofold. First, the New Incorporation threatened to encroach on the basis of all City privilege, its jealously guarded 'freedom'. In 1636, the Recorder and some of the Aldermen on hearing of the proposed terms approached the Privy Council in alarm and temporarily persuaded them to order that the Incorporation should not press freemen of the City to join. Four days later, however, the Privy Council changed its view and issued the Order-in-Council of March 19 1637, which stated that the Incorporation should enrol '. . . as well freeman of London as others [of] the King's subjects, denizens or aliens, using any occupation, art, or mystery, or trade by retail, inhabiting within the said precincts'.[97] Journeymen who were considering trading or working in the liberties were unlikely to take up their City freedom[98] when they had also to enrol with the

[95] Bankes Papers, 12/46.

[96] Brett-James mistakenly saw the New Incorporation as a political body which he described as 'a veritable precursor of the London County Council', *The Growth of Stuart London*, p. 231.

[97] P.C.R. 2/47, fols. 242-3.

[98] The right of conferring the freedom had rested with the City magistrates since the time of Edward III. It could be conferred for apprenticeship, through patrimony or by redemption. Freedom by redemption could be granted if a breach of the indentures had taken place, as a reward for special services or exceptional skill, or by presentment by the Chamberlain. No one in the City or liberties who had not taken up the freedom was allowed to keep shop or employ journeymen. The prohibition was reaffirmed in 1606, although provisos were made for citizens dealing in certain trades to employ foreigners, such as cording, spinning, felt-making, capthicking, knitting and brewing. With this exception, the City government took stern measures to enforce the taking up of the City freedom. Archer, op. cit., pp. 148 seq.

New Incorporation of Westminster to whom they would pay
their fine. The City, which had looked with hostility at Charles'
policy of granting incorporations to new Livery Companies,
saw also in this New Incorporation of the suburbs an ultimate
threat of the same character. One of the clauses in the Letters
Patent mentioned the lack of enough Companies to which
apprentices could be bound.[99]

Secondly, the Incorporation was unpopular because it included in its area even those liberties over which the City
government had acquired jurisdiction by the Charter of 1608.
One of the four wards included 'the parishes and precincts of
Blackfriars and St. Martin's le Grand and the other places on
the north side within three miles between the Western Ward
and the parish of St. Botolph's, Aldgate on the east'.[100] The
Order-in-Council of March 1637 stated that since it had been
alleged that Duke's Place, Whitefriars, Blackfriars and Coldharbour were not within the precincts of the New Incorporation as they had been granted to the City by the Charter of
1608, the inhabitants of these places should not be interfered
with until further order.[101] But in spite of this, the Incorporation continued to claim jurisdiction in these precincts.

These disputes were never settled by Charles I. The absence of any mention of the New Incorporation either in the
list of 'Things desired by the City to be granted'[102] or in the
Charter of 1638 indicates that neither Charles nor the Privy
Council were prepared to yield on these points. Moreover, the
matter became more embittered when, in June 1638, the dispute between the City and the Incorporation over the right
to operate within the City's newly acquired liberties was decided in favour of the new body. 'If the City of London shall
find themselves aggrieved thereat', the Privy Council decided,
'they may bring their action at law against any able freemen
of the new Corporation inhabiting in those places and not free
of London, whereupon it may be decided by a legal trial
whether those places be within the freedom of London or
no'.[103] Thus, between 1638 and 1640, there was a succession

[99] Patent Roll, C.66.2744, 12 Charles I.
[100] Ibid.
[101] Rem. vii, fol. 191. P.C.R. 2/47, fol. 254.
[102] Bankes Papers, MSS. 48/9. J.Co.Co. 38, fols. 103-7.
[103] P.C.R. 2/49, fol. 251.

of suits between the City and the new body, concerning 'free-men' and 'privileged places'. On November 27 1638, the Court of Aldermen agreed to take action on behalf of the inhabitants of Duke's Place who were imprisoned for refusing to enter the New Incorporation.[104] In the following year, there was a dispute between the City and the new body concerning the inhabitants of Blackfriars.[105] The arrest of Thomas Williams in June 1638 for refusing to pay a fine to the Incorporation because he already held the freedom of the City, showed that the dispute over this subject was still a vital issue.

Opposition to the Incorporation was as strong outside the City as within. Garrard, writing at the beginning of the project, said it was 'much opposed by the Londoners and many others. . . . Where profit may come to the King, let them pass, but to enrich private men, they have not my wishes'.[106] At the end of the first year, the officers of the Incorporation presented a disappointing report. There was widespread opposition to taking up the freedom, and many other obstructions had been encountered in the City and the suburbs. In 1640, the City government considered the New Incorporation a major grievance. One of the earliest official petitions to the Long Parliament from the City mentioned in its records was against John Reading, one of the Chamberlains of the new body for 'procuring the late Letters of Incorporation'.[107] Unfortunately, there is no record of either the details of the petition or the Commons' reply, but the whole project must have fallen into abeyance, to judge from a petition of 'the inhabitants of Westminster and the suburbs of London in the county of Middlesex' on July 21 1641, complaining of the absence of government in these areas since the dissolution of the Star Chamber.[108]

THE IMPENDING CRISIS: THE PROBLEM RESTATED

The rapid growth of London's population in the first half of the seventeenth century transformed the face of the metropolis. It also presented the City's magistrates with new problems

[104] Rep. 53, fols. 28-28v.
[105] Rep. 54, fol. 322.
[106] Knowler, op. cit., ii, p. 55.
[107] Rep. 55, fols. 18-18v.
[108] H.M.C. House of Lords MSS., Fourth Report, Part I, p. 90.

of government, placing great strain on the City's traditional machinery and weakening the authority and power of the magistrates. It weakened also the Livery Companies, because of the difficulties in the densely populated liberties and sub-urbs, of enforcing the 'search', the ancient investigation and regulation of trade and manufacture. Many of the new indus-tries which were established here did not come within this purview of the old traditional Companies and, as in an earlier age, town air had 'made free', so, in a sense, did suburban air now. The growth of industry with its recurrent periods of de-pression, provided new social problems; in particular, the state of semi-permanent depression which existed in the cloth trade between 1620 and 1640 brought social dislocation to the northern and north-eastern suburbs, whose population was almost entirely dependent on the work it provided. A rough and lawless population living in slums could only intensify the problems. Perhaps the loss of open spaces and amenities, lamented by Stow, was also a factor in this general instability and discontent, as some authorities believe it was in the next two centuries, when a much worse deprivation is said to have accounted for part of the unrest in large and rapidly growing towns. The suburbs had long been notorious as a refuge for rogues and vagabonds. In 1592 they were described by Henry Chettle, a London compositor and dramatist, as 'in many places no other but dark dens for adulterers, thieves, mur-derers and every mischief worker'.[109] The liberties, to a some-what lesser extent, shared this evil reputation. Whitefriars, which included a wild place nicknamed 'Alsatia', was feared as a haunt of thieves, although it also harboured sober Puri-tans.[110]

The City poor in their tenements and the suburban slum-dwellers in their jerry-built houses and flimsy shacks (even 'paper-built' at Mile End, it was said in 1642),[111] much as they might become brutalized and atomistic in these surround-ings, were also subject to unifying factors which brought them closer together and placed their violence at the service of

[109] *Shakespeare's England*, op. cit., ii, p. 179.

[110] See below, Chapter V, pp. 179-80.

[111] Probably of plaster. F. H. W. Sheppard, ed., *Survey of London*, vol. xxvii, 1957, p. 238.

whoever was fittest to command it. On occasion, sedition and riot became as contagious as the plague and disease which periodically swept through the narrow streets, and great crowds would quickly gather against authority. It was the opponents of Charles who had most, if not everything, to gain from these *sans-culottes* of the English Revolution. But not all was gain. Ardent Protestants and patriotic citizens noted the alien Catholic residents in their midst, their numbers often grossly exaggerated amid the current atmosphere of xenophobia and insecurity. Even the refugees from an intolerant Catholicism, popular as they were at times, evoked mixed feelings. When the 'stranger' was a Roman Catholic tradesman, the conflict was less complicated. To economic fears and rivalries was added the threat of a potential Fifth Column, while who could say with certainty in what direction the native Catholic mob might not be driven? The leaders of the parliamentary puritans may have wondered if it was from this source that a force of two hundred armed men of Westminster was gathered outside Parliament in December 1641, by supporters of the King.[112] Earlier, in September 1640, the citizens had included in a petition of grievances to Charles, a complaint about the 'great concourse' of Roman Catholics in the liberties and suburbs.[113] In January 1642, they had enlarged their complaint to cover 'those many thousands of unknown persons who are sheltered [and not questioned] in Covent Garden'.[114] A curious document, 'gross forgery' to Clarendon, proof of a Papist conspiracy to others, boasted of the strength of Royalist and Catholic support: 'Our Party is strong in the City, especially Holborn, the new buildings and Westminster. We are afraid of nothing but the Scots appearing there again.'[115]

But most of this, although widely believed, was rodomontade. A force of a sort might be recruited from retainers and some Catholics, and for a larger affray criminals and outlaws might join in; strong Royalist sympathies were to be found also in

[112] W. H. Coates, ed., *The Journal of Sir Simonds D'Ewes*, New Haven, 1942, p. 263.

[113] Harl. MSS. 7162, fol. 101.

[114] *A Speech delivered at a Conference with the Lords, January 25th 1641* [*1642*]. *By occasion of the Petitions from the City of London*, John Pym. 1641 [1642], p. 2.

[115] *A Letter directed to Mr. Bridgman, 4th January, and a letter to one Master Anderton . . .* 1641 [1642] [Bodleian], Clarendon, *History*, i, pp. 513-14.

the newly built areas to the west of the City which had been developed by courtiers. Clarendon noted how Westminster, St. Martin's and Covent Garden have always undergone 'the imputation of being well affected to the King'.[116] But the main religious and political sympathy and strength of the outskirts lay elsewhere. The suburbs and some of the liberties very quickly earned a reputation for Puritanism and, after 1640, for radicalism. Puritanism was, perhaps, particularly strong because the magistrates of these areas were much less well organized than the City Aldermen and less likely to report seditious preaching to the Privy Council. Stepney and Wapping were disturbed throughout the sixteen-twenties and -thirties by sailors' riots. Stepney, in particular, the home of some eminent Huguenot refugees, had a long tradition of Puritan preaching;[117] in 1639 the Privy Council was informed that a group of Covenanting Scotsmen were meeting together in the Flushing Inn in Wapping.[118] In 1642, the inhabitants of the eastern suburbs of London, 'mariners, soldiers, or private persons' petitioned against the removal of their own Trained Bands from the Tower and the violence which had been used against Puritans and Brownists and two of their favourite preachers, Jeremiah Burroughs and William Greenhill.[119] Southwark was another suburb with a radical reputation, not enhanced among the friends of order by the distant memory of the part it had played, with its vital command of the Bridge, in earlier civil disorders. Here, the tanners, glovers and brewery workers were notorious for lawlessness and sedition. In May 1640, as we shall see, they joined with the sailors of Bermondsey in a great demonstration against Laud.[120] Some of the poorest outparishes, crowded with craftsmen and labourers, were those bordering the Fleet river. Hugh Peter, a leading Puritan preacher, was active in St. Sepulchre's, one of these parishes. Two of the most radical and Puritan areas of all were the liberties of Blackfriars and Whitefriars. In Blackfriars, vast

---

[116] Clarendon, *History*, ii, p. 430.

[117] G. W. Hill and W. H. Frere, ed., *Memorials of Stepney Parish . . .* , Guildford, 1890-1891, *passim*.

[118] S.P.Dom. 16/418/55.

[119] R. R. Steele, ed., *Bibliotheca Lindesiana*, 1910, i, p. 234.

[120] See Chapter IV, pp. 107-8.

crowds assembled to hear a popular preacher,[121] while in Whitefriars, so opponents alleged, most un-puritanlike hospitality was offered to visiting preachers.[122] Even the theatre reflected this radicalism, although its dramatists were often extremely anti-Puritan in sentiment and were themselves under constant attack by the Puritans. Situated in the liberties and outparishes, the playhouses were close enough to the people who flocked to them to express this opposition to authority and good order. The Red Bull, in St. John's street, Clerkenwell, was well known for its turbulent audiences and in 1638 it got into trouble for putting on a play lampooning one of the notorious monopolists of the City, Alderman William Abell.[123] It is significant that some of the opposition to theatres arose not so much from the contents of the plays or the moral character of the players as from the political danger in permitting large and excited assemblies to gather.[124]

Many of the parliamentary puritan leaders had houses in the suburbs. A prominent group were close neighbours in Holborn, where Robert Greville, the second Lord Brooke, one of the main architects of the opposition, lived in Brooke House, at the corner of Holborn and Gray's Inn lane, not far from the home of the second Earl of Warwick, who lived further along to the west in Warwick House.[125] Both provided a convenient meeting-place for the Providence Island Company. Nearby also, John Pym had lodgings in Gray's Inn lane, and from 1637 to 1643, Cromwell lived in Long Acre in the same suburb of Holborn.[126] Hackney was another suburb where a number of parliamentary puritan leaders lived. Originally, the residence of Fulke Greville, the first Lord Brooke, before he moved to Holborn, it had among its inhabitants, Owen Rowe, the regicide, and Lady Mary Vere, the great friend and protectoress of Puritan ministers, who had prevailed on the patron of the living to appoint her nominees as the incumbents.[127]

[121] See Chapter V, pp. 162-3.
[122] *Persecutio Undecima, The Churches Eleventh Persecution* . . . , 1648 [anon.], pp. 27, 54, 55. [Thomason Tracts.]
[123] S.P.Dom. 16/429/51, 52.
[124] *Index to Remembrancia*, op. cit., pp. 355-6.
[125] J. P. Malcolm, *Londinium Redivivum*, 1802, ii, pp. 208, 209. E. Williams, *Early Holborn and the Legal Quarter*, 1927, i, pp. 526-9.
[126] G. H. Cunningham, *London: A Comprehensive Survey* . . . , 1927, p. 427.
[127] S. Clarke, *The Lives of sundry Eminent Persons*, 1683, p. 145.

One of these was Calybute Downing, who became vicar of
Hackney in 1637. Preacher of a momentous sermon to the
Honourable Artillery Company in September 1640, he was
later a fiery Army chaplain nicknamed 'Hugh Peter the
Second'.[128] The Earl of Holland, according to Clarendon, a
Puritan intriguer out of pique because of his rebuff at Court,
held private meetings of the 'factious party' at Holland House,
his residence in Kensington.[129] Around the same time, Pym
moved to the nearby village of Chelsea, where he had as
neighbour Lord Mandeville. In Westminster, conveniently
near Parliament, 'in a little court behind Westminster Hall',
Pym also had an office in 1641 at the house of Sir Richard
Manly,[130] while not far away, Lord Saye occupied a similar
office, a kind of early party headquarters. In Westminster too,
in Hampden House near Whitehall, the Puritan Elizabeth,
mother of John Hampden, lived for over forty years.[131] In
Covent Garden, in the midst of the suburban district they had
developed, dwelt the Bedfords, early giants in the long line
of Puritan estate builders and promoters.[132] In the sixteen-
forties, the younger Sir Henry Vane became a resident in the
district. But it would be rash to read too much into these facts.
The suburbs also attracted men whose opinions differed radically from those of the parliamentary puritans. Many wealthy
City Aldermen and later Royalists lived there. One can only
speculate whether in subsequent revolutionary times the presence of a concentration of powerful leaders in the suburbs
brought some influence to bear on the march of events.

It is small wonder that the City magistrates found the problem of the suburbs practically insoluble. Some of the poorest
and most radical areas were those where their jurisdiction did

128 Anthony à Wood, *Athenae Oxonienses*, ed. P. Bliss, 1813, iii, col. 107.

129 Clarendon, *History*, i, pp. 387-388.

130 Clarendon, *The Life of Edward, Earl of Clarendon*, 1827, i, p. 90.

131 M. H. Cox and G. T. Forrest, ed., *Survey of London*, xiv, 1931, p. 107-9.

132 The property of the dissolved priory of St. Bartholomew's Smithfield was
developed by Robert Rich, first Earl of Warwick in the fifteen-nineties. E. A.
Webb, op. cit., ii, p. 293, William Wheeler, a Puritan member of the Long
Parliament, was responsible for laying out the northern part of Spitalfields.
F. H. W. Sheppard, ed., *Survey of London*, xxvii, 1957, p. 97. Another Puritan
builder after the Restoration was Dr. Nicholas Barbon or Barebones, son of a
more famous father. But in the early seventeenth century, there were also estate
developers of Royalist sympathy, such as William Newton who built up part of
Lincoln's Inn Fields. N. G. Brett-James, op. cit., p. 155.

not reach. But they faced a dilemma. Even if their powers were
extended to cover these areas, such burdens of office were bound
to prove heavier than could be borne by merchants, usually
fully engaged in trade. These burdens were already heavy and
increasing. This probably helps to explain the growing reluctance to hold office in the first half of the seventeenth century.
On the other hand, it was in their interest to preserve good
stable government if trade was to flourish. It was natural that
they should look to the Privy Council for help in solving their
problems. Lord Burghley had begun the practice of holding
regular conferences with Recorder Fleetwood on the City's administrative problems. The Tudor Privy Council had also considerably enlarged the magistrates' powers to deal with one
aspect of their problem—the growing burdens of vagrancy and
poverty. But at no point was the crown able to agree with the
municipality on the larger and intractable issues—who was to
control the expanding, turbulent liberties and suburbs and
what rights and privileges were to be given to their inhabitants.
We have seen how the Privy Council's proposals for an Incorporation, largely motivated by financial considerations, fell to
the ground after antagonizing both the City government and
the dwellers in the suburbs. The suburbs, without any clear
or unanimous voice, had proved 'refractory' in their response.
If they wanted anything, they wanted to be left alone to enjoy
without payment liberty to trade or manufacture. A considerable number pleaded that they were too poor to take up their
freedom, while able men, presumably loath to take office,
pleaded the plague as a reason for their unwillingness to 'meet
promiscuously with multitudes'.[133] As for the Aldermen, probably only a feudal type of overlordship, such as they enjoyed
over Southwark, would have satisfied them. For here the City
government faced another dilemma. It claimed jurisdictional
rights over the liberties and suburbs but it was not prepared to
grant them political privileges in return. Nor did it want to
alter the social composition of Common Council by giving
representation to districts which were often radical and socially
inferior, and it refused to do anything to weaken the obligation on City traders to take up the City freedom.

The natural allies of the City government in preserving and

[133] S.P.Dom. 16/363/88.

increasing its powers of jurisdiction and its traditional privileges in the London area should have been the Privy Council. Such a partnership would have been a formidable one. But under James I and Charles I, short-term financial expedients took the place of statesmanship and the City magistrates found themselves alienated from those who shared their political and social outlook and with whom they might be expected to have a natural affinity. In 1641 and 1642, when they reaped the whirlwind, the Privy Council and the City Aldermen were to rue this failure to achieve more efficient government in the London area.

CHAPTER II

The Constitution of the City of London

HISTORIANS of sixteenth- and seventeenth-century London will inevitably feel the lack of an adequate treatment of the City's constitution in this period. A history of the City's constitutional development does not exist. With the important exceptions of John Strype and William Bohun, eighteenth- and nineteenth-century historians of the City were concerned either to describe its constitution and government as they existed in their day or, if a historical treatment was intended, to describe them primarily in formal terms of the growth of the City's chartered privileges. William Maitland[1] and Alexander Pulling[2] in the eighteenth and nineteenth centuries respectively, carefully described the functioning of City government as it existed in 1756 and 1849. George Norton,[3] in his *Commentaries* on the constitution, dealt almost entirely with its chartered privileges. The brief account of the constitution which Margaret James included in her *Social Problems and Policy of the Puritan Revolution* (1930) is too slight for our purpose and was intended only as a short introduction to an account of the radical reforms of the constitution that were proposed during the Commonwealth.[4]

The sources for a historical account of the City's constitutional development are to be found in the records of the City councils, mainly in the Repertories of the aldermanic Bench

---

[1] *The History of London . . . including the several parishes*, W. Maitland and others, 2 vols., 1739. A later addition in 1756 includes much additional material.

[2] *A practical Treatise on the Laws and Customs of the City of London . . .* , 2nd edition, 1849.

[3] *Commentaries on the History, Constitution and Chartered Franchises of the City of London*, 1829.

[4] An excellent account of the City government and constitution after 1688 exists in S. and B. Webb, *The History of Local Government . . .* , Part II, 1908. In *The Corporation of London*, Oxford, 1950, published under the auspices of the Guildhall Library Committee, there is a brief and valuable historical introduction to the City constitution, but it has little material relating directly to the sixteenth and seventeenth centuries.

and the Journals of the Court of Common Council, which until 1640 also included notices of Common Hall elections and copies of mayoral precepts. Although the Letter Books, a transcription of the most important passages of the Journals, have been calendared for the thirteenth, fourteenth and fifteenth centuries by R. R. Sharpe,[5] no such work exists for the sixteenth and seventeenth centuries. It is almost impossible, therefore, for the historian to present a detailed accurate account of the practical functioning of the constitution without a minute examination of the original manuscript records, a formidable task since, from 1600 at least, the Repertories contain nearly 300 folios for every year, while the records of Common Council, although very much briefer, are interspersed with notes on orphans and mayoral precepts, which increase the difficulties of finding the relevant material.

Some information can, of course, be gained from contemporary accounts, but on the whole their yield is disappointing. In the sixteenth and seventeenth centuries, the love of tradition and reverence for the law weighed heavily on the minds of men, with the result that lawyers and historians alike described the City constitution as it existed centuries earlier, in terms of antiquated Acts and Ordinances, and not in accordance with its contemporary functioning. John Stow, who was strongly imbued with this reverence for the traditional, was more eager to describe thirteenth- and fourteenth-century constitutional practice than the customs of his own day, and appended to his work the twelfth-century essay of Fitzstephen on the City of London. His work included only the briefest reference to the constitution, for, as he says, he had thought of dealing with it at greater length, but, hearing that James Dalton was preparing such a work, he put it aside. When Dalton died, however, without producing this work, Stow decided to add to his book the few notes he had gathered on City government. But this sketchy outline provides little information.[6] Anthony Munday and Humphrey Dyson, who continued and enlarged Stow's Survey in 1633, only partly fulfilled his original intention; they were more interested to describe

---

[5] *Calendar of letter-books preserved among the archives of the Corporation . . . , A–L,* ed. R. R. Sharpe, 1899-1912.

[6] Stow, *Survay,* ii, p. 186.

the ceremonial and pageant associated with civic offices than the working of the constitution, and described the machinery of City government in the briefest and most formal terms.

In 1642, when the parliamentary puritans of the City were challenging the contemporary working of City government, a tract was published, written by Sir Henry Calthrop, Recorder of the City from 1635 to 1636, entitled *The Liberties, Usages and Customes of the City of London.*[7] Published at a time when constitutional and political ideas, as well as practice, were being thrown into the melting-pot, it might have been expected to throw some light on the constitutional conflicts of the day. This work, however, is a great disappointment to the historian of London's constitution in the seventeenth century. It is content to select relevant passages from *Liber Albus*,[8] John Carpenter's famous account of City government written in 1419, and from early charters and Acts of Parliament, and makes no reference to the conflicting claims of, for example, the Court of Aldermen and the Court of Common Council, or to other contemporary disputes. Moreover, on closer examination, it appears to be almost identical with a manuscript tract by Recorder Fleetwood, included in the Liber Fleetwood, which he presented to the City in 1576.[9] But it may be of some significance that this work was first published in 1642, since it contains a literal interpretation of early City charters, a method much in fashion among Puritan and parliamentary lawyers; on the subject of the election of the Sheriffs, for example, the Charter of 2 Henry III is quoted in these words: 'It is granted to the citizens of London to make elections of their Sheriffs,

[7] *The Liberties, Usages and Customes of the City of London; confirmed by especiall Acts of Parliament, with the time of their confirmation. Also, Divers ample, and most beneficiall Charters, granted by King Henry the 6, King Edward the 4, and King Henrie the 7th not confirmed by Parliament*, 1642.

[8] John Carpenter, *Liber Albus: The White Book of the City of London*, 1419, trans. H. T. Riley, 1861.

[9] 'Liber Fleetwood', Guildhall Record Office. Fleetwood's manuscript is headed: 'All the Libties, usages and customes hereafter following are confirmed by an especiall Acte of Parliament made at Westm. A° 7 regem regis Rici Secundi Albo Libro 43.a.' The tract published in 1642 added references to the later confirmations of these privileges, but appears to have no other additional information. The close similarity of these two works, as far as I am aware, has never been commented upon in print.

and after to remove them at their pleasure.'[10] It was evidence
of this nature that the parliamentary puritans of the City must
have used to illustrate their claim, described in a later chapter,
that the Lord Mayor had usurped the right of electing one of
the Sheriffs.

*The City Law, or, The Course and practice in all manner of juridicall
proceedings in the Hustings in Guildhall,* published in 1647, was,
as its title suggests, mainly concerned with describing the legal
rights of City freemen and the chartered privileges of the City.[11]
*The Reports of Speciall Cases touching severall customs and liberties of
the City of London,* collected by Sir Henry Calthrop and published in 1655,[12] was a treatise concerned, according to the
introduction, with 'the privileges and immunities granted unto
the merchants of London'. On the election of City officers it
was content to quote the earlier selections from *Liber Albus,*
reprinted in *The Liberties, Usages and Customes.* The reprint of
The City Law in 1658 has no additions. *Lex Londinensis; or,
The City Law*—published in 1680, although purporting to correct, as it states in the preface, the inadequacies of the earlier
editions of *The City Law,* adds much to our knowledge of the
workings of the City law courts, but very little to the constitutional procedure of the City.

Only John Strype in his continuation and enlargement of
Stow's *Survay* and William Bohun in *Privilegia Londinis* (3rd
ed., 1723) described the evolution of the City's constitution.
Both of them were aware of the constitutional struggles of the
mid-seventeenth century. But although Strype quoted valuable passages from contemporary civil war pamphlets on the
disputed claims made by the Court of Aldermen on the one
hand, and the Courts of Common Council and Common Hall
on the other, in the main he illustrated these conflicts from

[10] *The Liberties, Usages and Customes,* p. 16. There is a similarly anachronistic
reference to the election of the Aldermen: 'Upon the feast day of St. Gregory
yearly shall every Aldermen be removed from their place, and new in their place
shall be chosen. (lib. alb. fol. 42a, b. 50, E. 3). Note that this is changed since by
Act of Parliament', ibid. p. 2.

[11] In spite of being 'englished' from an old French manuscript, it incorporated
some reference to recent constitutional changes. On the election of Sheriffs, it
states that 'One shall be chosen by the Mayor . . . and the other by the Commons',
p. 16.

[12] According to the introduction, it was written in 1618 and dedicated to
Alderman Sir Thomas Lowe.

the crisis of 1680-2 and the years following, with which he would naturally have been more familiar. Nevertheless, William Bohun and above all John Strype contain the most useful of the printed accounts of the City constitution. But printed sources alone could not provide the historian with more than a cursory sketch of the development of the constitution in the seventeenth century. This can only be derived from a first-hand examination of the voluminous City Repertories and Journals.

Nothing could be more misleading than to suggest that the constitution of the City of London was well defined either in theory or practice. Except among a few antiquarians and lawyers, the form of the constitution was of small interest to those concerned in the working of the City government. They had no Whiggish preconceptions about fixed methods of procedure or 'constitutional rights', but adopted what lay to hand in the way that best suited their immediate purposes. For that reason, the historian will discover many conflicting precedents in City government during the sixteenth and seventeenth centuries, which make any general statement about the constitution subject to many qualifications. The summary description of the City constitution which follows aims therefore at giving a general impression, and it must be remembered that in practice there was probably a great deal more fluidity and elasticity in their methods of government than can be conveyed in a short account.

The executive government and legislature of the City of London in the seventeenth century was organized into three main Courts[13] or Councils: the Court of Lord Mayor and Aldermen, the Court of Common Council and the Court of Common Hall. For the sake of a general classification (there were many exceptions in detail), the Court of Lord Mayor and Aldermen was the executive governing body of the City, the Court of Common Council performed the functions of a legislative body, while Common Hall was not a deliberative council, but acted solely in an electoral capacity.

[13] No account will be made here of the complexity of minor courts which were part of the City's government, such as those whose functions were primarily judicial, i.e. the Lord Mayor's Court, the Sheriffs' Courts, the Court of Requests, the Chamberlain's Courts, the Court of Conservancy of the Thames, and the Coroner's and Escheator's Courts, nor of those whose functions were little more than a survival of the past, such as the Court of Hustings.

COMMON HALL

Common Hall was by far the largest and most popular of these assemblies. It included all the liverymen of the City, who were said to number about 4,000 in the middle of the seventeenth century.[14] Its origin probably lay far back in the Folkmoot. In the thirteenth century, it was still attended by all the householders of the City who paid scot and lot. Gradually its membership was restricted, first of all to freemen of the City, and then, by ordinances of 1422 and 1443, to Common Council men and 'other powerful and discreet citizens specially summoned'.[15] With the multiplication of Livery Companies towards the end of the fifteenth century, its membership was enlarged again. In 1467, the Master and Wardens of Companies were added, together with 'other good men specially summoned'. In 1475, the liverymen of the Companies were substituted for the 'wealthier and wise' men of the wards.[16] In the sixteenth and seventeenth centuries, with the incorporation of many new gilds, some of which were representative of craftsmen working in humbler trades, Common Hall had a wide, popular composition. In official records, it continued to be called by its ancient title of the 'Congregation' until 1738. Clarendon, referring to 1643, after Common Hall had temporarily strengthened its position in the City constitution,[17] described it 'as the most general assembly of the City, the meanest person being admitted'.[18]

Clarendon was, of course, greatly exaggerating popular influence over Common Hall. The power of the liverymen was considerably limited by a system of indirect election to some of the more important offices, such as those of Lord Mayor and City Chamberlain; the power of calling Common Hall and dissolving it rested solely with the Lord Mayor. But there may have been some grounds for Clarendon's insinuation that men of lower rank than liverymen were accustomed to attend the meetings. In the normal way, there was no means of ascertaining whether others than liverymen were present, unless in

[14] House of Lords MSS., Victoria Tower, Petition of the six persons, July 29 1641, Vol. July 26th-August 14th. [Folios unnumbered.]
[15] *The Corporation of London*, op. cit., pp. 9-10.
[16] Ibid.   [17] See Chapter IV, pp. 120-2, 199, 248.
[18] Clarendon, *History*, Bk. vi, p. 222.

a disputed election a poll was demanded by the electors, when every voter could be checked with the Beadle's lists.[19] Otherwise, the Common Sergeant ordered all those to depart who had no right to vote, but no steps were taken to enforce his command, and, judging by contemporary complaints, men who were not entitled to vote frequently stayed and took part in elections. Since voting was usually by show of hands, there was no systematic way of checking on the voters' qualifications. For this reason, Common Hall could at times of political crisis become the mouthpiece of a greater body of opinion than might be deduced from a formal account of its composition.

Since at least 1406, it had been customary in the election of the Lord Mayor for the Common Hall to send up to the Court of Aldermen (who sat separately in the east end of Guildhall) two nominations from which the Aldermen were to choose one. Although not specifically enacted by City ordinance, it was customary for these nominations to include the senior Alderman under the chair who was normally elected. On the day of election, September 29th, the Recorder addressed the assembly reminding them of the purpose of their meeting, after which the Aldermen retired into the Inner Chamber. Then the nominations were conducted by the Sheriffs and Common Sergeant, 'who first maketh a brief rehearsal of those former precedents which Master Recorder had before delivered to them'.[20] The Sheriffs, Common Sergeant, other City officers and 'certain of the Prime Wardens of the chief Companies' carried the nominations to the Aldermen. Their choice was then signified to Common Hall by the Recorder, who demanded of them 'whether it be their free election, or no'.[21] The Common Hall affirmed it and the assembly was dissolved. The same procedure was followed in the election to the lucrative post of City Chamberlain which took place annually on June 24th. Two Bridgemasters, Aleconners and Auditors of Accounts were also chosen on the same day by the Lord Mayor and Aldermen from four nominations for each office sent up by Common Hall.

[19] *The Method and Rule of Proceeding upon all Elections, Polls and Scrutinies at Common Halls, and Wardmotes within the City of London . . .* , 1743, p. 29.

[20] Stow, *Survay*, cont. Munday, p. 652.   [21] Ibid.

The procedure for electing the Sheriffs was somewhat different. It had been customary from the fourteenth century for the Lord Mayor to choose one Sheriff and the liveries the other. One method of nomination adopted by the Mayor was to drink to his chosen nominee at a public banquet held just before the election. Even before his nominee was confirmed at Common Hall, he normally signed bonds to hold the office, or paid his forfeiture.[22] In the election of the other Sheriff, 'the Sheriffs, Master Chamberlain, Master Common Sergeant, Master Town Clerk and the Councillors of the City, and other Officers . . . take and receive the name of him, that shall seem (by their judgments) freely . . . to be nominated and elected, and justly tried out, not only by voice, but also by hands' at the meeting of Common Hall.[23] The election day for the Sheriffs was June 24th, and they were sworn in on September 28th.

While the reigning Lord Mayor summoned and dissolved Common Hall, it was the Sheriffs who conducted the proceedings in the election of the Lord Mayor, the Sheriffs and minor offices. This was a fruitful source of dispute and disturbance,[24] which may have been one reason for the turbulence which marked Common Hall proceedings in 1640 and 1641 and which, as will be seen, enabled the parliamentary puritans in the City to pursue their policy at first with greater success in Common Hall than in Common Council, which was more rigidly dominated by the Lord Mayor and Aldermen.

Besides the officers already mentioned, Common Hall in the seventeenth century also elected the four City Members of Parliament. Originally, they had been appointed by the Lord Mayor and Court of Aldermen. From the fourteenth century to the sixteenth, it had been the custom for the Court of Aldermen to nominate two of the Members and Common Hall two, the four nominations subsequently being confirmed in Common Council. Early in the sixteenth century, the right of election was entirely transferred to Common Hall, which acquired the power both to nominate and to elect the Members of Parliament, and the strict division of representation between the

[22] *The History of the Sheriffdom of the City of London and County of Middlesex . . .*, 1723, p. 23.

[23] Stow, *Survay*, cont. Munday, p. 651.   [24] *The Method and Rule*, pp. 15-16.

Aldermen and the Commoners ceased.[25] Nevertheless, it was
observed in all the elections of the early Stuart period, with
the important exceptions of 1628 and 1640. It should be noted
that the Sheriffs alone had power to call, dissolve and conduct
the assembly for this purpose: 'They therefore are solely the
masters of all these proceedings, and the Lord Mayor has no
authority of interposing.'[26] This may partly account for the
election of well-known parliamentary puritans as City Members of Parliament in 1640, at a time when the Lord Mayor
and Aldermen and many wealthy merchants of the City were
more disposed to side with the King.[27]

Common Hall, with its early traditions as a popular assembly, offered the supporters of the parliamentary opposition in
the City a ready instrument. In the disputes of 1641 and 1642,
there were complaints by liverymen that outsiders were voting
at Common Hall, foreshadowing, perhaps, the claims made
later under the Commonwealth that according to ancient tradition Common Hall should be attended by all freemen. In
1641 and 1642, there were attempts to give the assembly deliberative functions, in particular, the right to consent to the
raising of City loans. Common Hall was summoned in January
1641[28] to debate whether a loan should be raised for Parliament, and again in November and December to discuss the
proposed loan for suppressing the Irish rebellion.[29] It also
claimed to elect both Sheriffs without the intervention of the
Lord Mayor and Aldermen.[30] Evidence of its increasing powers
in the constitution is found in the fact that Common Hall
gained its own Journal for the first time in 1642. Previously,
its meetings had been recorded together with the minutes of
the Court of Common Council.

COURT OF COMMON COUNCIL

The Court of Common Council, the City's legislature, was
a much smaller assembly than Common Hall, but in theory
it represented the entire body of freemen. Elections to the

[25] *The Corporation of London*, p. 14.
[26] *The Method and Rule*, p. 19.
[27] See Chapters IV and V, *passim*.
[28] The Diary of Sir Thomas Peyton, fol. 67-68 [Bodleian Library, microfilm,
no. 39], J.Co.Co. 39, fol. 167.
[29] *D'Ewes*, ed. Coates, p. 133.   [30] See Chapter IV, pp. 120 seq.

Court of Common Council were conducted yearly at a meeting of the wardmote. The function of the wardmote was primarily to elect ward officers, the clerk, the beadles, the constables and the inquest, but it also took part in electing Common Councilmen and in nominating its Alderman. Although attendances at the wardmote was originally compulsory on all householders and males over the age of fifteen years, from at least 1419,[31] it was only the freemen who were allowed to vote in elections for Aldermen and Common Councilmen.[32]

In the fourteenth century, the Common Councilmen were the *probi homines* of the wards and their numbers varied according to the matters on which they were called to deliberate. The Court of Common Council was first mentioned as having a permanent basis in 1346, when each Alderman was required to cause to be elected in his ward 'eight, six or four of the better men, according as his ward be great or small, to be at the Guildhall as often as they might happen to be summoned to treat of the arduous affairs of the commonalty'. Elections were at first entirely in the hands of the Aldermen and the wealthiest of the ward, for in 1437 the Aldermen were directed to choose with 'the advice of the worthiest men of the ward, the most sufficient men of good and wisest discretion to be of the Common Council'.[33] In the seventeenth century, the Aldermen still exercised great influence over Common Council elections, and in the disputed elections of December 21 1641 there was much complaint that the Aldermen had insisted on electing their own nominees.[34] Although any freeman and householder of the City paying scot and lot was eligible to be a Common Councilman, in practice there seems to have been a strong feeling that liverymen should be elected, and that they should sit until elected to a higher office. Thus, in 'A Breef Description of the Famous Cittie of London', written in 1558, it was

---

[31] *The Corporation of London*, p. 29.

[32] There was a tendency for elections to be controlled by small groups in the precincts. The Committee which judged the disputed elections of 1641, re-emphasized that Common Councilmen should be chosen by all the freemen of the ward. See below, Chapter IV, pp. 138-9. The Lord Mayor's precept issued on December 19 1642 reiterated this statement, adding that the names of all the freemen should be entered on a roll to be read at the wardmote by the Clerk and called out by the Beadle. Common Hall, Bk. i, fol. 15.

[33] *The Corporation of London*, pp. 23, 49.

[34] See Chapter IV, pp. 138-9.

stated that Common Councilmen were liverymen of their companies who 'continue in their office, so long as they live (except they be called to some higher office)'.[35]

From early times, the wardmotes had been organized into divisions, known as precincts,[36] the smallest unit of City government and, in theory, ward officers were nominated here before going for final election to the wardmote. The boundaries of the precinct did not usually coincide with those of the parish;[37] nevertheless, there was a tendency in the seventeenth century for the precincts to be controlled by the vestry[38] of the neighbouring parish church. In some cases, vestries were claiming the right to conduct the entire election and refused to permit the wardmote the right of making the final choice.[39] In at least ten[40] of the parishes whose vestry minutes are extant for the early seventeenth century, precinct meetings are entered as a matter of course in the vestry minute books, and the men chosen as Common Councillors were sometimes declared elected before the wardmote had even met.[41] From the middle of the century, there was also a parallel movement to by-pass altogether the powers of the precincts and wardmotes in the

[35] Harl. MSS., 6363. In *Method and Rule* the author suggests that it is 'esteemed proper' for Common Councilmen to be liverymen, since 'they not only pass laws which must bind all the rest, but frequently control the proceedings of the livery men, and do many acts under the notion and authority of their being a selected part of Common Hall', p. 52.

[36] The origin of the precinct is unknown. It is not mentioned in the fourteenth-century *Liber Albus* and probably developed in the fifteenth century. S. and B. Webb, op. cit., p. 586.

[37] Half of the City parishes stretched across ward boundaries, and nine-tenths of them were in more than one precinct.

[38] There is evidence that 'select vestries' existed in some London parishes (see Chartae Miscellanae, vii, *passim*, Lambeth Palace Library) and in these cases, their usurpation would have been a particular grievance. But even when vestries were 'general' or 'open', it rarely implied before 1640 that all parishioners who were freemen and householders could or did attend; it appears that voting at elections was often confined to those who had served or fined for parish office. Vestry Minute Bk., St. Dunstan's in the West (MSS. 3016:1, fol. 224, 229, 230, &c.). First Precinct Book, Aldgate Ward (MSS.: 142:3). Vestry Minute Book, St. Dunstan's in the East (MSS. 4887:1, fol. 500).

[39] J.Co.Co. 40, fols. 21 seq.

[40] St. Stephen's, Coleman Street; St. Benet's, Paul's Wharf; St. Augustine's; St. Andrew Hubbard by Eastcheap; St. Bartholomew, Exchange; St. Botolph, Billingsgate; St. Nicholas Acons; St. Margaret, New Fish street; St. Alphage, Cripplegate; St. George, Botolph lane; St. Mary, Aldermanbury.

[41] St. Bartholomew, Exchange, Vestry Minute Bk., MSS. 4,384:1, fols. 523, 562, 509.

elections of Common Councilmen, by substituting for them the
'Common Council of the Ward', an unofficial committee of·
the wardmote containing the Alderman, his deputy, the Common Councilmen and a few of the wealthiest inhabitants.[42]

The numbers of Common Council had increased between
the fifteenth and seventeenth centuries, from about 100 under
Richard II, to 187 in Edward VI's reign, to 196 at the time
of Stow's Survey, and to 237 in 1646.[43] The Court of Common
Council was evolved in the fourteenth century as the response
of the citizens to the financial exactions of the Aldermen.
Their earliest claim, therefore, was to control finance. But
their privileges only seem to have extended (and this imper-
fectly) to the right of assent to municipal assessments (for royal
loans and civic purposes), that were imposed on the wards.
Assessments were frequently made on the Livery Companies,
such as the loan to the crown in October 1640, and in these
cases, Common Council was not summoned. Moreover, the
Court of Aldermen frequently ordered payments out of the
Chamber without the assent of Common Council, which frequently protested and reasserted its right.[44]

Common Council also claimed some supervision over transactions which concerned municipal property. Since 1558, all
documents sealed with the Common Seal of the City had to
be signed in the presence of some members of Common Council.[45] By an Act of Common Council of April 24 1592, this
power was conferred on four Aldermen and six Commoners
elected in Common Council.[46] This body, later known as the
Lands Committee, was the most important City committee,
and was often authorized to deal with other matters of importance which were to be discussed prior to their debate in
Common Council. The members of Common Council who
were elected to it were normally the senior and wealthiest
members of the Court who had either fined for the positions

[42] After the Restoration, particularly between 1660 and 1674, there was a
movement to avoid the popular, turbulent assemblies of precinct and wardmote,
by establishing in their place a meeting of the influential men of the locality known
as the Common Council of the ward.

[43] MS. 169:9, Guildhall Record Office.

[44] J.Co.Co. 37, fols. 202v-203.

[45] Rep. 14, fols. 20v, 30v, 32, &c.

[46] *A List of the Bye-Laws of the City of London unrepealed*, 1769. no. 205, 34 Eliz.
April 24 1592.

of Alderman and Sheriff, or were soon to occupy these places. The members of the Lands Committee usually sat on every other important committee elected by Common Council. The impression is gained from the Journals of Common Council that some of the members of this Committee, together with a few other senior Aldermen and leading Commoners, prepared reports and made decisions on important matters in a way that sometimes usurped the functions of the Court as a whole.[47]

Although, by long tradition, the Court of Common Council claimed to make by-laws independently of any other power in the kingdom,[48] their actual legislative power was far from independent of the Court of Lord Mayor and Aldermen. Although the Court of Aldermen sat as part of Common Council and took part in its deliberations, they voted separately and exercised a veto over its proceedings. Only those measures proposed to the assembly on the initiative of the Court of Aldermen were in fact discussed: according to a contemporary there were 'several precedents where the Mayor and Aldermen have decried Bills offered by the Commons (though it cannot be expected there should be many of such precedents, for wherever they gave a direct negative the thing was thrown out, seldom or never entered, unless where part agreed and part denied').[49] The Common Council minutes were read (although they did not require confirmation) at the following meeting of the aldermanic Bench.[50] Moreover, the Court of Aldermen judged disputed Common Council elections, a privilege which was not successfully claimed by Common Council until 1642.[51] According to an order of 1544, it was the practice in the sixteenth and seventeenth centuries for a Court of Aldermen to be held directly before Common Council, and in the sixteenth

[47] Before 1640, there were very few cases where Common Council rejected or even amended reports prepared by its committees, there being no equivalent in procedure in the Court to the third reading of Bills in the House of Commons.

[48] This claim existed by prescription and included the right to alter its constitution without reference to Parliament, though it was not claimed that an enactment could be made contrary to statute.

[49] Small MS. Box 4, no. 3, Guildhall Record Office.

[50] Stowe MS. 796, fol. 21. Undated MS. report in a seventeenth-century hand on aldermanic power in the Court of Common Council.

[51] See Chapter IV, pp. 137-8.

century, there are many examples of Bills being discussed and
prepared before being submitted to the Council.[52] In 1618, the
Court of Aldermen reasserted their claim that they should 'debate and conclude all matters' 'before they were presented to
Common Council',[53] and stated again on June 12 1628, 'that
no matter was to be offered to the Common Council that had
not been first debated, thought necessary and convenient
by a full Court of Aldermen or a special committee'.[54]
Finally, as it was in the sole power of the Lord Mayor or
his *locum tenens* to convene and dissolve Common Council,
it enjoyed very little initiative independent of the senior
magistrates.

Common Council sat much less frequently than the aldermanic Bench. Whereas the Aldermen sat twice a week, on
Tuesdays and Thursdays, except in vacations, Common Council, in the first half of the seventeenth century, was usually
called about five or six times a year, and sometimes as infrequently as twice. It was not unusual for the Lord Mayor and
Aldermen to summon a hybrid assembly, on some occasions,
which by-passed Common Council altogether and included
themselves and the wealthiest commoners and liverymen of
the City chosen at their discretion.[55] As Charles I was known
to be opposed to the calling of Common Council, the Lord
Mayors occasionally resorted to this expedient between 1629
and 1640, particularly when an unpopular royal request for
loans was under discussion.[56]

[52] S. and B. Webb, op. cit., p. 631.

[53] Rep. 33, fol. 322.

[54] S. and B. Webb, op. cit., p. 631. This power of the Court of Aldermen was
successfully challenged by Common Council in March 1642. See Chapter IV,
pp. 147 seq.

[55] The confusing practice appeared in the fifteenth century of referring to all
sessions of the Court of Aldermen at which commoners were present as meetings
of 'Common Council'. Many of these sessions were clearly not properly constituted
Courts of Common Council at all. There may sometimes have been more outsiders than Common Councilmen present, since it had been decided in 1425 that
'all substantial persons' who had been allowed to resign from the office of Alderman or Sheriff should sit on all City 'councils'. S. L. Thrupp, *The Merchant Class
of London*, Chicago, 1948, pp. 81-82.

[56] See Chapter III, pp. 102-3.

COURT OF ALDERMEN

The third and by far the most powerful of the City Councils was the Court of Aldermen. The Aldermen, who numbered twenty-six, were nominated by the wardmote, at a specially convened meeting presided over by the Lord Mayor. Originally they were nominated by all who paid scot and lot, but from at least 1419, it had been established that only freemen could take part in the proceedings. The wardmote had the right to nominate four candidates from which the Court of Aldermen chose one. If the nominations of the wardmote were considered unsuitable, the Court of Aldermen had the right to reject them, and if three successive nominations were not approved, the Court chose its own candidate on the fourth occasion.[57] The part played by the wardmote in the election was even further reduced, since there was a tradition that the Lord Mayor and the eldest knight on the Bench had the first choice of a vacancy and normally transferred—'if it be an easy and quiet ward'.[58] In the sixteenth and seventeenth centuries, it was not at all clear that even freemen had the right to submit nominations. John Strype asserted that 'The Aldermen . . . are chosen by the Common Councilmen and others of the livery residing in the respective ward'.[59] Finally, the Court of Aldermen could override the wardmote entirely, by its claim to dismiss members of the Bench at its own discretion, a power which they could and did use to silence opposition to their policy.[60]

Except for a period between 1354 and 1394, the Aldermen were elected for life and could only be removed by a decision of the aldermanic Bench. The qualifications of the Alderman were that he should be a freeman of the City, have been born within the kingdom and be the son of an Englishman. He did not have to be a householder or resident within the City. The rule that Aldermen should belong to the livery of one of the

[57] A. B. Beavan, *The Aldermen of London*, 1908, ii, p. xx. Strype, op. cit., Bk. v, p. 88.

[58] *Reports of Speciall Cases*, p. 179. The author relates this custom, adding optimistically 'yet the election is in the ward absolute of themselves, whom they will choose'.

[59] Strype, op. cit., Bk. iv, p. 156.

[60] *Index to Remembrancia*, p. 437. See also Chapter III, p. 75.

twelve great Companies was gradually relaxed in the seventeenth century, although the majority still belonged to one of
the great twelve.[61] There was a high property qualification of
£10,000 for the office, and a fine of between £600 and £1000,
was imposed on those who refused to serve.

Chosen for life from among the wealthiest citizens, by the
indirect election of the Aldermen themselves, the Court was
oligarchic and almost self-perpetuating. It enjoyed immense
executive and judicial power. It also exercised, as we have
seen, important legislative functions in the Court of Common
Council. The Recorder and some of the senior Aldermen acted
as Judges of Oyer and Terminer, and Gaol Delivery, and as
Justices of the Peace. The Bench as a whole was responsible
for the Court of Hustings, the Sheriffs' Court and the Orphans'
Court. They fixed the meetings of the Courts of Conservancy
of the Thames which the Lord Mayor held eight times a year.
They heard pleas of debt and issued ale-house licences for the
City. In *The Reports of Speciall Cases*, the Court of Aldermen
and Lord Mayor was said to 'treat, determine and discuss . . .
the pleas, and matters, touching Orphans, apprentices, and
other businesses of the same City. And there are redressed and
corrected the faults and contempts of those which do against
the custom and ordinance of the City, as well at the suit of the
parties, as by inquest of Office . . . and there they use to justify
bakers, victuallers and tradesmen, and to treat and ordain for
the government of the City, and for keeping the King's
peace . . .'.[62] Since 1487, all Ordinances made by the gilds
of the City were subject to the approval of the Court of Aldermen, as well as every aspect of their proceedings, a right which
was enforced by imprisonment of their Wardens, in cases of
recalcitrance.[63] Constituted as a Court of Orphans, it was responsible for the management of minors' estates and for the
safe-keeping of their property. The Court of Aldermen enjoyed the special privilege of presenting petitions to the throne,

[61] A. B. Beavan, op. cit., ii, p. 322. He estimated that in the first half of the
seventeenth century, there were elected from the minor companies, eleven leathersellers, five dyers, four girdlers, three for each of the stationers, scriveners, barber-
surgeons, and brewers, two weavers, two wood-mongers and one from each of the
following gilds, apothecaries, coopers, innholders, pewterers, plumbers, upholders: forty-two in all.

[62] *Reports of Speciall Cases*, p. 153.   [63] Ibid.

and at the hands of the Sheriffs, to the House of Commons.

Procedure in the Court was chiefly by petition, but its deliberations were private, and the Aldermen were not obliged to give reasons for their decisions. The ballot box had been in use in the Court since 1525,[64] but was prohibited in 1637 on the orders of the King, who declared 'his utter dislike thereof'.[65] The senior Aldermen who had held the mayoralty and those immediately next in succession exercised a disproportionate influence over the proceedings of the Court. Not only were they Judges and Justices of the Peace, but they sat on all the most important committees, and above all, on the Committee for letting the City and Bridgehouse lands.

Unpopular with some of the citizens because of its secret deliberations, its lifelong membership, and its great power and privilege, the Court also incurred opposition as a result of its disposal of a vast patronage. In the middle of the seventeenth century there were over 140 offices to which the Lord Mayor and Aldermen enjoyed the right of election and reversion,[66] while they also claimed and exercised the right to grant freedoms by redemption. Common Council disputed the right of the Court of Aldermen to nominate to some of the more important City offices, and by an order of Common Council made in 1597, they asserted that the Lord Mayor and Aldermen were to grant only one reversion a year.[67] Although this order was re-enacted in the following year, it was far from strictly observed. By the third decade of the seventeenth century, the sale of offices was again a major grievance.[68] Not only were offices exercised by deputy, but by means of reversions they were in some cases passing from father to son. Thus, the system tended to establish a hard core of vested interests within the municipality, directly dependent on the Lord Mayor and Aldermen, and naturally antagonistic to any major political changes in City government. The crown, in turn, used the utmost influence with the Aldermen to appoint its own nominees to some of the more lucrative positions, and if these

[64] *Calendar of Letter Books, L.*, pp. xvi, 246.
[65] Rem. vol. vii, fol. 201.
[66] 'A Table of Sundry Offices and Roomes in the City of London, within the Lord Mayor's Guift', appended to *The City Law.*
[67] *A List of the By-laws of the City of London unrepealed*, 1769, no. 194.
[68] J.Co.Co. 38, fols. 109, 161 and 303.

positions were already filled, Charles I had no hesitation in urging the Bench to create new offices.[69]

As well as prestige and dignity, there were material advantages in holding the office of Alderman. The Court enjoyed the wardship of Orphans' estates. Individual Aldermen could borrow from the City Chamber for a long stretch of years at below the current rates of interest,[70] and were in a favourable position to secure leases of City properties which could be sublet at a handsome profit. Influence at the King's court often came even without seeking, since the crown and nobility were always in need of aid from the financial circles of the City, and the Aldermen in their turn enjoyed the advantage of securing the leases of customs farms, or industrial and commercial monopoly patents. Close connections with the court could also, however, bring disadvantages. It meant lending to the King at his request, when refusal might entail loss of privileges. The Aldermen, as City magistrates, were obliged to execute unpopular royal policies, such as the collection of Ship Money;[71] the wealth of the City, with its proximity to Whitehall, ensured the watchfulness of the Privy Council against slackness or neglect of duty. These disadvantages must have been increasingly felt by merchants of middle rank in the sixteen-thirties, and partly account for the growing number of refusals to serve the office. The amount of time which the Aldermen were obliged to devote to matters of government and administration, as has been pointed out, was irksome for merchants whose business interests were all absorbing.

LEADING OFFICERS OF THE MUNICIPALITY

No account of the City constitution would be adequate without a brief reference to the functions of some of the most important executive officers of the municipality, the Lord Mayor, the Sheriffs, the City Chamberlain, the Recorder, and the Remembrancer.[72] On the authority and dignity of the City's

[69] *C.S.P.D., 1635*, vol. 289/2, 302/121, 299/80. J.Co.Co. 37, fol. 192.

[70] See Appendix III, p. 338.

[71] This often involved City magistrates in long-drawn-out and expensive suits, Chamb. Acc., 1638-9, fol. 52v.

[72] There were other important City officers, of course, particularly the Town Clerk and Common Sergeant. But I have described here only those who exercised functions of major constitutional importance in the municipality, or represented the City at the court and the Privy Council, and in Parliament.

first officer, James Howell in 1657 remarked, '. . . concerning
the magnificence, gravity and state of the chief magistrate,
neither the Praetor of Rome or the Prefect of Milan, neither
the Proctors of St. Mark in Venice or their Podestas in other
cities, neither the Provost of Paris or the Margrave of Amsterdam, can compare with the Lord Mayor'.[73] Yet, his status
in the kingdom, although high, had not reached the degree
of elaborate respect with which he was treated after 1688, and
he could still be bullied and insulted by the crown. Nevertheless, he ranked next to the Privy Councillors and took part
in entertaining distinguished foreign visitors. His authority in
the City knew no bounds and seemed to be increasing. The
full title of 'Lord Mayor' had been assumed in the early sixteenth century.[74] As chief magistrate of the City, he had power
to call and dissolve the City Councils and he presided over
the more important judicial courts. He chose one of the City
Sheriffs. His power over the City Companies had greatly increased in the sixteenth century, until in James I's reign he
claimed to be Master of all the Companies.[75] So powerful was
the Lord Mayor in the middle of the seventeenth century,
that it might almost be said that in the Civil War, the policy
of the City varied from one year to the next, according to the
opinions of the Alderman who held the mayoralty.

To offset the expenses of office, the Lord Mayor enjoyed
four-fifths of the price of offices in his gift, as well as over £500
which was paid to him from the profits of rent farms and
market leases.[76] His nominations to office were normally accepted by the Court of Aldermen, and most of the 'profits'
accruing from the sale of offices went into his own pocket.[77]
He had the right to grant three redemptions for the freedom
of the City, and even the Lady Mayoress had the right to
grant one of these privileges. Both Alderman Sir Morris Abbot,
Lord Mayor for the year 1638-9, and Alderman Sir Henry

[73] *Londinopolis*, 1657, p. 395.

[74] *Calendar of Letter Books*, L., p. 232.

[75] G. A. Unwin, *The Gilds and Companies of London*, 1908, p. 232.

[76] Strype, op. cit., Bk. v, p. 154. This figure probably relates to a period some
years earlier than Strype was writing, as elsewhere Strype comments that the
current value of these fees and rent farms amounted to £2,000. The figure quoted
here is similar to that given in *The City Law*, pp. 67-69.

[77] In 1697, the 'profits' of the mayoralty were estimated to amount to £3,527
per annum. Webb, op. cit., p. 673, n. 3.

Garway, who held office after him, used their positions to establish their sons and relations in some of the more lucrative offices. In October 1639, Sir Henry Garway's third son, John, was granted the reversion of the office of Common Sergeant or of Under-Sheriff of the Sheriff's Court, whichever fell vacant first, while his fourth son, Thomas, was granted the reversion of the office of Town Clerk or Secondary of one of the City Compters, depending again on its prior vacancy.[78]

The office of Sheriff offered no such opportunities to recoup the expenses which it entailed. The entertainments which the Sheriffs were expected to give to the Aldermen at assizes and sessions reached the limits of extravagance. In the sixteen-thirties, the cost of holding the shrievalty was estimated at around £3,000.[79] This was a considerable sum even for those citizens worth £10,000 in lands and goods, which was the property qualification for holding the office.[80] To meet the costs, the Sheriffs were allowed about £150 from market and rent farms,[81] and the value of one-fifth of the prices of offices in their gift,[82] but this in no way covered their expenses. It included the right to appoint officers in their own household (subject to the confirmation of the Court of Aldermen), the Sergeants-at-Mace and the Yeomen; they claimed also to appoint the more lucrative positions of the Keepers of the Compters and the Under-Sheriffs, but the Lord Mayor and Aldermen contested their claim in 1638 and won the right to make the appointments.[83]

According to William Bohun, the Sheriffs had 'both a judicial and a ministerial power lodged in them, for with respect to their own Courts they are the sole Judges, but in the Court

[78] Rep. 54, fol. 319v.

[79] *C.S.P.D. 1636-1637*, vol. 342/38. In 1588, it was estimated at £2,500. Harl. MSS. 6,363, fol. 12. Alderman Richard Chambers complained that in 1644-5 it had cost him £4,000. See Appendix II, p. 314. This may represent the gross cost before the deduction of his official allowances, although he may have exaggerated his expenses. Thomas Cullum's shrievalty has been estimated to have cost him, after deducting allowances, between £2,000 and £2,394. A. Simpson, 'Thomas Cullum . . .', *Ec.H.R.*, xi, 1958-9, pp. 30-31. The expenses of the office had been somewhat reduced by Common Council in 1643. See below, p. 246.

[80] J.Co.Co. 35, fol. 335v.

[81] Strype, op. cit., Bk. v, p. 155.

[82] S. and B. Webb, op. cit., p. 680, n. 1.

[83] Rep. 53, fol. 119. P.C.R. 2/50, fol. 129.

of the Hustings they are not Judges alone, but are the Ministers to execute the judgments and precepts of the Lord Mayor . . .'.[84] As representatives of the crown in judicial proceedings, they served the King's writs, compelled men to answer a summons to the courts, kept the public peace, and 'in all cases where the King is party, they may break open doors . . . upon escapers and [outlaws] after judgments'.[85] They also empanelled juries. Besides their judicial functions, the Sheriffs exercised important political powers. They presented petitions of Common Council and the Court of Aldermen to the House of Commons and they were returning officers at Common Hall elections and at the election of the City Knights and Burgesses. In the later sixteenth century and the first half of the seventeenth, there is evidence of a growing distaste among City merchants to hold the office. So great was this feeling that in 1592, Common Council passed an Act bestowing £100 on the citizen who accepted the shrievalty after all other nominees had refused.[86] Prestige accompanied the position, but the expense could be ruinous. Thomas Smith wrote to Sir John Penington in October 1638, 'yesterday, I was with your kinsman, Sheriff Penington, who lives like a prince; my business was to let him know that the Lord Chamberlain had four does to send him . . .'.[87] But in November 1641, Penington was complaining about his financial difficulties to his cousin, Sir John. 'The shrievalty did pinch me', he protested.[88]

The City Chamberlain was 'an officer of great repute and trust', according to Strype: 'Though annually chosen on Midsummer Day, [he is] yet not displaced, but continues during life, if no just and great crimes are made out against him.'[89]

[84] William Bohun, op. cit., pp. 51-52.

[85] Ibid. pp. 53-54.

[86] It is difficult to estimate from the Chamberlain's Accounts whether the number of men who preferred to fine rather than serve the office was increasing during the seventeenth century (although contemporary comment suggests this) because the system of fining was used by the City government as a method of raising funds. It is often in times of financial crisis that the greatest numbers of men are recorded to have fined: e.g. from 1625-1630 and in 1639 at times when the City government was trying to raise loans for the crown and in 1651, 1652, and 1653 when the Chamber was heavily indebted. MS. Shelf 150. Guildhall Record Office. Thirty-six men fined in 1627, twenty-eight in 1630, twenty-one in 1633, eleven in 1637, forty-one in 1639, ten in 1640, and eighty-four in 1651.

[87] S.P.Dom. 16/400/49.

[88] S.P.Dom. 16/485/104.   [89] Strype, op. cit., Bk. v, p. 162.

He was responsible for keeping an account of the estates of the City Orphans, and had special cognizance over apprenticeship enrolments and disputes. He was not paid a fee, but normally made a substantial profit from having at his disposal the cash balances of the Chamber's accounts. He sometimes combined his position with the Treasurership of one of the great trading Companies. Robert Bateman, Chamberlain from 1625 to 1643, was also Treasurer of the East India Company.

The Recorder was the chief legal adviser of the municipality. According to Strype (who was quoting from *Liber Albus*), he was usually 'one of the most skilful and virtuous apprentices of the law of the whole kingdom, whose office is always to sit on the right hand of the Mayor in recording pleas and passing judgments; and by whom records and processes had before the Mayor and Aldermen at Great St. Martin, ought to be recorded by word of mouth before the Judges assigned there, to correct errors'.[90] He was elected for life by the Court of Aldermen. An Order made by the Bench in the reign of Philip and Mary stated that he was to be chosen from the 'old and learned officers' of the City.[91] In fact, in the early seventeenth century, the Recorders were not usually men who had previously held legal positions in the City. One of his main functions was to act as representative of the City in negotiations with the crown and Privy Council; Strype, still quoting *Liber Albus*, described it thus: 'The Mayor and Aldermen have . . . used commonly to set forth all other businesses, touching the City, before the King and his Council . . . by Mr. Recorder, as a chief man, endowed with wisdom and eminent for eloquence.'[92] This meant that the crown was always anxious to see one of its own nominees appointed to the office. During every vacancy in the first half of the seventeenth century, there is evidence of royal interference in the elections, the crown's nominees being elected in practically every instance.[93] Thomas Gardiner, Recorder from 1636 to 1642, had

[90] Ibid. Bk. v, p. 159.

[91] *Second Report of the Commissioners of Inquiry into the Municipal Corporations of England and Wales*, Parliamentary Papers, 1837, vol. xxv, p. 37.

[92] Strype, op. cit., Bk. v, p. 159.

[93] Rem. vol. viii, fol. 21: Vol. iv, fol. 49; Vol. v, fols. 95, 97, 99: Vol. vii, fol. 42, 87, 137, 174.

been recommended by the crown to the Court of Aldermen as a suitable candidate.[94]

The Remembrancer was in many ways an assistant to the Recorder and a personal attendant of the Lord Mayor, his main function being that of an agent of the municipality at the Privy Council and at the King's court.[95] It was in the royal interest to procure the appointment of a nominee to this position, and Thomas Wiseman, Remembrancer during the critical years from 1638 to 1642, was also a figure at court in this period.[96] So entirely was it an appointment to conduct negotiations with the crown, that the office was abolished in 1642 after the rise to power of the parliamentary party in the City, as an unnecessary post which it was expensive to maintain.[97]

It will be seen from the above account that popular opinion in the City was only to a small extent reflected in the municipality. While the crown was able to bring pressure to bear through the persons of the Recorder and the Remembrancer, the Lord Mayor and Aldermen because of their constitutional position exercised ultimate control over Common Council, and even to some extent over the Livery Companies. Common Hall, it was true, was under the control of the Lord Mayor and Aldermen to a lesser extent, and at times of political crisis, it could become a platform for popularly held views. But here, too, the system of indirect election and the restriction of the franchise to liverymen exerted a restraining influence. So skilfully balanced was the City constitution that the Privy Council in 1621 commended it to the magistrates of Norwich (one of the few corporations where the citizens as a whole still exercised substantial influence) pointing out the admirable advantages of the constitution in excluding the lower orders, while maintaining a show of more liberal government. The Privy Council urged the Aldermen of Norwich to amend their own constitution upon London's pattern.[98] In times of crisis, however, claims were made in the City for more effective rights,

---

[94] Rem. Vol. viii, fol. 177.

[95] In Strype's time, he also attended Parliament during the session and reported on its proceedings to the Lord Mayor. Strype, op. cit., Bk. vi, p. 163.

[96] See Chapter IV, pp. 129, 247.

[97] J.Co.Co. 40, fol. 48.

[98] *C.S.P.D. 1619-1623*, vol. 108/80. W. L. Sachse, ed., *Minutes of the Norwich Court of Mayoralty, 1630-1631*, Norfolk Record Society, 1942, p. 18.

and if the reforming party could not find precedents for their claims in early practice, they could always point to the vague general statements in early charters which seemed to support their arguments. Moreover, the oligarchic character of City government meant that once a change had been made amongst the senior officers and the Aldermen, say, by the introduction of men who were parliamentary puritans, it would be difficult for new policies to be reversed and for the new men to be removed. These were to be important political factors in the City after the revolution of 1642.

CHAPTER III

The City Government and the Crown, 1625-40

THE highly privileged status of London (partly but not solely the result of its many favours from the crown) was too obvious to excite much comment in the sixteenth and seventeenth centuries, though its predominance in the economy was fully recognized and fiercely denounced by contemporaries. 'A head too big for the body' which drained the fat of the land and reduced the rest of the kingdom to decay and poverty, was one of many similar expressions used to describe the City's fortunate position. 'The merchants are so tied unto Companies, the heads whereof are citizens of London', another protested, that 'by means of the said Companies (the government whereof is ruled only in the City of London) all the whole trade of merchandise is in a manner brought to the City of London.'[1] The City had gained this ascendency partly as a result of natural geographical advantages, its proximity to England's earliest export market, the Netherlands, and an unrivalled position which commanded the Thames but was protected from the sea.[2] Another fundamental factor in the City's predominance was its closeness to the court in Westminster and the intimate financial connexion which had grown up between the monarchy and the King's 'royal chamber'. The chartered privileges and grants which had been so richly bestowed on the City strengthened the power of London as against the rest of the kingdom, but drew it also into dependence on the monarchy.[3] It was not

[1] Quoted by E. F. Hecksher, *Mercantilism*, 1935, i, p. 425, from an unnamed sixteenth-century author.

[2] Stow repeats a famous story (of which there were many current versions) of an Alderman in the reign of Mary Tudor, who on being told that the Queen intended to move Parliament and the law courts to Oxford to show her displeasure with the City, asked whether she also intended to divert the Thames. On being told no, the Alderman replied in that event they would manage well enough in London, wherever Parliament and the law courts were held. *Survay*, ii, p. 200.

[3] Stow dismissed the fear that the large population and the power of the City would breed sedition. Provided it was well governed, he wrote, it was more likely 'to impeach any disloyal attempt' . . . for 'as London hath adhered to some rebellions, so hath it resisted many, and was never the author of any one'. *Survay*, ii, p. 206. He seems to refer here to the City government.

F

unnatural, in the early seventeenth century, that the bitter struggle of the outports under James I against the monopoly privileges of the chartered companies of the City, became intimately bound up with Parliament's attack on the prerogative power of the crown.

In contrast, the City's contribution to national government and administration and its overwhelming influence on them, were seldom the subject of attack or even comment, although they were perhaps no less striking. The Privy Council depended on London's Trained Bands and its merchant ships in time of war, it called on the services of City officials to sit on royal commissions and take part in embassies abroad, it influenced the Lord Mayor and Aldermen to bestow offices in their patronage on king's servants and courtiers,[4] and it tested new fiscal and administrative measures in the City before imposing them on the rest of the country. The dependence of the crown on the municipality was not a one-sided affair. The City government rendered its services in return for the confirmation and supplementation of its chartered privileges, some of which provided a necessary if declining part of the municipal revenues. The municipality, moreover, depended on the goodwill of the crown to strengthen its jurisdiction in governing the City, and to provide it with the necessary judicial powers to carry out royal policy within its jurisdiction.

This collaboration between the City and the crown in matters of government was in many ways taken for granted.[5] Royal influence in the City government had always been powerful. The crown had long since surrendered the right to choose the Lord Mayor and the City Chamberlain, but it still interfered in City elections, particularly in the case of permanent

---

[4] City offices were often conferred on royal nominees, both minor lucrative offices such as 'seacolemeators', and influential offices such as that of Recorder. See *C.S.P.D. 1635*, vol. 289/2, 299/80, for a petition of Lady Carew for the right of appointing two extra 'seacolemeators'. When the Court of Aldermen turned down her request, the King intervened in her favour, although unsuccessfully on this occasion. Ibid. vol. 302/121. For the King's attempt to appoint to the places of Common Hunt and Common Packer, see Rem., vol. vi, fol. 160, vii, 98. Other references, Rem., iii, 1; iv, 23; vi, 56; vi, 92. *C.S.P.D. 1637*, vol. 366/66.

[5] It was not unknown for a courtier to be chosen to the highest positions in the City: Sir Peter Proby, Lord Mayor from 1622 to 1623, was described by the Recorder as a courtier and one-time barber to Secretary Walsingham. *The Letters of John Chamberlain*, 1939, Philadelphia, ed. N. E. McClure, ii, no. 416.

officials, to secure a sympathetic candidate. The City Recorder[6]
and Remembrancer, as we have seen, were nearly always royal
nominees, and it was common for the crown to appoint the
Recorder as Speaker of the House of Commons. The King also
interfered in aldermanic and mayoral elections whenever a disputed election occurred. The Lord Mayor and Aldermen were
frequently invited to the Privy Council to express their views
and were nominated to national commissions on matters of
trade and finance. Although the crown frequently abused and
insulted the City magistrates in private negotiations, it was
very careful that their outward dignity and the ceremonial of
their office should be strictly upheld, and it was always ad-
monishing them to wear their gowns,[7] and hold their feasts
with due solemnity. It had become customary for the King
to bestow knighthood on the Lord Mayor and, more recently,
baronetcies on those who served him well, while the City
government banqueted the royal family, entertained ambas-
sadors and celebrated royal anniversaries with true regal
splendour.

According to Clarendon, the crown alienated the City by
exploiting this relationship with the City government and neglecting to regard their interests. 'The City of London', he
wrote, 'was (by the court) looked upon too much of late time
as a Common Stock not easily to be exhausted, and as a body
not to be grieved by ordinary acts of injustice.'[8] The history
of these years shows that the most excessive demands and
attacks, unprecedented in scale, were made on the City government. Yet in spite of repeated demands and assaults on its
chartered priviléges, united opposition to the crown was not
achieved even in the financial and political crisis of 1639 and
1640, although the instability of trade and politics forced
the Court of Aldermen to refuse the crown's appeal for a
City loan.

[6] The Recorders who held office between 1625 and 1640 were all appointed at
the suit of the crown. Thus, Sir Edward Littleton in 1631 (Rem. viii, 87), Robert
Mason in 1633 (Rem. viii, 174), Sir Henry Calthrop in 1635 and Sir Thomas
Gardiner in 1636 (Rem. viii, 177).

[7] P.C.R. 2/43, fol. 322. An order of Privy Council enforcing strict observance
of dress.

[8] Clarendon, *History*, i, p. 499.

1625-30

The reign of Charles I opened, as far as the City was concerned, in a burst of goodwill, a reflection of improving trade after slump, and an endorsement, perhaps, of a more active foreign policy. The City granted him a loan of £60,000, and Charles in return gave mortgage security for the loan and for the sum of £100,000, together with interest which had been lent to his father.[9] But this goodwill was soon dissipated when the crown failed to pay the interest; and the King's request for a further loan of £100,000 in June 1626 was turned down by an extra-constitutional meeting of 300 wealthy citizens who had been specially summoned to consider it.[10] Characteristically, the Court of Aldermen then offered him £20,000 to be repaid within a year on the security of the Farmers of the Petty Customs.[11]

Contemporary observers found many reasons for the City's refusal to lend the full sum. Some thought that the royal dissolution of Parliament and the failure of the Cadiz expedition were partially responsible.[12] No evidence for this appears in the City's journals. In view of the City's willingness to lend to the crown in the following year, it was more likely that the dispute between the City and the King revolved around the question of security. In the Parliament of 1625, tonnage and poundage had been granted to the crown for the limited time of one year. This had had a severe effect on credit in the City, since anticipations on the Customs Farms were the most acceptable form of security. In addition, the unsettling effect of the war, particularly the retaliatory measures of the French in response to the seizure of prizes, brought about a temporary trading depression that made money scarce.[13]

The King was not discouraged by an initial refusal, and he

[9] S.P.Dom. 16/1/66. Lands to the value of £216,310 were conveyed to the City. The money was raised by twenty Aldermen and 100 Commoners who in groups of one Alderman and five Commoners each stood bound for £3,000. The Court of Aldermen ordered £14,000 to be paid out of the Chamber as an advance on the loan. Sharpe, op. cit., ii, pp. 92-93.

[10] Rep. 40, fol. 272.

[11] Ibid. fol. 278v.

[12] R. F. Williams, *The Court and Times of Charles I*, 1848, i, pp. 115-16.

[13] W. R. Scott, *The Constitution and finances of . . . joint-stock Companies*, 1912, Cambridge, i, p. 186.

continued to negotiate with the City throughout the summer of 1626. The problem was to find a form of security that would be acceptable to City lenders. The municipality was in no position to make advances out of the Chamber. According to a critical report on the state of the Chamber in 1626, it was already running into debt and spending money that it held on trust for the Orphans of the City.[14] Nor was it anxious to pledge its bond for repayment, unless the securities were impeccable, for if the crown defaulted, as happened too often, the Chamber was liable to be sued by the creditors.[15] Even the crown's offer of the royal jewels and the estates of the Duke of Buckingham and other leading courtiers as security, was refused.[16] But the King's need was overwhelming, so in April 1627, he made a new offer: to compound for the sum of £160,000 outstanding to the City, together with a new loan of £120,000, by passing over to them a vast quantity of crown lands.[17] Here was that more tangible security that the City desired. Even so, certain points had to be made clear. The negotiations between the City and the crown turned primarily around the right of the City to sell the lands to repay the individual creditors, and whether the lands were to be sold by City or by crown commissioners.[18] According to the statement of the Attorney-General, Sir Robert Heath, the agreement finally reached on December 13th, stipulated that the lands were to be conveyed to the City to repay the crown's debts and also to cover the loan of £120,000, on the basis of twenty-eight years' purchase for their debt and interest, with a safeguard against compound interest.[19] The first £60,000 of the new loan was to be paid within ten days of the Contract being signed, and the other £60,000 six months later.

When news of this transaction reached the City parliamentary puritans, there was a cry of dismay. The loan had

[14] 'A Briefe declaration touching the State of the Chamber . . .', Misc. MSS. 166.1 [Guildhall Record Office].

[15] See order of the Court of Chancery in a suit of the executors of Alderman Thomas Bennett against the Corporation, June 11 1631. *Index to Remembrancia*, p. 197.

[16] *H.M.C. Eleventh Report, Skrine MSS.*, pp. 76-77. *Calendar of State Papers and Manuscripts . . . Venice*, ed. A. B. Hinds, 1913, vol. xix, p. 548.

[17] J.Co.Co. 34, fol. 80v.

[18] L.Bk. KK, fol. 92v.

[19] Royal Contract Estates Returns, C.R. 184/6.

been agreed upon less than two months after the overwhelming disaster to the English forces at the Isle of Rhé, at a time when there was great public protest against Buckingham's ill-judged policies, particularly his mismanagement of the war. For some months there had been a campaign for a new Parliament, but Thomas Taylor, a leading City Puritan and minister of St. Mary, Aldermanbury, now wrote in despair: 'We hear no more of any Parliament since the six score thousand pounds was promised to be lent by the City.'[20] He had underestimated Charles' need. The loan did not nearly cover the current anticipations on the revenue, and Charles was soon forced to summon Parliament, although the decision was not made until January 30 1628,[21] six weeks after the agreement, later to be known as the 'Royal Contract', had been reached.

The City parliamentary puritans had other reasons to complain of the municipality. Earlier, when the King had tried to persuade the counties to pay him the sum which Parliament had refused to grant in 1626 (a 'free gift', it was euphemistically called), there was opposition all over the country. At Westminster it was refused at a rowdy meeting, disrupted, it was said, by almost universal cries of 'A Parliament! A Parliament!' the only dissentients being some thirty 'King's servants'.[22] At Hicks's Hall, the subsidymen of Middlesex refused the levy. But when the crown decided to resort to a forced loan, under the name of Privy Seals, London, Middlesex, and Westminster all submitted to it, even after the Judges had attacked its legality. The Court of Aldermen agreed to subscribe to the loan personally and submit lists of those men in their wards who were prepared to contribute and those who refused.[23] This led to a demonstration of protest by parliamentary puritans who covered the City with placards denouncing the Guildhall as the 'Yield-all'.[24] Some of their leaders refused to pay the loan and twenty-one of them were

[20] H.M.C. Fourteenth Report, Duke of Portland MSS., 1894, App., part 2, iii, p. 22.

[21] S. R. Gardiner, op. cit., vi, p. 226. The loan of £120,000, of course, could not solve the Crown's financial requirements, since the anticipations on the revenue on December 29 1627 amounted to £319,000. Ibid. p. 200. In addition, £200,000 a year was needed to pay the soldiers and sailors levied for the Cadiz expedition.

[22] Court and Times of Charles I, i, p. 130.

[23] Ibid. i, p. 211. S.P.Dom. 16/71/39. S.P.Dom. 16/72/63.

[24] Court and Times of Charles I, i, p. 211.

imprisoned, including Samuel Vassall, City M.P. in 1640, and William Spurstow, a leading member of the Puritan congregation of St. Stephen's, Coleman street,[25] who sat as Member for Shrewsbury in the Long Parliament. The Aldermen met even greater resistance when they tried to raise the first instalment of the £120,000 loan early in 1628. They had decided to levy it from the Livery Companies, but they met with stiff opposition from some of the smaller and more radical liveries, and more surprisingly, from one of the major Companies. Prominent members of the Vintners' Company,[26] twenty or thirty members of the Saddlers', including the Master and Wardens, and the officers of the Founders', Glaziers', Plumbers', and Joiners' Companies, were committed to Newgate 'for not having used their best endeavours' in promoting the loan.[27] Even one of the Aldermen was imprisoned for daring to leave the City during the time that the assessments were being collected, and refusing to stand security for part of the quota of the Drapers' Company. He was subsequently fined £300 and, in the high-handed way in which the Aldermen dealt with opponents, he was discharged from the Bench, on the grounds that '. . . he would never perform the office of one of the Sheriffs of this City (which if he continued Alderman the next year must fall upon him) to the honour of the City, and that he was unlikely to be fit to govern others that in his own person and by his own example despised the government of the City'.[28] The widespread opposition among the liveries culminated in the resignation of two of the City's Committee of Trustees for the loan, Henry Waller, who was a friend and ally of Sir John Eliot, and Ralph Hough, ostensibly 'in regard of their extraordinary business and occasions',[29] but more likely because of the suspicion with which the City's transactions were regarded by the House of Commons, and the City parliamentary puritans.

When it met in 1628, the Commons was greatly displeased at this action of the City magistrates in granting a loan to the crown before the King had agreed to summon Parliament. Two petitions, one from Nicholas Clegate, a Vintner, and the

---

[25] Rushworth, op. cit., i, p. 477.   [26] Ibid. i, p. 287.
[27] *Court and Times*, op. cit., i, pp. 314-15.
[28] L.Bk. KK, fol. 108-108v.   [29] Ibid. KK, fol. 128.

other from Chapman, a Scrivener, complaining of their imprisonment for non-payment of their assessments towards the loan, were read in the Commons on March 26th and 27th and were referred to the Committee for Grievances.[30] In May, Sir Edward Coke reported that the two complainants were unlawfully imprisoned, and it was decided to send a petition to the crown for their release.[31]

Another grievance aired in this Parliament concerned the assessment imposed by the City magistrates two years earlier on the order of the Privy Council, towards the fitting out of twenty ships to attack the French fleet.[32] The Aldermen had at first opposed the order, suggesting instead that merchants be allowed letters of marque against the French. But the Privy Council turned down the suggestion, and the City magistrates eventually yielded. The collection of the money had been undertaken by a compulsory assessment on all inhabitants who paid towards the relief of the poor, and those who refused to pay were to have their goods distrained and sold. But popular opposition to the levy was overwhelming. The collection of money proceeded so slowly that the City Chamberlain was ordered to lend £13,000 towards the fund, to be repaid when the sums had been gathered. In May 1627, £11,000 was still owing, and resistance was rising all over the City. The magistrates were compelled to petition the King that 'they had been forced to disburse large sums of Orphans' money out of the Chamber, expecting to be forthwith reimbursed by the citizens. Divers persons, out of opposition to that service, would not contribute and had been distrained upon for non-payment, and vexed and molested the Constables and Officers with suits at Common Law, who in defence were forced to plead long pleas which were chargeable and troublesome to them and the City'.[33]

These early years of Charles' reign were marked in the City by growing turbulence and defiance of authority. In 1626, sailors from the ill-equipped and mismanaged expedition against Cadiz, mutinied in the London docks because of their

[30] C.J., i., pp. 875-6.
[31] Ibid. p. 876.
[32] Melville Wren, 'London and the twenty ships, 1626-1627', Am.H.R., 1949-1950, pp. 321-335.
[33] Index to Remembrancia, op. cit., pp. 466-7.

arrears of pay. Three hundred seamen attacked the house of
Sir William Russell, Treasurer of the Navy, broke down his
gates, and 'would have plucked him out by the ears, had he
not given them fair words'.[34] Two companies of Trained Bands
had to be sent for his protection. These riots were followed by
even more bitter demonstrations against the Duke of Buckingham. On one occasion the mob got out of hand and murdered
one of his followers, Dr. Lambe, a necromancer. Soon after
Lambe's murder, a placard was posted up in Coleman street,
a radical area of the City later in 1641 and 1642, which read,
'Who rules the kingdom? The King. Who rules the King? The
Duke. Who rules the Duke? The Devil.'[35] The Aldermen,
partly as the result of royal pressure, treated this affair with
a severity out of all proportion to the deed, hanging a man
who said he had taken down one of the placards merely to
read it and then had put it back again.[36] Buckingham finally
met his death at the hands of an assassin in Portsmouth. Charles
planned an impressive state funeral, but for fear of demonstrations and tumults by the citizens it could not be carried out,
and the procession was finally forced to wind its way through
the City at night.

Opposition to the crown was not confined to the turbulent
mariners and the labouring classes of London. Some City merchants were now beginning a campaign against increases in
impositions and the unparliamentary levy of tonnage and
poundage. The Merchant Adventurers and the Levant Company were the only chartered trading companies to become
directly involved as organizations, but they were backed by other
individual merchants. The Levant Company refused to submit
to the increased imposition of 2s. 2d. on currants. By the end
of 1628, thirty 'prime merchants' were under arrest.[37] At least
one of the leading officers of the Levant Company was involved in the demonstrations against the impositions,[38] and
the cautious suggestion of the Governors of the Company that

[34] *Court and Times*, op. cit., i, p. 175.
[35] Ibid. i, p. 368.
[36] Rep. 42, fol. 217v.
[37] *Court and Times*, i, p. 432.
[38] William Garway, the Treasurer of the Company. Sir Morris Abbot, Governor
of the East India Company, and an important trader to the Levant, was also
involved.

the remedy lay in private petitions to the crown and Privy Council was overruled by the General Court, who insisted on laying their petition against all increased impositions before the House of Commons.[39] The attitude of the merchants was not, however, supported by the municipality, and Sheriff William Acton was imprisoned in the Tower by the Commons for his refusal to grant a *replevin* to a citizen and burgess, John Rolle, who had been imprisoned at the suit of the customs officers.[40]

But although some leading Levant merchants, Samuel Vassall, Richard Chambers and John Fowke (all of whom were later to be active supporters of Parliament), continued to maintain their opposition and were imprisoned within a year of the dissolution of Parliament, the majority of the merchants were all too ready to follow the lead of the municipality and to resume their trade when it became clear that successful opposition could no longer be sustained.[41] Sir Dudley Carleton, newly created Viscount Dorchester and Secretary of State, noted that there was even talk among the Merchant Adventurers' Company, who had refused to ship any cloths at all in March 1629 in protest against impositions, that a petition should be dispatched to the Council asking for royal protection against future Parliaments if the merchants paid their duties. The merchants trading to France, who had so recently opposed the increased impositions on wine, now asked the help of the Privy Council in disposing of large quantities of wine that had been left on their hands and suggested an increase in duties to counter a similar increase on English products imposed by the King of France.[42] After the depression of 1630, trade revived and for a few years the chartered trading companies enjoyed a period of expansion. When Daniel Harvey, a wealthy East India merchant, organized a petition against the abuses of the Customer Sir Abraham Dawes, 'to obviate

[39] Court Book of the Levant Company, vol. 1617-31. S.P. 105:148, fol. 163, 194v.

[40] Rushworth, op. cit., i, pp. 419-20.

[41] S. R. Gardiner stated that opposition from the merchants continued until the summer of 1629 (*History*, vii, p. 108) and no evidence of more prolonged resistance has been found.

[42] F. C. Dietz, *English Public Finance*, 1932, New York, p. 256. Also S.P.Dom. 16/250/5.

the calumny concerning refusing to pay, or stealing customs', the petitioners declared that 'they were all willing to pay all duties to his Majesty and would never refuse the same', a statement which Edward Hyde pointed out 'would have been much valued a year or so before'.[43] Nevertheless, the memory of the merchants' campaign of 1628 and 1629 remained; while Weston was Treasurer, the customs were not substantially altered and royal revenue was raised at the expense of the City government rather than at the expense of the merchants of the chartered trading companies.

1631-8

The behaviour of the City government in complying with the crown, therefore, far from protecting it against royal attack, encouraged the King and his advisers to increase their revenue at its expense, since they knew that concerted opposition from the City government was far less likely and more easily curbed than from the general body of merchants. Had not the City government also shown itself compliant to authority in another sphere—that of religion? Until 1629, the City Aldermen had a strong reputation for Puritanism. Although Puritans may have been in a minority among those appointed to fill the benefices in the gift of the municipality or to preach Fast Day sermons at Guildhall, they were staunch upholders of Sabbatarianism, an essential feature of the movement in the early seventeenth century. Furthermore, from 1622 they had contributed while it was safe to do so towards the St. Antholin lectures, the long-established and most notable Puritan endowment in the City. But their support dried up when the Feoffees of Impropriations, the leaders of City Puritanism, who had taken over the management of the lectures, were seen to be coming under attack from Laud and the government.[44] After 1630, the Aldermen not only stopped their Puritan activities, including their subscriptions to St. Antholin's and their Sabbatarianism, they reversed the process and began to contribute towards Laud's favourite scheme for rebuilding City churches, particularly St. Paul's.

[43] Clarendon, *The life of Edward, Earl of Clarendon*, 1857, i, pp. 22-23.
[44] D. A. Williams, 'Puritanism in the City government', *The Guildhall Miscellany*, no. 4, pp. 3 seq.

If the Aldermen could be so obedient to their Bishops, they would no doubt be equally submissive to their King. So the Privy Council calculated, when faced with the vexed problem of raising revenue. Every possible device was tried by the government to fill the exchequer in these years without a Parliament, and it decided to question all titles and privileges that could on one pretext or another be claimed for the crown. The municipality, with its extensive privileges extorted from needy kings in return for financial aid, was an obvious source of supply. Sir John Coke, one of the Secretaries of State, a courtier closely connected by marriage with influential City circles,[45] was as determined to raise revenue from the City of London, by challenging 'defective' titles and breaches of charters, as the Earl of Strafford was concerned to extort feudal revenue from Anglo-Irish landlords.

Partly on Coke's initiative,[46] persistent attacks were launched on the City's chartered privileges and grants. This policy was not new, although it was to be greatly intensified. Under James I, the Livery Companies had been attacked for owning 'concealed' lands that should have been surrendered to the crown under the terms of the dissolution of the chantries, and for maintaining 'defective' claims to their properties.[47] The proceeds of Justice, such as the Issues of Jurors and the City's title to the Greenwax fines,[48] had also been questioned. In 1619, during the negotiations over a new City charter, the recently drawn up Letters Patent of the City were annulled on the ground that the Attorney-General corruptly and without

[45] Throughout his life, he had close connexions with highly placed citizens and had married in 1624 Joan Gore, widow of Alderman William Gore and daughter of Sir Robert Lee, who was Lord Mayor in 1603. Dorothea Coke, *The Last Elizabethan, Sir John Coke*, 1937, p. 108.

[46] Many of these attacks on the City's privileges were embodied in schemes which were drawn up or endorsed by Secretary Coke. S.P.Dom. 16/220/65; S.P.Dom. 16/250/51. Sir John Coke, in spite of his reputation as a Puritan, was thought to be a supporter of 'Thorough' and the fullest claims of absolute monarchy. He had a special interest in financial questions, and Strafford praised him for the care with which he looked after the King's financial interests. W. Knowler, ed. *The Earl of Strafforde's letters and despatches*, 1739, i, p. 492.

[47] In 1609, the City companies were fined under a Proclamation against 'defective' titles, and in January 1619 £6,000 was demanded from the Livery Companies, as a composition for arrears in payment on concealed lands. A. H. Johnson, *History of the Worshipful Company of Drapers*, Oxford, 1922, iii, p. 85.

[48] Notestein, Relf and Simpson, ed., *The Parliament of 1621*, Yale Univ. Press, 1935, vii, p. 387, and pp. 373-4.

warrant introduced certain clauses granting the citizens forfeitures for treason and exempting them from serving at muster
outside the City.[49] The question of 'concealments' dragged
on until 1624, when an Act was finally passed protecting all
subjects from further inquiries.

The measures to be taken by Charles to sequestrate the
lands belonging to the City's Irish Society had also been foreshadowed earlier. Disputes between the City and the crown
had, in fact, continued ever since the estates had been passed
over to the Society in 1609. A sequestration of the rents and
profits of the lands had been ordered in September 1625,[50]
on the information of Sir Thomas Phillippes that the Londoners
had failed to plant their lands with English settlers. After a
petition from the municipality, the sequestration was revoked
in August 1627 and a new inquiry ordered.[51] In 1629 and
1630, he sent in his evidence against the City to Secretary
Coke, who agreed that it would now provide material for a
successful attack on the municipality. In this way the King
might 'both break the confidence of the times that hath
encroached upon him and increase his royalties and revenue
in an ample and fair manner'.[52] In 1630, the Attorney-General
filed an information in the Star Chamber against the Irish
Society for having extorted its charter from an unwilling James,
for having failed to send out English settlers and Protestant
clergymen, and for neglecting to build houses. On March 29
1631, a committee was elected by the Court of Common
Council to intercede with the crown.[53] Next year, the attack
on the Society was followed by an attack on the Royal Contract estates, a, matter in which Coke also took the offensive
against the City.[54] The municipality was ordered to make a
list of the Commissioners or Trustees for the estates and a copy
of all the Acts of Common Council concerning the lands.[55]
An information against the City was then brought into the
Court of Exchequer by the Attorney-General alleging that the

[49] Sharpe, op. cit., ii, p. 88.
[50] A. H. Johnson, op. cit., iii, p. 132.
[51] Patent and Close Rolls, Ireland, Car. I., p. 308.
[52] S.P.Dom. 16/172/72.
[53] L.Bk. LL, fol. 90v.
[54] *H.M.C. Twelfth Report, Cowper MSS.* 1888, i, p. 394.
[55] L.Bk. MM, fol. 15.

citizens had undertaken to return to the crown those lands
that remained after the debt had been settled.[56] The Trustees
were accused of selling the lands far below their value, of refusing to pay more than six per cent interest to the lenders,
and sometimes remitting the interest altogether, and of refusing to sell lands to the tenants even when offered a reasonable
price.[57] The Trustees in their depositions before the Exchequer,
naturally enough, denied the charges as strenuously as they
could.

The municipality was, perhaps, in no position to make an
absolute stand against the claims of the King. Its terms of
agreement with the crown were sufficiently vague for a legal
case to be made out against the City. The attack on the Irish
estates was not a sudden affair, but the culmination of a long
process of haggling between the two parties. The City, by this
time, was already disposed to bargain with the King, rather
than endure continuous sniping. But it was probably too ready
to seize at the chance of a settlement and too little disposed
to make a stand against the royal claims, to stand much chance
of succeeding in its case. The negotiations which followed between the King and the City illustrate the eagerness of the
magistrates to reach an agreement, a feature of the dispute
which has not been given due emphasis, and which throws
much light on the relationship of the crown and the municipality in this period. The series of attacks on the City's
charters and estates could have been based only on the belief
that the municipality would in the end be prepared to come
to an understanding, on terms that would be financially ad-
vantageous to the crown. The negotiations which were carried
on by the Lords of the Privy Council and a committee of
Aldermen and the Recorder at the Council Board, were conducted in circumstances that subjected the City's representatives to direct pressure from the crown throughout the process
of bargaining.

In March 1633, the Court of Aldermen petitioned the King
in protest at the number of suits which were being threatened
against the City government in respect of their Irish lands,

[56] S.P.Dom. 16/220/64.
[57] 'Information and Answers Concerning the Sale of the Royal Contract
Estates.' Shelf 185/6, no. 79. [Guildhall Record Office.]

their Royal Contract estates, and their charters. If relief was not granted, they said, 'your royal chamber, the City of London, and the petitioners are like speedily to fall into a more deplorable estate in regard they are much indebted'.[58] In April, they offered the Privy Council £20,000 in return for a cessation of the suits. Negotiations proceeded on this basis and by January 1634 the offer had increased to £30,000, providing the King stopped all action against their Irish estates. They were not at first prepared, however, to surrender the customs of Londonderry and Coleraine, though Strafford had already made it clear to Sir John Coke that these customs, for which the City paid no rent, were to be taken from them: 'at least', he wrote, 'you take that feather from them again, as not fit to be worn in the round cap of a citizen of London'.[59]

So the negotiations broke down. In 1635, the Attorney-General started proceedings against the City in the Star Chamber over their title to the Irish lands alleging their failure to keep to the terms of the original agreement. Judgment was given against the City. It was ordered to pay a fine of £70,000, its charter was cancelled and its property sequestrated.[60] In August 1635, a writ was ordered out of the Court of Exchequer and delivered to the Sheriffs of London for distraining upon the land and goods of the City for the fine of £70,000. The Aldermen, in great confusion and panic, at once begged the crown to come to a settlement with them: Strafford's well-informed correspondent, George Garrard, laconically remarked that the City magistrates 'are most willing to do their duties and have sent often to his Majesty's Attorney-General to advise them how to proceed'.[61]

The City's desire to negotiate was enthusiastically taken up by the Lords of the Privy Council, who ordered the City to 'make such an offer as should be fit for his Majesty to receive'.[62] At first, at the wish of the crown, these negotiations were carried on independently of Common Council. So powerful was royal authority over the City magistrates that it could even prevent its constitutionally elected councils from sitting. It was not until May 1636 that the crown gave the Aldermen

[58] Rep. 47, fol. 148v-149.   [59] Knowler, op. cit., i, p. 200.
[60] T. W. Moody, *The Londonderry Plantation, 1609-1641*, Belfast, 1939, p. 366.
[61] Knowler, op. cit., i, p. 463.   [62] Ibid. i, p. 467.

permission to call a Common Council to take part in the negotia-tions.[63] The City desired to make a settlement of all outstanding differences, including, besides its title to the Irish estates and lands of the Royal Contract, a host of other matters on which it had been attacked: 'the Estreats under Greenwax, upon forfeiture of Recognisance, and for non-appearance of Jurors[64] and concerning buildings and pretended encroachments made upon the wastes[65] and also concerning the claim made unto the City's lands or manor of Blanche Appleton'.[66] On June 23 1636, the Committee of Common Council which had been elected to consider what propositions should be made to the King, suggested a grant of £100,000 to the crown to be paid in five instalments. In return, the City's estates in Ireland were to be restored, the proceedings taken off the file and the land to be formally released from all plantation covenants. They were to be 'discharged of all trusts and ex-pectation of surplusage and other pretences upon the Royal Contract'[67] and to enjoy the fines for building on waste grounds within the City, and issues of Greenwax; their charters were to be confirmed and 'some things for government to be added'; fines and recognizances for the conservancy of the Thames

[63] J.Co.Co. 37, fol. 257.

[64] The 'estreates of greenwax' were the profits arising as casual revenue to the Crown collected by the Sheriff of the County (in contrast to the certain or fixed revenue), and had been nominally enjoyed by the City since the Charter of 23 Henry VI. Fines and forfeitures of recognizances, and issues lost before Jurors, were amongst the most profitable items of the greenwax. It was claimed that in thirty-two years, the profits of the greenwax amounted to £429,049. 11s. 8d. Bankes MSS. 50/50.

[65] Fines for building on the wastes, streets, and public places had also been granted by the Charter of 23 Henry VI. The grants made by this Charter were declared void by a statute passed in 28 Henry VI but were confirmed again by charter in 20 Hen. VII. James I in 1614 and 1618 challenged the City's right to this privilege, but confirmed them again soon after. Rem. iv, fol. 126. In 1636, the King ordered a commission to be prepared to Thomas Doughtie, to com-pound with offenders who had encroached on the streets and wastes of London. S.P.Dom. 16/377/107. Christopher Vernon also urged the crown to recover this privilege, asserting that it was worth at least £4,000 per annum. See above, pp. 21-2. But Vernon is a suspect source.

[66] Blanch Appleton (later 'corrupted to Blind Chapel Court) was a manor on the east side of Mark lane, near Fenchurch street. It had long been in the possession of the City, when the crown on some pretence to its ownership, granted it to Sir George Marshall. S.P.Dom. 16/348/44. This was one of the issues on which Charles refused to give way to the City at the time of the settlement of differences in 1637 and 1638. See below, p. 86n.

[67] J.Co.Co. 37, fols. 193, 202, 202v.

were to be granted,[68] together with the manors of Blanche
Appleton and Steward's Inn.[69] The Earl of Strafford, on whom
the King relied to assess the value of the Irish lands, was at
first prepared to accept the City's offer, although he thought
they should also surrender the fishing, customs and admiralty
rights, and the castle of Culmore.[70] But on his return to Ireland, he discovered that he had underestimated the value of
the estates.[71] He therefore urged the King to bid up the price.[72]
After several months of offers and counter-offers, in which the
crown pushed the price even higher,[73] the City government
decided to sacrifice the lands of the Irish Society rather than
pay the fine of £125,000 which was the final sum demanded
by the crown in composition for their property.[74] The municipality offered to surrender the lands and pay a sum of
£12,000 in return for the settlement of their other claims.
This offer was accepted by the crown on Strafford's advice
in June 1637; whereupon Common Council '. . . well approv-
ing of the aforesaid proceedings, and offer of the said Committees, and rendering all possible thankfulness to his Majesty,
for his gracious acceptance of the said offer, of the lands,
customs, fishings, arrears of rents, and monies, as aforesaid,
did with all willingness condescend for his Majesty having of
the same.'[75]

The City was well pleased with the outcome of the negotiations and preparations were made to lay before the Privy
Council a list of the other matters in dispute which the King
had promised to settle in their favour.[76] The crown proved

[68] A warrant to Sir Edward Wardour to collect these fines had been made out
in July 1636. Bankes MSS. 50/28. The City's right had been contested by the
Lord High Admiral under Elizabeth, but a verdict in 1587 was given in the City's
favour. But Sir Henry Marten, Judge of the Admiralty Court, challenged its
right early in the sixteen-thirties and attempted to ban Anthony Munday's enlargement of Stow's *Survay* because it contained a defence of the City's title against
the claims of the Admiralty. *H.M.C. Twelfth Report, Cowper MSS.*, 1888, ii, p. 38,
December 12 1633.

[69] Steward's Inn was an adjoining tenement.

[70] S.P.Dom. 16/346/92.   [71] Knowler, op. cit., ii, p. 41.

[72] Ibid.

[73] J.Co.Co. 37, fols. 257v-258.

[74] J.Co.Co. 37, fol. 307v.

[75] J.Co.Co. 37, fol. 345.

[76] J.Co.Co. 38, fol. 103. An identical list exists in the Bankes Papers in the
form of a royal order to the Attorney-General to prepare a Bill for the King's
signature. MS. 48/9.

amenable on nearly all the points desired by the City—there being only two exceptions of minor importance.[77] The fine in the Star Chamber over the Irish estates was taken off the file and the City was 'discharged of all trusts and expectations of surplusage and other demands upon the Royal Contract'.[78] The royal charter of 1638, in which most of the City's list of 'Things desired by the City to be granted' was embodied, gave enlarged powers of jurisdiction to the City as well as confirming the rights and privileges which had been challenged by the crown. In addition, new privileges were granted.[79] The Charter shows how much the City's privileges had been attacked. Apart from its title to Greenwax, to fines for encroachments on wastes and public places, and fines in the Court of Conservancy of the Thames, the City's right to garble, gauge and weigh certain commodities sold by retail had been disputed by the crown and was now reaffirmed. The City's power to prohibit markets within seven miles of London was also upheld. The municipality paid to the crown for the passing of its Charter, £12,000, which was levied on the Livery Companies, while a further sum of £2,355. 3s. 8d. was paid to Privy Councillors, courtiers and minor City officials for facilitating its passage.[80] Although agreement with the crown had been reached, and the City government had gained some advantages from its charter, many of the reaffirmed privileges were concerned with feudal rights and revenues which were

[77] P.C.R. 2/48, fols. 138 seq. Fines for building on streets and public places in the City were at first reserved to the crown, but then surrendered, although it was asserted that the Proclamations against new buildings were to remain in force. The crown refused to revoke its grant of Blanch Appleton to Sir George Marshall. As for fines and recognizances on the Thames, the crown amended the City's proposal to fines and recognizances in their own courts only.

[78] Doquet Books, Signet Office, vol. 6811 (11). December 1638.

[79] Both the Charter and the City's list of 'Things desired' contain twenty-four clauses, but four clauses of the Charter had not appeared in the City's list. The Charter contains additional grants of profits from fines imposed by the commissioners of sewers, the right to hold Moorfields and West Smithfield in free and common burgage, to hold a fair and markets in Smithfield and to forbid building there, and the right of the Recorder to plead the City customs without injury or inquiry. The clauses in the 'Things desired' which did not appear in the Charter concerned the Contract Estates, the request that the proceedings against the City in the Star Chamber should be taken off the file, and that the Companies which had been proceeded against for levying fees on admission to the freedom, should be pardoned.

[80] Chamb. Acc., 1638-9, fol. 49v.

either beginning to be obsolete, or which, being farmed out, brought profit to private men's pockets rather than to the Chamber. The settlement can have been no consolation to the Livery Companies and their members, whose subscriptions were now in effect seized by the crown. The Irish Society lost vast properties and had, besides, to pay the City's fine. The City government gained concessions which benefited a few City office-holders, and, to a lesser extent, the City Chamber. The members of the Livery Companies did not forget their losses, and when the City was asked by Parliament for a loan in November 1640, Samuel Vassall, one of the Members for London, reminded the House that the business of Londonderry 'sticks heavy upon them to £160,000'.[81]

A few grievances of the municipality even now remained unsettled. The Incorporation of the Suburbs still continued to interfere in the liberties of the City and to compel City freemen and their sons to take up their freedom with the 'New Incorporation'.[82] Charles' policy of compounding for new buildings also continued, having been specifically exempted from the grants made to the municipality in their charter. The crown still claimed to incorporate new London companies without the assent of the Court of Lord Mayor and Aldermen.[83] Although the magistrates persisted in their refusal to enrol the Company of Distillers they agreed to enrol a number of other incorporations which had been granted by the crown in this period. In 1639, however, the King further conciliated the City by cancelling some of the more unpopular charters—those of the Hat-band makers, Butchers, Horners, Gutstring makers, Spectacle makers, Comb makers and Tobacco-pipe makers.[84] The exigencies of the Scottish War encouraged a conciliatory policy. Freedom of election was restored to the Honourable Artillery Company. An agreement was arranged, concerning the City's privilege of imposing Package and Scavage on merchant strangers, which the King had previously granted to Mr. Kirke, an official of the Queen's bedchamber, and a second charter of confirmation and pardon was finally granted to the

---

[81] W. Notestein, ed., *The journal of Sir Simonds D'Ewes*, 1923, p. 37.
[82] See Chapter I, pp. 36-7.
[83] S.P.Dom. 16/230/59.   [84] *Foedera*, xx, pp. 340-1.

City in September in 1640.[85] Even the association of Sir William
Courteen for trade to the East Indies, so long the chief grievance of the East India Company, had its grants revoked.[86] But
on the many other issues which had provoked the trader and
the manufacturer in the City, no protest was forthcoming
from the municipality and no concession from the crown.
Some of the most obnoxious of the industrial monopolies
remained in force (without protest from the City government)
and the re-opening of the attack on the trading exporters and
importers in 1635 and 1636, with the increases in the Book of
Rates, also failed to provoke widespread resistance from the
merchants, although the East India Company had petitioned
the Council against these increases.[87]

It is noticeable that throughout the negotiations between the
crown and the City government, the municipality was concerned to discuss only those questions which directly affected
the City's estates and privileges. Ship Money, which the leaders
of the parliamentary opposition chose as the issue on which
to oppose Charles, was not fought by the City government.
After the failure of the Court of Common Council's protest in
December 1634, 'that by their ancient liberties and charters
and Acts of Parliament they ought to be freed' from the levy,[88]
it was no longer the subject of protest and was collected
rigorously by the City magistrates. The municipality made no
high constitutional claims denying the right of the crown to
tax the subject at its will. At a later stage, the City authorities
under royal pressure, far from countenancing the opposition
to the tax, committed to Newgate those who refused to pay
their assessments. Occasionally, a Sheriff sympathetic to the

[85] The right of the City to impose dues on goods imported and exported by
merchants who were not free of the City was unpopular and was frequently the
subject of remonstrance to the Privy Council. In 1632, the Council appointed a
Commission to inquire into Package, Balliage and Scavage dues. Rem. viii, fol.
106. As the result of the inquiry, the office of collecting the dues was granted by
the crown to Mr. Kirke, a groom of the Queen's bedchamber. This grant was
contested by the City, and Mr. Kirke was bought off with £4,000. S.P.Dom.
16/342/33. Meanwhile, part of the dues had been granted to Lord Holland. The
City, therefore, declined to accept the agreement with Kirke and a final settlement was not reached until January 1640. Rep. 54, fol. 2, 50v, 91v-92, 323v-324.

[86] *Court Minutes of the East India Company*, ed. E. B. Sainsbury, Oxford, 1907,
vol. 1635-9, pp. xxix-xxx.

[87] Ibid. pp. 206-7.

[88] L.Bk. MM. fols. 165-5v.

parliamentary puritans, such as Alderman Soames, would deliberately refuse to commit to prison for failure to pay and
would gain considerable popularity thereby.[89] As on other occasions, the City's legal counsel helped to undermine any signs
of opposition to royal policy. The Master of Charterhouse
wrote, '. . . the Mayor of London received some reprimand
for being so slow in giving answer to the writ sent unto the
City about the shipping business; afterwards the City Council
were called before the Lords, and received some gentle check,
or rather were admonished, to take heed how they advised
the City in a case so clear for the King, wherein his Majesty
had first advised with his learned Counsel, and with his Council
of State. It wrought this effect, that they all yielded and instantly fell to seizing in all the wards of London. It will cost
the City at least thirty-five thousand pounds.'[90]

The sum originally demanded from the City had been
£35,118, but it was reduced on representation from the City
to £32,163,[91] and a committee was set up by the Court of
Aldermen to undertake the collection of money and the provision of ships. The absence of further protests is surprising,
since the committee became immediately involved in disputes
with citizens who refused to pay and who brought continual
suits in the King's Bench,[92] while the difficulty of raising the
money forced the Court of Aldermen to make up the sum by
large loans from the City Chamber, only a small part of which
was later recouped.[93] The Sheriffs and officers of the City
were given specific authority '. . . to enter the houses of . . .
persons [who refused to pay], take their goods in distress and
sell them for satisfying the sums assessed upon them',[94] and
the extent to which goods were seized is evident from the
Repertories of the aldermanic Bench in 1640 and 1641,
when Parliament's condemnation of Ship Money encouraged

[89] See Chapter V, p. 192.

[90] Knowler, op. cit., i, p. 358. Garrard in a letter to Strafford.

[91] M. D. Gordon, 'The Collection of Ship Money', *Transactions of the Royal
Historical Society*, 1910, Third Series, iv, p. 141.

[92] For the year 1638-9, the Chamber paid out over £34 for prosecuting such
suits. Chamb. Acc., 1638-9, fol. 52v.

[93] In the Chamberlain's Accounts for 1641-2, £11,611. 11s. paid out by the
Chamber was still owing.

[94] Rem. vii, 170.

citizens to petition the Aldermen for the restitution of their possessions.[95]

On the issue of a second writ of Ship Money to the City government, the Privy Council complimented them '. . . for furnishing ships . . . more sufficiently and with better provisions and equippage and much cheaper than any of his Majesty's ships was provided'. The Council expressed the hope '. . . that the like would be done this year through the skill and good husbandry of the present Sheriffs and committees appointed to take care of the business'.[96] On this occasion, however, not only did the money come in much more slowly, but the members of the City committee were accused in the Exchequer Court of peculation and of setting out ships that were undermanned and undervictualled. The crown finally withdrew its charges against the Lord Mayor and the senior Aldermen on the committee, but persisted in its prosecution of a lesser member, William Bushell, who had acted as agent of the committee.[97] The arrears of Ship Money increased yearly between the issue of the first and third writs, in spite of the zealousness of the Sheriffs and their weekly attendance at the Privy Council to report on the collection. The opposition of a large proportion of the citizens nullified the activities of the magistrates. The collection for the final ship demanded in November 1638 could not be raised except by a levy on the twelve leading Livery Companies, seven of which contributed £100 each and the other five £60.[98] Later, in the Long Parliament, it was asserted that this levy was suggested by the Recorder, Sir Thomas Gardiner, and pushed through Common Council despite protests from some of its members.[99] At the end of 1639, £13,189. 18s. was still uncollected from London, in spite of continued precepts from the Lord Mayor, strongly supported by the Aldermen in their wards, enjoining its immediate collection. In June 1640, the crown made a last attempt to raise Ship Money in London. The Lord Mayor and Sheriffs, in order to show their willingness, conducted a

[95] Rep. 55, fols. 32v, 58, 58v, 63, 63v, 75, 100, 100v, 127v, 135, 135v.
[96] P.C.R. 2/45, February 14 1636.
[97] S.P.Dom. 16/378/99. January 17 1638.
[98] S.P.Dom. 16/417/110.
[99] *Articles of Impeachment by the Commons . . . against Sir Thomas Gardiner.* May 23 1642. [Thomason Tracts].

house to house visitation.[100] But they failed to collect the full sum and were brought before the Exchequer to answer for their 'neglect of duty'.[101] The political crisis, however, which overtook the crown in the summer and autumn of 1640, engendered caution, and nothing more was heard of the proceedings against the City officials.

THE CRISIS OF 1639 AND 1640

Until the crisis of the Scottish War, the municipality had on the whole been prepared to accept royal policy (as over Ship Money), and to negotiate with the crown on matters in dispute, such as the City's title to the Irish estates and some of its ancient chartered privileges. Opposition amongst the Aldermen was bound to be slow in forming, since most of them at this time had close ties with the crown and the court through their functions as City magistrates and holders of public offices, customs farmers, lenders to the crown and, in a very few instances, as holders of monopoly patents. Mostly, they combined more than one of these functions. All the senior Aldermen had been involved in executing unpopular royal policies. They had collected Ship Money and had carried out Laud's ecclesiastical policy by implementing the orders of the Court of High Commission: Aldermen Edmund Wright, Sir Edward Bromfield and William Abell were all reprimanded by the Long Parliament for their part in harrying leading parliamentary puritans in the City.[102] Many of the Aldermen were nominated to royal commissions on commercial and governmental matters and so were often involved in these years in policies that were under fire from the parliamentary puritans. Alderman Henry Garway sat on the Committee for rebuilding St. Paul's, one of Laud's cherished projects, and on the Commission for New Buildings,[103] whose activities were included in the Grand Remonstrance as amongst the citizens' grievances.

At least nine[104] of the Aldermen had held the leading offices

---

[100] *C.S.P.D. 1640*, vol. 457/36.   [101] Bankes Papers, MS. 5/41.
[102] See Chapter IV, p. 118-9.   [103] See Appendix I, p. 300.

[104] Aldermen Abbot, Abdy, Cambell, Clitherow, Cordell, Garway, Gayre, Garrard, and Highlord held office in the East India Company. Garway, Cordell, Gayre, and Abdy had held office in the Levant Company. See Appendix I, pp. 285 seq., for the biographies of these men.

in both the Levant and East India Companies, and a good number held the highest offices in other trading companies, though the disappearance of minute books for the Eastland, Muscovy, and French Companies makes a thorough analysis impossible. Many of the office-holders in the large trading companies were closely connected with the crown. Royal pressure was frequently brought to bear (not always successfully) at the elections of these highly placed officials, usually by influencing important individuals to support a candidate favoured by the crown. The leading officers of these Companies depended in turn on royal support to uphold their chartered privileges against interlopers in their trades. This was particularly so in the East India Company,[105] where leading Directors frequently invoked royal aid against critics within the Company (led by the Puritan Lords Brooke and Saye and the Earl of Warwick), and where, in spite of the royal licence granted to Courteen's Association and the raising of the Book of Rates, the crown's influence was extremely powerful.[106] Nearly all the leading Directors of the Company were at this time also Aldermen, and the Treasurer of the Company, Robert Bateman,[107] was also from 1625 to 1643 Chamberlain of the City—a significant concatenation of office-holders. Eight Aldermen[108] are known to have been either Customs Farmers or Undersharers, including

[105] In the Levant Company, the powers of the General Court were much greater than in the East India Company, and the policy of the Directors was not so easily impressed on the Company as a whole. Most of the major decisions were made in the General Court of the Levant Company, which occasionally took decisions against the advice of its Directors. Court Book of the Levant Company, S.P. 105:149, fol. 194v. The tenure of office in the Levant Company was limited and the ballot box was in use in elections until Charles forbade it in 1637.

[106] The desire to keep on good terms with the crown is emphasized in many ways in the records of the Company. In 1635, a Court of Committees agreed to accept the King's price for saltpetre, since 'there will be many occasions to ask the King's favour it will not be wise to give distaste in a business of this consequence'. *Court Minutes, E.I.C., 1635-1639*, pp. 51-52. For royal influence in the Company on more important matters, see below p. 101.

[107] Incorporator of the East India Company in 1600 and of the North-West Passage Company in 1612. M.P. for London, 1621-2 and 1624-5. Member of the royal commission for winding up the Virginia Company in 1624. Treasurer of the East India Company from 1620 and Chamberlain of the City of London, 1626-43. A. Brown, *The Genesis of the U.S.A.*, 1890, p. 826.

[108] Aldermen Abbot, Garway, Abdy, Cordell, Gayre, Whitmore, Pratt, and Acton. See Appendix I, pp. 285 seq.

Sir Henry Garway who was descended from a famous City family of Customers and was himself head of a Customs' ring. Some of these Aldermen, like Sir Edward Bromfield,[109] lent to the crown on their own account. Only two Aldermen, Sir Edward Bromfield who ran the London Soap Company and William Abell, the hated wine monopolist, were involved in accepting monopoly patents.[110] Probably the financial risks involved were too great to tempt the really wealthy, while industrial monopolies of basic products tended to interfere with the trading operations pursued by the merchants of the City. In some instances, also, these Aldermen, substantial landowners themselves with the aid of fortunes accumulated mainly in trade and sometimes from inheritance, were closely connected with the landed gentry and officialdom. Aldermen Sir George Whitmore and Richard Gurney had important landed connexions, and Alderman Sir Morris Abbot was the brother of the Archbishop of Canterbury and the Bishop of Salisbury. Many of them were members of those long-established, wealthy City families, all closely interconnected by marriage, who dominated the big trading companies —such as the Garways, Abdys, Whitmores, Clitherows, Cambells, and Abbots—and their attachment to the court inherited from their fathers was sometimes handed down to later generations. The name Abdy as borne by the Alderman's descendants passed into early eighteenth-century pamphleteering as a by-word for Toryism.[111]

It must be said, however, that the Aldermen of Charles' reign, despite the connexions with the crown described above, were not so closely involved with the government as the greatest Customs Farmers of the time, Sir John Wolstenholme, Sir Job Harby, and Sir Paul Pindar, or as the financial tycoons of the previous reign, Sir Baptist Hickes and Sir Lionel Cranfield, the complex structure of whose business and governmental interests earned them royal exemption from serving the office of Alderman. But at this time attachment to the court was by no means confined to the greatest merchant princes of the City or to those, such as the Customs Farmers, who were primarily government

109 See Appendix I, p. 294.
110 See Appendix I, pp. 289-91, 293-4.
111 See Appendix I, p. 289.

officials.[112] This is shown by the political sympathies of the major Livery Companies in these years. Their ruling councils, usually known as Courts of Assistants, appear to have shown little opposition to Charles's government. They accepted Common Council's decision to forfeit the Irish lands to the crown in return for the grant of a municipal charter in 1637, though it brought the Companies themselves little benefit, and they lost their entire investments in Ireland. Few of the major companies complained to the crown at this time or in the Long Parliament about monopolies. Most of them contributed to Laud's scheme for the rebuilding of St. Paul's.[113] In 1640 and 1641, the crown had strong support among the Wardens and Assistants of the Liveries,[114] and after the outbreak of the Civil War, a minority of the twelve greater Livery Companies, as far as can be deduced from their all too reticent records, showed any consistent evidence of support for Parliament.

But in the political and financial crisis of the Bishops' War in March 1639, when the crown turned desperately to the City government for aid in soldiers and money, it met with the first signs of real opposition, not at first from the Aldermen who were as compliant as ever, but from Common Council. Initially, Common Council had agreed that the citizens of every ward should be urged to contribute to the loan, partly through the persuasion of the Recorder, Sir Thomas Gardiner, a close friend of the court, who told the Council that the crown could, if necessary, compel the citizens to lend the money.[115] Only £5,000 was raised from this source, and no

[112] The distinction drawn by David Matthew in *The Age of Charles I*, 1951, between 'those few possessors of great mercantile fortunes who had attached themselves not only to the Court, but to the landed interest' and 'those of the second rank who still lived in the old town houses' (p. 177) was perhaps not quite so clear as he suggests. Most eminent merchants had both a town house and a country estate, as indeed had Sir Christopher Clitherow, whom David Matthew mentions as a merchant of the second rank.

[113] Calendar, Court of Assistants, Grocers' Company, ii, pp. 752-3. Court of Assistants Minute Book, Haberdashers' Company, 1583-1652, fol. 268v. Repertories of the Mercers' Company, 1631-7, fol. 129v. Orders of Court, Salters' Company, 1627-84 (Transcripts), p. 93. Court Book, Skinners' Company, 1617-51, fol. 150. Court Book, Vintners' Company, 1629-38, fol. 42. John Nicholl, *Some Account of the Worshipful Company of Ironmongers*, 1866, pp. 219-20.

[114] See below, pp. 116-7, 207.

[115] *Articles of Impeachment . . . against Sir Thomas Gardiner*, 1642.

agreement at all could be reached in Common Council whether
to raise 3,000 men from the Trained Bands for the war with
Scotland.[116] It then decided on the revolutionary step of drawing up a petition of grievances to the crown. No such general
petition of grievances had ever been sent to Charles before
from Common Council, and it was known that the crown strongly
opposed such actions. According to the remarkably well-
informed letter-writer, Edward Rossingham, the petition was
moderate in its contents. It complained of the 'extreme dearness
of all things in so much that the poor householder had much ado
to subsist', of the multitude of patents and monopolies, and
of the infringement of the City charters in requiring that citizens should be compelled to march out and fight other than
in the defence of London.[117] But 'the main part of the Aldermen and the moderate men of the Common Council' were
'utterly against the petition', he wrote, 'and the rather because the sum to be given was contemptible, especially to be
given from so rich a City'. After much discussion, it was agreed
by the majority of Common Council that the petition should
be presented with the £5,000. On the following Friday, a
committee was appointed to draw up the petition and, continued Rossingham, 'since the Aldermen refused to present the
money and the petition both together, some of the commoners
undertook it, but the same Friday at noon, the King, having
notice of the former day's proceedings, sent a command to
that committee, that they should forbear to meet upon that
business for he would receive neither their £5,000 nor their
petition.[118] It was said later in 1642 that it had been the
Recorder who was mainly responsible for the failure of the
citizens to present the petition, that he disclosed their intention to the crown, and then informed the persons appointed
to deliver the petition that the King would not receive it.
But Rossingham's account shows that the opposition of the
majority of the Aldermen allied with some 'moderate Common
Councilmen' was also important in preventing even the mildest
action on the part of citizens who were opposed to royal policy,
and the episode throws much light on the reasons for the

---

[116] J.Co.Co. 38, fol. 224.
[117] Add. MSS. 11,045, fol. 6.
[118] Ibid. fols. 7v-8.

ineffectiveness of the parliamentary puritan party in the City government before 1642.[119]

While Common Council was debating its petition, money was being raised elsewhere in the City, through the efforts of the Customs Farmer, Sir Paul Pindar, who, in April 1639, was said to have lent the crown £100,000.[120] It seems likely that the wealthy merchants who were accustomed to make loans to the government, preferred to subscribe on the security of the Customs Farmers, rather than lend directly to the crown or through the City Chamber. The great sums raised for the crown in the summer of 1640 were found by the Customs Farmers, who seem to have had little difficulty in raising money, as was shown by the competition for the Great Farm in 1638, which lifted the price from £150,000 to £172,500. But in less exalted financial circles, people were holding back. Rossingham reported a discussion in Common Council on the apparent scarcity of money in March 1639: some said '. . . that there was little trade and little money stirring, the Dutch having called in two hundred thousand pounds which merchants had of them at use; besides that other monied men called in their debts'; but others answered '. . . that the City was never richer than at the present time, and more abounding in money, but that the money was hoarded up, which after some very short time, when the money mongers looked upon it, that it brought no profit, they would bring it out again'.[121]

Credit, other than for the wealthiest City tycoons, was bad and political stability was shaken by the crisis of the Bishops' War. It is not surprising that the City government, and even some of the Aldermen who were staunch supporters of the crown, were still hesitant about raising loans. When the crown wanted a loan of £100,000 in June 1639, the Privy Council thought it wise to prepare the ground first by treating with individual Aldermen and wealthy citizens: Alderman Henry Pratt, Alderman Sir James Cambell, Alderman Sir George Whitmore, Alderman Sir William Acton, Mr. Delane, the apothecary, Mr. Cropley,[122] a silkman, and Mr. Henley of the

---

[119] Since the petition was not ultimately accepted by the Court of Common Council, the Journals characteristically do not mention the debate.

[120] S.P.Dom. 16/417/3.

[121] Add. MSS. 11,045, fols. 7v-8.

[122] Probably Edward Cropley, an Undersharer of the Customs Farms.

King's Bench. Alderman Cambell,[123] a member of an old City
family, a Governor of both the French Company and the Merchants of the Staple, and a leading East India merchant, declined to speak to the Lord Treasurer. But Aldermen Sir George
Whitmore and Sir William Acton, both Undersharers of the
Customs Farms, and closely connected with the Court, agreed
to see the Treasurer. Alderman Henry Pratt, who owed his
election to the City Bench in 1633 to royal pressure and who
was a close friend of Sir Francis Windebank, Secretary of State,
did not refuse to lend, 'but gave no hope, considering the scarcity of monies and the great damp of trade, the merchant
strangers having all called in their monies, and shut up their
banks'.[124] On June 8 1639, the Lord Mayor, Sir Morris Abbot
and the Aldermen were summoned to the Privy Council, but
only two Aldermen and the two Sheriffs appeared.[125] Abbot's
refusal to appear was a great blow to the crown. Well connected,
he was one of the Petty Farmers of the customs and had been
knighted in 1626 for the part he played in helping to raise the
City loan of £60,000 in 1625. As Governor of the East India
Company, he had, with the Privy Council's backing, fought
for many years the claims of an opposition party led by Lord
Saye and Lord Brooke for a greater voice in the allocation of
stock.[126] At the same time he could be of an independent turn
of mind and, as a member of the St. Stephen's, Coleman street
vestry, he was known to be Puritanically inclined in religion.
Three days later, the Lord Mayor was called back and ordered
to bring the Aldermen with him. This time, twenty-four Aldermen appeared and the Privy Council ordered them to raise
£30,000 in a month from amongst themselves and wealthy
commoners, 'always provided that they did not call their
Common Council, nor put it to the Commons, which his
Majesty would by no means endure'.[127] Their reply was un-
favourable; in anger, Secretary Windebank ordered the Lord
Mayor to put their refusal in writing and send it to the King.
Fifteen Aldermen besides the Lord Mayor had refused to lend.
Only four of these Aldermen, Isaac Penington, John Wollaston,
Thomas Atkins and Thomas Soames, later gave positive sup-
port to the parliamentary opposition. Six of them were Royalists

[123] For Cambell and the Aldermen mentioned below, see Appendix I, pp. 285 seq.
[124] *C.S.P.*, ii, p. 46.　[125] Ibid. p. 53.　[126] See Appendix I, p. 286.　[127] *C.S.P.*, ii, p. 54.

by the end of 1642: Henry Garway, Sir Edmund Wright, and Sir Richard Gurney (all in the immediate succession to the mayoralty), and Sir Jacob Garrard, the East India merchant who was knighted in 1641, John Cordell, the Royalist candidate at the mayoral election of August 1642, and John Gayre, at first sympathetic to Parliament, but probably a Royalist by December 1642. The other four Aldermen, who had all either died or resigned by 1642, were closely connected with the court at this time, and one of them, Anthony Abdy, was one of Charles' staunchest allies in the City government. Seven Aldermen had agreed to raise money: Henry Pratt, Sir William Acton, Sir James Cambell, Sir George Whitmore, Gilbert Harrison and two men heartily disliked as monopolists, Sir Edward Bromfield and William Abell.[128] Edward Rossingham wrote on June 25th, 1639, 'I hear all the Aldermen do not agree to raise their proportions of this sum, but only some few monied men of them, which are willing to lend reasonable good sums, what they can well spare upon less security than the aforesaid [the wine and soap impositions] which hath been offered'.[129]

The refusal of the majority of the Aldermen to finance Charles was based not merely or, perhaps, not even chiefly, on doubts about its political wisdom, but on dissatisfaction about the securities. The Venetian Ambassador wrote that the revenues of the crown were pledged until the end of 1644.[130] The wine and soap impositions were bound to be attacked should Parliament be assembled. Even the mortgage of royal estates may have been a doubtful attraction to prospective lenders. Those who had lent to James I and Charles in the previous decade and had been repaid out of the Royal Contract estates, claimed to have discounted their bonds at 90 per cent. of their value.[131] There were political considerations too. The rumours of an intended pacification with the Scots made the City unwilling to tempt Charles to a more warlike policy.[132] As a cautious gesture, the Court of Common Council on July 31 1639,

---

[128] See Appendix I, pp. 285 seq.
[129] Add. MSS. 11,045, fol. 31.
[130] *V.S.P. 1636-1639*, p. 545.
[131] 'Information and Answers Concerning the Sale of the Royal Contract Estates.' Shelf 185/6, no. 79. [Guildhall Record Office].
[132] Clarendon MSS. 16,104.

gave a free gift of £10,000 to the King.[133] According
to Rossingham, Sir Morris Abbot, the Lord Mayor, proposed to Common Council that a further £5,000 should be
raised from the Bench of Aldermen, 'but that would not be
agreed unto'.[134]

In the spring of 1640, after the calling of the Short Parliament, the City was again approached for a loan. This time,
with the temporary improvement in the political crisis, the
crown hoped for better success. But again the stumbling-block
was the security and a genuine lack of credit. The Dutch having
again called in their money, noted Rossingham, 'the exchange
of money between England and Amsterdam' was raised 3 per
cent.[135] Early in April, the Lord Mayor, Sir Henry Garway,
was ordered to present to the King a list of the richest men in
the City, 'provided the Common Council, with which he had
no desire to meddle, were not consulted about it'.[136] The
Privy Council placed great reliance on Garway's ability to get
things done in the City. The son of Sir William, one of the
wealthiest Customs Farmers of the century, Henry Garway was
a Petty Farmer under Charles. He was a leading Director and
then Governor of the East India, Levant, Greenland and Russia
Companies, and he had long been an adamant opponent of
the opposition party in the East India Company.[137] In 1639,
he had managed to impress men to reinforce the Berwick garrison, even though Common Council was opposed to the levy,
by refusing, so Rossingham said, to put the matter to a vote.[138]
Garway presented the list of the City's richest men at a meeting of the Privy Council to which the Aldermen were specially
summoned, called in one at a time and interrogated. To some,
the proceedings must have had a flavour of Muscovite or
Turkish government, familiar through trading connexions,
rather than the treatment customarily afforded to London
Aldermen and citizens with their proud dignities and rights.

---

[133] J.Co.Co. 38, fol. 303. The £10,000 was raised from Sheriff's fines. Forty-
one men fined in the summer rather than serve the office.

[134] Add. MSS. 11,045, fol. 43v.

[135] Ibid. fol. 109v.

[136] S.P.Dom. 16/450/88.

[137] See Appendix I, p. 299.

[138] Add. MSS. 11,045, fol. 101v. Transcripts of the French Ambassador. P.R.O.
31/3/72.

Edward Bromfield was reminded that he had promised last summer to lend £3,700. He denied it but, after some argument, undertook to lend £1,000, although only on good securities. Six or seven thousand pounds was said to have been raised in this way. A week later, the Aldermen were summoned again but with no more success, though the King said that the sum 'would do him more good at present than if so be the Parliament would give him twenty subsidies'.[139] Finally, it was suggested that wealthy commoners should contribute to the loan on the basis that 'every Alderman who has been Lord Mayor shall lend £1,500, those who have not passed the chair £1,000, and all those commoners who have fined for Sheriffs of London £500 apiece, of whom there are near a hundred'.[140]

The Lord Mayor, Sir Henry Garway, and the Aldermen were sent away to prepare detailed lists of the richest men in each ward, who would be compelled to contribute. Such was the fear of the King's retribution that all but seven Aldermen agreed to submit their lists,[141] although they refused to set a rate for the levy. Three of those who did not send in their lists were the well-known City Puritans, Aldermen Isaac Penington, John Warner, and John Wollaston. The other four were more prominent senior members of the municipality, Aldermen John Gayre, Sir Nicholas Rainton, Thomas Soames and Thomas Atkins. With considerable courage, these men made a public refusal when they were called before King's Bench. Soames became a popular hero in the City when he told the Judges that his becoming an Alderman would not affect *his* honesty: 'he was loath to be an informer', he told them, 'he was an honest man before he was an Alderman, and desired to be an honest man still'.[142] Strafford, in exasperation, told Charles that he should make an example of some of the Aldermen and hang them for their refusal. The prosecution was to remind him of this ill-advised remark at his trial.

But the crown still had other sources of finance in the City. The Customs Farmer, Sir John Harrison, was approached at

---

[139] *C.S.P.D. 1640*, vol. 450/88.

[140] Ibid. Transcripts of the French Ambassador, P.R.O. 31/3/72.

[141] S.P.Dom. 16/453/75. These returns made by nineteen Aldermen have been printed in Vol. 2, Series 2, of *Miscellanea Genealogica et Heraldica*, by Dr. Howard, 1886-7, pp. 35 seq.

[142] Bankes Papers, MS. 18/31.

this time by the King, begging him 'for God's sake' to lend him money. The Customs Farmers did what they could. According to Harrison, 'besides what each partner supplied out of his own private money or cash, they borrowed upon their joint bonds very great sums of money, and advanced and paid aforehand upon account of the Rents by the said Contract then agreed to be paid . . . £250,000'.[143] At least five Aldermen,[144] as well as other wealthy City merchants, contributed to raising this sum. In July, the Merchant Adventurers were prevailed upon to lend the crown £40,000 on the security of the Customs Farmers, rather than suffer Charles' proposal to seize the bullion at the Tower.[145] In August, Lord Cottington, on behalf of the Privy Council, prevailed upon the Governor of the East India Company to sell him a consignment of pepper on the security of the Farmers. Alderman Sir Christopher Clitherow, the Governor of the Company, supported by Alderman Abdy (who agreed to buy £3,000 worth of the total), forced the proposal through the Court without putting it to the vote.[146] By this method, the crown raised £50,000 in ready cash.

The crown found it more difficult to bring pressure to bear on the more popular assemblies of Common Council and Common Hall. In the Common Hall elections of City

[143] Stowe MSS. 326, fol. 72. 'Discourse of sundry affaires in 1640 and 1641 concerning the Contract farme of the customs.' The total sum which the Farmers raised, £253,242. 13s. 5d. (ibid. fols. 55v-56), included the £50,000 together with interest for which they gave their bond to the East India Company, on the occasion of the pepper sale to the crown, and which was not paid over to the Company by the Farmers for some years. It would have been more accurate if the Farmers had said they had given bonds for a quarter of a million pounds, rather than that they had raised this sum in cash. It is not possible to check the sum from the Receipt Books of the Exchequer, since the practice that had grown up of assigning tallies meant that money borrowed by the crown was often issued straight to a crown creditor and not entered as a loan at all. In 1640, the value of tallies assigned amounted to £102,381. 7s. 2d. (compared with sums varying between approximately £124,000 and £60,000 between 1636 and 1639), but only £63,000 of it was entered as loans to the crown. F. C. Dietz, 'The Receipts and Issues of the Exchequer during the reigns of James I and Charles I', *Smith College Studies*, vol. 13, no. 4, 1928.

[144] Aldermen Abdy, Acton, Cordell, Pratt, and Whitmore. Stowe MSS. 326, fol. 108.

[145] Rushworth, op. cit., iii, p. 1216. As this sum was raised on the security of the Farmers, it should not be considered an additional loan to the crown above the £253,000. Stowe MSS. 326, fol. 72.

[146] *Court Minutes, E.I.C., 1640-1643*, pp. 82, 88.

Burgesses to the Short Parliament, there were chosen 'not only Puritans but those who in the past have shown most boldness in opposing the king's decrees'.[147] On June 11th, when Common Council was approached for the levy of 4,000 men for the Army, with coat and conduct money, '. . . they stood much upon it that it belonged not to them, as Common Councillors, to covenant to any such levies, so my Lord Mayor would not put it to the question, but will find out some other way to raise and coat the men'.[148] At the same time, a petition for the calling of Parliament and the redress of grievances was circulating in the City and receiving great acclaim from the citizens. When the leaders later asked Sir Henry Garway to present it to the King, he refused and told them to do it themselves.

On July 23rd, the crown made another fruitless attempt to raise a loan from the City government. The Lord Mayor called together a hybrid assembly of the Aldermen, Sheriffs, and two representatives from every ward,[149] but the assembly denied that it had power to raise a loan, despite the fact that 'the Lord Mayor and Aldermen would willingly have either given or lent his Majesty £20,000 . . . but it would not be accepted'.[150] The King, therefore, ordered the Lord Mayor to levy the sum from the Companies, adding a special assurance, 'that this money was not to make war, but only that his Majesty might make the more honourable peace with the Covenanters, with the sword in his hand'. Rossingham related that the Lord Mayor 'advances this service as much as he can, having rated every Company according to their wealth, his own Company, being the Drapers', at £4,500; many of the Companies have met at their halls upon this business, but almost all the principal Companies pleaded inability, because Londonderry has consumed their stocks. Yet the Salters' were so far prevailed upon that they yielded to lend £2,800 if ten of the principal Companies did first lend; the Barber-Surgeons', a poor Company, lend £300 willingly, but all the Companies have not met to return their answer; nevertheless, by those which have, it is collected that his Majesty will not be able to

---

[147] *V.S.P., 1640-1642*, p. 25.   [148] S.P.Dom. 16/457/36.
[149] Transcripts of the French Ambassador. P.R.O. 31/3/72.
[150] S.P.Dom. 16/461/32.

prevail with the City for a tenth part of what he demands.'[151]
Even the King's direct appeal to the Livery Companies had
failed to win a response.

Once Charles had promised to call Parliament and the Peers
had pledged their security for the loan, the City finally agreed
to raise the money. The parliamentary puritans of the City,
however, were not so anxious to entrust the King with a large
loan which might tempt him to break his promise to call Parliament. But the Lord Mayor and Aldermen did all that could
be desired to help. The Peers were invited to dine with Sir
Henry Garway, and after that, a Common Council[152] was
called, 'amongst which', they said, 'we mingled divers Commoners that were not of the Common Council, such as we
knew well affected and powerful in the City. This was stuck
upon as not standing with their forms, but the business not
the forms, was to govern us'; their instructions, explained the
Peers, would not be 'satisfied' unless 'some commoners of
good sort . . . were called, though not all the commonalty
. . . which we overruled'.[153] The Lord Mayor, Recorder, and
Aldermen were particularly active in pushing the loan, they
said. The Privy Council laid great stress on securing it, as the
only way out of their financial impasse and the only way of
humbling the Scots. The Army's Commissary-General wrote to
Windebank, 'the complying of the City of London with the
King will now be a means either speedily to abate their [the
Scots'] pride by arms, or to terminate their rebellious war by
their submission'.[154]

But the Privy Council had not reckoned with the strength
of the parliamentary puritan opposition in the City. They were
not going to allow the government to pay off the Scots before
Parliament assembled. 'God send us the first £50,000 at the
day', wrote Sir Henry Vane to Windebank on October 11th,
'the rest to follow, and that you agree upon the security, for
we have many Thomases amongst us.'[155] Money was slow to

[151] S.P.Dom. 16/463/33.

[152] For the practice of holding 'hybrid' assemblies which were called Common
Councils, see Chapter II, p. 58. Rossingham wrote: 'This was no Court of
Common Council, though all the Court of Common Council were commanded
to be there, because many rich citizens that were no Common Councillors were
also at this meeting.' Add. MSS. 11,045, fol. 123.

[153] S.P.Dom. 16/469/22.   [154] S.P.Dom. 16/469/77.   [155] S.P.Dom. 16/469/85.

come into the City Chamber. The City parliamentary puritans were already bringing influence to bear upon City government. The Court of Aldermen needed several promptings from the Privy Council before they officially condemned the citizens' petition of grievances that was circulating in the City. Sir Thomas Gardiner, the Recorder, was again rejected in the parliamentary elections and the four parliamentary puritans who had sat in the Short Parliament were re-elected; Common Hall refused to elect a close friend of the court, Sir William Acton, as Lord Mayor—all these events were ominous straws in the wind. Earlier in September, the crown had suffered another blow by the death of one of the monarchy's most steadfast supporters on the aldermanic Bench, Anthony Abdy. Windebank wrote to Charles, 'your Majesty will have a great loss of him, being a very able and outstanding citizen, and one whose judgment had lately swayed him to become a great servant to his Majesty'.[156] When the Peers asked the City for another £150,000 they met with a repulse. Sir Henry Garway, 'not finding that forwardness that he desired in the Commons and withal being very unwilling that there should be any denial',[157] was forced to propose that they should wait until after the sitting of Parliament before they gave their answer.

The crown and the Privy Council already found themselves faced by the dilemma in the City which was to overwhelm them in the turbulent days at the end of 1641. The City government, even when sympathetic to the crown, found it impossible to ignore the rising temper of the majority of citizens. To confer authority and power on even loyal magistrates could be dangerous at such a time; who was to say that they might not be successfully challenged by the citizens, and the machinery of government taken over by the parliamentary puritan party? Secretary Windebank faced this quandary in August 1640. The desirability of arming the City now that the Scots were again on the march had to be weighed against the disadvantages 'of suffering any considerable forces . . . to be drawn together at this present, unless the City were in better temper'.[158] The Lord Mayor and Aldermen had made every effort to suppress riots and demonstrations during the year and had been congratulated on their work by the Privy Council. But

[156] *C.S.P.* ii, p. 116.   [157] Add. MSS. 11,045, 131v.   [158] *C.S.P.* ii, p. 95.

the Trained Bands were a citizen army. As events were to prove, without trusted soldiers of a different temper from the citizens, the City magistrates were ultimately powerless. The King was already being compelled to fortify the Tower and fill it with a sympathetic garrison as a precautionary measure against a possible armed uprising. So desperate had the state of affairs become by 1640. But it can be argued that the crisis of 1639-40 was precipitated by the crown's great blunder in bringing about the unpopular and financially crippling Scottish war. Had this crisis not occurred, the compliancy of the municipal government and financial circles with the crown from 1631 to 1638 suggests that money might still have been raised from London, while the oligarchic constitution of the City government might well have considerably delayed the time when popular feeling against royal policy would become effective.

*   *   *

These fifteen years from 1625 to 1640, fall into three periods, culminating in the crisis of 1639 and 1640. But although each of these stages from 1625 to 1630, 1631 to 1638, and 1639 to 1640, has its own historical importance, one main theme with many variations runs through them all: the incessant and overriding demand of the crown for loans and revenue, and the complex response of powerful men and groups in the City towards that demand. The first five years demonstrate the divisions between the City government and the parliamentary puritans. A pattern begins to emerge which is repeated more powerfully after 1640: the City government's readiness to compromise with the crown; its reluctance, if not abhorrence, in putting political conditions to the King; and its opposition to the campaigns of the parliamentary puritans, who appeal successfully to Parliament to support their stand against contributions to the forced loan and to the loan upon which the Royal Contract is based. The alliance of forces and the clash of opinions is almost a dress rehearsal for the events of the first two years of the Long Parliament. In the next period we see again the pliability of the Aldermen in face of increasing demands by the crown. Encouraged by their submission, Charles and his advisers turn the screw. The City government must now pay for ancient chartered privileges and grants as well as new-found rights. This is not a new quarry in the royal chase—other Kings have exacted payments for privileges—but now the hunt is intensified and broadened. But still the City government submits, giving up its valuable Irish lands in return for a new Charter, empty of any real concessions. The crown calls off its attack on the City's privileges, but the Irish estate is lost, and an even vaster sum of money has to be found. The struggle against Ship Money organized at this time by the parliamentary puritans throws into sharper relief the contrast between their actions and those of the leaders of the City government. In the final crisis, although the City government as a body cannot raise money for the crown because of political instability and lack of adequate securities, some wealthy Aldermen and, of course, the Customs Farmers, can still be found to provide for the royal needs. By 1639, there is beginning to be a small group of parliamentary puritans in Common Council. As yet they are ineffective, but the events of the next two years will bring them to power. We must now trace the City government's response to these first years of the Long Parliament and consider the circumstances which allowed the opposition party to challenge and overcome the ruling group in the municipality.

CHAPTER IV

The Constitutional Crisis, 1640-2

By 1640, London was a hotbed of discontent. The Puritan opposition to Laud's religious policy which, the Venetian Ambassador remarked, would finally disturb the peace of the land,[1] had now become part of a more general unrest caused by trade depression, unemployment and the plague. The Scottish war brought a new element of political insecurity as the cause of the Covenanters was espoused by their Puritan brethren in the City. Rumour attributed more sinister plans to the King. There was a scare that French soldiers were to be landed on English soil and that 50,000 Frenchmen were already lurking in the City's suburbs. To allay this particular fear, the Middlesex Justices, on the order of the Privy Council, went to the length of preparing a census of foreigners dwelling in the outskirts of the City.[2]

The apprentices, called out by their traditional cry of ''prentices and clubs', were frequently prone to riot, particularly on holidays and festivals, when they would burst the bonds of discipline in youthful bouts of destruction. Now more serious causes intervened. During Whitsun 1639, John Lilburne organized the distribution of petitions against his imprisonment among discontented and unemployed cloth-workers at a meeting on Moorfields. It ended in a considerable demonstration against Laud.[3] The calling of Parliament in April 1640, only to end in an abrupt dissolution, inspired it was rumoured by Laud, brought popular feeling to fever pitch. In May 1640, placards suddenly appeared throughout the City urging the apprentices to rise and free the land from the rule of Bishops. At a great public meeting on St. George's Fields, Southwark, the City apprentices, and the glovers and tanners of Bermondsey and Southwark on holiday for the May Day celebrations, joined up with the sailors and dockhands, now idle through

[1] V.S.P. 1636-1639, p. 242.
[2] H.M.C., Ninth Report, Appendix, p. 498. C.S.P.D. 1638-1639, p. 562.
[3] M. A. Gibb, John Lilburne, 1947, p. 57.

lack of trade, to hunt, as they put it, 'Laud, the fox'. The
Trained Bands were ordered to attend the proposed assembly
place, but they could not prevent five hundred citizens from
marching on Lambeth Palace, only to find that their victim
had escaped.[4] On the night of May 14th, the prisons were
broken open by the apprentices, and the whole City was
aroused by the night watch to take up arms and preserve
their lives and property. The apprentices tried to free Alderman Atkins, one of the four Aldermen imprisoned by Charles,
but he managed to calm the crowd and returned to prison,
from which he was released next day.[5] The rioters also planned
to attack the house of the Earl of Arundel, the recent commander of the army against the Scots, because, it was said,
he had mounted guns in his gardens on the north bank of
the Thames and turned them in the direction of the apprentices' assembly place on St. George's Fields.[6] The failure of
the City magistrates to deal with the riots prompted the intervention of the Privy Council, who, in mistrust no doubt of
the City's militia, ordered up 6,000 foot from the Trained
Bands of Essex, Kent and Hertfordshire. On May 21, the
Judges declared that the recent disturbances amounted to high
treason, and John Archer, a glover of Southwark, said on the
flimsiest evidence to be the ringleader, was brutally tortured
before his execution.[7] This show of force did not deter the
rioters and placards continued to be posted up, calling on the
citizens to kill Rossetti, the Papal Ambassador, and defend
the true faith.

In June, the news that the citizens were busy circulating a
petition to be presented to the King brought the Privy Council
clumsily into action again. They arrested for 'seducing the
King's people'[8] the two men who were thought to be the
leaders, Richard Chambers and Samuel Vassall, both of whom
were soon to play a prominent part in the parliamentary puritan cause. Vassall's house had been searched earlier and among
his papers was found a pile of covenanting literature and a

---

[4] Laud, *Works*, iii, p. 235. Rushworth, op. cit., iii, p. 1173.

[5] *Winthrop Papers*, Massachusetts Historical Society, 1929-44, iv, p. 248.

[6] S.P.Dom. 16/451/85.

[7] S.P.Dom. 16/454/39. This was the last attempt in England to use the rack
as a means of extorting confession.

[8] S.P.Dom. 16/460/43.

'remonstrance against Ship Money'.[9] Those citizens who had
refused to pay Ship Money were already lodged in Newgate.[10]
Thomas Foxley, a leading Puritan amongst the City clergy,
who had been connected with the Feoffees of Impropriations,
was imprisoned in the gatehouse 'in a chamber not four yards
square'.[11] Calybute Downing and Cornelius Burges, who were
circulating a petition among the ministers in opposition to the
Laudian Canons,[12] had their houses searched and their papers
seized. But a policy of half-hearted repression was not without its dangers to a harassed and debt-ridden sovereign. The
strength of popular feeling and the crown's desperate need for
money from the City induced a more moderate policy. Secretary Windebank at first advised the King to imprison the
authors of the two petitions,[13] but caution prevailed, and it
was finally considered advisable to let them go free, and to
concentrate on procuring an official disclaimer of the petitions
from the Court of Aldermen.

Popular and Puritan opposition to the government of Charles
I was not confined only to the propertyless or the non-freemen
of the City, for well-to-do freemen and liverymen were also
involved. This widespread discontent and turbulence disturbed
the delicate mechanism of the City's constitution. Even in less
critical years it was a precariously balanced instrument. While
the citizens enjoyed a fairly wide franchise, popular influence
was severely limited by the Court of Aldermen's power over
Common Council and over elections to the most important
offices. But in times of political crisis the citizens occasionally
challenged the control of the Aldermen. In October 1628, at
the height of the merchants' campaign against increased impositions, a dispute occurred in the election of the Lord
Mayor.[14] In 1632, the citizens refused to elect Sheriff Henry
Pratt to a vacant aldermanry.[15] On both occasions, the crown

---

[9] S.P.Dom. 16/429/38.

[10] Among those still lodged in Newgate was Stephen Estwicke, Common
Councilman and later a supporter of Parliament and Militia Commissioner for
the City. *H.M.C., Fourth Report, Part I, House of Lords MSS.*, p. 29. See also
Appendix II, pp. 315-6, below.

[11] I. M. Calder, 'The St. Antholin Lectures', *The Church Quarterly Review*, clx,
no. 334, p. 54.

[12] S.P.Dom. 16/463/54.   [13] *C.S.P.*, ii, p. 117.

[14] *Index to Remembrancia*, op. cit., p. 208. clx, *C.S.P.D. 1628-1629*, vol. 118/80.

[15] *C.S.P.D. 1631-1633*, vol. 224/10.

interfered to remind the Lord Mayor and Aldermen in sharp tones of their failure to preserve 'quiet government'. In an attempt to stave off similar conflicts in April 1640, the crown ordered the Lord Mayor not to call Common Council to discuss the proposed royal loan. But when the crown later decided to pursue a conciliatory policy and resort to Parliament, opportunity was again seized by the parliamentary puritans of the City to pursue popular policies through a constitutional medium.

In the first stages of the campaign, it was in Common Hall rather than in Common Council that these policies achieved success. The domination of the Lord Mayor and Aldermen over Common Council was bound to make it at the outset an ineffective instrument for furthering parliamentary puritan designs. Not so with Common Hall. Here the Aldermen as a Court had no power of veto and the lack of formality in its voting procedures gave greater opportunity for an opposition party to make headway. Since Common Hall was primarily an electoral body, however, the main disputes in City government in 1642 (with the exception of the Common Council election of December 1641) revolved around the elections of the Mayor, Sheriffs and the City Burgesses.

The first City election to be held after Charles's submission to the proposals of the Peers occurred on September 28 1640. This was the annual election of the Lord Mayor, which took place in Common Hall. At least a week before, Secretary Windebank had been informed by the City Remembrancer, Thomas Wiseman, that it would be disputed,. and the Privy Council sent for the Recorder 'to advise upon some course to direct the City from such an irregularity'.[16] There was a movement afoot in the City to set aside Sir William Acton, the senior Alderman, and to elect in his place one of his younger colleagues. Acton, a known adherent of the court, was an unpopular citizen. An Under-officer and Undersharer of the Customs Farms, he had been imprisoned in 1629 on the order of the House of Commons, while City Sheriff, for denying a *replevin* to the merchants detained by the crown for their refusal to pay customs duties.[17] Charles had rewarded him with the first baronetcy to be conferred on a City dignitary during his

---

[16] *C.S.P.*, ii, p. 124.   [17] Rushworth, op. cit., i, pp. 419-20.

reign,[18] an honour that was more marked since knighthood
and other distinctions were usually conferred only on the
Alderman who held the mayoralty. In 1635, he was a witness
for Sir James Bagg in one of the most sordid Star Chamber
cases of the period.[19] After the outbreak of the Bishops' War,
when the municipality was refusing to lend to the crown,
Acton, it was rumoured, lent the King a 'cartload of money'.[20]

On the day of the election, Guildhall was full from eight
in the morning until three in the afternoon. A number of
young 'mechanics', so we are told, made such an uproar that
nothing could be heard. When they came to the choice of
Mayor, they refused to consider the senior Alderman, 'but
cried "no Acton, no Acton", three several times, and told my
Lord Mayor he had honour enough already, he need not be
a Lord, and would not be persuaded by any means to choose
him'.[21] Instead, they nominated Alderman Thomas Soames
and Alderman John Gayre, two of the four Aldermen who had
been imprisoned in the previous May for their refusal to submit a list of wealthy inhabitants as a basis for a forced loan.
Gayre was also popular because it was said that he had opposed the aldermanic decision to condemn the citizens' petition
of grievances.[22] But neither of these candidates was close to his
turn for the office. The final list that was sent from the body
of the Hall to the Court of Aldermen included Soames and
Alderman Edmund Wright, while Acton, who had received
only 200 of 1,500 votes cast, was not named.[23]

Windebank wrote in great alarm to the King, pointing out
the unprecedented nature of this dispute. 'These three hundred years', he told him, 'no one Alderman hath been rejected
or put out of his order, but in case of poverty, infirmity of age
or sickness. . . . If this be permitted, the government of the
City is utterly lost; and if Alderman Soames be chosen, besides his disaffections and disabilities, all the Aldermen his
seniors, which are seven or eight, will disclaim to come into

[18] *Complete Baronetage*, ed. G.E.C. 1902, Exeter, ii, p. 72.

[19] S.P.Dom. 16/300/34.

[20] *C.S.P.D. 1640*, vol. 468/69.

[21] *H.M.C. Twelfth Report, Part IV, MSS. Duke of Rutland*, p. 524.

[22] *H.M.C., Sixteenth Report, MSS. Lord Montagu of Beaulieu*, 1900, p. 128. Add.
MSS. 11,045, fol. 122.

[23] S.P.Dom. 16/468/97.

the place after him.' His conclusion was: 'this falls out most
unhappily now that the State hath so much cause to use the
City.'[24] Windebank did not exaggerate the unprecedented
character of this break with City tradition. So much for granted
did the senior Alderman take his election to the mayoralty,
that Alderman Acton had already re-furnished his house to
fit it for the scale of entertainment that would be required of
him.[25]

The Lord Mayor, Sir Henry Garway, hurried to the Privy
Council to find out what action he should take, adding that
if they thought it necessary he would continue as Mayor until
the King deposed him.[26] The Privy Council decided that he
should hold another election meeting a week later, before
which he was 'to dispose by treaty, some of the most discreet
of the Companies to conform themselves to the ancient course
of election', and on the day 'to be careful that none be admitted to give their voices, but such as shall bring tickets from
their Companies that they have power to vote'. Garway seems
to have had some success at the postponed election, for a compromise candidate was chosen, Alderman Edmund Wright,
who was the next Alderman in seniority to Sir William Acton.
Windebank and the Privy Council thought it wise to accept
this election in the circumstances, commenting that 'though
the election be irregular, yet it is not altogether so disorderly
as if they had chosen Soames'.[27] Although Sir William Acton
had been rejected, victory on the whole lay with the crown.
Alderman Wright was by no means popular with the parliamentary puritans; the citizens were reputed to be 'as mad
against him being chosen, as against the others'. 'All the exceptions I can learn they have against him', wrote Rossingham, 'is he was one of those Aldermen that had joined with
the Lord Mayor to have written the letter to disavow the City's
petition.'[28]

This election was followed by a meeting of Common Hall
to choose the City's Burgesses for the new Parliament. The
Recorder of the City, Sir Thomas Gardiner, was again rejected
as he had been in the previous March; three well-known Puritans who were known to be antagonistic to the government were

[24] C.S.P., ii, p. 127.   [25] Add. MSS., 11,045, fol. 122.   [26] S.P.Dom. 16/468/97.
[27] C.S.P., ii, pp. 127, 128.   [28] Add. MSS. 11,045, fol. 122.

elected, Alderman Penington, Samuel Vassall and Mathew Cradock, together with Alderman Soames, the 'popular' candidate at the mayoral election. After the proceedings, which according to custom were conducted by the Sheriffs, the petition of the citizens' grievances was handed up to the platform to the newly elected members so that they might present it to Parliament. This caused great confusion. Traditionally, petitions from the citizens to Parliament had first to receive the approval of the Lord Mayor and Aldermen, and the same petition had been rejected by them a few weeks previously. A heated debate was therefore held as to whether it should be read out or not. It was finally decided by a show of hands not to read it in Common Hall. Agreement was reached, however, that it should be read in Parliament, 'where many of them', as they declared, 'would appear to prove all true set down in that petition';[29] and within the first few days of the Long Parliament it was duly read to the Commons by Alderman Penington. Not realized at the time was the tremendous advantage gained to the parliamentary puritan cause by this last election. But in the coming months, as the City members claimed to speak for the City and acted as a link between the citizens and the parliamentary opposition, this advantage appeared ever more strongly.

The paradox of the situation was that the City government never identified itself with the views of its members of Parliament. The municipal and parliamentary records for these years do not show that the Court of Aldermen or Common Council supported, explicitly or implicitly, the policies of Pym and the parliamentary opposition before the crisis of January 1642. Although Clarendon, writing of London in 1640 and 1641, described it as 'the sink of all the ill-humours of the Kingdom',[30] there is no evidence in his History that he was including the officers and representatives of the municipality in his condemnation; elsewhere, indeed, he hints that the City government was sympathetic to the crown. The Court of Aldermen which exercised decisive power in the constitution was composed in September 1640 of men who, as the issues between the King and Parliament emerged, were predominately Royalist; a considerable change in personnel on the Bench took

29 Ibid. fol. 128v.   30 Clarendon, History, i, p. 264.

place before Parliament gained complete control of City government. An analysis of the careers of the twenty-four Aldermen[31]
and Lord Mayor who held office in September 1640 shows that
five[32] had died by the late autumn of 1642 in the early months
of the Civil War, of whom at least four[33] had been closely connected with the court; two[34] had been discharged from the
Bench for 'delinquency', and one[35] for neglect of duty; three[36]
had been discharged from the Bench at their own request
(probably because of the political crisis); by the winter of
1642-3, seven[37] more Aldermen had been imprisoned as 'delinquents' for persistent refusal to pay their assessments, three[38]
of whom were discharged as 'malignants' by the summer of
1643. Nearly all were either senior Aldermen, or were near in
succession to the mayoralty. In contrast, only five[39] Aldermen
who were members of the Bench in September 1640 became
energetic supporters of the parliamentary opposition (of whom
three[40] had sat only for a year); the remaining six Aldermen[41]
(and I include here four men who were in occasional trouble
with Parliament for refusal to pay assessments since in the
context this does not imply active 'royalism') adopted a middle
position, at first perhaps sympathetic to the parliamentary
opposition, later turning towards the crown, but preferring to
suffer the victory of the opposition than risk the financial
disadvantages involved in leaving the City to join the
King.

The Court of Common Council, as an official body, also
appears to have had little sympathy with Pym and the

[31] Two vacancies on the Bench had not yet been filled.

[32] Aldermen Sir Morris Abbot, Anthony Abdy, Sir James Cambell, Sir Christopher Clitherow and Edward Rudge. See Appendix I, *passim*, for these Aldermen
and those mentioned below.

[33] Aldermen Abbot, Abdy, Cambell and Clitherow.

[34] Aldermen William Abell and Sir Richard Gurney.

[35] Aldermen Sir Edward Bromfield.

[36] Aldermen Sir Henry Pratt, John Highlord and Gilbert Harrison.

[37] Aldermen Sir William Acton, Sir John Cordell, Sir George Clarke, Sir
Henry Garway, Sir John Gayre, Sir Jacob Garrard and Sir George Whitmore.

[38] Aldermen Sir William Acton, Sir Henry Garway and Sir George Whitmore.

[39] Aldermen Thomas Atkins, Isaac Penington, Thomas Soames, John Warner
and John Wollaston. Even Soames was lukewarm in his support by 1643. See
Appendix II for these Aldermen.

[40] Aldermen Penington, Warner and Wollaston.

[41] Aldermen Edmund Wright, John Gayre, Sir Jacob Garrard, Sir Nicholas
Rainton, Thomas Adams and John Cordell.

parliamentary opposition. It was, of course, extremely limited in its sphere of action by the force of the aldermanic veto which has been shown to have been used against the parliamentary puritans in 1639 and 1640. Nevertheless, between November 1640 and January 1642, no record has been discovered of the veto being challenged, and no measures in support of Pym and his party (with the exception of the 'Protestation') are recorded as even having been introduced into the Court. Common Council did not sponsor any of the citizens' petitions, not even the more moderately phrased petitions, such as the one calling for the execution of the Earl of Strafford, although the Court had no reason to look kindly on the Earl. It held up the taking of the 'Protestation' in the City parishes by quibbling over the authorization of the order.[42] It urged Parliament to release from imprisonment a City tradesman, Thomas Philips, who had embarked on legal proceedings against the Earl of Warwick, one of the leaders of Pym's party in the Lords, for his use of parliamentary 'protections' to cover the debts of a servant.[43] In November 1641, Common Council concurred with the Court of Aldermen in preparing the royal banquet on the King's return from the north, in spite of Captain Venn's efforts to dissuade them. The Committees who were elected during 1641 by Common Council included as many men (occasionally more) who later became Royalists as Parliamentarians.[44] It is not intended to suggest that there was not a strong group of Puritans and supporters of the opposition within Common Council. It has been shown that strong opposition to royal policy existed in the Court in 1639 and 1640. Moreover, since the Journals of Common Council only very occasionally record measures that were discussed but voted down in that assembly, it is not possible to discover with

[42] J.Co.Co. 40, fol. 2v.

[43] Ibid. fol. 5, 5v.

[44] 'The Committee for Parliamentary Affairs', whose election was first mentioned in the Court of Aldermen and confirmed in Common Council at a later date, consisted of eight Aldermen and fourteen Commoners, of whom the majority later supported the King, although it also contained a minority of parliamentary puritans. See below, Ch. V, p. 196. The City Committee appointed to discuss Protections with a Committee of the House of Commons was similarly composed. J.Co.Co. 40, fol. 4. A majority of the Committee set up to welcome the King in November 1641 was composed of men who are later known to have been Royalists. J.Co.Co. 40, fol. 8.

certainty whether the citizens' petitions were introduced into
Common Council, or what degree of support they would have
won. But the fact that the supporters of Parliament were not
able to challenge the Court of Aldermen with success until
the revolutionary months of 1642, when they had the open
support of the House of Commons for their claims, serves as
some indication of the relative strength of the parties in the
preceding years.

In contrast with the citizens' petitions, so often wrongly
ascribed to the City government, none of the official petitions
presented by the Court of Aldermen and Common Council
were concerned with controversial national issues, while Parliament, overwhelmed with urgent national business, found
little time to deal with them. The forfeiture of the Irish lands
(an issue on which the City Members of Parliament had been
very active) was declared to be unwarranted and was annulled,[45] an important gesture, but Parliament was slow to
deal with other issues. The City government could not have
been unaware that whereas the unofficial petitions of the citizens, the Root and Branch petition, one calling for the execution of Strafford, and another to exclude the Bishops from the
House of Lords, were well received by the opposition leaders
and given lengthy consideration, no action at all was taken
on some of the petitions which originated in the Court of
Aldermen and Common Council. The measures sponsored by
the municipality were mainly of a governmental or administrative nature. They petitioned against Charles's Incorporation of the Suburbs and in favour of an Act prohibiting new
building in and around the City; they presented a draft Bill
to strengthen their jurisdiction over Southwark, and another
'for setting the poor on work'.[46] No legislative action was taken
on any of these proposals during the first two years of the
Long Parliament. Moreover, it is also significant that only
three of the twelve leading Livery Companies (from whose
numbers the overwhelming majority of Aldermen and Common Councilmen were drawn) petitioned Parliament against

[45] Harl. MSS. 164, fol. 62v.

[46] Chamb. Acc. 1640-1, fol. 51. This shows the money paid to the City's solicitor
towards his expenses in preferring the City's Bills. Unfortunately, only the titles
of the Bills are mentioned here, and not the contents.

monopolies or presented their grievances to the House in 1640 and 1641. More petitions might have been presented, were it not the custom in the City to submit petitions first of all to the Lord Mayor and Aldermen for their approval. The Skinners' Company presented a petition to the City Committee on December 15 1640,[47] hoping that it would then be presented to Parliament, but no trace of it can be found in the journals or diaries of these early years.

As the months passed and Parliament still continued in session, the City became increasingly concerned about the possible abuse of Protections, a device which granted to Members of Parliament and their servants immunity from arrest for debt while the Houses were sitting. In May 1641, the Court of Aldermen and Common Council set up a Committee to discuss this grievance and a petition was presented to the House of Commons on June 2nd by Alderman Richard Gurney, a staunch supporter of the crown who a few months later was to be elected Lord Mayor. The Committee established to consider the petition reported in October that 'there was near a million of money owing to the City from the Members of the two Houses and from their servants and from the servants of the King, Queen and Prince; that those debts if they were received would drive a greater trade than was now driven by all the merchants in London . . . and in fine concluded that this grievance was greater to the City of London than all the projects of salt, soap and leather had been, and than the Ship Money itself'.[48] The Committee proposed to abolish Protections for Members' servants and suspend them for Members. Their suggestions led to heated debates in both Houses and aroused great opposition particularly in the Lords. No Bill was passed in the early years of the Long Parliament, although some minor adjustments to parliamentary privilege were made by order of the House of Commons. The failure of Parliament to do more than modify the worst abuses of the system was used later by City Royalists as propaganda to denounce Pym and the parliamentary opposition.[49]

[47] Court Book, Skinners' Company, vol. 1617-1651, fol. 186.

[48] D'Ewes, ed. Coates, pp. 42-43.

[49] See below the charges brought against Sir George Benion in March 1642, pp. 105-1.

Again, in contrast to the welcome it afforded to the citizens' petitions, the House of Commons not only neglected to remedy the grievances of the City government, but openly attacked its leading magistrates. Complaints about the municipality poured in to the Committee for Grievances from London citizens. Nicholas Clegate, a Vintner, petitioned Parliament for redress against certain of the senior Aldermen of the City, including Sir Nicholas Rainton and Sir George Whitmore, for committing him to prison for his refusal to contribute towards the loan which the City government raised in return for the Royal Contract estates.[50] Several citizens complained of their treatment at the hands of City officers, who had imprisoned them for refusal to pay tonnage and poundage and Ship Money; where distresses had been taken in place of Ship Money, the City government was ordered to return the articles seized, and the Repertories of the aldermanic Bench contain many references to citizens reclaiming property that had been taken away by the Sheriffs and placed in the Chamber.

Many individual Aldermen and a few Common Councilmen found themselves personally attacked for their actions as City magistrates by the parliamentary Committee for Grievances. The Committee dealing with Ship Money voted that Sir Edward Bromfield, Lord Mayor from 1636 to 1637, had 'violated the law and liberty of the subject' in imprisoning in Newgate, Robert Oake and William Newitt, collectors of Ship Money, for negligence in performing their office, and ordered that reparation should be paid to them.[51] Richard Chambers also complained of his treatment at Bromfield's hands. Alderman William Abell was attacked for having assisted the order of the Court of High Commission, by breaking into Henry Burton's house and using force to carry him off to prison.[52] Even the Lord Mayor, Alderman Edmund Wright, was brought before the Committee and attacked for ransacking Dr. Alexander Leighton's study and seizing his papers, which he had done as Sheriff on the order of High Commission. When the

[50] Chamb. Acc. 1640-1, fol. 51.

[51] Rep. 55, fol. 32v. Samuel Vassall, M.P., was one of those who had returned to him a quantity of silver which had been seized by Sir Robert Parkhurst, Lord Mayor, 1636-7, for his refusal to pay Ship Money. Also fols. 58, 58v, 63, 63v, 75, 100, 100v, 127v, 135, 135v.

[52] D'Ewes, ed. Notestein, pp. 218, 194. Rushworth, op. cit., iii, p. 301.

Committee told him that his action was against the law as declared in Parliament, Wright replied that 'it had been as good that the Parliament had never spoken at all of the law nor the liberty of the subject'.[53] The Recorder, Sir Thomas Gardiner, would probably have been made Solicitor-General by the crown,[54] had it not been for the unpopularity he incurred for his part in reprieving the Jesuit, John Goodman. Some of the Aldermen were attacked for their earlier commercial activities. Alderman William Abell, 'the most unhappy, hated object of three kingdoms', was fined and imprisoned for his management of the notorious wine monopoly. Complaints were made about Sir Edward Bromfield's conduct of the London Company of Soapboilers, which bought out the Westminster Company in 1637 and was given the same monopolistic rights to test all manufactured soap and suppress any unauthorized by the Company. A number of Aldermen who were either Farmers or Underwriters of the Customs were directly or indirectly involved in the Commons' investigation into the Customs in 1641, including Aldermen John Cordell, Sir George Whitmore, Sir William Acton, and Common Councilman Sir Nicholas Crispe (who was also connected with unpopular industrial and commercial monopolies). Alderman Sir Henry Garway suffered the severest financial blow. As one of the Petty Farmers, he was amongst the seven leading Customs Farmers who were condemned by the Commons as delinquents and he was ordered to pay £15,000, his share of the collective fine of £150,000.[55] Although he was elected Governor of the East India Company shortly afterwards, the rumour quickly spread in the City that he was bankrupt.[56]

The Lord Mayor and Aldermen also discovered that it was becoming increasingly difficult to preserve law and order now that the parliamentary opposition showed such favour to the citizens' petitions and demonstrations. The Trained Bands could not deal effectively with demonstrators: they were a citizens' militia, averse to arresting their own neighbours, and little could be expected from the routine watch and ward. So the Lord Mayor's precepts, forbidding citizens to go down to Westminster, were disregarded with impunity. Established

[53] D'Ewes, ed. Notestein, p. 517.   [54] Baillie, op. cit., i, p. 292.
[55] C.J. ii, p. 163. Harl. MSS. 163, fol. 279.   [56] S.P.Dom. 16/483/74.

authority in the City was crumbling. When a member of the
Company of Watermen was told that he ought to be obedient
to law, order and the Lord Mayor, he answered that 'it was
Parliament time now, and the Lord Mayor was but their
slave'.[57]

Popular agitation was accompanied by renewed activity on
the part of the opposition among the liverymen of the City.
A dispute broke out at the meeting held on June 24 1641 to
elect the Sheriffs, the Chamberlain, the Bridgemasters and the
Auditors of the Accounts. The elections had to be postponed,
and it was two months before they were settled. On June 28th,
the Lord Mayor and Court of Aldermen delivered a petition
to the King and Privy Council. For 300 years, they said, the
Lord Mayor had elected one Sheriff and the Commonalty the
other. But now Common Hall claimed to elect both. They
asked the King to intervene on their behalf.[58] Charles was unwilling to interfere personally at so critical a time, and referred the case to the House of Lords. On June 29 1641, the
Lords ordered the Mayor to summon a Common Hall for
July 2nd, 'which is to consist of the Master, Wardens and
liverymen and no others', to settle their differences. When the
meeting failed to reach agreement, the Peers ordered six citizens to be elected to discuss the matter with the Lord Mayor
and Aldermen. At least five of the six elected were strong
opponents of Charles's government. Four of them, Captain
Mainwaring, Captain Bradley, John Fowke and Stephen Estwicke, were shortly to play a prominent part in organizing
citizens' petitions to Parliament, and together with Francis
Peck, another of the six, they later became members of the
City Militia Committee, Parliament's chosen instrument in
the City. The party in the City which was challenging the
Lord Mayor and Aldermen on this occasion was evidently
closely identified with the parliamentary puritans who, as will
be seen, came to power in the City in the crisis of January 1642.

In the next two months, both parties in the City were busy
organizing support and searching precedents to establish their
case in the disputed election. The party supporting the Lord
Mayor drew up a petition in his favour signed by 172 of the

[57] H.M.C., *Fourth Report, Part I, MSS. House of Lords*, p. 61.
[58] *L.J.* iv, p. 292.

wealthiest and most prominent merchants in the City.[59] Among
them were a leading group of East India Company merchants,
William Garway, Nicholas Backhouse, Robert Abdy, Daniel
Harvey, Richard Bateman and William Cockayne. Other signatories were the wealthy Customs Farmer Sir Nicholas Crispe,
the Spanish trader Marmaduke Rawden, and Andrew Riccard,
all later Royalists. At least five of them were prominent Common Councilmen, some of whom were to lose their seats in the
decisive elections of 1641. Their petition attempted to discredit
the popular party by alleging that they were 'not well affected
to the present government'.[60] This was strongly denied by the
six representatives of Common Hall, who pointed out that the
petition had been organized by Thomas Wiseman, the Remembrancer, 'an officer', they said, 'who was chosen and maintained
by the Lord Mayor and Aldermen'. They could obtain thousands of signatures to support their claims as against hundreds
to the contrary, they added, and suggested that the dispute
should be settled at Common Hall by a show of hands.[61]

Five weeks had now passed since the dispute began. The
House of Lords, thinking it was high time the affair was
settled, elected a committee to negotiate with representatives
of the Court of Aldermen and Common Council, and the six
members of Common Hall. Again there was stalemate. Reluctantly the Lords came to a decision. Since the election had not
been performed on the appointed day, the right of election,
they said, now lay with Common Hall, though they hoped
that to avoid dispute, Common Hall would elect the Lord
Mayor's candidate.[62] The Upper House was probably being
guided in its decision by the tradition that Common Hall had
the right to elect both Sheriffs if the Lord Mayor's candidate
refused to accept office on election day or died during his year
of office.

The case of a disputed election, however, hardly fell within
these terms. Although Common Hall proceeded to elect the
Lord Mayor's candidate, the Lord Mayor and Aldermen were
highly displeased with the Peers' ruling. On August 26th, they
appeared before the Lords and threatened to give up their

[59] House of Lords MSS. Victoria Tower, vol. July 17-26, 1641. July 26th.

[60] H.M.C. Fourth Report, Part I, House of Lords MSS., p. 91.

[61] Ibid. p. 92.   [62] L.J. iv, p. 373.

offices unless the order was revoked: adding prophetically: 'This being as may be justly feared but a beginning to destroy and dissolve the ancient government of the City. . . . and to bring the magistracy of the City into contempt and disesteem.'[63] The Lords answered that they considered their order prejudicial to neither side. 'As for the government of the City, the Lords are very careful of it', they said, 'and command the Lord Mayor . . . to be so likewise.' According to Edward Nicholas, the Officer of the Privy Signet, the Lord Mayor and chief citizens 'were much troubled' at the answer of the House. They had good reason to be alarmed. Recent ordinances of the City had all confirmed the right of the Lord Mayor to choose one of the Sheriffs,[64] and the magistrates of the City not unnaturally considered the declaration of the House of Lords to be a direct challenge to their authority.

In August and September 1641, it was evident that the City government was becoming openly sympathetic to the crown. The judgment of the House of Lords in the case of the disputed shrievalty hastened this development, and the crown on the advice of Edward Nicholas began belatedly to take positive steps to encourage such sympathies. An opportunity was provided when Parliament passed an Act granting tonnage and poundage to the King, which did not include provision for the abatement of duty on re-exports. The value of this provision to City merchants was very great, and the shortsightedness of the Commons stimulated the East India and Levant Companies to petition them that the omission might be rectified. The crown was well aware of the importance of establishing amicable relations with the directors of the East India Company and earlier in the year had made a special effort to end the negotiations with the Dutch concerning damages which the Company claimed against their counterparts in Amsterdam.[65] Parliament, on the other hand, had countenanced the petition of an opposition group in the Company, led by the unpopular

---

[63] House of Lords MSS, Victoria Tower, vol. August 14-28, 1641. Petition of the Lord Mayor and Aldermen, August 26 1641.

[64] *The History of the Sheriffdom of the City of London and County of Middlesex*, 1723, pp. 17, 18. In 1639, the Commons had elected both Sheriffs, but only because the Lord Mayor's candidate, Robert Charlton, refused to accept office on the day of election. J.Co.Co. 39, fol. 99.

[65] *Court Minutes, E.I.C., 1640-1643*, pp. 134-5.

Thomas Smethwicke.[66] On July 23rd, Alderman Sir Henry Garway, Governor of the Company, told the General Court that the King had promised to recommend to Parliament a renewal of their charter.[67] The occasion of the Companies' petitions to Parliament concerning duties levied on re-exports was turned to advantage by the King, who on September 7th commanded the Lord Keeper to 'tell the City in my name, that though their own burgesses forget them in Parliament, yet I mean to supply that defect out of my affections to them, so that they may see that they need no mediators to me, but my own good thoughts; for as yet I assure you that I have not been sued to in this particular by any on their behalf'.[68]

According to Edward Nicholas, the King's action was well received by the Lord Mayor, who said he would 'make known your Majesty's great goodness to all the merchants of this City'. The King had achieved a victory and it bore immediate fruit. On September 29th, Nicholas wrote to Charles, 'yesterday the Remembrancer of the City of London came to me from the Lord Mayor and Court of Aldermen and desired me to present to your Majesty the humble and dutiful thanks of the City for your Majesty's great grace and goodness in the business of tonnage and poundage. I assure your Majesty that your gracious letter concerning that matter has wrought much upon the affections, not only of the merchants, but of diverse others of this City.' The Remembrancer, inquiring the date of the royal return from Scotland, thereupon suggested that the City should prepare a public reception and banquet for him on his return to London. Nicholas was overjoyed and wrote to Charles that it would be of great assistance to the King to have this opportunity 'to cheer and encourage [the City] in their dutiful affections to your royal person'.[69]

Meanwhile, the summer months had brought growing disorder to London. The return of the plague disorganized the settled government of the City, already disturbed by the burden of great numbers of disbanded soldiers returning from the northern army. The magistrates of the City, the Aldermen,

[66] *Court Minutes, E.I.C., 1640-1643*, p. 156.
[67] Ibid. p. 180.
[68] *Diary and Correspondence of John Evelyn*, ed. William Bray, n.d. p. 759.
[69] Ibid. pp. 767, 771.

had returned for the summer to their country houses as was customary. Turbulence was exacerbated by the order of the House of Commons on September 8 1641, permitting the removal of the rails from the communion table, and prescribing the abolition of images and the discontinuance of the practice of bowing at the name of Jesus. Violent disputes broke out between the Puritans and the orthodox clergy. Disorder in the parish upset the smooth working of the precinct, normally controlled by the vestrymen, and disturbed the routine of the ward. Nicholas wrote to the King on October 5th: 'I am credibly assured that the City of London grows very weary of the insolent carriage of the schismatics, finding their way of government to be wholly arbitrary.'[70]

The election of the Lord Mayor which took place on September 28th reflected this feeling of the City officials. Every effort was made to ensure that the senior Alderman was elected, and they were successful in spite of considerable opposition from the body of Common Hall. Secretary Nicholas wrote to Charles highly commending the conduct of Sheriff George Clarke, who nominated Alderman Richard Gurney, carried his name up to the Court of Aldermen, and dismissed the Court, without heeding the cries of 'No Election!' from the Hall.[71] It appears that the popular candidate was once again Alderman Thomas Soames, one of the City Burgesses. Another Member of Parliament, Sir Peter Wroth, thought the election was evidence of the growth of Royalist sympathy in the City which would in turn 'infect' the whole kingdom. 'If London turn proselyte', he wrote, 'you need not doubt the general conversion.' Firm action on the part of those in authority, he thought, was all that was required. 'Believe me', he continued, 'the late choice of the Mayor, . . . was triumphantly victorious, because each party put themselves in battle array; and the Puritans, if I may give that name to factious people whom you and I know, and disliked honest men were branded with, were overcome with hisses. The effect of courage was seen in that particular; for when the noise began, and they would not go to the election, the new honest stout Sheriff took the paper out of the Sergeant's hands, forgot to make an oration, but bid them hold

[70] *Diary and Correspondence of John Evelyn*, ed. William Bray, n.d. p. 768.
[71] Ibid.

up their hands who would choose Gurney; then proposed three more, carried up two, Gurney and Soames; then the present Lord Mayor came down and informed them that he and the Court of Aldermen had chosen Gurney, whereat the other party called out "No Election". The aforesaid Sheriff dismissed the Court, and so authority silenced noise, and might do so in other and greater things if practised.'[72]

The divisions between the magistrates of the City and the parliamentary puritan citizens were intensified by the election of Sir Richard Gurney, a silk merchant married into a wealthy landed family and described by Clarendon as a man of 'wisdom and courage . . . who expressed great indignation to see the City so corrupted by the ill artifices of factious persons'.[73] When the City government was approached early in November 1641 for a loan towards the suppression of the Irish rebellion, the Recorder, Sir Thomas Gardiner, complained of Parliament's failure to uphold the authority of the City magistrates and officials against its turbulent inhabitants. 'There is now such a slighting of the government of the City', he told the House, 'that there is an equality between the Mayor and the Commons, the power of the Mayor being no more than that of the commoners of the City; they desired but countenance from their lordships, and their lordships shall have service from them.'[74] William Pierrepont, in his report to the Commons on the attitude of the City government towards the proposed loan, made the same point, saying, 'the Common Council did find themselves aggrieved by a disrespect shown to the Lord Mayor and the magistrates of London, by divers people who refuse to give any obedience to any warrant to appear before the Lord Mayor, declaring they would not come'.[75] Meanwhile, Common Council on October 21st had set up a committee of six Aldermen and twelve Common Councillors to make a collection of those acts of Common Council concerned with the government of the City and arrange for their publication so that all might know what these laws were.[76]

---

[72] S.P.Dom. 16/484/63.
[73] Clarendon, *History*, iv, p. 78. Clarendon, *The Life* . . . , i, p. 108.
[74] John Nalson, *An Impartial Collection of the Great Affairs of State*, 1682, ii, p. 597.
[75] Ibid.
[76] J.Co.Co. 40, fol. 6.

The dominant party amongst the Aldermen now rallied around the Lord Mayor to push ahead the preparations for the City banquet which they proposed to give in Charles's honour on his return from the north. The Court of Aldermen and Common Council persisted in their intention, 'notwithstanding', Nicholas told the King, '. . . there have been practices underhand to divert them from their settled purpose'.[77] Captain John Venn, M.P. for the City, tried unsuccessfully to dissuade Common Council from entertaining the King 'as a thing displeasing to the Parliament'.[78] The City's gesture came at the worst possible time for the parliamentary opposition. Pym was about to make what was up to that time his greatest attack on royal power by launching the controversial Remonstrance. The junketings in the City could not have been less appropriate. Common Council, unperturbed, confirmed the election by the Court of Aldermen of a committee of six Aldermen and twelve Common Councillors (many, but by no means all, of whom later became Royalists) to attend to the arrangements of the banquet.[79] On November 25 1641, the King made his entry into the City and was greeted with elaborate pomp and festivity. It was said that Alderman Sir George Whitmore, owner of the magnificent Italianate Balmes House in Hoxton, cut a roadway through his estate to smooth the journey for the royal family.[80] The City Companies lined the streets with guards of honour. Besides the official celebration, the Lord Mayor also entertained the King privately in lavish style at the cost it was reported of £4,000.[81] So many 'libels' protesting

[77] William Bray, op. cit., p. 793.

[78] H.M.C., Twelfth Report, Coke MSS, ii, p. 295.

[79] The Court of Aldermen elected the Committee on November 17th and Common Council confirmed the names at its meeting two days later. Rep. 50, fol. 227, J.Co.Co. 40, fol. 8. The Aldermen were Sir George Whitmore, Sir Edward Bromfield, Jacob Garrard, John Wollaston, John Gayre and Thomas Adams. Whitmore and Bromfield were later Royalists and Garrard, Gayre and Adams were supporters of 'accommodation' with the crown by 1643. See Appendixes I and II. The Commoners included Roger Drake, Roger Gardiner, Sir George Benion, Roger Clarke and Robert Alden who were all Royalists in 1642. Three members, John Langham, James Bunce and William Gibbs became parliamentary supporters. The remaining Commoners were Mr. Ashwell, Mr. Goldsmith, David Edwards, and Mr. Isaacson.

[80] 'Ovatio Carolina. The triumph of King Charles', Harleian Miscellany, 1810 p. 91.

[81] Daniel Gurney, The Record of the House of Gournay, 1848, p. 534.

at the banquet had been scattered about the City previously, that two Companies of the Trained Bands were ordered to stand ready on the day.[82] There is no evidence, however, that disturbances took place.

It is perhaps some indication of the sympathies of Common Council that both the Recorder's speech to the King on this occasion and his reply are fully recorded in the Journal of the Court. Sir Thomas Gardiner, on behalf of the City government, assured the King of their loyalty and affection, and of their devotion to 'our established religion', which he called on Charles to cherish and defend. He then turned to the subject of City government and begged the King to strengthen the authority of the Lord Mayor and Aldermen, in order, as he put it, that they 'shall be thereby the better enabled to serve your Majesty and constantly to render to you the fruits of a true obedience'.[83] After his speech, the City presented the King with a gift of £20,000 which had been placed in a great cup of gold, and £5,000 to the Queen contained in a golden basin.[84]

The King's reply was carefully phrased; as a contemporary remarked, the crown and his advisors had 'a policy in it to see if they can gain the City'.[85] Charles thanked the Recorder and the citizens for their expressions of loyalty. 'I now see', he continued, 'that all those former tumults and disorders have only arisen from the meaner sorts of people and that the affections of the better and main part of the City have ever been loyal and affectionate to my person and government.' Referring to the almost daily rumours of Popish-Irish and even Scottish plots implicating the King, he continued, '. . . it comforts me to see that all those misreports that have been made of me in my absence have not had the least power to do me prejudice in your opinions as may be easily seen by this day's expression of joy.' He proceeded to bestow certain favours on the City. He promised to restore prosperity to their trade and to return to them their Londonderry estates, which he admitted, 'as that kingdom is now, is no great gift. But I intend first to recover it and then to give it to you whole and

[82] *Ovatio Carolina*, p. 90.

[83] J.Co.Co. 40, fol. 9.

[84] *Diurnal Occurrences*, November 25 1641.

[85] *H.M.C. Buccleuch MSS., Vol. I, Lord Montagu of Boughton*, 1899, p. 286.

entirely.' Finally, he agreed to uphold the City in their full liberties and to maintain 'the true Protestant religion according as it hath been established in my two famous predecessors' time, Queen Elizabeth and my father'.[86] At the end of his speech, Charles conferred a knighthood and baronetcy on the Lord Mayor and a knighthood on the Recorder.

The tone of the Recorder's speech with his plea for the defence of 'our established religion', and the royal reply, dissociated the Court of Aldermen and Common Council as a body from the parliamentary puritan opposition. The City's gesture caused many contemporaries to conclude that the City government had now openly espoused the royal cause; indeed, the citizens in their petition of December 11 1641, calling for the exclusion of the Bishops from the House of Lords, found it necessary to make the vigorous assertion that 'whereas it had been divulged upon the King's late entertainment in the City that the City had deserted the Parliament they abhorred the same and should always be ready to spend their estates and lives for our [Parliament's] safety'.[87]

Nevertheless, it was clear that the official municipality was not of their mind. The Court of Aldermen and Common Council declared itself gratified by the royal gesture over the Londonderry estates and ordered the City's Committee for parliamentary affairs to consider how a 'Bill may be preferred to Parliament for the confirming thereof to the Companies of this City'.[88] There were other issues on which it might have been wise for the King to make a gesture. In a list of recommendations submitted to Secretary Nicholas on the content of the royal speech, it was suggested that the King should make some statement on the abuses of Protections, which Parliament had been notoriously slow to reform. The last petition of the City government on this subject had been rejected by the House of Lords on November 15th.[89] The City government was also beset with problems of administration. 'He must take their last Charter into consideration', continued the compiler of the list of recommendations, 'to make some alterations which he intends shall be for the honour, profit and quiet of the kingdom: as the bringing their election to a less company and adding all

---

[86] J.Co.Co. 40, fol. 9v.   [87] S.P.Dom. 16/486/42.
[88] J.Co.Co. 40, fol. 9v.   [89] L.J. iv, p. 438.

the suburbs to their government'.[90] However, when the City sent a deputation to the King to present him with their petition, these points were not included. They prayed the King to continue to dwell at Whitehall, which 'would give a good quickening to the retailing trade', and implored him not to impute the disorders about Westminster to the municipality. 'We held it a misfortune', they continued, 'and a scandal upon us, that when those disorders were mentioned, the City was named with it.' Many of the trouble-makers, they thought, came from the unregulated and disorderly suburbs: 'The skirts of the City, where the Lord Mayor and magistrates of London have neither power, nor liberty, are more populous than the City itself', they explained, 'fuller of the meaner sort of people; and if any dwellers in the City should be actors in it, as who can deny, but among millions of people some there may be, yet their purpose was unknown to us.'[91]

The City deputation which visited the King at Hampton Court on December 3 1641 consisted of the Recorder, Sir Thomas Gardiner, Aldermen Sir George Whitmore, John Cordell, Thomas Soames, John Gayre, Jacob Garrard, John Wollaston, the two Sheriffs and eight commoners. The King received them warmly, granted their petition, and knighted the five Aldermen and the two Sheriffs.[92] Thomas Wiseman, the City Remembrancer, remarked to Sir John Penington, that his cousin, Alderman Isaac Penington, was not one of those knighted, for his 'ways you partly know are rather to please himself than to strive to do any acceptable service to the King, if it stand not with the sense of the preciser sort of the House of Commons'.[93] But the deputation had included Alderman John Wollaston, who had earlier signed the Root and Branch petition and was later to become a leading supporter of Parliament, and Alderman Thomas Soames, M.P., the popular candidate at the mayoral elections of both 1640 and 1641. Wollaston finally rallied to the parliamentary cause despite his knighthood; Soames, however, who was said to have voted against the Grand Remonstrance, became only a lukewarm

[90] S.P.Dom. 16/485/109.   [91] *Ovatio Carolina*, p. 101.   [92] Ibid. p. 102.
[93] S.P.Dom. 16/486/29. Thomas Wiseman was a frequent correspondent of the Admiral, who left £50 in his will to 'Thomas Wiseman, Remembrancer of the City'. Egerton MSS., 2,533, fol. 95. His letters to Sir John Penington show his close sympathies with the King.

adherent of Parliament and was not chosen to sit on many of
the major parliamentary or City committees. It is not surprising that the King felt he had won the City to his side and that
he could therefore make a resolute stand against the demands
of Parliament. Many contemporaries saw the City's entertainment as a possible turning-point in the King's affairs which,
as Wiseman hoped, might bring about 'a great alteration in the
affections of the City' and 'make the sectaries look about them'.[94]
But within the short space of a month, their hopes of a
'general conversion' to the side of the crown, had proved to
be ill-founded. The demonstrations of the citizens against the
Bishops in the first week of December revealed that sympathy
with Royalist policy in the City was confined in the main to
the leaders of the municipality, some City officials and some
of the wealthiest citizens. A correspondent of Sir John Penington
remarked: 'Since the King's coming all things have not happened so much to his contentment as by his magnificent entertainment was expected. The factious citizens begin to come
again to the House with their swords by their sides, hundreds
in companies.'[95] After the tumultuous days of December, another letter-writer prayed that 'we find not that we have
flattered ourselves with an imaginary strength and party in
the City', and could only conclude on hearing about the City
demonstrations 'that the power of the City magnates . . . was
already broken'.[96]
The City magistrates tried unsuccessfully to stem the tide
of popular feeling. In the first week of December, a fresh petition was circulating in the City, demanding the removal of
the Bishops from the House of Lords, the punishment of delinquents, and the reform of abuses that 'are crept into the ancient
government of the City'.[97] This open attack on the government of the City magnates aroused the Lord Mayor, the three
senior Aldermen, the Sheriffs and the Recorder to take puni-
tive measures against the organizers and supporters of the
petition. The petition was presented to the House by John
Fowke, a merchant of 'very good fortune'[98] living in Mark
lane who was already known as a leading parliamentary

[94] S.P.Dom. 16/485/92.   [95] S.P. Dom. 16/486/14.
[96] S.P.Dom. 16/488/30.   [97] S.P.Dom. 16/486/42.
[98] *D'Ewes*, ed. Coates, p. 271, quoting the Diary of Sir John Holland.

puritan in the City, having been elected one of the six representatives of Common Hall in the case of the disputed shrievalty some months earlier. In a speech introducing the petition
at the Bar of the House, he complained of the obstructions
which had been used to prevent the collection of signatures[99]
and the House of Commons set up a committee to investigate the
charges. On December 20th, George Peard, Member for Barn-
staple, reported to the House that the Lord Mayor had declared
that only ignorant and idle people subscribed to it, while the
Recorder, 'when they came to that part of it, that declared
the Common Council the representative body of the City,
[and] did desire the removal of the Bishops and Papist Lords
from the Lords' House, . . . swore . . . that it was a lie; and
said further that this petition did tend to sedition, and to set
men together by the ears'.[100] The Lord Mayor and Recorder
were out of favour with the Commons. They had already been
attacked there for their failure to provide a suitable house in
the City for the Scottish commissioners, and the task had been
delegated instead to Captain John Venn, one of the City
Burgesses.[101] On December 18th, when an Order for a Public
Fast in London was under discussion, some members of the
House 'spoke against our sending to the Lord Mayor or having any thing to do with him (in respect that he would have
hindered the petition lately preferred to us by the citizens of
London) but that we should send to the Aldermen of every
ward',[102] and the responsibility for the Order was left to the
City Members of Parliament.

In the last days of December, it seemed that government in
the City was dissolving. In the mounting confusion of petitions
and demonstrations, even the Lord Mayor was forced to tell
the King that unless Colonel Lunsford (the newly appointed
Royalist Constable of the Tower, who was thought to harbour
violent designs on the City) was dismissed, he could not
answer for the consequences in London. On December 31st,
at the bidding of Secretary Nicholas, the Court of Common
Council met to disclaim the demonstrations, promised
to do their utmost to restore order, and threatened to
punish those, particularly members of the Trained Bands,

[99] *D'Ewes*, ed. Coates, pp. 319-20.   [100] Nalson, op. cit., ii, p. 763.
[101] *D'Ewes*, ed. Coates, p. 220, n. 4.   [102] Ibid. p. 316.

who were failing to do their duty and suppress the rioters.[103]

These measures, however, proved useless; nor was the declaration of Common Council evidence of future support for the crown from that body. Until January 1642, Common Council had concurred with the Court of Aldermen on general policy, either through the wishes of the most influential members of Common Council or as a result of pressure exerted by the aldermanic veto. They had campaigned against Protections, had consented to take their full part in banqueting the crown on November 25th, and had repudiated the City demonstrators. It is erroneous to assert that in 1641 'most of the questions which then divided the nation were first threshed out in the Common Council'.[104] As we have seen, there is no evidence that any of those petitions of a controversial nature on important political or religious disputes either originated in or were discussed in the Court of Aldermen and Common Council in this period. The House of Commons tacitly recognized the character of Common Council in 1641, by calling Common Hall whenever it required a new loan from the City. Even in 1642, there was probably still a large minority of Common Councilmen who were 'neutralist' in their attitude to Parliament or antipathetic. How was it then that from the time of the arrest of the five members by Charles I at the beginning of 1642, the City government became the most prominent ally of Pym and the parliamentary opposition?

Contemporaries of both Royalist and parliamentary puritan opinion were unanimous in attributing the decisive change which took place early in 1642 to the results of the annual Common Council elections held on December 21 1641, which they said excluded the old leadership of Common Council, in favour of men of active parliamentary puritan sympathies. These elections transformed the political scene in London, and Clarendon went so far as to attribute to them the King's departure from Whitehall early in January 1642. In the *History of the Great Rebellion*, Clarendon wrote that the City 'at their election of Common Councilmen (which is every year before Christmas, and in which new men had rarely used to be chosen except in case of death, but the old still continued) all

103 J.Co.Co. 40, fol. 10.
104 W. D. Hamilton, ed., *C.S.P.D.*, *vol. 1641-1643*, 1887, p. x.

the grave and substantial citizens were left out, and such chosen as were most eminent for opposing the government and most disaffected to the Church, though of never so mean estates: which made a present visible alteration in the temper of the City'.[105] Clarendon was writing some time after the events. But another observer who was more in a position to know what had happened was Nehemiah Wallington, a Puritan who followed the turner's trade in St. Leonard's, Eastcheap, and had himself taken part in some of the citizens' demonstrations; he wrote that those Common Councilmen who were 'not well affected' were removed and 'very wise and sound Common Councilmen' were chosen in their place, which 'was a great mercy of God'.[106] Two contemporary writers suggested that these changes were a political affair. The highly tendentious, although exceedingly well-informed author of A Letter from Mercurius Civicus to Mercurius Rusticus, wrote that the citizens 'accuse the old Common Councilmen as men not zealous for religion, ready to comply with the court for loans of money, and which was worse, many . . . were active in promoting the intended petition for Episcopacy and the Book of Common Prayer'.[107] Some of the evidence that he then gives on the

[105] Clarendon, History, i, p. 275. The date, given here as December 1640, is obviously a mistake: elsewhere he refers to the Common Council elections at which important changes took place as those of December 1641. Ibid. i, p. 501.

[106] Nehemiah Wallington, Historical notices of events occurring chiefly in the reign of Charles I, R. Webb, ed., 1869, i, p. 274.·

[107] A Letter from Mercurius Civicus to Mercurius Rusticus: Or London's Confession but not Repentance, Oxford, 1643, reprinted in Somers Tracts, 1750, i, p. 407. This tract was attributed by the editor of Somers Tracts to Samuel Butler. But the most authoritative editors of Butler's works do not include it among his writings and we must look elsewhere for its authorship (A. R. Waller and R. Lamar, The Collected Works of Samuel Butler Cambridge, 3 vols., 1905-28). The pungent, witty style resembles the writing of Sir John Birkenhead in Mercurius Aulicus. If Birkenhead was the author, the intimate knowledge of City affairs shown in the tract suggests that he had an informant in the City. This could have been Peter Heylin who had close City connexions, was said to have been in London in 1643, and at one time worked on Mercurius Aulicus. But this is conjecture. 'Mercurius Civicus' shows a considerable knowledge of both the leading individuals and the workings of City government. Professor H. R. Trevor-Roper has pointed out to me that the Appendix to the Oxford edition of Sir John Spelman's, The Case of our Affaires in Law, Religion and other Circumstances, 1643-1644, although entitled, A Discoverie of London's Obstinacie and Miserie, is in fact taken bodily from A Letter from Mercurius Civicus. This Appendix does not appear in the London editions of Spelman's work. Although the D.N.B. attributed it to Spelman, F. Madan in his Oxford Books, a Bibliography, 1912, thought it differed stylistically. Professor Trevor-Roper points out that neither noticed that it is in fact part of an earlier independent work.

activities of the parliamentary puritan party in the newly
elected assembly can be corroborated from City and parliamentary records. The author of *Persecutio Undecima*, who was
also knowledgeable about City affairs, saw these elections as
the culmination of a long parliamentary puritan campaign to
capture all City offices, however humble. 'Not an office in the
City', he wrote, 'though chargeable and troublesome; yet how
ambitious were the faction of those places, even to a constable-
ship.'[108] The activities and sympathies of the newly elected
Common Councilmen certainly support the view that they
were enthusiastic supporters of Parliament. Another contemporary writer said that the old Common Councilmen had
been publicly arraigned and accused them of assessing taxation unfairly, so that it weighed unduly on the poor, and of
prosecuting poor parishioners for failure to pay. 'All the Common Councilmen', he wrote, 'were arraigned by the citizens
and consequently a select committee was appointed to meet
at Guildhall, to regulate these abuses, which have been by
them committed; and being accused, they were found so inex-
cusable delinquent and peccant, they were . . . excluded from
their corrupt offices, and new Common Councilmen elected
in their places.'[109] This pamphlet was answered by another
which denied that the Committee set up to investigate the
elections arraigned the old Common Councillors, and stated
with truth that it merely inquired into the validity of the
elections.[110] The report of this Committee is extant in the
Journal of Common Council and there is no evidence that
the old Common Councilmen were arraigned or accused of
abusing their office. What evidence does this report throw on
the wider issue of the extent to which the personnel of Common
Council changed at this election?

This question has been investigated by Melvin Wren in his
article 'The Disputed Election in London in 1641'.[111] His

[108] Anon., *Persecutio Undecima. The Churches Eleventh Persecution*, 1648, p. 58
[Thomason Tracts].

[109] J. Bond, *The Downfall of old Common Councilmen, being their great repulse at
Guildhall last Friday by the Committee, who extruded the old out of their corrupted offices,
and elected new in their places*, 1642. [Guildhall Library.]

[110] *An answer to a late scurrilous and scandalous pamphlet, entitled The downfall of the
old Common Councilmen*, 1642. [Guildhall Library.]

[111] *E.H.R.*, vol. lxiv, 1949, pp. 34-51.

conclusion was that few changes took place and that Common
Council's opposition to Charles had been growing steadily
since 1625. His methods, however, can be seriously criticized.
In the first place, he has made generalizations on the change
of personnel in the Court of Common Council from the election returns of 1641, when evidence for approximately only
fifty-seven members is extant[112] out of a total membership of
237. In these fifty-seven cases, twenty-five 'new' Common
Councilmen were elected.[113] There were also disputes in other
wards besides these, for it was discovered that the Alderman
had failed to return the full number of Common Councilmen
in the ward of Farringdon Within (where two extra members
were ordered to be elected) and also in Aldersgate Ward,
where two extra members were ordered to be elected to Common Council. In Langbourne Ward, the whole election was
declared invalid and the ten members ordered to be re-
elected.[114] Thus, disputes or changes in personnel are known
to have taken place in connexion with over half of the extant
returns. It would seem, therefore, that such evidence as exists
on the changes in the personnel of Common Council in December 1641, suggests that the elections aroused considerable
conflict in the precincts and wards. In at least four precincts,[115]
there was an entire change in the personnel of Common Council. Although Clarendon was wide of the mark in stating that
Common Councilmen held office for life, the same men often
held office for many years, and it was unusual for precincts to
change all their representatives in one election. Melvin Wren
asserts that in the precincts where new Common Councilmen
were elected, such changes did not indicate differences of policy
between the old and the new representatives, since many of
the newly elected councillors had previously held parish
offices.[116] But it is unlikely that political conflicts would have
affected the election of parish officers before the political

[112] For a list of those wards and precincts for which information on Common
Council returns is extant, see Bibliographical Note II, pp. 344-5.

[113] For changes in the personnel of Common Council in December 1641, see
Bibliographical Note II, pp. 344-5.

[114] J.Co.Co. 40, fols. 21-23.

[115] St. Dunstan's in the West, St. Stephen's, Coleman street, St. Benet, Paul's
Wharf and St. Benet Fink.

[116] Wren, op. cit., p. 48.

turmoil of 1640 and 1641, as much as wealth and status; in any case, men were compelled to serve the more menial offices. On Wren's own evidence, it appears that in many instances the new members had not held the most important parish offices, and since nearly all citizens of any substance held or fined for the minor ones, it would be surprising to find men elected to Common Council who had held none of these offices. The election of men beneath this status would indeed have heralded a social as well as a political revolution in the City in 1642.

Since the nature of the extant evidence makes it impossible to generalize accurately on the changes in the total membership of Common Council in December 1641, a more fruitful approach to the problem can be made by an analysis of the changes in the personnel of its leading members who served as members of committees. The leaders of Common Council who sat on its committees exercised a great influence over the assembly. Changes in this leadership might be of as great significance for the future policy of the City as changes in the total personnel of Common Council. From the evidence of the Committee which investigated the elections, it is clear that it was some of the leaders of Common Council who were defeated, men who had sat on the City Lands Committee, had served as Auditors of the Chamberlain's and Bridgemasters' Accounts, and were members of every other important committee, until the end of 1641. Such were Roger Clarke and Sir George Benion,[117] a wealthy silk merchant of Cheapside, who had taken a leading part in the opposition to Protections, and was later responsible for circulating a petition in London against Parliament's proposed Militia Ordinance;[118] both had been leading members of Common Council committees. On

[117] On August 14 1641, Oliver Lord St. John petitioned the House of Lords against Sir George Benion, who since 1631 had abused his position as the King's Receiver-General for the Counties of Northampton and Rutland, to recover his own debts, and had seized the petitioner's estates. *H.M.C. Fourth Report, Part I, House of Lords MSS*, p. 97. He was elected to the City Lands Committee in July 1640. J.Co.Co. 39, fol. 111. See below for his opposition to Protections, pp. 150-1. He was later concerned in Edmund Waller's conspiracy in the City in May 1643. David Lloyd in his *Memoires of the Lives, Actions, Sufferings*, 1668, p. 634, said that his house in Highgate was pulled down to the ground in the Civil War.

[118] Roger Clarke was elected to the City Lands Committee in July 1637. J.Co.Co. 38, fol. 107. He is mentioned as a Royalist in *Mercurius Civicus*.

the day of the election, they were greeted at the wardmote of Farringdon Within with cries of 'No Benion! No Clarke!'[119] Although their names were returned on the Indenture by the presiding Alderman, the investigating committee decided that it was a false return and that a new election should take place. Thomas Lusher,[120] an important Common Councilman from 1635, was opposed in Cornhill Ward in 1641 and finally defeated by the parliamentary puritan, John Bellamy.[121] The author of *A Letter from Mercurius Civicus* refers also to the defeat of those 'grave, discreet, well affected citizens', Roger Drake, Roger Gardiner, Deputy John Withers[122] and Mr. Cartwright, all of whom, as can be seen from the Journal of Common Council, had been leading members of the Court and sat on its most important committees. Since the names of none of these men occur again in the Journals and they were later declared Royalists,[123] there is no reason to reject his evidence. Three of the men denounced by 'Mercurius Civicus' as leaders of the parliamentary puritan party in the City gained their seats as a result of these disputed elections, two of them, William Perkins, 'Lord Saye's tailor', and Alexander Normington, 'the Cutler', in the radical precinct of St. Dunstan's in the West,[124] and Owen Rowe in St. Stephen's, Coleman street.[125]

Apart from Wren's failure to consider all the evidence of contemporaries, who were unanimous that significant changes of personnel had occurred, he makes no mention of the constitutional issues which were raised by the inquiry into the conduct of the elections, and which revealed major conflicts within the municipality, as indicative of political dispute in the Court of Common Council as changes of personnel. Whereas disputed elections had hitherto always been judged by the Lord

[119] J.Co.Co. 40, fol. 22.

[120] Cornhill Wardmote Bk., fols. 210-220v. He was a Warden of the Fishmongers' Company from 1638 to 1640. Transcripts, iii, part 3, p. 581. He was elected to the City Lands Committee in June 1641. J.Co.Co. 40, fol. 3v.

[121] J.Co.Co. 40, fol. 21v. John Bellamy was a parliamentary 'trier' for the province of London from 1645 to 1648. Wren, op. cit., p. 40, n. 2.

[122] Both Drake and Gardiner were concerned in the presentation of Benion's petition against Parliament's Militia Ordinance; a John Withers was Treasurer of Bridewell from 1631 to 1637. O'Donoghue, op. cit., pp. 274-5.

[123] D. Lloyd, op. cit., p. 634.   [124] J.Co.Co. 40, fol. 22v.

[125] Previous to 1638 Owen Rowe had sat as Common Councilman for another precinct. V.M.Bk., St. Stephen's, Coleman street, fol. 106.

Mayor and Court of Aldermen,[126] these disputes were now investigated by a Committee of Common Council. The author of *A Letter from Mercurius Civicus* asserted that although 'formerly all controversies of this nature were submitted to the determination of the Lord Mayor and Court of Aldermen, only now by the impetuousness and clamour of Fowke and his adherents, it must be referred to a committee of the Common Council'.[127] On January 19th, Common Council appointed its Committee of Safety to receive complaints about the conduct of the elections,[128] although previously on January 10th, the Court of Aldermen had also appointed a day, January 27th, to hear two disputes which had been brought to its notice.[129] The appointment of the Common Council Committee on January 19th must therefore have been in direct opposition to the aldermanic Bench. The Committee presented its report to Common Council on March 2nd, when it was confirmed, and the Lord Mayor was ordered to direct the Aldermen of those wards where disputes had taken place to proceed immediately to a new election.[130] The Lord Mayor and Aldermen, despite earlier precedents in their favour, had taken no part as a separate body in the investigations of the elections.

Common Council not only decided these disputes in the face of all precedents, but also criticized abuses that had crept into the machinery of the elections. They particularly attacked the oligarchic control of small cliques in the precincts and vestries over ward elections. The Committee stated clearly that Common Councilmen should be elected at the meeting of the wardmote by all the freemen of the City who paid scot and lot, and not at a previous meeting of the precincts. 'Although precincts do meet on or before St. Thomas's Day, to consider who they think are fit to be Common Councilmen, . . . yet we conceive their power therein extends only to present the names of such persons to the wardmote', they declared, 'and that then the said inhabitants of the ward may in part or in whole approve or reject that nomination or name others to be in

---

[126] 'Instances of the exercise of the jurisdiction of the Court of Mayor and Aldermen of the City of London over Elections for Common Councilmen' (1536-1825). Guildhall Small MS. Box 47, H.2. In the seventeenth century there were precedents from 1607, Rep. 28, fol. 149, and 1624, Rep. 39, fol. 89.

[127] *A Letter from Mercurius Civicus*, op. cit., p. 410.

[128] J.Co.Co. 40, fol. 16.   [129] Rep. 55, fol. 352.   [130] J.Co.Co. 40, fol. 23.

election with them as they find cause.' This statement marked
a short-lived attempt to prevent the wardmote being robbed
of its authority by the ruling groups of the precincts and
parishes. In particular, it struck at the power of the vestries,
with whom the rulers of the precincts were practically synony-
mous.[131] The collaboration of some Aldermen with these ruling groups to get their own nominees elected was another
major grievance which emerged from the Committee's reports.
In Cornhill Ward, the presiding Alderman, Sir Nicholas
Rainton, opened the meeting of the wardmote by saying that
he 'neither would nor could spare' two of the Common Councilmen, Mr. Mosse and Thomas Lusher. When there were
protests, he retracted and agreed to submit the names of the
six old Common Councilmen as well as some other nominations for election. After a show of hands he declared that the
six had been re-elected. According to the investigating Committee, many inhabitants of the ward then shouted 'no choice!
no choice!' and demanded a poll. Rainton refused, saying ' "he
would not do and undo", and refused to suffer it to be tried
by the poll or to permit them to have a negative voice'.[132]
Elsewhere, as in Broad street Ward and in Langbourne, the
Aldermen had refused to return the full number of Common
Councilmen.[133]

There is some evidence to suggest that the newly elected
Common Councilmen took up their seats before Plough Monday (the first Monday after Twelfth Night), which was the
traditional date for their swearing into office. This would be
of great significance, since the first six days of January were
decisive in determining which side the City government would
take in the breach between King and Parliament, and the
presence of newly elected citizens who were ardent supporters
of the parliamentary puritans might well be the deciding factor.
The author of *A Letter from Mercurius Civicus* asserted that they
took up their seats before time.[134] That this was probably so
is suggested by Common Council's election of a Committee of
Safety on January 4th, having been directed to take this step
by order of the House of Commons. Such a Committee was
without precedent in the history of the City and proved to be

<hr/>

[131] See Chapter II, p. 55.   [132] J.Co.Co. 40, fol. 21v.   [133] Ibid. fols. 22-23.
[134] *A Letter from Mercurius Civicus*, op. cit., p. 408.

as revolutionary as its name suggests. Its composition, as well
as its functions as will be shown below, contrasted markedly
with those of previous committees of Common Council. Only
one of the six Aldermen elected was senior, Sir Nicholas
Rainton, and three of them were prominent parliamentary
puritans.[135] On January 19th, Rainton asked to be discharged
because of his many commitments (amongst which he weakly
alleged were his duties over the collection of poll money)[136]
and the leading parliamentary puritan, Alderman John
Warner, who was said to have signed the Root and Branch
petition, was elected in his place.[137] All the Common Councilmen elected to the Committee were prominent supporters of
Parliament and included Captain Randall Mainwaring, later
Deputy Lord Mayor to Isaac Penington, John Fowke, who
presented the citizens' petition of December 11 1641, Stephen
Estwicke, signatory of more than one citizens' petition, together with Alexander Normington, the Cutler, denounced for
his part in these events by 'Mercurius Civicus', and Owen Rowe,
the radical Puritan vestryman of St. Stephen's, Coleman
street.[138] The election of Normington and Rowe to Common
Council were amongst those in dispute.[139] The constitutional and political significance of the work of the Committee
is perhaps reflected in the fact that two of the elected Aldermen,

[135] Aldermen Thomas Atkins, John Towse, and Sir John Wollaston. The other
two members were Sir Jacob Garrard and Sir John Gayre, who did not sign the
report of the Committee's investigations into the Common Council elections, and
were taken off the Committee in September 1642 for having 'wholly deserted
the . . . service'. J.Co.Co. 40, fol. 37v.

[136] This was probably an excuse, since the collection of Poll Money was practically finished. Moreover, his resignation coincided with Common Council's decision
to refer the disputed elections to this Committee. J.Co.Co. 40, fol. 16.

[137] Ibid.

[138] For Mainwaring, Estwicke, Normington and Rowe, see Appendix II. For
the possible identity of 'Mercurius Civicus', see p. 133n. The author had no
connexion, of course, with the London news-sheet, Mercurius Civicus . . . , 1643-6,
which favoured the parliamentary cause.

[139] Among the other Commoners were William Gibbs, Captain James Bunce,
and Samuel Warner, who were made Aldermen in 1642 and 1643 during the
mayoralty of Alderman Isaac Penington. The remaining members of the Committee were James Russell, Nathaniel Wright and William Berkeley, all of whom
were to become supporters of Parliament. Melvin Wren in his article in E.H.R.,
vol. lxiv, 1949, p. 37, says that all but one of the Committee had been members
of Common Council for many years. But no evidence has been found that John
Fowke, James Russell, Alexander Normington or Samuel Warner had previously
been members of Common Council.

John Gayre and Jacob Garrard, at this time lukewarm or 'neutralist' in their attitude to Parliament, did not sign the Committee's recommendation on the elections.

The Committee of Safety was elected at a time of tremendous crisis in the City and kingdom. It would not have been surprising if the normal constitutional machinery of the City had been disturbed. In the last week of December, it was evident that the King was planning to resort to strong action. On January 4th, he attempted to arrest five leading Members of the House of Commons; they had been forewarned, however, had fled to the City and were sheltered in that radical centre, Coleman street. The citizens were angry but also fearful at the King's action; for although Colonel Lunsford had been dismissed from the Tower, his successor, Sir John Byron, continued to fill it with soldiers and ammunition, while Whitehall was being similarly stocked up with arms. With a sense of impending danger, the whole City shut shop and provided themselves with weapons. Nehemiah Wallington described the tension of the previous night when the Tower was filled with cannon and artillerymen; it spread such fear in the City 'that the Aldermen and the Sheriffs were up that night and the gates looked unto and the chains pulled across the streets, with knocking at the doors for men to stand upon their guard, and the next day our shops were shut up close, with every man his halberd and weapons in a readiness, and it was much feared that that night would have been a bloody night, but God of his mercy kept us'.[140]

On January 5th, the King attended Common Council to ask for the extradition of the five Members. On his journey through the City and at Common Council itself, the cry was continuously heard, 'Privileges of Parliament! Privileges of Parliament!' At Common Council, the cry of 'God save the King!' was intermingled with them. Charles asked that the members should speak their minds. 'It is the vote of this Court that your Majesty hear the advice of your Parliament,' cried one. 'It is not the vote of this Court,' cried another; 'it is your own vote.'[141] That evening, Charles chose to dine with the Sheriff who was less sympathetic towards him, George Garrett. On his way out of the City, he was attended by the Lord

[140] N. Wallington, op. cit., i, p. 280.   [141] C.S.P.D. 1641-1643, vol. 488/19.

Mayor and Aldermen to Temple Bar, 'who returning back, about Ludgate, some rude persons pulled the Lord Mayor off his horse, and some of the Aldermen, and forced them to go home afoot'.[142]

On the previous day, the King had sent a message to the Lord Mayor, complaining that the guns and cannon from the Artillery Yard had been taken into Leadenhall and that the ordinary citizens of 'mean quality' were harbouring muskets in their houses.[143] The least incident could set off the greatest disturbance in the City. On January 6th, an alarm was raised and the Trained Bands were assembled without the authority of the Lord Mayor. Rumour had it that troops of soldiers were threatening the City. Nehemiah Wallington wrote in his diary that he hoped that night would never be forgotten: 'for in the dead of night there was great bouncing at every man's door to be up in their arms presently and to stand on their guard, both in the City and suburbs, for we heard (as we lay in our beds) a great cry in the streets that there were horse and foot coming against the City. So the gates were shut and the cullisses let down, and the chains put across the corners of our streets, and every man ready on his arms. And women and children did then arise and fear and trembling entered on all.' We have a characteristically different view of the causes of the panic from 'Mercurius Civicus', who said that he was present at the Lord Mayor's house on this momentous night. It was the royalist charge that a false scare had been manufactured by the parliamentary puritans: 'Mercurius Civicus' alleged that he had occasion to judge by their demeanour which Aldermen were acquainted with the raising of a panic in the City about a Cavalier attack. For Nehemiah Wallington there were no such doubts. Some people, he said, died that night of shock, as did his neighbour, the wife of Alderman Adams. Although their fears soon proved to be groundless and some scoffed at them for their panic, yet he felt 'it is certain enough, that had not the Lord of His mercy stirred us up to bestir ourselves, it would have gone hard enough with us'.[144]

Be that as it may, there is some doubt as to how close Londoners

[142] N. Wallington, op. cit., i, p. 282.
[143] C.S.P.D. 1641-1643, vol. 488/14.
[144] N. Wallington, op. cit., i, p. 289-90.

stood to a holocaust of savage repression and sanguinary
insurrection on these winter nights of January 1642. Perhaps
the odd, undisclosed chances of history saved them. Or a fortunate combination of factors—the self-imposed discipline of
the citizens, which evoked the admiration of the French Ambassador, the far from desperate character of the populace,
and the somewhat restrained and ambivalent attitude of the
leading classes of society, may together have prevented a
bloody conflict in the streets. But whatever the many differences, parallels with other revolutions are difficult to resist.
At any rate, on the surface, all the makings of such a conflict
appeared to be there and with them all the heroic and melancholy preparations. Almost 150 years later, when Paris rose
to storm the Bastille, one seems to hear echoes of revolutionary
deeds which earlier were about to engulf London but, fortunately, passed her by unharmed. Paris had her Bastille,
London her fortified Tower, but the Tower passed peacefully
into the hands of Parliament's nominee and then to Alderman
Isaac Penington, Fishmonger, the leader of the revolution in
the City. Paris had her 10,000 women, so many Judiths, as
Camille Desmoulins saw them, who swept the National Guard
aside, seized guns and cannons, attempted to hang a minor
municipal official in default of the Mayor, and threatened the
Hôtel de Ville with their torches. London rehearsed all this,
but distantly and as in a play that was never performed. Cheapside and other main streets were barricaded with benches,
while women who entered sometimes violently into the political
struggle, as we shall see again,[145] boiled cauldrons of scalding
water to pour on the heads of marauding Cavaliers who never
arrived.

The crisis in the City and kingdom was reflected in the
changed temper and leadership of Common Council. On
January 5 1642, the newly elected Committee of Safety presented a draft of a petition to Common Council, which was to
be sent to the King. It expressed regret at the removal of
Balfour, the predecessor of Lunsford, from the Lieutenantship
of the Tower, at the continuation of the war in Ireland, at
the steps taken to fortify Whitehall, and above all at the
King's attempt to seize the five Members of Parliament.[146] It

[145] See below, p. 226.   [146] J.Co.Co. 40, fol. 12.

was accepted by the Court of Common Council. A radical change had taken place in that body. This petition from the municipality was the first to bear directly on political issues of national importance. Moreover, it was obviously a direct criticism of royal policy, and the first indication that the 'unofficial' citizens and leading parliamentary puritans had won the leadership of Common Council.

But there is no evidence that the Court of Aldermen had changed its attitude towards the crown. Most probably it felt that under the circumstances it was wiser not to veto the petition presented to Common Council by the Committee of Safety and preferred to submit to popular pressure, or it was overridden by the new and resolute leadership amongst the Common Councilmen. The King's blunders forced the House of Lords, also, to submit temporarily to popular pressure from the Commons and the citizens. The Royalist Lord Mayor was unable even to issue the royal proclamation in the City impeaching the five Members, because of the strength of popular feeling. Common Council proceeded to put the City into a state of defence. Serjeant Major Skippon (and not the Lord Mayor) was given power to raise the Trained Bands to defend Parliament and the City, on the grounds that 'the Commission of the Lord Mayor being but a Commission of Lieutenancy . . . [was] . . . illegal'.[147] The Trained Bands were increased, reorganized and put on a war footing. The six regiments were put under the command of the leading parliamentary puritans, Aldermen Isaac Penington, Sir John Wollaston, Thomas Atkins, John Warner, John Towse and a more lukewarm supporter of Parliament, Alderman Thomas Adams. Some of their officers were men newly elected to Common Council or soon to be prominent in the parliamentary cause in the City, Lieutenant-Colonels Randall Mainwaring, Francis West and Rowland Wilson, Captains Edward Bellamy, John Booker, and Thomas Player, and the ubiquitous Captain Owen Rowe and his brother, Francis,[148] who held a commission in the same regiment. Ammunition from Vauxhall and Lambeth Palace was moved into Leadenhall. The King, probably at the

[147] J.Co.Co. fols. 14v-15.

[148] H. A. Dillon. 'On a MS. List of Officers of London Trained Bands in 1643', Archaeologia, 1890, vol. 52, pp. 129-44.

Queen's prompting, fled from Whitehall on the night of January 10th, though the story went that the Lord Mayor, Aldermen Sir George Whitmore and Sir Henry Garway, seeing how much this would weaken their cause in the City, did everything in their power to persuade them to stay. They even offered him, it was said, a guard of 10,000 men if he would remain in the City.[149] Next day, the five M.P.s who had been sheltering in Coleman street, embarked on a barge accompanied by flotillas of seamen from the Port of London, to return amidst cheering crowds of supporters to Westminster. There they were met by Philip Skippon and the Trained Bands in full military regalia, each soldier waving a copy of the Protestation, which they had stuck in their hats, or on the top of their pikes, 'hanging like a little square banner'.[150]

The victory of the parliamentary puritans in the City seemed complete. Common Council's petition of January 5th was followed by another asserting that City merchants would not bring their bullion into the Tower, because they had no confidence in its Lieutenant, Sir John Byron.[151] On January 24th, the municipality presented a petition to Parliament expressing radical political demands which revealed that they were now in full agreement with 'King Pym' and the majority of the Lower House. As a counterpoise to the Lords' refusal to join in a request for parliamentary control of the militia, it urged Parliament to assume the power of the sword; and to relieve Ireland 'by disarming of Papists, by putting the forts and strength of this kingdom by land and sea into safe hands, as the Parliament shall confide in'. A barbed reference to the Lords' refusal to agree to the exclusion of Bishops called for 'the speedy passage of Bills conceived by the House of Commons and sent up into the Lords'.[152] It seemed now as though the wheel had turned full circle, and the City government was in the forefront of the parliamentary party. But this would be a premature conclusion: the Court of Aldermen, many influential City officials and perhaps a substantial minority of Common Council had not been converted. The driving force

[149] Roger Coke, A Detection of the Court and State of England, 1694, p. 134.
[150] N. Wallington, op. cit., i, pp. 291-2. Harl. MSS., 162, fol. 318v.
[151] J.Co.Co. 40, fol. 17.   [152] Ibid. fols. 18-18v.

behind the arming of the City and the petitions to Parliament had come from the recently elected Committee of Safety. The power and significance of this Committee in the early months of 1642 has never been commented on by historians. Yet, not only was the composition of the Committee, as we have seen, radically different from that of previous committees, but it was given very great authority. In the first few months after its election, it drew up practically every petition of the municipality, and all important business was referred to it. The tax of four-fifteenths voted for the defence of the City, was ordered to be paid into this Committee, and issued out on its warrant.[153] On January 8th, it was given special authority to confer with the House of Commons, on behalf of the City, on matters concerning the defence of the kingdom.[154] To prevent any opposition from the Lord Mayor and Aldermen, the House of Commons, on January 13th, conferred on it a radically new power which struck a direct blow at their authority. Since Common Council had appointed a Committee to consider the safety and defence of the City and since its decisions could not take effect until presented to Common Council, Parliament therefore ordered that 'the Lord Mayor shall call a Common Council as often and at such times as shall be desired by the said Committee'. Further, the Lord Mayor was to inform the Committee of any orders received from either House of Parliament.[155]

The Lord Mayor's traditional right to call Common Council was indisputable, and had been unchallenged for centuries. The author of *A Letter from Mercurius Civicus* described this innovation of the Commons with characteristic abuse. Whereas this power had always rested with the Lord Mayor and Aldermen, he said, now by orders from the House of Commons 'at the instance of Penington, Venn and Vassall', it is no longer left to the Lord Mayor's judgment, but he must call it as often as 'the men of this faction shall command him'. Venn and Fowke had used this 'usurped power' with such insolence, he continued, that 'when they have required Sir Richard Gurney to call a Common Council, and he hath demanded a reason, they vouchsafed him no other answer, than . . . that

<hr />

[153] J.Co.Co.40, fol. 12.   [154] Ibid. fol. 14.
[155] *C.J.* ii, p. 376.

when he came hither he should know' [156] On January 19th, as we have seen, this Committee was also authorized to judge the disputed elections to Common Council,[157] a right which had also previously been exercised by the Lord Mayor and Aldermen. Finally, its members were invested with power over the City Militia. The Commons Committee at Grocers' Hall ordered that the City Militia should be entrusted to persons chosen by Common Council, and on January 22nd they elected the members of the Committee of Safety to act as Commissioners of the Militia.[158]

In the next few months, what appear to be the acts of the Lord Mayor and Aldermen were often, in fact, the responsibility of this powerful parliamentary puritan Committee. Sir John Coke informed a correspondent that 'what comes from the Committee to the Common Council comes with much recommendation, and being carried with plurality of voices passes as the act of the Lord Mayor and Aldermen'.[159] The Common Council, to which the Committee owed its position, also assumed a new importance in the government of the City. It met much more frequently, sometimes more than twice a week during January. All important business was referred to it for its agreement while the aldermanic Bench neither summoned the meetings nor was able to limit the discussions. For the first time, Common Council gained a Journal of its own and its written proceedings were separated from those of Common Hall. Its records thus become much fuller and more interesting. The new stature which Common Council was assuming is evident not only in its arbitration of the disputed Common Council elections, but also in its attempt to interfere in a disputed aldermanic election in Vintry Ward, against the Court of Aldermen who had refused to accept the nomination made by the inhabitants.[160] On March 14th, it exercised another power, previously enjoyed by the Court of Aldermen, the right to dismiss one of its members, Robert Alden, ostensibly

[156] *A Letter from Mercurius Civicus*, op. cit., p. 411.

[157] J.Co.Co. 40, fol. 16.

[158] Ibid. fol. 17v.

[159] *H.M.C. Twelfth Report, Appendix, Part II, Coke MSS.*, ii, p. 304.

[160] J.Co.Co. 40, fol. 21. See Chapter II, p. 59, for the Alderman's claim to reject the nomination of the wards if they thought fit.

for neglecting to take the Protestation.[161] To at least one contemporary, these constitutional innovations seemed so radical and violent that he assumed them to mark, unjustifiably, as will be shown,[162] a transference of social power. 'The Puritan faction', wrote 'Mercurius Civicus', '. . . having thus gotten the power to call Common Council, power to continue them, power to put the question what they please, and power to determine all by a major part, my Lord Mayor having no more sway than Perkins the tailor,[163] Rily the bodicemaker, or Nicholson the chandler,[164] they may dispose of the wealth and power of the City as they please.'[165]

The Lord Mayor and Aldermen did not submit to these constitutional changes without a struggle. They chose as their battle ground the subject of the Militia, a choice dictated as much by its crucial importance in national affairs as by its importance in the City constitution. But involved in the question of the Militia was also that of the aldermanic veto,[166] the most irksome of the weapons by which the Lord Mayor and Aldermen controlled the Court of Common Council, and the central point of dispute in the City constitution. When the subject of the Militia was discussed in the City in January 1642, with the election of the Committee of Safety as Militia Commissioners, the Lord Mayor and Aldermen had not at first, according to 'Mercurius Civicus', considered that the influence of the Lord Mayor was to be altogether

[161] J.Co.Co. 40, fol. 26v. Robert Alden, Salter, was deputy to Sir John Cordell, Alderman of Basinghall Ward. He had been a Common Councilman since at least 1640, J.Co.Co. 40, fol. 6, and he was on the Committee that welcomed the King, ibid. fol. 8. In May 1643 he was concerned in Waller's conspiracy in the City and was named in Sir Nicholas Crispe's Commission of Array. His dismissal from Common Council may have been political discrimination, since the Court of Aldermen recorded that he took the Protestation before the Bench on March 15 1642. Rep. 55, fol. 395v.

[162] See Chapter VII, pp. 245-6, 249-50.

[163] William Perkins, said to be Lord Saye's tailor, later signed Common Council's petition of July 9 1642 complaining of Sir Richard Gurney's interference in its proceedings. He may have been the Perkins who invested £50 in the Massachusetts Bay Company. Rose-Troup, op. cit., p. 151.

[164] Nicholson also signed the petition of July 9th. See also p. 155 n.

[165] A Letter from Mercurius Civicus, op. cit., p. 412.

[166] R. R. Sharpe in his London and the Kingdom mistakenly asserted that 'until the year 1645 the right of the mayor and aldermen to veto an ordinance made by the commons in Common Council assembled appears never to have been disputed'. See below, p. 248.

excluded;[167] but at a later meeting of Common Council when the orders of the previous meeting were read, they protested strongly at the exclusion of the Mayor and at the placing of so much power in that Committee.[168] Hence a petition against Parliament's ordering of the Militia was drawn up by the Recorder and the City's counsel, and brought into the Court of Aldermen on February 15th.[169] The Remembrancer, Thomas Wiseman, giving evidence on behalf of the Lord Mayor at his trial in the following July, said that the substance of the petition was agreed upon by fifteen or sixteen Aldermen, and signed by fourteen. He said that he did not know whether any Aldermen had protested against the petition, although he knew that some did not agree with it, but he was certain that the majority were in favour.[170] Alderman John Warner who gave evidence against Gurney agreed that the petition was accepted by the majority, and that some protested, as he did himself. He tried to walk out, but the Lord Mayor ordered him to stay. He remembered Gurney particularly urging support for the petition.[171]

The petition was presented to the House of Lords on February 16th, signed by Sir Richard Gurney and thirteen Aldermen.[172] It stated that the Lord Mayor and Aldermen had agreed to the establishment of the Committee of Safety, only on the condition that it should not exercise 'sole power'. Now Parliament intended to settle on it the power of the Militia which time out of mind had been under the rule of the Lord Mayor and Aldermen.[173] On February 22nd, Walter Long

[167] Framlingham Gawdy in his notes on Parliament gave a different reason for the Lord Mayor and Aldermen's delay in protesting. 'The citizens at first', he wrote, 'fearing the government of the militia would have been troublesome in the City, therefore named the meaner men, but now things are more quiet they would have it put into better hands.' Add. MSS. 14,828, fol. 51.

[168] A Letter from Mercurius Civicus, p. 413.

[169] Rep. 55, fol. 373.

[170] L.J. ii, p. 246.

[171] Ibid.

[172] Aldermen Whitmore, Rainton, Abbot, Garway, Wright, Gayre, Cordell, Garrard, Adams, Reynardson, Acton, Garrett and Clarke. House of Lords MSS., Victoria Tower, vol. February 1-18, 1642. Petition of the Lord Mayor and Aldermen, February 16th.

[173] H.M.C. Fifth Report, House of Lords MSS., p. 8. From 1617, Commissions of Lieutenancy had been conferred on the Lord Mayor, Recorder and senior Aldermen. Previously, however, the Trained Bands of the City had been under the control of a Committee of the Court of Aldermen and Common Council, called the 'Committee for Martial Causes'. The Corporation of London, op. cit., pp. 213 seq.

brought a copy of the petition into the Commons. William Strode alleged that Robert Gardiner, Deputy Alderman for Cripplegate Without[174] until he was defeated in the elections of 1641, was one of the main promoters of the petition. When Gardiner refused to answer questions, he was dispatched to the Tower. The petition was again brought to the notice of the House two days later by Alderman Penington,[175] who pointed out the gravity of the situation since there were 200 signatures to it, some of them very wealthy men. He under-estimated the support for the petition. There were over 330 signatures, and they included some of the most prominent merchants and Common Councilmen in the City: three members of the wealthy Bateman family, several influential members of the East India and Levant Companies, besides William Cockayne, Robert Abdy, Daniel Harvey, Eliab Harvey and Andrew Riccard, and ex-Common Councilmen Roger Drake and Thomas Lusher.[176] The House of Commons did not need to be reminded of the dangers of a royalist 'counter-revolution' in the City. According to D'Ewes, most members spoke against the petition, 'showing it to have been a most dangerous design plotted by the Recorder of London, [Sir George] Benion, [Robert] Gardiner and other citizens to hinder the settling of the Militia there according to the ordinance of Parliament . . . and they had drawn by secret and false informations and prac-tises divers of the very wealthy citizens of London as well as others to subscribe to the said petitition, so to set a division in the City and by their example to induce other places to do the same'.[177]

In order to conciliate these potentially dangerous enemies in the City, Parliament decided to punish only the authors of the petition, who were declared to be Sir George Benion, the silk mercer of Cheapside and ex-Common Councilman, and the Recorder, Sir Thomas Gardiner. From Benion's Articles of Impeachment, it is clear that he was being attacked for a long record of opposition to Parliament. He was said to have insulted the House of Lords at the time when they were

[174] *The Visitation of London, 1633-35*, i, *Harleian Society, 1880-1883*, p. 300.
[175] Harl. MSS. 162, fol. 402v.
[176] House of Lords MSS., Victoria Tower. Petition of the citizens of London. February 24 1642.
[177] Harl. MSS. 162, fol. 402v.

discussing the City's Bill against Protections, saying, 'he saw no reason the Lords should have any privilege; he swore, by God, he would have it [the Bill] pass, and if not, there should be no money lent out of the Chamber of London, he would not leave a groat in it'. The Lords, he said, should be as liable to arrest as they were in other countries, otherwise the 'multitudes' must come up to Westminster as they had done against Strafford.[178] Serjeant Wilde, reporting from the Committee that was investigating Benion, said that he behaved in this way 'on purpose to make a bustle in the City'.[179] Clarendon described Benion as 'a citizen of great reputation for wealth and wisdom . . . a very sober man whom the House of Peers adjudged . . . to be disfranchised and incapable of any office in the City, to be committed to the common gaol of Colchester (for his reputation was so great in London that they would not trust him in a City prison) and fined him three thousand pounds'.[180] According to another Royalist source, his house in London was plundered in a shameless way, including his 'fine wainscot' and 'goodly leads'.[181] Five of the Articles of Impeachment against Sir Thomas Gardiner were concerned with earlier misdemeanours in 1639 and 1640 when he was said to have urged Common Council to lend to the crown and tried to prevent the calling of Parliament.[182] On the subject of the Militia, Parliament accused him of having first agreed to the appointment of the Safety Commissioners, and then of deliberately changing his attitude 'to hinder the proceedings in Parliament'.[183] He was found guilty and imprisoned in the Tower.

The introduction into the Court of Aldermen and Common Council on February 17 1642 of the petition against the Militia brought into prominence the most critical of the constitutional conflicts within the municipality: the claims of the Aldermen

---

[178] R. Verney, *Notes of Proceedings in the Long Parliament*, Camden Society, 1844, p. 170.

[179] Ibid.

[180] Clarendon, *History*, ii, pp. 27-28.

[181] 'A Speech made by Alderman Garroway', *Harleian Miscellany*, 1810, v, p. 229.

[182] *Articles of Impeachment by the Commons . . . against Sir Thomas Gardiner*, May 23 1642, pp. 2-3 [Thomason Tracts].

[183] Ibid. Among those who gave evidence against him were the leading City parliamentary puritans, Captain John Venn, Captain Randall Mainwaring, Samuel Warner and Alderman John Towse.

to register their votes separately from the Commoners and to veto Common Council proceedings. When the Recorder proposed that the petition should be read, opinion was divided, and it was agreed that a poll should be taken. The result was that eighty-five Commoners and five Aldermen voted against the reading of the petition, and sixty-one Commoners and eight Aldermen, including the Lord Mayor, in favour.[184] If the aldermanic veto had been applied, the petition would have been read, since seven Aldermen constituted a majority of the thirteen required for a quorum. Instead, the total votes on both sides were declared, 'whereby', proceeds the Journal, 'it appeared that the greater number were against the reading of the said petition, and so the said petition was forborne to be read'. When this issue became prominent again in 1645, John Bellamy, the champion of Common Council, quoted this instance as a precedent for their claim to dispense with the aldermanic veto.[185] 'Mercurius Civicus', fishing for an apt comparison, saw one in the levelling of the House of Lords with the Commons. 'The itch of incorporating two in one', he wrote, was as great in the City as in Westminster, but with 'better success' than in Parliament, for the 'faction' had 'cast all into a common huddle', and while the outward show of a separate body was preserved, Aldermen and Commoners had been made equal in power by the mingling of their votes.[186]

The Court of Aldermen, however, was no more prepared to surrender on this issue than they had been on the question of the control of the Militia.[187] On March 10th, it was ordered in the Court of Aldermen that 'no petition shall hereafter be presented in the Common Council before it be first read and approved of in this Court'.[188] This order was an attempt both to uphold their own authority over Common Council and to

[184] J.Co.Co. 40, fol. 20v.

[185] J. Bellamy, *A Plea for the Commonalty of London, or A Vindication of their Rights* (*which hath been long withholden from them*) *in the choice of sundry City officers*, 1645, pp. 11-12. [Thomason Tracts.]

[186] *A Letter from Mercurius Civicus*, op. cit., p. 412.

[187] But on the question of the Militia, the Lord Mayor and Aldermen were eventually forced by Parliament to capitulate and, as a Court, they made no further stand. The Venetian Ambassador thought the Aldermen preferred to submit to Parliament than give up 'the privileges of their office' or risk their 'rich fortunes'. *V.S.P. 1642-1643*, p. 19.

[188] Rep. 55, fol. 393v.

prevent it from reading a petition that was to be presented to
Parliament, in condemnation of the attitude of the Lord Mayor
and Aldermen to the control of the Militia. On March 13th,
the Lord Mayor refused to accede to the request of the Committee of Safety to call a Common Council, with the excuse
that he was ill.[189] The Committee was not satisfied and reported his behaviour to the House of Commons, who ordered
him to appoint a *locum tenens*. The next day, Common Council
met to consider the draft of a petition which was to be sent
to both Houses of Parliament. It was read, but not voted upon
on the decision of the majority of Aldermen present, headed
by Alderman Sir George Whitmore, who was acting as *locum
tenens*.[190] On March 15th, Common Council protested to the
House of Commons, and a Committee was set up to consider
their grievances.[191]

The investigations of this Committee brought out clearly the
nature of the constitutional dispute between the Aldermen and
the Common Council. First, the citizens complained that 'a
member hath not the liberty . . . to propose or put a question,
but he or they must first acquaint the Lord Mayor and Court
of Aldermen. Secondly, that if . . . [they] dislike of it, it shall
not be put to the vote. Thirdly, that they give them little or
no time to consider thereof, if it be upon the greatest and
weightiest affairs of the City, and by this means . . . [Common
Council] are often surprised and have not time to answer.'[192]
The spokesman for the Committee then questioned Alderman
Henry Garway on the customs of the City in these matters.
Garway explained that the Aldermen and Common Council
sat apart. When asked whether they voted together, he replied, 'that in case the Common Council were divided', the
Aldermen could mediate 'and settle the matter, according as
it hath been since Edward III's time'. The spokesman persisted and asked what would happen if the Aldermen were
divided amongst themselves, 'as for example, suppose there be
fourteen Aldermen of one opinion and twelve of another and
with these twelve there be three hundred of Commons who
should carry it'. The Alderman, plainly confused, gave a con-
tradictory answer, agreeing at first that the twelve and the

[189] *C.J.* ii, p. 476.   [190] J.Co.Co. 40, fol. 26v.   [191] *C.J.* ii, p. 479.
[192] *A True Diurnal of the Passages in Parliament*. March 14-21, 1642. March 16th.

three hundred should carry it, but then adding that, nevertheless, the ultimate power of decision rested with the Lord Mayor and Aldermen, and that before this power should be taken from them, he would resign from the Bench. At a further meeting, two days later, the right of Common Councilmen to introduce a subject of debate not on the order paper was discussed. The counsel for the Aldermen claimed that this right could only be exercised in times of great danger to the City. The Committee therefore adjudged, since it was a time of crisis, that the Court of Aldermen had infringed the rights of Common Council.[193] The decision of this Committee of the House gave Common Council authoritative support. On March 18th, the petition was read and voted upon in Common Council, even though a quorum of Aldermen was not present.[194] By this action, the petition of the Lord Mayor and Aldermen against the Militia Commissioners was condemned and approval was given to the proposals of Parliament on the Militia.

The Court of Aldermen realized that this limitation of their traditional powers involved a complete surrender of policy-making in the City to Common Council. This, they could not accept and an appeal was made to Parliament. On March 24th, they ordered the City's solicitors to be retained to advise in the dispute with Common Council.[195] Although the Aldermen gave the parliamentary Committee permission to search the records of the City,[196] it was some time before the Committee produced its report. Finally, on June 30th, the House of Commons asked the Lords to join with them in an order to the Lord Mayor to call Common Council as often as 'by the committee chosen by Common Hall [sic] he shall be desired'.[197] But the Lord Mayor still refused to submit, and on July 9th a petition was read in the House of Lords signed by sixty-four Common Councilmen, complaining of obstructions in their proceedings. Among the signatories were four members

---

[193] *A True Diurnal of the Passages in Parliament.* March 18th.

[194] Eleven Aldermen were present: Aldermen Whitmore, Gayre, Garrard, Atkins, Wollaston, Adams, Warner, Towse, Reynardson, Andrewes and Clarke. All the senior Aldermen absented themselves, except Whitmore, who was acting as *locum tenens.* J.Co.Co. 40, fol. 27.

[195] Rep. 55, fol. 400v.

[196] Ibid. fol. 408.

[197] *C.J.* ii, p. 645. Common Hall, here, is obviously a mistake for Common Council.

of the Militia Committee, Captain Venn, Captain Mainwaring, William Berkeley, and Owen Rowe, and also two men who, as we have seen, were said by 'Mercurius Civicus', derisively, to be part of the leadership of the parliamentary puritan party, William Perkins ('Lord Saye's tailor'), and Christopher Nicholson ('the chandler').[198] The Lord Mayor, they said, had refused to put to the vote Parliament's order for the unloading into the City's magazine of the arms taken from Hull and for mobilizing the citizens in arms;[199] 'whereupon', continued the petitioners, 'one of the members of the said Court, professing his readiness to give his consent to obey the said ordinance of Parliament, many of the Aldermen then present and all the Commons with one consent, cried out, "And so do we all!" and declared it by holding up their hands, as is accustomed to declare the votes of that Court'. Sir Richard Gurney, acting it was said, on the directions of the King, had refused to submit to the popular will and paid for his loyalty by being sent to the Tower.[200]

The Lord Mayor was already under attack in Parliament for proclaiming the Royal Commission of Array in the City on June 10th. The proclamation of this Commission was brought to the notice of the Commons by the two City Sheriffs, who disclaimed all responsibility for the action by the Lord Mayor.[201] They were accompanied by representatives of the Militia Committee. Their spokesman, John Fowke, pointed out the dangerous situation created by the proclamation, for 'notwithstanding himself and all the said Committee were fully persuaded that this Militia was settled according to the fundamental laws of the realm, yet they could not tell what operation the publishing of the late proclamation yesterday might have in respect of others'. Fowke, therefore, asked the House to consider a way of preventing 'any mischief or inconvenience that might arise'.[202]

[198] See pp. 137, 148 n., 169, 253 n.

[199] These were the main points of six propositions sent by Parliament to the City. *A Perfect Diurnal*, July 11-19, 1642. July 11th.

[200] Ibid.

[201] Harl. MSS. 163, fol. 157v. But a MS. note in Thomason's hand to a printed copy of the Royal Commission of Array adds: 'The Sheriffs knocked off their horses proclaiming it.' Steele, op. cit., i, p. 263.

[202] Harl. MSS. 163, fol. 157v.

On July 5th, therefore, the Commons sent up a request to the Lords to join with them in an impeachment of the Lord Mayor.[203] His trial opened on July 22nd. Serjeant Wilde outlined the charges, prefacing his remarks with the statement, 'this Lord Mayor is a person great and eminent, and of great power and authority in . . . [the City]; that he is one of the greatest offenders of his predecessors, and is a great burthen and nuisance to the City and Commonwealth'.[204] There were five principal charges against him: for issuing the Commission of Array, for subscribing to the petition against the Militia, for suppressing a petition in favour of the Militia, for refusing to call Common Council, and for failing to suppress anti-parliamentarian rioters in Cheapside. It is an indication of the sympathies of the aldermanic Bench that some of the leading Aldermen of the City appeared at his trial as witnesses in his defence. Aldermen Sir Henry Garway, Sir Nicholas Rainton and Edmund Wright asserted that it had always been the duty of the Lord Mayor to publish royal proclamations.[205] Alderman Sir John Gayre and one of the Sheriffs, Sir George Clarke, took the view that the Lord Mayor was not more guilty in assenting to the petition against the Militia than the rest of the Aldermen.[206] The Remembrancer, Thomas Wiseman, and other prominent City officials, Clement Mosse, Mr. Herne and Mr. Mitchell, also appeared in his defence. On the charge that Gurney had refused to call Common Council, Clement Mosse who was Controller of the Chamber, was able to describe the constitutional practice of the City from long personal experience. He had been a Clerk in the City government since 1599, and it had always been the custom, he said, for the Aldermen to decide whether Common Council should be called and to appoint a convenient day.[207] He was supported by Mr. Mitchell.[208] Evidence against Gurney was provided by two prominent parliamentary puritan Aldermen, Thomas Atkins and John Warner, and also by Common Councilmen and Militia Commissioners, Captain Mainwaring, John Venn, James Russell, Stephen Estwicke and Owen Rowe.[209] But there is no record that they supported their case by reference to constitutional precedents. On August 12th, he was

[203] C.J. ii, p. 653.   [204] L.J. v, p. 230.   [205] Ibid. p. 247.   [206] Ibid. p. 256.
[207] Ibid. p. 267.   [208] Ibid.   [209] Ibid. pp. 246-7.

adjudged guilty of the charges against him: 'to be put out of his office of Lord Mayor of London; to be utterly incapable of bearing office in City or kingdom; incapable of all honour and dignity; and to be imprisoned during the pleasure of the two Houses of Parliament'.[210]

The senior Aldermen were evidently sympathetic with the Lord Mayor's stand against Parliament. When Gurney, during his trial and detention, refused to appoint a *locum tenens*, Aldermen Sir Henry Garway, Sir Nicholas Rainton and Sir George Whitmore would not perform the office, excusing themselves for reasons of health.[211] They were upheld in their refusal by the Clerks of the Lord Mayor's Court, who declared that only the Lord Mayor could exercise this power.[212] On July 14th, the House of Lords ordered Whitmore to call a Court of Aldermen to make an appointment.[213] A week later, fifteen Aldermen informed the House that the Aldermen had never before performed this function and could not do so now. The fifteen included not only the senior Aldermen, but also Aldermen Sir Thomas Soames, Sir John Cordell, Sir John Gayre, Sir Jacob Garrard, Sir Thomas Adams, Sir John Wollaston and Thomas Atkins.[214]

On August 12th, the day of the Lord Mayor's deposition, the Court of Aldermen began to prepare for a new election, and a week later, Alderman Rainton called a meeting of Common Hall.[215] The commonalty nominated John Wollaston and Isaac Penington, and the final choice fell on Alderman Penington.[216] The crown and Royalist party refused to accept this election and referred hereafter to Penington as 'the pretended Lord Mayor'. The aldermanic candidate appears to have been Alderman Cordell, who was next in succession to the mayoralty.[217] Not only was he passed over, however, but also Aldermen Soames, Gayre, Garrard and Atkins who were all senior to Penington.[218] Gurney was loyal to Charles to the end. He

[210] Clarendon, *History*, op. cit., ii, p. 246.   [211] *L.J.* v, p. 200.

[212] Ibid. p. 209.   [213] Ibid. p. 210.   [214] Ibid. p. 229.

[215] *L.J.* v, p. 297.   [216] J.Co.Co. 40, fol. 34v.

[217] *Court Minutes of the East India Company*, vol. 1640-3, p. 262.

[218] Both the City government and the Commons were aware that the legality of the election might be challenged. The deputy Recorder, on presenting Alderman Penington to the Barons of the Exchequer, quoted precedents from the reigns of King John and Henry III to show that on a Lord Mayor's deposition, it was

refused to give up the insignia of his office, claiming that 'they were at his house in London, locked up, and he could not come at them', and these and the City sword had to be taken from him by force.[219] He was imprisoned in the Tower, his estate was sequestered, Gurney House was turned into a garrison, and he died, still in the Tower, in 1647.[220]

In Clarendon's view, Alderman Isaac Penington had been made Lord Mayor 'by the voice and clamour of the common people, against the customs and rules of election'.[221] Clarendon's judgment reflected his own prejudices, but it contained a kernel of truth. If not by the 'common people', he *had* been elected by the City parliamentary puritans. It was evident from Alderman Penington's career in Parliament that the City, if not necessarily committed to radicalism, would nevertheless be strongly subject to its influence. Penington had support from Common Hall and a substantial number of Common Council for the policy of Pym. The Court of Aldermen had undergone changes in its composition and was to suffer further changes[222] which made it, if not an out and out supporter of Pym and his 'middle group', at least a moderate adherent of the parliamentary cause. Five Aldermen had died or retired between September 1640 and December 1641, and four[223] of the men who replaced them became parliamentary supporters. Between January and late autumn 1642, Aldermen Sir Morris Abbot and Sir James Cambell died, and Aldermen William Abell, Sir Edward Bromfield and Sir Richard Gurney were discharged for delinquency and failure to carry out their duties. Four of the men by whom they were replaced were also adherents of Parliament.[224] So, in September 1642, the parlia-

customary for a new election to be held immediately. Penington, he stressed, had many qualifications for the office, having been Sheriff and held many other offices, as well as having made a notable contribution as City Burgess in Parliament. *M. Deputy Recorder's Speech at the Exchequer Bar . . . at the Lord Mayor's taking his oath . . . on 18 August 1642* [Thomason Tracts]. According to *England's Memorable Accidents*, September 26-October 3 1642, (p. 30). Alderman John Towse was also a candidate but Penington had the majority.

219 *L.J.* v, pp. 297, 298.
220 M. A. E. Green, ed., *Calendar of the Proceedings of the Committee for Compounding*, 1889, ii, pp. 858-60.
221 Clarendon, *History*, ii, p. 246.
222 Aldermen Abdy, Clitherow, Highlord, Harrison and Pratt.
223 Aldermen Towse, Garrett, Langham and Andrewes.
224 Aldermen Fowke, Gibbs, Chambers and Bunce.

mentary puritan Aldermen on the Bench were almost equal in strength with those who either openly sympathized with the crown or acquiesced in parliamentary rule from *force majeure*. In 1643, four[225] of the remaining senior and royalist Aldermen were discharged and Alderman Wright died, tipping the balance in favour of those who were at least moderate supporters of Parliament. Even after such a succession of changes, the main support for Pym's policy in the City did not come from the Aldermen (most of whom remained 'moderates' and supporters of accommodation with the King), but from the powerful Militia Committee. With the discharge of Alderman Sir John Gayre and Sir Jacob Garrard from the Committee on September 6 1642, and their replacement by the Lord Mayor and the two Sheriffs, it appeared to be a fitting instrument for the execution of Pym's policies in the City.

*   *   *

We have seen that until December 1641, the Court of Aldermen and Common Council showed no support for Pym's policy in Parliament. They obstructed rather than supported the citizens' petitions. Many leading City magistrates were attacked for earlier support of Charles' government. Encouraged by the example of the parliamentary opposition, the parliamentary puritans in the City began a campaign to win City office. They put forward candidates at elections and began to make new claims for more popular control of Common Council and Common Hall. Their campaign culminated in December 1641 at the time when the dispute between the King and Parliament had also reached its crisis. The newly elected Common Councilmen elected a Committee of Militia which was dominated by the City parliamentary puritans and seized the political initiative in the City government. They took over the Trained Bands, challenged the aldermanic veto, provided evidence for the impeachment of Sir Richard Gurney, and elected Alderman Penington, the leader of the parliamentary puritans, as Lord Mayor in his place. We must now discover who these parliamentary puritans were who had swept all before them in the City.

---

[225] Aldermen Acton, Garway, Whitmore and Windham.

CHAPTER V

The City Parliamentary Puritans before the Long Parliament

THE Puritan Revolution, said 'Mercurius Civicus', was conceived near Banbury, shaped in Gray's Inn Lane and 'put out to nurse' in London.[1] The purpose of this chapter is to identify and describe the foster-parents. The evidence leaves little doubt that it was the Puritan citizens and clergy of the metropolis, and some of the less wealthy City merchants as well as a number of merchants of middle and upper middle rank, who nourished the cause of the parliamentary opposition in the years before 1640. It is necessary now to retrace our steps in time to discover how the City parliamentary puritans exercised influence and disseminated information in the decade before 1640.

Contemporaries in London in the sixteen-thirties were unanimous that the great majority of the citizens were Puritan. What did they mean by this term? In the early days of Elizabeth's reign, when the terms of the Church settlement were still fluid enough to allow of possible modification, they were a clearly defined group who hoped to reform the Church from within in a Calvinist direction. The word Puritan had no ambiguity. From the time of Archbishop Bancroft, however, when the Church finally set its face against further Calvinist reform, the Puritan movement was forced to turn its energies from agitating within the Church to bringing pressure on the crown through Parliament. So arose again that momentous alliance between the constitutional opposition in Parliament and the Puritan movement in the Church This alliance assumed a recognizable form in the sixteen-twenties when the leaders of the Puritans, John Preston and his clerical friends, became associated with the parliamentary opposition led by John Pym, William Fiennes, the first Viscount Saye and Sele, Fulke Greville, the first Lord Brooke, Sir Richard Knightley, Robert Rich, the

---

[1] *A Letter from Mercurius Civicus to Mercurius Rusticus*, op. cit., p. 399.

second Earl of Warwick, and his brother, Sir Nathaniel Rich. After Preston's death, contacts between the two wings of the movement continued in organizations like the New England Plantation Companies and the Feoffees of Impropriations. These two wings of the movement coalesced in the sixteen-thirties and were swelled, through Laudian persecution, by a small group of Separatists who wanted to secede from the Church altogether. Therefore, although the word 'Puritan' was still sometimes used in its original precise sense by contemporaries, it was also beginning to have political overtones. It was being frequently used to denote those, as John Davenport defined Puritan, 'who secretly encourageth men in opposition to the present government'.[2]

The looseness of the term, Puritan, in the sixteen-thirties reflected the heterogeneous character of the movement. It did not imply that the citizens were strict Calvinists although in 1645, there appears to have been wide support for Presbyterianism in the City. Many were far less orthodox in their views. Nearly all were attracted to some aspects of the Puritan movement: a preference for lectures and disapproval of tithes and Laudian ceremonies were sentiments shared by the majority of the citizens. But it would be difficult to attribute a set of doctrinaire opinions to them. Some citizens were certainly heterodox in their religious outlook: a few of the greater Livery Companies, for instance, showed sufficient zeal to appoint Puritans to their endowed lectureships, while at the same time being prepared to contribute to a new St. Paul's, a plan to which Laud was devoted.[3] Nor did being a Puritan imply necessarily being a supporter of the parliamentary opposition. Not all those who favoured Puritan lectures and disliked tithes and Laudian ceremonies were supporters of Parliament in 1642. Alderman Richard Gurney, Lord Mayor in 1641, strongly opposed the suggested increase in City tithes in 1638, but he was a supporter of the King from 1641. Alderman Sir Nicholas Rainton, chairman of the Feoffees of Impropriations from 1632 to 1633, was a lukewarm adherent of Parliament in 1642.

[2] I. M. Calder, *Letters of John Davenport*, New Haven, 1937, p. 14.

[3] Court Book Skinners' Company, vol. 1617-51, fol. 150. Orders of Court, Salters' Company, vol. 1627-84 [Transcripts], p. 93. Calendar Court Minutes, Grocers' Company, ii, pp. 752-3.

But there was undoubtedly a strong party among the City Puritans, who later became not only supporters of the parliamentary opposition but active participants in influencing policy. How did these men, so highly organized in 1641 and 1642, form the basis of their association in the decade before 1640? Probably the Puritan clergy of the City, their leading parishioners and the Society of the Feoffees of Impropriations formed the most broadly based movement and the most effective method of spreading parliamentary puritan ideas in the City. The merchants who later gave their support to Parliament appear to have been far less successful in proselytizing. There was their own particular protégé, the Massachusetts Bay Company, which was entirely managed by merchants later to be preeminent among the financiers and organizers of the parliamentary cause. Apart from the New England Plantations, however, they achieved very little success in penetrating the older commercial companies, although lack of adequate records for many of these organizations makes it impossible to state this with certainty. One exception was the Levant Company, where there was evidence of an opposition party which was campaigning against increased impositions in 1628 and whose members became leading adherents of Pym and his party in the first two years of the Long Parliament. It has been seen earlier that the parliamentary puritans in the City achieved very little influence in the municipal councils before 1640. But 'Mercurius Civicus' accused them of having captured a City organization of another character, the Honourable Artillery Company, a kind of military academy for training officers of the Trained Bands; with what justification he made this accusation will be discussed below.

Since the early sixteen-twenties, the Puritan movement in London had been associated with a number of prominent Puritan clergymen, who, although they were in a minority among the City clergy, enjoyed great influence and popularity with the citizens. Three parishes which had long been pre-eminent in this respect were St. Anne's, Blackfriars, All Hallows, Bread street, and St. Stephen's, Coleman street, and in all three parishes the parishioners enjoyed the right of presentment to the livings. The rector of St. Anne's, Blackfriars, from 1621 was William Gouge, who for more than thirty years drew huge crowds, more than his church could accommodate, to his Sunday sermons and his Wednesday lectures. Richard Stock, who was one of the first to suggest a London society for buying up impropriations, was rector of All Hallows, Bread street, until his death in 1626. His work was carried forward by the Puritan lecturer, George Hughes, until his sermons gained him unwelcome publicity with Archbishop Laud. The vicar of St. Stephen's, Coleman street, from 1624 to 1633 was John Davenport, an acknowledged leader of the Puritan movement, who helped to edit John Preston's sermons and who counted William Fiennes, first Viscount Saye and Sele, as an 'honourable and faithful' friend.[4] After his emigration in 1633, he was succeeded by the Puritan John Goodwin. These men had been popularly elected to their office by their congregations, among whom were some of the leading Puritan laymen in the City, in particular, Alderman Penington of St. Stephen's, Coleman street, and Captain John Venn of All Hallows, Bread street. This right to elect their own ministers, with the power also of granting or withholding augmentations, gave the City Puritans in these parishes a great hold over their ministers: it was little wonder that their sermons so often reflected the political temper of the London citizens.

Perhaps even more important than these ministers was Charles Offspring, from 1617 the Puritan rector of St. Antholin's, who helped to administer the famous St. Antholin lectures. These six lectures, founded in 1559, in full Genevan fashion, and supported mainly from parish funds (except for the five years when they were managed by the Feoffees of Impropriations), had made this parish the centre of Puritan social and religious activities. The tolling of the bells at five in the morning for a whole hour to summon Puritans to the lectures at six was a familiar sound in Budge Row, and a source of great vexation to their anti-Puritan neighbours. Each day the church was filled with an eager citizen audience whose enthusiasm directed by Offspring and his Puritan vestrymen soon promoted St. Antholin's to a kind of 'missionary' headquarters in the heart of London. Not least among its activities was its money-raising efforts, carried out by the rector and his vestrymen, who canvassed and conducted house-to-house

---

[4] *Letters from John Davenport*, op. cit., p. 190.

collections in order to augment the lecturers' stipends.[5] One purpose of the lectures was to provide a testing ground for young Puritan preachers. According to 'Mercurius Civicus', the Feoffees of Impropriations had this aim in mind. Under their management, the lectures provided a spiritual counterpart to the Artillery Garden, 'a place to train up their young emissaries . . . from which most of their bought impropriations were filled'.[6]

The Feoffees who bought up impropriations were a society of Londoners suppressed by Laud in 1633 for attempting to undermine the Church.[7] Plans for a society of this kind had been mooted in 1612 but came to nothing through lack of money. The idea was kept alive by Richard Stock, rector of All Hallows, Bread street, and was adopted and developed by the Feoffees in 1626. They consisted of four merchants, four lawyers and four clergymen, who bought up lay impropriations, advowsons and presentations, to establish lectureships and supplement the incomes of the 'godly' clergy all over the country. They also took over the management of the St. Antholin lectures with the purpose of training men to fill their newly purchased livings. The Puritan clergy and lecturers financed by the Feoffees were bound to reflect the general outlook of those on whom they depended for their stipends. The Feoffees were among the chief supporters of Pym and the parliamentary opposition according to Peter Heylin, a well-placed observer, since his uncle, Alderman Heylin, was for a time the Society's chairman. 'They were appointed by a secret combination of the brotherhood to advance their projects', he wrote, and 'there was not one man among them that wished well to the present government'.[8] The Society, in turn, depended for its financial support on the charity of the wealthier City Puritans. It was from these men that the Feoffees were themselves drawn. Nearly all the lay and legal members of the Feoffees were Adventurers in one of the New

[5] D. A. Williams, 'Puritanism in the City government, 1610-1640', *The Guildhall Miscellany*, no. 4, 1955, p. 5.

[6] *A Letter from Mercurius Civicus*, p. 401.

[7] I. M. Calder, 'A Seventeenth Century Attempt to Purify the Anglican Church', *Am.H.R.*, 53, pp. 760 seq. I. M. Calder, *Activities of the Puritan Faction of the Church of England*, 1957, *passim*.

[8] Peter Heylin, *Examen Historicum*, 1659, pp. 208-9.

England Companies, seven of them in the Massachusetts Bay Company, of which one of the Feoffees, George Harwood, was Treasurer.[9] Two of the Feoffees, Gabriel Barbour and Christopher Sherland, were members of the Providence Island Company. Another, Francis Bridges, was a leading vestryman of St. Antholin's and a collector for the St. Antholin lectures.[10] Four of the clerical Feoffees were the leading clergymen already mentioned, Charles Offspring, John Davenport and Richard Stock, who was succeeded on his death by William Gouge. This Society by their meetings and campaigns to raise money for purchasing impropriations and endowing lectureships helped to bring together the City Puritans into an active community. They financed lecturers in the City who promoted the cause from their pulpits. When one of their lecturers, George Hughes, was silenced by Laud, he fled from London to Warwick Castle, to become chaplain to Robert Greville, the second Lord Brooke,[11] one of the national leaders of the parliamentary opposition who was described by Edmund Calamy as 'a great patron and Maecenas to the pious and religious ministry': a connexion between the City Puritans and the parliamentary opposition, and an example of the way in which the influence of the Feoffees was perpetuated after their suppression.

No other London parish besides St. Antholin's supported a lecture for every weekday. A few, however, supported one or at most two Puritan lecturers, in some instances partly financed until 1633 by the Feoffees. That eloquent republican, Hugh Peter, gained his first audiences at St. Sepulchre's, Holborn; Thomas Foxley, Clerk to the Feoffees, drew large crowds at St. Martin's-in-the-Fields as well as at St. Antholin's; and John Archer, another St. Antholin's lecturer, also preached a Sunday afternoon sermon at All Hallows, Lombard street.[12] There was of course a small number of other parishes in London where Puritan clergy held sway, especially in those parishes where the advowson was vested in the parishioners. No definitive study or even enumeration has yet been made of those City parishes that were Puritan in this period. But it is certain

---

[9] Christopher Hill, *Economic Problems of the Church*, Oxford, 1956, p. 255.
[10] *Activities of the Puritan Faction of the Church of England*, op. cit., p. 34.
[11] *D.N.B.* George Hughes.
[12] I. M. Calder, 'The St. Antholin Lectures', *The Church Quarterly Review*, January-March 1959, p. 54.

that one of them was St. Mary Aldermanbury, where Thomas
Taylor, 'that brazen wall against Popery', was minister and
John Stoughton rector; Stoughton was succeeded in 1639 by
Edmund Calamy, the eminent Puritan and protégé of Robert
Rich, the second Earl of Warwick. After Calamy's election,
Warwick, one of the foremost leaders of the parliamentary
puritan party, applied to the vestry for a pew in this church.[13]
In the parish of St. Matthew, Friday street, the indomitable
Henry Burton preached his 'seditious lectures' until in 1636,
he was deprived and brutally punished by Laud. His Puritan
parishioners signed a petition to the King for his pardon, but
Charles immediately imprisoned the two men who presented
it. When Burton set out for Lancaster Castle, where he was
to be incarcerated, he was followed by a procession of 500 of
his 'loving' friends from London. John Downham, one of the
leading Puritan clergymen who signed the petition against
Laud's Canons in 1640, was rector of Allhallows the Great and
a lecturer at St. Bartholomew, Exchange, while Cornelius
Burges, who presented the petition to the King at York, and in
1641 was said to be one of the leaders of the City apprentices,
was rector of St. Magnus, London Bridge. The Puritan City
clergy were supported by their brethren at the Inns of Court.
The famous sermons of Pym's friend, Richard Sibbes, at Gray's
Inn had caused the supporters of Arminianism considerable
annoyance. John Preston, as Preacher of Lincoln's Inn, had
established there yet more firmly a Puritan tradition going back
to the fifteen-eighties. He was the centre of a group of Puritan
Benchers[14] who were to become active for the parliamentary
cause after 1640, and he influenced William Prynne, the re-
doubtable and voluminous pamphleteer who championed Puritan theology and suffered from Laud's particular venom.
Preston, it was said, had also 'formed a strong party in the
City',[15] so that after his death in 1628, the memory of his work

[13] V.M.Bk., 1610-1763, St. Mary Aldermanbury. Folios unnumbered, September 10 1639. J. P. Malcolm, *Londinium Redivivum*, 1802, ii, p. 119. Calamy's
weekday lecture was attended by 'persons of the greatest quality' for the next
twenty years, 'there being seldom so few as twenty coaches outside his church'.
D. Neal, *The History of the Puritans*, 1793, iv, p. 424.

[14] S. R. Gardiner, ed., *Documents relating to the Proceedings against William Prynne*,
Camden Society, 1877, p. xxv.

[15] P. Heylin, *Cyprianus Anglicus*, 1668, p. 150.

remained among his Puritan associates there and helped to create the climate of opinion that led to the parliamentary puritan victories in 1641 and 1642.

'Mercurius Civicus', who was in no doubt about the part played by the Puritan clergy of the City in providing 'fire from the pulpit', asserted that the 'faction' deliberately imported ministers to London for their purpose. They had been trained, he claimed, at two kinds of seminary: one, the 'initiatory' for novices, was in the universities; the other, St. Antholin's, was, as we have seen, for 'practique', or practical training. He mentioned, as initiating seminaries, Magdalen College and New Inn Hall at Oxford and Emmanuel College and Catharine Hall at Cambridge. This was a typical shot in the pamphleteering war, but there was fire beneath the smoke. A great number of zealous Puritans had received their education at these colleges. Moreover, when John Warner, as Sheriff in 1639, wanted a chaplain, he wrote to Henry Cornish, a tutor at New Inn Hall under Christopher Rogers, the Principal. Both Oxford men were noted for their support of the 'godly' cause in the University and they provided as chaplain, Christopher Love, a young Welsh Puritan preacher, already notorious for refusing to be ordained by his Bishop. Even closer bonds were created with the Warner household when he married the Sheriff's ward, Mary Stone.[16] In 1640, Love was the first to refuse publicly to subscribe to Laud's Canons and two years later, as a result, he was expelled from the University. He was shortly appointed chaplain to John Venn's regiment and became a popular City preacher at St. Anne's, Aldersgate.

Half-way between the initiating and practical seminaries described by 'Mercurius Civicus' was another kind of training found nearer the metropolis and elsewhere. This was the private academy or school, usually conducted by a Puritan minister, aided by 'assistants' who might be young clergymen. In Rotherhithe,

[16] Wood describes Cornish as a poor scholar who was employed for a time in the buttery at New Inn Hall, became a 'puling preacher', was appointed to a canonry of Christ Church by the Parliament, and lived to 1698, preaching at the end as a very old man of more than eighty years in a barn at Bicester. Rogers, who had fled from Oxford in 1643, was appointed a canon of Christ Church and deputy Vice-Chancellor in 1649. *Athenae Oxonienses*, op. cit. (*Fasti Oxonienses*), ii, cols. 118, 157-8. For Warner and Love, see Sloane MSS. 3945, 'Mrs. Love's Memoir of her Husband'. Christopher Love was later an extreme Presbyterian who was executed in 1651 for plotting against the Commonwealth.

part of the eastern and south-eastern purlieus of London, whose radicalism and Puritanism we have noticed, such a 'private seminary', a precursor of the dissenting academies, was conducted by the learned rector, Thomas Gataker. Thomas Young, tutor to Milton and a Smectymnuan, was one of his assistants. Gataker's work in the suburbs was quiet and inconspicuous, although he had achieved early prominence in the Puritan movement as a young Cambridge don and Preacher at Lincoln's Inn. Long resident in Rotherhithe where he had been rector since 1611, he was widely respected.[17] Royalist critics needed a shriller and more easily recognized opponent. They found one in the figure of the public preacher imported, they said, into the City from areas near London. One such was Calybute Downing, vicar of Hackney, who after preaching a remarkable sermon at the Artillery Garden in September 1640, which was understood by his opponents to have upheld the legality of taking up arms against the King, retired secretly to the Earl of Warwick's house in Essex for fear of being questioned. Yet, Downing, often selected by Royalists as a representative figure of the irreconcilable and factious Puritan divine, had another side. In the summer of 1641, when Charles showed signs of conciliation, and Parliament had won many of its demands, he wrote a striking pamphlet, optimistic in the belief that the King would effect a 'universal reformation'.[18] But few pamphleteers on either side wasted words on the subtleties of their opponents' ideas or the more sympathetic aspects of their characters: to 'Mercurius Civicus', Downing remained one of the 'faction' who had been deliberately set on to utter wild words to 'feel the pulse of the City'.

Although the Providence Island Company contained among its undertakers nearly all the early leaders of the Long Parliament, it was not sponsored by the parliamentary puritan merchants of the City; those City merchants who had been connected with it, with the exception of Thomas Barnardiston, who retained his connexion a few years longer, withdrew after 1632, probably because of the inadequate financial return.[19]

[17] Simeon Ashe, 'The Narrative of the Life and Death of Mr. Gataker', in *Gray Hayres Crowned with Grace*, 1655, p. 54 [Thomason Tracts].

[18] *A Discoursive Coniecture upon the reasons that produce a desired event . . .* 1641.

[19] A. P. Newton, *The Colonizing Activities of the Early Puritans*, New Haven, 1914, pp. 125, 127. A Brown, op. cit., ii, p. 852.

It was the more successful Massachusetts Bay Company which bought out the Dorchester Company founded by west country-men, that attracted these merchants. It combined religion with trade, stating its purpose as 'the propagation of the Gospel of Jesus Christ and the particular good of the several adven-turers'.[20] Its members included three of the City M.P.s in 1640, Matthew Cradock the first Governor of the Company, Samuel Vassall and Captain John Venn; two men who were Aldermen in 1642, and supporters of Parliament, Thomas Andrewes and Thomas Adams; and at least five merchants who, as Common Councilmen and members of the Militia Committee, became leading supporters of Parliament, Nathaniel Wright, Christopher Coulson, William Spurstow, Owen Rowe and William Perkins, as well as three prominent Puritans, John Davenport, Vicar of St. Stephen's, Coleman street, Hugh Peter, and John White, the Puritan lawyer and one of the Feoffees of Impropriations. Many of these men were to become prominent in 1642 as leaders of the parliamentary puritan party in the municipality. The early meetings of the Company, therefore, held at Matthew Cradock's house in St. Swithin's lane in the City, must have provided a centre for parliamentary puritan organization comparable with that in Gray's Inn lane where the undertakers of the Providence Island Company had a meeting-place. Among those who later emigrated to Massa-chusetts in 1637 was a group of parishioners from St. Stephen's, Coleman street, including John Davenport. In 1638, they founded the colony of New Haven, an offshoot of Massa-chusetts, on land granted by the Council for New England to Robert Greville, Lord Brooke.[21] As we have already seen, and shall see again, Lord Brooke, who himself at one time considered emigrating to Massachusetts, was a man who enjoyed many and varied connexions with the parliamentary puritans of the City.

Another organization in the City which was subject to the in-fluence of the parliamentary puritans was the Levant Company. It in no way resembled the Massachusetts Bay Company, how-ever, in being under the leadership of the City parliamentary puritans; the Customs Farmers and wealthiest merchants

---

[20] F. Rose-Troup, *The Massachusetts Bay Company and its Predecessors*, New York, 1930, p. 19.

[21] Godfrey Davies, *The Early Stuarts, 1603-1660*, Oxford, 1959, p. 342.

of the City were predominant here as they were in the East
India Company. But some of the parliamentary puritans who
later captured the municipality sat on the Court of Assistants;
John Fowke, Richard Chambers and Samuel Vassall did so,
while Alderman Penington and Matthew Cradock, later City
M.P.s, had moderate trading interests in the Company.
Their campaign can be traced both at the Court of Assistants
and at the meetings of the Generality (who had greater constitutional power as against the Directorate than did the Court
of Committee in the East India Company). It culminated in
1628 when they secured the agreement of the Company,
strongly opposed by that staunch supporter of the government,
Alderman Abdy, to petition Parliament not only against increased impositions on currants but on all commodities.[22] In
1640 and 1641 they were also successful in persuading the
Company to present a petition of their grievances to Parliament.[23] In the East India Company there was a much smaller
opposition party led by a few of the less influential City merchants, including Matthew Cradock,[24] and supported by Lord
Saye and Sele, Lord Brooke and the Earl of Warwick, who
were fighting to limit the power of the Directorate over the
allocation of the Company's stock. Unfortunately, the records
do not tell us the names of more than one or two of these merchants; but as they were allied with some of the future leaders
of the parliamentary opposition, they may have included a
nucleus of parliamentary puritan citizens.

'Mercurius Civicus', looking back 'on those times when this
Rebellion was but an embryo', describes the Artillery Garden
as a prominent centre of the secular activities of the Puritans.
At first, they considered such activities profane, he says, but
when they saw that 'the blessed reformation intended could
not be effected but by the sword . . . they began to affect, yea,
and compass the chief offices of command, so that when any
prime Commanders died new men were elected wholly devoted
to that faction'.[25] The Honourable Artillery Company, which
claimed to have been incorporated in the reign of Henry VIII,

[22] Court Book of the Levant Company, vol. 1617-31. S.P. 105:148, fol. 194v.
[23] Ibid. vol. 1631-1640, S.P. 105:149, fol. 398.
[24] Court Minutes, E.I.C., 1640-1643, p. 1.
[25] A Letter from Mercurius Civicus, op. cit., p. 399.

was revived and reorganized around 1610. Both the Privy
Council and the Lord Mayor and Aldermen felt it necessary
to keep a close watch on a Company devoted to exercising arms
and practising military discipline. In 1614, the Privy Council
allowed the Company to increase its membership from 250 to
500, provided only men of 'good means, well-affected in religion and to his Majesty' were enrolled[26]. To keep the Company
under control, the election of officers was vested in the Lord
Mayor and Aldermen, except the office of Treasurer, to which
the Company had the right of nomination. But this did not
prevent many leading parliamentary puritans enrolling in the
Company. From the book of enrolment, it appears that four
of the Company's Treasurers[27] between 1620 and 1635 were
leading supporters of the parliamentary opposition: Captain
Henry Waller, City Member of Parliament in 1628 and 1629
and close friend of Sir John Elliot and John Hampden, Richard
Chambers who had been imprisoned for his refusal to pay tonnage and poundage and was subsequently elected to the revolutionary Militia Committee of 1642, Alexander Normington who
was also elected to that Committee, and Captain Randall
Mainwaring, who became Deputy Lord Mayor to Isaac
Penington in 1642. In 1630, a dispute broke out between the
Company and the Lord Mayor and Aldermen over the right
to nominate to the office of Captain Leader. The crown seized
upon this dispute as an excuse for intervening and established
its own right to nominate to this post and to approve of the
nominations made by the Lord Mayor and Aldermen to the
other offices.[28] Previously, the Puritan M.P. Captain Henry
Waller had held the office of Captain Leader. Before 1631,
a number of leading parliamentary puritans had enrolled in
the Company: John Towse and John Wollaston, later Aldermen and financiers of Parliament, and Owen Rowe the
regicide. In addition, Nathaniel Wright, Francis Peck, Alexander Normington, Randall Mainwaring and James Bunce,[29]
all members of the revolutionary Militia Committee, were

[26] G. Gould Walker, *The Honourable Artillery Company*, 1926, p. 26.
[27] G. A. Raikes, ed., *The Ancient Vellum Book of the Honourable Artillery Company
Being the Roll of Members from 1611-1682*, 1890, p. 4.
[28] G. A. Raikes, *The History of the Honourable Artillery Company*, 1878, i, pp. 71-75.
Index to Remembrancia, op. cit., pp. 22-23.
[29] For these members of the Militia Committee, see Appendix II.

members of the Company, with John Venn, Maurice
Thompson and Samuel Vassall.[30] Military drill and sport were
becoming popular recreations among the citizens, not only at
the Artillery Garden but in other places about the City and
suburbs. To the simple pleasure of bodily exercise was added
the sterner satisfaction of performing a patriotic duty. According to an eminent authority, even the great and solitary Milton,
tireless in study, seems to have taken part in March 1642 in
similar 'useful and generous labours' which served 'the cause
of religion and our country's liberty'.[31] How much more so
the citizens and their parliamentary puritan leaders. Writing
of the sixteen-thirties, the well-informed author of *Persecutio
Undecima* tells us that these leaders were joined at their exercises in the City's 'military yards' by Lord Brooke, who was in
the habit of spending much time there.[32] His activities were
probably the 'manly' and healthy 'recreations', begun at this
time, according to a sympathetic contemporary.[33] Although
Brooke's name does not appear among the Artillery Company's
enrolled members, his younger son, Fulke Greville, who was
closely associated with the City 'radicals' in 1643, joined the
Company a few months before the outbreak of war.[34]

But the records of the Company do not show that it was
entirely the preserve of the future supporters of Parliament,
and particularly after the crown's interference in the Company, few parliamentary puritans enrolled. Moreover, such
men as Captain Marmaduke Rawden who were later to become Royalists were prominent members, while some of the
leading supporters of Parliament, Alderman Penington, John
Fowke and Matthew Cradock were not enrolled in the Company at all. After 1639, however, when the crown restored
freedom of election to the Company, the parliamentary puritans consolidated their position. Alderman Soames was chosen
President and Captain John Venn, his Deputy, both of whom

---

[30] *The Ancient Vellum Book, passim.*

[31] J. Milton, *An Apology against a Pamphlet . . . against Smectymnuus,* 1642, (Every-
man's Library ed., . . . *Prose Works,* 1927, p. 117). See D. Masson, *The Life of
John Milton,* 1894, ii, p. 402; but Leslie Stephen in his article on Milton in the
D.N.B. criticized the evidence as being 'apparently very inadequate'.

[32] *Persecutio Undecima,* p. 56.

[33] S. Clarke, *A Generall Martyrologie,* 1651, p. 2.

[34] *The Ancient Vellum Book,* p. 65.

soon became prominent as supporters of Pym in the Long
Parliament. At the same time, according to *Persecutio Undecima*,
Captain Matthew Forster, 'one of the faction', brought over
the Puritan Philip Skippon from Holland to be their Captain
Leader;[35] Skippon was a veteran in Sir Horace Vere's regiment which had been sent to assist the Dutch to maintain their
independence. The value and perhaps the purpose of the 'faction's' military enthusiasm was shown in January 1642, when
the City parliamentary puritans took over entire control of the
City Trained Bands.

'Mercurius Civicus' also asserts that Puritan influence was
beginning to permeate the City Councils, although he adds
that this was confined to the election of men from other corporations, such as Alderman Thomas Atkins, who came from
Norwich, a breeding-ground of Puritanism, and to a few 'beggarly' citizens of London who, he claims, could not afford to
maintain the offices to which they were elected.[36] His remarks
seem to be partly corroborated by evidence from the Journal
of Common Council. In 1639, a number of parliamentary
puritans are found as members of Common Council Committees
who had not been mentioned as members earlier: Randall
Mainwaring, one of this author's 'beggarly captains', William
Gibbs, John Langham and John Towse.[37] Matthew Cradock sat
on Common Council Committees from 1637, and Captain Venn,
another 'beggarly captain', as well as Francis Peck, from
1638.[38] As we have seen earlier, no evidence for organized
parliamentary puritan activities appeared in the municipality
until March 1639, when a moderate petition of grievances was
defeated by a majority of Aldermen and Common Councilmen.[39]

But the appearance of the petition marked the revival of a
weapon (disused since the early years of James I) which was
to become the strongest in the parliamentary puritan armoury.

[35] *Persecutio Undecima*, p. 56. Captain Matthew Forster was a Vintner and a
prominent vestryman in the Puritan parish of St. Bartholomew, Exchange. The
parishioners paid Dr. Grant, their orthodox rector, gratuities for allowing them
to invite Puritan ministers to lecture in the parish. E. Freshfield, *Vestry Minute
Book of . . . St. Bartholomew Exchange*, 1890, p. xx.
[36] *A Letter from Mercurius Civicus*, pp. 399-400.
[37] J.Co.Co. 39, fol. 227.
[38] See Appendix II, p. 323.
[39] See Chapter III, pp. 95-6.

At the same time that the petition of grievances was being discussed in Common Council, five hundred apprentices of the Grocers' Company (which in 1642 contained more eminent parliamentary puritans than any other of the leading twelve companies) were petitioning the King against Lord Goring's licence for selling tobacco.[40] It was rejected by the Privy Council, but once the habit of petitioning had been revived, this form of political activity was increasingly adopted and achieved some decisive victories. In August 1640, there followed the petition of the Puritan City clergy, led by Calybute Downing and Cornelius Burges in denunciation of the new Canons and Oath that had been promulgated by Convocation, and in September, one from the citizens demanding that Parliament be called and grievances redressed. The petition of the citizens marked a new phase in the parliamentary puritan campaign. It was organized on a mass scale, bearing, it was said, over 10,000 signatures.[41] A movement of these proportions could not fail to cause alarm in the Privy Council. In spite of repeated promptings from the Council, the Lord Mayor and Aldermen were unable to suppress the petition. Nevertheless, the magistrates of the City did not give it countenance. According to Rossingham, it had at first been presented to the Lord Mayor 'desiring his Lordship to present it to Parliament' but he 'rejected the petition bidding them to deliver it themselves'.[42] On September 22nd, the Court of Aldermen officially disowned it.[43] The Privy Council still had cause for alarm. Although only four Aldermen had signed, the manner of its circulation among the citizens and its wide support revealed the strength of popular feeling. The Council's fears were justified; two of the leaders of the citizens who presented their petition to the King at York were Richard Shute[44] and Maurice Thompson,[45] both of whom became prominent supporters of the parliamentary opposition in the Court of Common

[40] Add. MSS. 11,045, fol. 7v.

[41] S.P.Dom. 16/467/135.

[42] Add. MSS., 11,045, fol. 126v.

[43] Rep. 54, fol. 307. P.C.R. 2/52, fol. 365v.

[44] Richard Shute was connected with the 'war party' in the City in 1643 and presented some of the more radical petitions. See Chapter VII, pp. 252 seq.

[45] Later a Commissioner for Customs. Before 1640, he was notorious as an interloper in the East India trade.

Council, while Captain John Venn, who was also associated with the petition, became well known later for his ability to mobilize the citizens.

The citizens' petition of September 1640 was a fuller document than that presented by the Peers to the King, or than the petition of grievances which had been presented to the Court of Common Council in the previous year. It ranged over a wide field and revealed deep-seated opposition to Charles' policy. The petition combined opposition to Ship Money, impositions and monopoly patents, with protests against innovations in religion, opposition to the Scottish War, and complaints about the sudden calling and dissolution of Parliaments without the redress of grievances. It became apparent later that the outcome of the election of the City Burgesses marked an even greater disaster for the crown. Instead of returning their Recorder, Sir Thomas Gardiner, and one or more of the senior Aldermen, the four citizens who had represented the City in the Short Parliament, Aldermen Penington, Alderman Soames, Samuel Vassall and Matthew Cradock, were re-elected.[46] The return of leading parliamentary puritans as Burgesses for the City must have alarmed those members of the Privy Council who remembered the parliamentary sessions of 1628 and 1629. Then, as now, the Recorder had been rejected by Common Hall. Captain Henry Waller, Captain Leader and Treasurer of the Artillery Company, had been elected a Burgess for the City. A prominent Puritan,[47] he had played a leading part in supporting the policy of the parliamentary opposition, as an opponent of Arminianism and of the unparliamentary levy of tonnage and poundage. As a result of their political co-operation in this Parliament, a close friendship was formed between Captain Waller and Sir John Eliot, leader of the opposition, and while Eliot was in the Tower, Waller acted as his personal 'convoy to all parts'.[48] Waller was also a friend of John Hampden.

[46] 'Return of the names of every member returned to serve in each parliament.' *Parliamentary Accounts and Papers*, 1878, vol. 62, Part I, pp. 485 seq.

[47] His funeral sermon was preached by George Hughes, Lecturer of All Hallows, Bread street, and was entitled, *The Saints Losse and Lamentation. A Sermon Preached at the Funerall of the Worshipfull Captaine Henry Waller, the Worthy Commander of the Renowned Martiall Band of the Honourable City of London exercising Armes in the Artillery Garden*, 1631.

[48] John Forster, *Sir John Eliot*, 1865, ii, pp. 338-49, 533, 592.

These friendships continued until Waller's death in 1631, and set a precedent for the alliance of the City Burgesses and the leaders of the parliamentary opposition in 1640. A brief account of the earlier careers of the City members returned in 1640 will show that a similar alliance was to be formed in the Long Parliament.

THE CITY MEMBERS OF PARLIAMENT

Alderman Isaac Penington,[49] the eldest son of Robert Penington[50] of London, merchant, and Judith, daughter of Isaac Shetterden of London, was a well-known figure among City Puritans. Although for many years a substantial trader in the Levant Company, shipping out broad cloths and kersies and returning with silks and grograins,[51] he was not prominent, unlike his colleagues Matthew Cradock and Samuel Vassall, among those who opposed the impositions on currants, and the unparliamentary levy of tonnage and poundage. He had a moderate financial stake in the East India Company, but appears to have sold out his shares by the end of 1635.[52] He also traded to France.[53] He was not connected, as far as it is possible to discover, with the Plantation trades in America or the West Indies. Apart from these moderate interests in the export trade, he owned jointly with Lewis Young a brewhouse in Whitefriars,[54] and in 1644 he rented from the City a brewhouse

[49] 1587(?)-1661. He married first Abigail, daughter of John Allen of London, merchant, and, secondly, Mary, daughter of Matthew Young, a brewer of London. He had six children by his first wife. Isaac, the eldest, became a leading Quaker and author. The Alderman was a second cousin of the Admiral, Sir John Penington, of Muncaster, whose financial affairs he managed while the Admiral was at sea. Throughout this work, I have spelt the Alderman's surname as he usually wrote it.

[50] Robert Penington was the second son of William Penington of London, citizen and Grocer. He died on April 18 1628, and in his will, he made a number of charitable bequests and appointed his eldest son, Isaac, his chief executor. He left all his properties in Suffolk and Norfolk to Isaac Penington and charged them with annuities payable to his other relatives. P.C.C. Skynner 36. He had considerable interests in the East India trade from its foundation. *C.S.P. East Indies, 1613-1616*, p. 173.

[51] Ledger of the Levant Company, vol. 1627-35. S.P. 105:158, fol. 33.

[52] *Court Minutes E.I.C., 1635-1639*, p. 121.

[53] On more than one occasion, he presented petitions to the House of Commons from merchants trading to France and Spain in wines.

[54] House of Lords MSS., Victoria Tower, House of Lords, vol. April 27-May 6 1647, Petition of Alderman Isaac Penington and Lewis Young, May 6 1647.

in Broken Wharf.[55] He was not among the biggest merchant princes of the City, although he was a substantial citizen, described in May 1640 by Sir Morris Abbot as among the eight wealthiest citizens of his ward.[56] He did not become prominent in City government before 1638, nor had he held the most important parish offices[57] (he is first mentioned in the vestry minutes as one of the general vestry which elected John Goodwin as vicar)[58], and he was not returned as a Common Councilman for his ward. In 1638, however, he was elected Sheriff at a time when there appears to have been increasing reluctance among citizens to hold the office.[59] In the following year he was elected an Alderman,[60] and from 1640 to 1642, he held the position of Prime Warden of the Fishmongers' Company. When he was first elected to Parliament, therefore, in 1640, he had held high office for a short period only, was one of the junior Aldermen, and although he had held the leading offices in his Livery Company,[61] he

[55] Rep. 57, fol. 15.

[56] *Miscellanaea Genealogica et Heraldica*, vol. ii, 2nd Series, 1888, pp. 35 seq. These returns which are extant for nineteen of twenty-six wards give the names of those citizens who were thought by the Alderman of the ward to be most able to contribute to a royal loan in May 1640. There does not appear to have been any fixed standard of wealth by which the Aldermen decided who was or was not capable of lending. This reduces the value of the returns for the historian. Neither is there any means of knowing how a man adjudged to be amongst the wealthiest citizens of a well-to-do ward would compare with a wealthy citizen of a poorer ward. But the returns can provide a very general indication as to who were considered the City's richest men, and when the returning Alderman divided the wealthy citizens into degrees of wealth, as happened in some instances, comparisons can then be made between those in the first and, say, in the fourth class.

[57] There is no record, that is, after 1622, the date from which the Vestry Minute Books are extant for this parish. Vestry Minute Book, St. Stephen's, Coleman street, MSS. 4458:1. He was, however, admitted to the committee for parish business on December 27 1633 (fol. 89), elected a Collector for the Poor on April 10 1636 (fol. 101) and an Auditor of the Churchwardens' Accounts on February 26 1638 (fol. 105).

[58] Ibid. fol. 86v.

[59] Rep. 52, fol. 159. £100 was ordered to be paid to Penington in accordance with an Act of Common Council of 1592, for accepting the office of Sheriff after a number of the Lord Mayor's previous nominees had refused. Chamb. Acc., 1638-1639, fol. 57v.

[60] Rep. 53, fol. 79v. The *D.N.B.* antedates his election to the Bench by a year.

[61] He was made a liveryman of the Company on November 4 1613, and an Assistant on May 22 1622. He served the office of third Warden in 1634, and was elected Prime Warden in 1640. Transcripts of the Fishmongers' Company, Court of Assistants, ii, pp. 130, 660, iii, part 3, pp. 305, 751.

had not served as a Churchwarden or Common Councillor.

His recent advent to municipal office did not mean that he had not previously taken a deep interest in public affairs. In his letters to his cousin, Captain John Penington, later Admiral, for whom he seems to have acted as secretary for a time, he had many comments to make on day to day events. He was glad to see the end of the war against the Huguenots of La Rochelle.[62] He was not afraid to state his alarm at the misdirected administration of naval affairs, the evils of impressment and the appointment of ignorant courtiers as sea-captains.[63] He had himself heard at first hand about the sufferings of the sailors, having had a cargo in one of the ships trading to France. Perhaps his sympathies with them now gave him contacts with the world of turbulent mariners who rose and demonstrated so frequently in the London docks in 1641 and 1642. Certainly at the time he was already a parliamentary puritan. In 1627, he wrote to his cousin, that he hoped King and Parliament would be reconciled. 'I pray God incline the heart of the King to yield that which may further God's glory . . . and tend to the reformation of that which is amiss, that so we may live and enjoy peace and prosperity under him. I mean peace with all the world but war with Spain for I am confident that we shall never have peace with them but to our prejudice.'[64] War with Spain: here was one of the main tenets of the opposition's programme, particularly of that most important pressure group, the Providence Island Company. Penington did not comment so freely to his cousin in the sixteen-thirties. Their sympathies were perhaps already diverging. But in 1637, he remarked on the Star Chamber proceedings then in progress against the City: 'News I have not worth your knowledge, neither is it safe to write of anything that passes, all the discourse is now of the great Star Chamber business, of which passages I know you shall have better information than I can give you: but this I can report for a truth thereof I am both an eye and ear witness, these proceedings cause much dejection among many good and loyal subjects, make many fly and make many more think of providing for their safety in other places.'[65]

[62] S.P.Dom. 16/20/49.   [63] S.P.Dom. 16/22/95.
[64] S.P.Dom. 16/24/43.   [65] S.P.Dom. 16/363/120.

Penington's reputation and popularity with the citizens of London arose from his activities as a leading Puritan. He was a man of the first importance in the Puritan movement and was connected with a number of its campaigns. He took part in arousing support for the attempt, initiated by a familiar group of London clergymen, Thomas Taylor, Richard Sibbes, John Davenport and William Gouge, to create a public fund for the relief of the distressed Protestants of the Palatinate.[66] At the Court of the livery of the Fishmongers' Company, Penington tried to arouse sympathy for the victims of the Spanish and Imperial wars on the Continent, even though such appeals were forbidden by royal proclamation.[67] It was said that he was elected to Parliament because of his 'known zeal, by his keeping a fasting Sabbath throughout his shrievalty'.[68] But his contacts with the Puritan movement went even further. There is evidence that he was directly associated with its acknowledged leaders and that he and his wife were accustomed to entertain them on their visits to London. Penington's second wife was Mary, the daughter of Matthew Young, a London brewer, and even before their marriage she was unusually prominent as a Puritan hostess. The author of *Persecutio Undecima* tells us that whenever one of these clergy came to town 'they found entertainment in the City. For whose rendezvous a widow (whom Alderman Penington married) kept an ordinary at Whitefriars (where many of them lodged in Dr. Preston's day)'.[69] It is tempting to see their inn as both a refuge and an organizing centre for ardent Puritans. Whitefriars still enjoyed ancient rights of sanctuary, the Peningtons could be trusted, and after their marriage the house may well have continued to receive and sustain guests visiting London on 'godly' business.[70] Penington, in partnership with Lewis Young, a merchant who was perhaps related to Mary, owned a brewery in Whitefriars, which he may have acquired through his marriage; possibly the eating-house or inn was attached to it.

A sidelight on the opposition to industrial development

[66] *C.S.P.D. 1627-1628*, vol. 56/15.
[67] Transcripts, Fishmongers' Company, op. cit., iii, part 3, p. 245a.
[68] *Persecutio Undecima*, p. 57.   [69] Ibid. p. 55.
[70] Compare a house at Bristol which received from all over England poor families who had come to embark for New England. Masson, op. cit., ii, p. 581.

in the City, somewhat obscured by a hint of official dislike of Penington, is revealed in a curious episode in which the brewery was closed down in 1637 at the suit of the Judges of Serjeant's Inn and the Inner Temple because of the smoke nuisance it created by the burning of 'sea-coal'. The partners submitted petitions in 1641 and 1647 for the compensation promised to them and claimed a loss of £2,000. In the later petition, they made a point of mentioning the presence of the Earl of Dorset, Lord Maltravers and his father, the Earl of Arundel (Earl Marshal of England) at the original hearing.[71] Penington may have felt that his political enemies were taking advantage of his smoky chimneys to blacken his reputation and damage his interests. He said in his petition that it was common for 'sea-coal' to be used in London. But both earls lived nearby—Dorset in Dorset House, a fine mansion in the same district, and the Earl Marshal in his palatial Arundel House not far away—and this may be sufficient explanation of their action. A more scandalous affair a year later involved a fellow brewer, Mr. Bond of Westminster, who was charged with a similar offence by Laud. The Archbishop, it was alleged, offered to drop the proceedings against him if Bond gave £1,000 towards the rebuilding of St. Paul's. When Bond refused to pay, he was sent to the Fleet, his houses were pulled down, and he paid a fine of £1,000, having lost, it was said, thrice this sum. Penington sheltered him on his release.[72] The two brewers, if they reflected on any political implications of these actions and consoled themselves with thoughts of ultimate justice, may well have seen their opponents as men antagonistic to them in every possible way, hindering even their industry. Nevertheless, God's will would prevail.[73] Subsequent events would have confirmed them in their views. The Earl Marshal in May 1640, was in danger of an attack on Arundel House, planned in revenge for the guns he had

[71] House of Lords MSS., Victoria Tower, Petition of Alderman Isaac Penington and Lewis Young, May 6 1647. *C.J.*, ii, p. 156. *H.M.C. House of Lords MSS., Fourth Report, Part I*, p. 67.

[72] *C.S.P.D., 1641-1643*, vol. 499/20.

[73] Cf. the case of Richard Chambers, a victim also of political repression, who published a curious petition and broadsheet thanking God's Providence for the restitution of his rights: *Humble Petition of Richard Chambers . . .* and broadsheet beginning *Now Right Honourable*, 1646 [Thomason Tracts]. But his rejoicing was premature. See Appendix II, p. 314.

mounted, ready, it was said, to fire on the London apprentices assembled across the river in St. George's Fields. Dorset in 1641, when he ordered the Westminster Trained Bands to fire on the London citizens demonstrating outside Parliament, met with opprobrium in the Commons.[74] Laud's action against Bond was cited when the Archbishop was on trial for his life. Compensation both financial and spiritual was eventually paid.

Penington, a little earlier, had been reported to Laud, over his proposal to establish a lecturer at Chalfont St. Peter in Buckinghamshire, where he had bought 'The Grange' as a country residence. His vicar, James Bradshaw, an orthodox clergyman, recoiled with horror from this suggestion of a lecturer in his peaceful parish and rebuffed the Alderman. Whereupon, he reported, Penington immediately began to abuse Laud and the local Bishop, insolently saying 'since this same pragmatical Bishop kept his Visitation, there is a great gap opened forth for the increasing of Popery and spreading of Arminianism'.[75] To Penington, as to so many extreme Puritans, Laud was the personification of much that they detested in Church and State. It might be thought that he had strong private reasons to hound him in the Long Parliament, but it was the 'godly cause' not private vengeance which inspired Penington throughout his career. There is high drama and tragedy in the last act of the relationship between the Alderman and the Archbishop, but it is not a tragedy of personal revenge. It was Penington, in his capacity as Lieutenant of the Tower, who brought the news to Laud in his cell that both Houses had condemned him to death and, in this capacity, he accompanied him in the last scene of all—the short journey to the scaffold on Tower Hill. But if Penington was not moved by feelings of revenge, he cannot be exonerated from the charge of religious and political intolerance. As Lord Mayor in 1643, he denounced three Royalist clergymen of the City to the Committee for Scandalous Ministers,[76] who thereupon sequestered them from their livings. He was then Lord Mayor in a City divided and at war, and he no doubt considered that there

[74] See Chapter VI, p. 221.

[75] S.P.Dom. 16/326/18. The *D.N.B.* wrongly states that Penington was reported to Laud for refusing to bow at the name of Jesus; in fact, it was his gardener.

[76] *H.M.C. House of Lords MSS., Fifth Report*, p. 78.

were compelling political reasons to oust 'malignant preachers' from the pulpit. When his Quaker son rebuked him many years later for his 'formal religion' and his attempts to silence opponents by fines and prison bars,[77] he was judging him by the lofty ideal of toleration, which must have seemed a visionary concept to men concerned with holding political power in a time of revolutionary upheaval and war.

In his public and personal affairs, Penington was a dedicated man. His portrait[78] reveals him as a slender figure ('little Isaac', royalist scribblers called him), with an austere intellectual face, a man whose conviction gave him an inner strength that belied his slight appearance. The scandals of the Commonwealth left his reputation untarnished. Even the coarsest, 'muck-raking', Royalist ballad writers and poetasters generally seem to have treated Penington as outside the class, so often caricatured, of crude, profit-seeking Puritans, paying off old scores. Even so, at a time when the State was torn by Civil War, it is not surprising that some libels against Penington were uttered. One versifier alleged that he grew rich from the fees on citizens' passes;[79] another spoke of Penington, 'who thinks store of good he doth' by imprisoning, plundering and hanging Royalists who refused to bring their contributions to the Guildhall.[80] This was a reference to the 'voluntary levy' of 1642, and no one, of course, was hanged for refusing to contribute, but it is significant that this extremely hostile witness seemed to recognize, however faintly, that Penington's deeds, although vile, were prompted by his conception of what was good. The treatment of Penington by other Royalist ballad writers and pamphleteers is similar, and there is nothing to compare with the savage attacks made on such a man as Alderman Fowke or others, for that matter, of greater integrity. There is even a certain amount of tolerant humour. One song writer who called on the Devil to take Pym and all his Peers

[77] Maria Webb, *The Penns and Peningtons*, 1867, pp. 78-82. John Penington's Collection of his father's MSS., vol. i, fols. 120-7, MSS. Collection, Friends' House, London.

[78] Attributed to Cornelius Jannsen, it is in the possession of the Fishmongers' Company, London.

[79] 'London's Farewell to the Parliament', *Rump: or an exact collection of the choycest poems and songs relating to the Late Times*, 1662 [reprinted 1874], i, p. 94.

[80] 'The Downfall of Cheapside-Crosse', ibid. i, p. 138.

was charitable enough to call Penington 'wise and old',[81] no
doubt with irony, but the reference is not unkind; similarly,
other writers give us glimpses of Penington and his remarkable
wife both to the fore in the fortification and entrenching of
the City in 1642 and 1643,[82] when a great mass of citizens
from all ranks of society, men and women, marched out with
trenching tools in defence of London.

In a sense, this great common action of the citizens, mirrored
Penington's own life and purpose. He participated in the Puritan movement in its highest conclaves but also at a much
humbler level—as an ordinary member of the vestry of St.
Stephen's, Coleman street. From at least 1633, Penington's
town residence was in this parish,[83] a centre of Puritanism—
the Faubourg St. Antoine of London. Coleman street was 'a
large fair street' but the alleys leading off it were filled with
poor craftsmen. The ward, long and narrow and densely populated on either side of its central thoroughfare, was notorious
for its lawlessness: its lack of constables disturbed the neighbouring parishes of St. Olave Jewry and St. Margaret Lothbury.[84] The vicar of St. Stephen's, as has been said earlier,
was John Davenport, one of the Feoffees of Impropriations
who became a Separatist by 1633 when he resigned his office
and emigrated to found the colony of New Haven. He was
succeeded by John Goodwin, that 'Great Red Dragon of Coleman street', who signed the ministers' petition against the
Laudian Canons[85] in September 1640 and was later a leading
Independent. Goodwin seems to have been on terms of warm
friendship with the leading parliamentary puritans. He dedicated his first sermon to appear in print to Isaac Penington
and the 'rest of my loving parishioners, and dear friends, the
inhabitants of St. Stephen's, Coleman street', and two of his
later works to John Pym and Mrs. Elizabeth Hampden, the
mother of John Hampden.[86] Penington lived in this strong-
hold of London Puritanism and revolution. It was here that

---

[81] 'The Cavaliers' Prayer', ibid. i, p. 112. See also *The Rebels Almanack* . . . ,
1660, pp. 4-5.

[82] 'A Western Wonder', *Rump*, op. cit., p. 135. 'On the demolishing the Forts',
ibid, i, p. 246.

[83] *The Visitation of London, 1633-1635*, ii, p. 151.

[84] J.Co.Co. 40, fol. 45v.   [85] Nalson, op. cit., i, p. 496.

[86] Thomas Jackson, *The life of John Goodwin*, 1872, pp. 16-19.

the Five Members took refuge, perhaps in his house. Cromwell and Hugh Peter met regularly at its Star Inn and, in the twilight of its revolutionary ardour, it was in the crowded alleys off Coleman street that the Fifth Monarchy men conspired and Venner's ill-fated rising broke out and was crushed.

Contemporary Royalist historians frequently asserted that Penington was a close personal associate of Pym and the leaders of the parliamentary opposition. It is clear that he was intimately connected with the national Puritan movement and the City Puritans with whom he waged common campaigns in London. His early connexions with the clerical friends of John Preston would have given him close contacts with the leaders of the parliamentary opposition and that his views coincided with theirs can be seen from his letters to his cousin. Clarendon asserted that Penington was 'a man in the highest confidence of the party'.[87] Robert Baillie, that zealous covenanting divine sent by the Scottish Church to London in 1640 to gather evidence against Laud, suggests in a letter[88] that there was already contact between the leaders of the House of Commons and Penington in the first weeks of the Long Parliament, though this causes no surprise since the Alderman had already sat in the Short Parliament. Penington's choice of a country seat at Chalfont St. Peter in Buckinghamshire in proximity to Hampden, Sir Arthur Goodwin and the other parliamentarians of this county, rather than at his paternal estates, may well indicate an acquaintance with these circles, or it may have resulted in such a friendship. Later, Penington's son, a Quaker in the same tradition but with very different beliefs, formed a coterie of Friends around the same house. Both Hampden and Penington were friends of John Goodwin, the minister of St. Stephen's, Coleman street, and Clarendon in his *History* described Hampden as one of the chief leaders of the Root and Branch party with which the Alderman was also prominently connected.[89]

---

[87] Clarendon, *History*, i, p. 284.

[88] David Laing, ed., *The Letters and Journals of Robert Baillie*, Edinburgh, 1861, i, pp. 271 seq., pp. 274 seq.

[89] Penington's political radicalism persisted throughout the Interregnum. His religious views are less clear. He appears to have supported the establishment of Presbyterianism in London in 1646, and he differed with John Goodwin's views on the sacrament. In 1649, however, he supported Goodwin's reinstatement as

Matthew Cradock did not play such an energetic part in the House of Commons as Isaac Penington, although before 1640 he was more eminent than the Alderman in City mercantile circles. The son of Matthew Cradock of Stafford and Dorothy Greenham, and brother of Samuel Cradock of Thistelton, Rutland, he married, first, Damaris, daughter of Richard Wyn of Shrewsbury in the church of St. Stephen's, Coleman street in 1622, and then Rebecca, daughter of Thomas Jordan, a merchant of London.[90] By his first marriage he had a daughter, Damaris, who married Thomas Andrewes, the eldest son of the parliamentary puritan Alderman and Lord Mayor.[91] Cradock's marriage with Damaris Wyn had already connected him with several leading Puritan families, the Spurstows, Alderseys, Moulsons, Parkhursts and Oldfields.[92] He lived in the parish of St. Swithin's, London Stone, another Puritan parish (in this instance the advowson was leased from the Salters' Company) where the congregation claimed the right of electing their ministers.

His association with the New England plantations began in the sixteen-twenties, probably with the Dorchester Company. He transferred his stock in 1628 to the newly formed Massachusetts Bay Company of which he was a foundation member and the first Governor. He saw the work of the Company as both a spiritual crusade and a commercial undertaking, concerning himself on the one hand with its evangelical mission to convert the Indians[93] and on the other with his shipbuilding interests which were one of his most important business activities. His particular achievement was the establishment of a shipyard on the river Mystic now called Medford in Massachusetts. Perhaps as one of the most prominent shipbuilders of his time, he was in touch with that group of Puritan

vicar. E. Freshfield, *Some Remarks . . . upon the History . . . of St. Stephen's, Coleman street*, 1887, pp. 9 seq. He sat on the Commission to try the King, although he did not sign the death warrant, and he became an energetic member of the Council of State. But he retired from politics after 1655, when he suffered severe financial reverses, and he was discharged from the aldermanic Bench in 1657. Imprisoned at the Restoration, he died in the Tower in 1661.

[90] Rose-Troup, op. cit., p. 139.

[91] See Appendix II, pp. 309-11.

[92] Rose-Troup, op. cit., p. 139.

[93] N. B. Shurtleff, ed., *Records of the Governor and Company of the Massachusetts Bay Company*, Boston, 1853, i, p. 384.

mathematicians and scientists who worked with Dr. Wells in the docks at Deptford. In any event, he would have been conversant with the scientific achievements in this field which were among the greatest technological advances of the early seventeenth century.[94]

Cradock's most important action as Governor of the Massachusetts Bay Company was his suggestion that its government should be transferred to New England. Astutely forecasting the trend of political events at home, he hoped to remove the new Plantation from the danger of royal interference. His judgment was sound: when Sir Francis Gorges with Charles's backing launched his attack on the Company in the Star Chamber, he was unable to take effective action against an absentee defendant. Cradock alone among the patentees refused to submit and was taken into custody by the King's Bench 'for usurping the government'.[95] It is not clear how he viewed the later separatist tendencies of the Company in New England, although many of his servants fell foul of the New England magistrates. As an Adventurer in England he claimed to have expended large sums for the benefit of the Company.[96] It was his knowledge of the Plantations which brought him into contact with the younger Sir Henry Vane, whose passage to Massachusetts he secured in 1635,[97] and who became Governor of the colony in the following year. This friendship became politically significant later. When next they met, it was as members of the Root and Branch party in the first months of the Long Parliament.

From at least 1628, Cradock also had substantial trading connexions with the East India Company. Throughout the later sixteen-thirties, he sat as a 'Committee' for the Company, but failed to be elected Deputy Governor in 1639. He became identified with the opposition party in the Company, as we would expect, supporting the criticisms made by a number of the smaller shareholders that policy was laid down by a caucus. In January 1640, at a Court of Committees, he supported the Court's claim to take a greater part in discussing and arranging

[94] F. R. Johnson, 'Gresham College; the Precursor of the Royal Society'. *Journal of the History of Ideas*, 1940, i, pp. 413-38.

[95] Bankes Papers, MS. 8/18. Cf. C. M. Andrews, *Colonial Self-Government 1652-89*, 1904.   [96] Rose-Troup, op. cit., pp. 29-30.

[97] *C.S.P. Colonial, 1574-1660*, vol. viii/70.

the new stock, but his proposal was defeated.[98] As a 'Committee' he was usually employed in buying up cloth for export to the Indies.[99] Cradock was one of the largest traders in the Levant Company.[100] He was elected as Assistant repeatedly throughout the sixteen-thirties, but failed to be elected Deputy-Governor in 1637, when he was nominated as a candidate against the highly unpopular Customs Farmer Sir Job Harby.[101]

Matthew Cradock had taken part in City Councils from at least 1637, when he was elected to most of the important Committees of Common Council, including the Committee for letting City Lands.[102] He had held office in the livery of the Skinners' Company, serving as second and first Warden in 1638 and 1640, respectively.[103] His Puritanism and his political opposition to Charles in the Gorges Star Chamber case, secured his election as Burgess for the City of London in the Short Parliament and in November 1640, until his death on May 27 1641, he was a close political ally of Alderman Penington.

Cradock was succeeded as City M.P. by Captain John Venn, by that time already well known for his part in sponsoring citizens' petitions. John Venn came of Somersetshire yeoman stock[104] which claimed to trace its ancestry back to the fourteenth century. He had been apprenticed by his father to the Merchant Taylors' Company in 1602, and gained his freedom in 1610. The later Royalist allegation that he was a 'decayed' merchant, 'a beggarly Captain', appears doubtful, for at the time he was a substantial trader in wool and silk with the West of England and Ireland.[105] From at least 1626, he occupied a silk shop in Bread street.[106] Like Matthew Cradock and Samuel Vassall, he was one of the original members of the Massachusetts Bay Company and was still a stock-holder in 1644. In 1635, together with Matthew Cradock and Samuel

[98] *Court Minutes, E.I.C., 1640-1643*, p. 1.
[99] At the time of his death, he owed several sums to clothiers. P.C.C. Evelyn, 81.
[100] Ledger of the Levant Company, vol. 1627-35. S.P. 105:157, fol. 90. He had been admitted to the freedom of the Company on July 12 1627. Court Minute Book, S.P. 105:148, fol. 169.
[101] Ibid. vol. 1631-40. S.P. 105:149, fol. 254.
[102] J.Co.Co. vol. 37, fol. 290; 345v: vol. 38, fol. 107, 133v, 173v.
[103] Court Book of the Skinners' Company, vol. 1617-51, fol. 169, 181.
[104] *The Visitation of London, 1633-1635*, op. cit., ii, p. 308.
[105] *C.S.P.D. 1637*, vol. 355/5.
[106] *D.N.B.*

Vassall, he was involved in the *quo warranto* proceedings against the Company. He stood his trial and disclaimed his offence.[107]

John Venn first rose to prominence in the City in 1631 as a result of a disputed election in the Honourable Artillery Company. In the dispute mentioned earlier which led to the intervention of the Privy Council, Venn had been nominated as an opposition candidate to Captain Marmaduke Rawden (the choice of the Court of Aldermen and later, after 1642, an ardent Royalist) for the position of Captain Leader. Neither candidate was elected, for the crown nominated a third candidate who was forcibly instituted. But in 1636 Venn was elected Captain Sergeant-Major by the Company and at some time between 1639 and 1641 he was made Deputy President under Alderman Soames.[108] Venn was also a prominent member of Common Council from at least 1638. In that year he was elected to the Committee for selling Contract lands,[109] and to nearly all important subsequent committees set up by Common Council. In July 1640, he was elected to the most important Common Council Committee, the Committee for letting the City Lands.[110] He was chosen one of the four Wardens of the Merchant Taylors' Company for the year 1641-2.[111]

Although Captain Venn had therefore held important civic offices by 1641, he was by no means among the wealthiest City merchants. In 1640, he was placed by the Alderman of Bread street Ward, William Abell, as among the third group of wealthy citizens, there being at least twenty-eight citizens in the ward who were richer than Venn.[112] He was a friend and correspondent of John Winthrop, and like Alderman Penington he was a well-known Puritan who lived in a parish

---

[107] Bankes Papers, MS. 8/18.

[108] M. Milward, *The Soldiers Triumph: and the Preachers Glory. In a Sermon preached to the Captains and Souldiers exercising Arms in the Artillery Garden . . . 31 August 1641,* p. 1.

[109] J.Co.Co., 38, fol. 107v.

[110] Ibid. 39, fol. 111.

[111] Court of Assistants, 1636-1654, Merchant Taylors' Company, fol. 125.

[112] *Miscellanea Genealogica et Heraldica,* op. cit., p. 37. When Venn died in 1650, however, he had been enriched by purchases of Bishops' lands and left in his will, besides properties in Candlewick street and Nicholas lane in the City, lands in Somerset, Lincolnshire and Northamptonshire. In addition he was owed £4,000 by Parliament and £140 by the Trustees for Bishops' lands. P.C.C. Pembroke, 123.

that also enjoyed a reputation for its Puritanism. As Church-warden of All Hallows, Bread street, in 1631, Venn quarrelled with the Salters' Company, who protested that he had assessed them to pay poor rate, though they had long claimed exemption.[113] As we have already seen, the rector of this parish until 1626 was Richard Stock, one of the Feoffees of Impropriations. From 1632, George Hughes was chosen to give a Thursday afternoon lecture by the parishioners of All Hallows and his stipend was augmented until 1633 by the Feoffees. In 1640, the sub-curate was Sampson Carrall, who was mentioned by Sir John Lambe, Dean of the Arches, as an 'unconformable' minister.[114]

The third member of Parliament for the City was Samuel Vassall, the son of John Vassall, a merchant of London of Huguenot origin, living in Stepney, who had equipped and commanded a ship against the Spanish Armada, and who was famed for his knowledge of navigation. Samuel Vassall followed his father's profession and became an eminent City merchant and shipbuilder. His trading operations lay in the American plantations, the West Indies, West Africa and in the Levant. As a wholesale clothier,[115] he traded his cloth for the colonial products of these lands: currants and silks from the Levant, and tobacco, hemp and flax from the plantations. Like his father and his father-in-law, Abraham Cartwright, he was interested in the colonization of Virginia and later of Carolina.[116] The Long Parliament subsequently appointed him one of the Commissioners for the Plantations.[117] With his colleague Matthew Cradock, he was one of the original Incorporators of the Massachusetts Bay Company, against whom *quo warranto* proceedings were taken by the crown in 1635.[118]

---

[113] Orders of Court, 1627-1684, Salters' Company (transcripts), p. 94.

[114] *C.S.P.D. 1640-1641*, vol. 474/67. After the outbreak of war until his death in 1650, Venn fought long and bravely as Colonel in the parliamentary army. From 1642 to 1645, he was Governor of Windsor Castle and was alleged to have ordered the plundering of St. George's Chapel. Although an admirer of the preaching of Christopher Love, the Presbyterian minister, he was a political independent and signed the King's death warrant.

[115] *C.S.P.D. 1629-1631*, vol. 175/105.

[116] *C.S.P.D. 1629-1631*, vol. 168/70. *C.S.P. Col.*, vol. v/90, vol. viii/3,

[117] *C.S.P. Col.*, vol. x/97.

[118] Bankes Papers, MS. 8/18.

Eventually Samuel Vassall and his brother owned jointly one-tenth of the whole of Massachusetts.[119]

Vassall was one of the most stalwart of Charles' opponents amongst the London merchants. In 1627, he was imprisoned by the Privy Council for his opposition to the forced loan. In 1628 he was among those Levant merchants who refused to pay the 2s. 2d. imposition on currants and forcibly broke open the warehouses to remove his goods. In 1630, he opposed the unparliamentary levy of tonnage and poundage, and in 1635, he was again imprisoned, for his opposition to the Ship Money levies, this time by the Sheriff of London, at the order of the Privy Council, and the City authorities seized a quantity of his plate.[120] Sir John Northcote summed up tersely Vassall's own account of his damages to the House of Commons on December 2 1640: 'Sixteen times committed £5,000 damages. Loss of his trade, £10,000 more. His credit impaired. Total £20,000.'[121]

Previous to his stand against Charles's impositions on currants, Vassall had been in trouble with the Levant Company for his failure to pay his impositions,[122] but in spite of it, he was elected an Assistant in 1625 and 1628. He was not elected an Assistant again until 1640.[123] It appears that Vassall avoided City offices. He was one of the Wardens of the Drapers' Company from 1636-7,[124] but as far as is known he was not a member of Common Council, and he fined rather than serve the office of Sheriff in 1639. His main concern was with the commercial world. Vassall must have been at this time a successful merchant in spite of Charles' persecution: the Venetian Ambassador mentioned his experiments in the Levant market with high quality fringed cloth which he was selling at a time

[119] Rose-Troup, op. cit., p. 156.

[120] Rep. 55, fol. 32v.

[121] A. H. A. Hamilton, ed. *The Note Book of Sir John Northcote*, 1877, p. 24.

[122] Court Minutes of the Levant Company, vol. 1617-1631. S.P. 105:148, fol. 152v. He was subsequently mentioned as having failed to pay his dues to the Company, ibid. fols. 70, 145, 223.

[123] Ibid. fols. 122, 181; vol. 1631-1640, S.P. 105:149, fol. 377.

[124] In the official returns of M.P.s he is described as a Clothworker. His Livery Company, however, was the Drapers'. He was one of the Livery from 1619 to 1636, and an Assistant from 1636 to 1659. During his lifetime, he employed eighteen apprentices, and nine at one time, between 1631 and 1638. A. H. Johnson, op. cit., iv, p. 419.

when trade was at a low ebb.[125] In 1640, after the calling of
the Long Parliament Vassall became the spokesman of the
City merchants in the House of Commons. He was elected to
the Committee for Trade,[126] and played the leading part in
presenting Levant Company petitions and securing the prohibition of the import of currants from Venetian territories.[127]
Although from 1643, Vassall became a member of the 'peace
party' and later a political presbyterian,[128] in the early years
of the Long Parliament on many issues, he worked with
Alderman Penington.

The fourth City Burgess, Alderman Thomas Soames, belonged, unlike his three colleagues, to one of the wealthiest
merchant families in the City, which had already held high
City office. He was the third son of Alderman Stephen Soames,
said by John Chamberlain, the gossip writer, to have died in
May 1619 worth £6,000 in land and £40,000 in goods,[129]
while his eldest brother, Sir William Soames, further augmented the family fortunes by his marriage into the well-
established aldermanic family of Barnham.[130] In 1640, Alderman Soames had not yet held aldermanic office long enough
to have acquired the greatest honour in City life, but he was
well on the path. He was elected Alderman in 1635, Sheriff
for the year 1635-6, and a colonel of the Trained Bands in
1638.[131] When the crown granted the Lord Mayor and Aldermen the power to elect to the office of President of the Honourable Artillery Company in 1639, they conferred the office on
Alderman Soames.

The Alderman had trading interests in the Levant[132] and

[125] *V.S.P. 1632-1636*, p. 461.

[126] Harl. MSS. 4277, fol. 1.

[127] Add. MSS., 34,485, fols. 81-82v.

[128] Like Penington and Richard Chambers, Vassall appears to have fallen on
bad times under the Protectorate and petitioned Cromwell for the sum of £20,000
which Parliament had awarded him for his sufferings under Charles's personal
government. Throughout the Interregnum, he retained his connexions with the
New England Plantations, for which he was a parliamentary Commissioner, and
he died in Massachusetts in 1667.

[129] *The Letters of John Chamberlain*, ii, no. 328.

[130] *The Visitation of London, 1633-1635*, ii, pp. 250-1.

[131] A. B. Beaven, op. cit., ii, p. 63.

[132] Ledger Book, Levant Company, S.P. 105:158, fols. 53, 110, 151. His trade
to the Levant increased greatly after 1640.

East India Companies, and served as one of the Committees for the East India Company between 1640 and 1643.[133] He was interested in the Russia Company and also traded to the Adriatic. He does not appear among the lists of those who opposed Charles I over impositions or tonnage and poundage, but he refused to pay the forced loan in 1627 and as Sheriff in 1638 he took no action against citizens for failure to pay Ship Money. In the same year, an order was issued to the Attorney-General to exhibit an information against him in the Star Chamber for depopulation on his estates in Nottinghamshire and converting land from tillage.[134] In May 1640, it will be recalled, he was one of four Aldermen who refused to draw up a list of the wealthy inhabitants of his ward likely to lend to the crown, and he added to his offence by stating that his reputation as an honest man, won while a commoner, was as dear to him now that he was an Alderman. His popularity with the citizens on this account caused him to be nominated as an opposition candidate to Sir William Acton at the mayoral election on September 29 1640, and as we have seen, he headed the poll. The Privy Council and the Lord Mayor, however, refused to admit the election, and a compromise candidate was found. Alderman Soames had connexions with other parliamentary puritans in East Anglia and in Parliament. He was acquainted with John Winthrop and was a brother-in-law of Sir Nathaniel Barnardiston. But in spite of his earlier history and connexions, Soames quickly became lukewarm in his adherence to Parliament (in November 1641, he was said to have voted against the Grand Remonstrance) and by 1643 he was reputed to support the 'peace party'. Nevertheless, although he never became associated with Alderman Penington and the radicals in the Long Parliament,[135] in 1640, he was known as an opponent of the court among the citizens.

All four City members had sat in the Short Parliament, but

[133] Court Minutes, E.I.C. 1640-1643, pp. 61, 177, 262.

[134] C.S.P.D. 1639-1640, vol. 435/21.

[135] Soames was secluded at Pride's Purge and he was dismissed from his aldermanry for refusing to take part in proclaiming the Act for the abolition of Kingship, which he said was against his judgment and conscience. In 1660, he was restored to the Rump and to the aldermanic Bench.

its duration was too brief for them to play a conspicuous part.[136] After its dissolution in May, Alderman Soames was committed to King's Bench for his provocative attitude towards the projected forced loan. Alderman Penington did not even attend the meeting of the Aldermen with the Privy Council, and in spite of the punishment meted out to the four Aldermen who had refused, did not send in the required list. In June, on the order of the Privy Council, Samuel Vassall with Richard Chambers was imprisoned far from London because they were contumaciously stirring up popular agitation among the citizens.

THE REPRESENTATION OF THE MUNICIPALITY IN PARLIAMENT

On the meeting of the Long Parliament, therefore, there could have been little doubt about the likely attitude of the four City members towards the issues dividing the King and the Commons. In most previous Parliaments, although not in 1628 and 1629, the Court of Lord Mayor, Aldermen and Common Council had been represented by their Recorder. In 1640, Sir Thomas Gardiner, who had held the office since 1636, was not returned for the City, nor for several other seats to which the Privy Council unsuccessfully tried to get him elected. His defeat was even more portentous, for the King had designed that he should act as Speaker in the forthcoming Parliament.[137] The City of London with its four members was, in view of its predominance in the commercial and financial affairs of the country, greatly under-represented in the House of Commons. The proceedings of the early Stuart Parliaments had served to emphasize the lack of voice in the Commons of the City's government and leading trading groups, particularly in comparison with the vociferous representation of the outports. Many Members of the Long Parliament had

---

[136] They sat on two Committees, the Committee for receiving the Accounts of the Treasurers of the subsidies and fifteenths granted 21 James I, *C.J.* ii, pp. 8, 15, and the Committee concerning needle-makers and steel wire-drawers, ibid. pp. 8, 17. A Committee was also established to investigate Samuel Vassall's grievances against the government, ibid. p. 8.

[137] Clarendon, *History*, i, p. 220. The Court of Aldermen prematurely presented him with £150 'as a loving token from this Court' when it was known that the King intended to make him Speaker'. Rep. 54, fol. 333v.

London connexions, of course, either as shareholders in commercial undertakings or indirectly through relatives who were City traders, while some provincial merchants had at one time served a London apprenticeship and retained some London interests.[138] But these men could not be said to reflect faithfully the views of the City government or of the ruling councils of the trading companies. In November 1640, only eleven men[139] who were primarily City merchants with important trading and livery company connexions, were elected for other seats than the City, and none of these had held high civic office in the municipality. Two of them, Sir John Jacob and Sir Nicholas Crispe, were subsequently 'disabled' as monopolists,[140] while a third, Sir John Harrison, kept his place (after much misgiving on the part of some of the Members) only because his son undertook to raise parliamentary loans in a period when the House of Commons was finding difficulty in raising money. At least five[141] of them were supporters of the parliamentary opposition, and so were the Members returned for Southwark and Westminster.

In Southwark was elected John White,[142] the Winthrop

---

[138] E.g. Sir Thomas Bludder (Reigate), Sir Robert Parkhurst (Guildford, Surrey) and Alexander Bence (Aldeburgh, Suffolk). M. F. Keeler, *The Long Parliament, 1640-1641*, Philadelphia, 1954, pp. 109, 296, 106.

[139] George Abbot (Guildford, Surrey), Edward Ashe (Heytesbury, Wiltshire), Anthony Bedingfield (Dunwich, Suffolk), William Bell (Westminster), Sir Nicholas Crispe (Winchelsea, Sussex), Sir John Harrison senior (Lancaster), Sir John Jacob (Rye, Sussex), Robert Jenner (Widhill, Wiltshire), Sir Arthur Ingram (Kellington, Cornwall), John Rolle (Truro, Cornwall), William Spurstow (Shrewsbury), D. Brunton and D. H. Pennington, in *Members of the Long Parliament*, 1954, do not include Bedingfield, the London Mercer, or Jenner, a leading Goldsmith, among their account of London merchants. They include George Lowe, M.P. for Calne (p. 59), though there is no evidence that he was a London merchant. They may have confused him with his London cousin. Cf. Keeler, pp. 257-8. Brunton and Pennington mention in their section on London merchants a number of monopolists who were debarred from sitting. But these men, William Watkins, Thomas Webb, Fitzwilliam Coningsby, Endymion Porter, Edmund Windham and George Goring, were primarily courtiers and royal officials who, while they helped to procure patents in which they had a financial interest, were not necessarily themselves London manufacturers or traders. Keeler, op. cit., *passim*.

[140] *C.J.* ii, p. 36.

[141] Ashe, Bedingfield, Bell, Rolle and Spurstow.

[142] White acted in close co-operation with Alderman Penington during the early years of the Long Parliament. He presided over two Committees (one to replace 'scandalous' ministers by Puritan preachers, the other the Committee of Plundered Ministers), on both of which Penington was a leading figure.

family lawyer, famous already for his activity as one of the
Feoffees of Impropriations and for his disputes with Laud.
His colleague Edward Bagshaw had also fallen foul of Laud
in 1639 for his discourses at the Middle Temple; he supported
Pym in the early days of the Long Parliament, although he
was a Royalist by 1642. At Westminster was elected John
Glynne, later one of the most active lawyer members of the
House. His ardent prosecution of the policies of the parliamentary leaders and the City parliamentary puritans led to
his election to the Recordership, after Sir Thomas Gardiner
had joined the King.[143] Finally, the Commons chose as
preachers for their fast days and sermons, City clergymen
who had in the main been outspoken in their opposition to
the Laudian Church and in particular to the new Canons and
Oath. The influence of these men in the Commons and in City
parishes, above all of Cornelius Burges, Calybute Downing
and Edmund Calamy, all of whom were intimately connected
with the City parliamentary puritans, was an important con-
tributory factor to the victory of Parliament over the King in
the minds of the citizens.[144]

Without their Recorder in Parliament and in view of the
background and history of the City Burgesses, the Court of
Lord Mayor and Aldermen may well have felt its representation inadequate. On December 1 1640, it elected a Committee
for parliamentary affairs, a procedure at least as old as Elizabethan times, which was to 'meet together . . . and consider
of all matters that may anyway concern the good and honour
of the City and be thought fit and requisite to be propounded
and presented to the Honourable House of Commons in the
behalf of the City'.[145] This Committee consisted of the Recorder and eight Aldermen, of whom three were senior.[146]
Only two of the eight Aldermen had yet made any stand
against the crown, and one of these finally gave his sympathies

[143] Rep. 56, fol. 198v. He was elected in place of Peter Pheasant, who held
office for a few months only.

[144] E. M. Kirkby, 'Sermons preached before the House of Commons . . . 1640-
1642', Am.H.R., 1938-9, vol. xliv, pp. 528 seq. W. Haller, Liberty and Reformation
in the Puritan Revolution, New York, 1955, pp. 16 seq.

[145] Rep. 55, fols. 18-18v.

[146] I.e. they had held the mayoralty. Sir George Whitmore, Sir Christopher
Clitherow and Sir Henry Garway.

to Charles soon after the outbreak of the Civil War.[147] There
were fourteen Common Councilmen elected to the Committee,
five or even six of whom had become Royalist supporters either
in December 1641 or by the time of the passing of the Militia
Ordinance in the following March, and four of whom became
prominent adherents of Parliament.[148] The Committee included some of the City legal officers, but the City Burgesses,
although their counterparts had been elected to a similar body
in 1624 and 1626, were not chosen to sit on the Committee.

It may seem surprising at first sight that the four City members acting without the authorization of the municipality,
which had its own Committee for lobbying the Parliament,
should have exercised so much influence on the proceedings
of the House of Commons. The reason lay partly in the close
political alliance which came to exist between them and Pym
and the parliamentary opposition. But their strength was also
derived from their ability to mobilize the petitions and demonstrations of the citizens, despite the fact that no citizen
of London was supposed to pursue any Bill or suit in the
House without the consent of the Lord Mayor and Aldermen,[149] a regulation that was entirely disregarded in the City
after 1640. But the petitions could not have achieved their
effect unless the House of Commons had been prepared to
receive them favourably, and to permit the citizens the liberty
of making speeches at the Bar of the Commons in support of
their petitions, a procedure which involved a wide extension
of constitutional practice. But that is to anticipate our story.

[147] Alderman Gayre and Alderman Atkins. Gayre later dissociated himself
from the City Militia Committee which had been established with parliamentary
authority.

[148] Roger Drake, Roger Clarke, Sir George Benion, Mr. Keightley and John
Withers were Royalists by the spring of 1642. William Cockayne was known to
have Royalist sympathies in 1643, and George Clarke was the Royalist Sheriff in
1641-2. Captain Venn, Captain Mainwaring, Francis Peck and Nathaniel Wright
became leading City parliamentarians.

[149] Rep. 13 (ii), fol. 323v.

CHAPTER VI

The City Members of Parliament and the Citizens, 1640-2

W E have seen something of the composition and activities of the parliamentary puritans before 1640 and how they were able to exert influence and spread their views before the calling of the Long Parliament. The years of preparation, the long seeding time which had brought this despised and harried opposition party to prominence, if not yet to power, had passed. They had weathered persecution and adversity, growing stronger in their reputation as martyrs in a righteous cause. At last, a Parliament had been summoned again, and the seed sown by the parliamentary puritan party was bearing its first harvest, demonstrated to all who could read the signs, by the return of four leading opponents of royal policy as Members for the City of London. We turn now to an examination of their use of the position they had won in the House of Commons, how they consolidated it, gaining allies and losing them, and how it was buttressed from outside by rapidly developed and sometimes daringly new forms of political agitation and organization.

THE CITY MEMBERS AND THE PROBLEM OF FINANCING THE LONG PARLIAMENT

When the Long Parliament assembled in November 1640, it was faced with the task of maintaining the English army in the north and, in accordance with the terms of the Treaty of Ripon, of assuring to the Scottish army an allowance of £25,000 a month. A loan was essential if Parliament was to prevent a hasty dissolution and avoid the immediate levy of a subsidy which, as Members of Parliament were quick to point out, might, owing to the uncertainty of the return, 'be raised above the intention'.[1] A paradoxical situation faced the House: if they could not raise money for the army they faced dissolution;

---

[1] *D'Ewes*, ed. Notestein, p. 35.

on the other hand, if they raised too much, Charles could presumably dispense with Parliament.

The City's M.P.s, particularly Alderman Penington, straight away canvassed the Court of Aldermen for a loan. The City government, faced by a financial debit in the Chamber and doubtful about the securities, hesitated, offering first a meagre loan of £25,000 and, after much cajoling from Penington, the promise of the same amount again if adequate security could be found.[2] However reluctantly granted, this promise of a loan helped to guarantee the continuance of the Scottish army in the north. Pym and the leaders of the parliamentary opposition were now able to use its presence and the monthly payments which it demanded as a bargaining factor with the crown. As Baillie wrote: 'They confess that army is their own, and a most happy mean for their desires; that the dissolving of it were their ruin; that for the keeping of it on foot and all our bygone losses, what they would not do.'[3] In other words, everything depended on keeping the army in being.

The policy of Pym and his supporters was to procure sufficient money to keep the Scottish army in the north, but not so much that it would be paid off before enough concessions had been wrung from Charles. This policy was made possible because of the slowness with which money came in from the financially embarrassed City Treasury[4] and reluctant City financiers. The policy owed its success, very largely, to the City M.P.s, who, in connivance, no doubt, with Pym and the leaders of the opposition, were quick to establish themselves as financial intermediaries between the House of Commons and the City. The significance of this has not been noticed by historians; yet the influence they gained was far-reaching. Instead of approaching the City government direct, the Commons used the City M.P.s as their emissaries. Moreover, on December 18 1640, Alderman Penington managed to secure the nomination of himself and one of the other City M.P.s, Alderman Thomas Soames, as Treasurers of the first City loan

[2] Penington suggested to the House that the loan should be guaranteed by individual M.P.s, with, if possible, two guarantors to each bond, an arrangement which appears to have satisfied the underwriters in the City. Ibid. pp. 51, 542.

[3] Baillie, op. cit., i, pp. 280-1.

[4] See Appendix III for the finances of the City Chamber.

and the four subsidies on which it was secured,[5] giving themselves the opportunity of withholding or hastening it, according to political expediency. When the full extent of the Scottish
claims were known in January 1641, a further loan of £60,000
was asked from the City. Alderman Penington suggested that
the question of raising this loan be referred to Common Hall,[6]
an assembly in which he had a considerable following, and to
which he owed his election to Parliament. Thus, in addition
to his powers as Treasurer of the loan, he was now provided
with a platform in the City from which to influence the liverymen to lend or withhold their money, as parliamentary tactics
dictated. Clarendon, whose account of the political manœuvres
of the opposition and Root and Branch men in these years is
far more valuable and accurate than has been allowed (it can
be corroborated by evidence in D'Ewes' diary and elsewhere),
neatly summed up the strategy of the opposition: 'The task
of borrowing money gave them opportunity of pressing their
own designs to facilitate their work; as, if anything they proposed in the House was crossed, presently the City would lend
no more money because of this or that obstruction.'[7] There
is no doubt that Alderman Penington saw the presence of the
Scottish army in the north, as did Pym and the parliamentary
opposition, as the key to their political strategy, and further,
that on this and other issues, he was in close touch with the
Scottish Commissioners in London. Baillie wrote home on
December 28 1640: 'This day Alderman Penington with a
number of his brethren came, with some also of the town
captains, and some from the Inns of Court, to our lodging
for complimenting our Commissioners: he told them roundly

[5] D'Ewes, ed. Notestein, p. 189.

[6] The Diary of Sir Thomas Peyton (Bodleian Library microfilm no. 39), fols.
67-68.

[7] History, i, p. 274. The value of his History for the first two years of the Long
Parliament is much greater than suggested by C. H. Firth in his article, 'Clarendon's History of the Rebellion' in the E.H.R., 1904, pp. 26-54. Although Clarendon
was undoubtedly attempting to prove that it was the parliamentary opposition
which was unconstitutional in the first years of the Long Parliament, and was
therefore obliged to explain 'popular' pressure on the House as though it was
all artificially contrived by Pym and his party, it does not follow that his account
is too biased to be useful. It provides valuable evidence of the early growth of
'parties' in the Long Parliament, substantially corroborated in other sources.
The wrong dating of which Clarendon was sometimes guilty can be corrected
from parliamentary journals and diaries.

that they were aughten us [beholden to us for] the redemption of their liberties, estates, religion and lives.'[8]

Penington was quick to put his power over the purse-strings to the test. Later in January, on the very day that the Commons voted to accept the Scottish demand for some additional financial assistance as reparations, Penington rose to tell the House that the loan of £60,000 had been collected but could not be paid over for a number of reasons, essentially political: 'Goodman the Jesuit was the other day reprieved when he should have been executed and that the late Lord Keeper was countenanced by the Queen of Bohemia at The Hague and was wafted over into the Low Countries in one of the King's ships; that Secretary Windebank was likewise countenanced in France by the Earl of Leicester, the King's Ambassador there; and that a Letter came lately from the Lords of the Upper House to the City for the countenancing of innovations; upon all of which grounds and reasons the said City was now resolved not to lend . . . the sum or any part of it'.[9] The immediate results of Penington's speech were that the Recorder of the City, Sir Thomas Gardiner, was brought in to the House and publicly rebuked for his share in the reprieve of Goodman (Penington thus helping to humiliate one of the City's leading officials), while the House was stimulated into retaliating against the Order of the Lords, by sending Commissions into the country to demolish 'relics of idolatry'.

On February 3rd, all possibility of a breach with Scotland was excluded by a final vote in the House of Commons of £300,000 to the Scots, which gave the Commissioners complete satisfaction. This sum, of which the greater part would have to be raised by City loans, strengthened the political position of the City Members, particularly of Alderman Penington, who had already established himself as intermediary between the Commons and London's money-bags. In the following weeks Alderman Penington used his financial power openly and with great pertinacity to promote political ends. These events are described below in some detail, not only to indicate the extent of his influence, but because they show his policy entering a new phase—a phase in which he became attached

[8] Baillie, op. cit., i, p. 288.   [9] D'Ewes, ed. Notestein, p. 277.

to the radical wing of the opposition. He began openly to promote the policy of the small radical Root and Branch group, with which he had been associated from the beginning by his presentation of the City's ecclesiastical petition in the previous December. On some occasions during February and March 1641, his extreme policy was publicly disowned by Pym and the leaders of the parliamentary opposition: for although Pym also felt more secure in his use of the financial weapon after February 3rd, he was not prepared to drive the House of Commons too far or too fast, nor risk disorders in the north which might result from the complete withholding of supplies from the army.

The first occasion on which Alderman Penington was deserted by his erstwhile allies concerned John Goodman the Jesuit. The radicals were greatly incensed by the King's reprieve of Goodman because they saw it as a preparation to saving the life of a much greater enemy to their cause, that of Strafford.[10] On February 6th, Penington announced to the Commons that the citizens of London 'were not satisfied with his Majesty's last speech without the said John Goodman, the priest, were executed'.[11] But the House was not prepared to follow his lead, and it was declared that the Speaker should write to the City 'to let them know that both the Houses of Parliament were fully satisfied with the same speech'. Even the radical Strode, one of the crown's most irreconcilable opponents, felt that it was not worth prolonging a struggle on this issue, and dissociated himself from the Alderman, comparing him and his supporters to the sons of Zeruiah, who were frequently rebuked by David for being over-zealous.[12]

Penington was not discouraged by this temporary defection of his earlier allies. He and the radicals had pursued the case of Goodman because his reprieve might save Strafford's neck. Now, as a bargaining counter to procure Strafford's execution, they tried to hold up the Bill of Subsidies, desperately needed to pay the Scottish army. So concerned were Pym and the majority of the House to prevent disorders in the army from lack of pay that the Subsidies Bill was pushed through the House despite a vociferous rear-guard action fought by Penington and the radicals. Even with the security of a further

[10] Baillie, op. cit., i, p. 295.   [11] D'Ewes, ed. Notestein, p. 333.   [12] Ibid. p. 334.

Subsidies Act, Penington made certain that the money promised by the citizens would be slow in coming in.

The political manœuvring of Alderman Penington was by this time clearly apparent. Those members of the Lower House who were concerned to see the Scottish army disbanded at the earliest possible date, and who saw that political conditions were being attached by Penington and the parliamentary puritan citizens to the grant of loans, decided to make a personal approach to the merchants of the City. The outcome of this journey to the City's money-bags, which pleased no one, provides an illustration of London's political division and the way in which politicians of both sides sought to exploit it. The House sent a deputation to visit some of the solid, leading citizens. It was headed by Arthur Capel, who later in the year was created a baron by the King and subsequently fought at his side, Sir John Strangeways, soon to compound heavily for his delinquency at Goldsmiths' Hall, and Edward Hyde.[13] On February 27th, Hyde reported that they had conferred 'with the most substantial and best reputed men of the City'[14] who had promised to raise the money but only on certain conditions. Then employing the same tactics as Penington, Hyde took the opportunity to attack the opposition policy of prolonging the Scottish army's occupation of the northern counties: the City, he asserted, was 'very much troubled and melancholy to see two armies kept on foot at so vast a charge within the bounds of the kingdom, when . . . all the danger of a war was removed; and that they who were very able to make good what they promised had frankly undertaken that if a peremptory day was appointed for being rid of those armies, there should not be want of money to discharge them'.[15] D'Ewes reported that Hyde had also told the House 'that he hoped of £50,000 from particular men, but they objected [to] a Scottish paper set out'.[16] This paper was a statement of the Scottish Commissioners assuring their Root and Branch friends of support and affirming that they wanted to abolish episcopacy in England. Originally printed for circulation in the House of Commons, the statement was allowed by a calculated indiscretion to fall into a Stationer's hands and was

[13] *D'Ewes'* ed. Notestein, p. 398.   [14] Clarendon, *History*, i, p. 283.
[15] Ibid. p. 284.   [16] *D'Ewes*, ed. Notestein, p. 417.

promptly published in the City. The opponents of the Scottish army rose up in indignation. Immediately after Hyde's statement, some of his political supporters demanded that the paper be read to the House and officially condemned. Alderman Penington was instantly on his feet to retort to Hyde 'that those that except at the Scottish paper are not a considerable number'.[17] The radicals, Sir Walter Earle and William Strode, gave the Alderman the strongest support, asserting that 'Mr. Hyde had done ill in reporting it seeing that £50,000 was lent by those very men notwithstanding that paper'.[18] The demand that the paper should be read was finally rejected, having caused 'one of the greatest distempers in the House' that D'Ewes had ever seen.[19]

On March 1st, in a very full House,[20] Alderman Penington determined to meet this challenge to his position as intermediary between Parliament and the City. He announced that £100,000 would be lent by the City on the security of the two new subsidies: but, he went on, 'for the £50,000 which was offered by some with a Remonstrance annexed to it', he thought it would prove but *colloquintida*—a 'polluted source', so other members interpreted him.[21] Penington then suggested that a delegation should be sent from the Commons to the City, men 'such . . . as the City had a good opinion of' and whom he magnanimously offered to name, if the House would give him leave. He named six prominent leaders of the opposition: John Pym, John Hampden, Denzil Holles, Nathaniel Fiennes, Sir Walter Earle and Sir Henry Vane, the last two being among his radical associates. After a great debate in which Hyde and others strongly opposed this proposition and 'made merry with the Alderman's *colloquintida*'[22] (Hyde, the professional lawyer, was highly amused by this heavy-footed classical excursion on the part of a City merchant and business

---

[17] Notebook of Framlingham Gawdy, Add. MSS. 14,827, fol. 8v.

[18] *D'Ewes*, ed. Notestein, p. 418.

[19] Harl. MSS. 164, fol. 271.

[20] In the debate on whether Dr. Chaffin should be sent to the Tower for his speech against Parliament, the House divided, the noes being 190 and the yeas 189. Penington's speech followed on immediately after the discussion on Dr. Chaffin. *D'Ewes*, ed. Notestein, p. 420.

[21] Ibid. pp. 420-1.

[22] Clarendon, *History*, i, p. 285.

man), Penington's suggestion was finally adopted by the Commons.

On March 3rd, however, it appeared that in order to discredit Hyde's financial propositions, Penington had overstated his case. He was now forced to announce to the House 'that he was mistaken the other day when he desired six members by him then nominated should be sent to the Lord Mayor and Aldermen to borrow £100,000 of them, as if he had been certain that the money would be lent: he only advised that the said means might be assayed; but he confessed that they had now found a repulse'. Therefore, he told the House, 'himself and some five or six others had met together and had agreed to lend each of them two thousand pounds apiece'.[23] The difference between his earlier promise of £100,000 and this meagre offer of £10,000 or £12,000 was not lost on his opponents. According to D'Ewes, 'the Lord Digby and some others laid great blame on the said Alderman for naming members of the House himself, and undertaking so much by himself, which he could not effect; and others excused him, and so much heat followed upon it, as had scarce happened before in the House'. Sir Thomas Jermyn proposed that in future Alderman Soames should negotiate loans in the City rather than Penington, while Edmund Waller struck a shrewd blow at the Alderman, saying, 'Penington made the City believe he was a great man here, but he was sure he shows himself no great man in the City.'[24]

On March 3rd and 4th, another attempt was made to circumvent Penington's position as financial intermediary between Parliament and the City. Some members of the Commons, together with a group of City merchants, offered either to be bound for, or provide in ready cash, a total sum of £60,000. Thereupon, on March 5th, Penington told the House that 'the £60,000 at first promised in the City was now gotten ready; and that for the £12,000 he offered yesterday he assured himself it would now be made £20,000'.[25] On the following day, he was asked to pay over the £20,000 to the Earl of Warwick, who was one of the Commissioners appointed by Parliament

23 *D'Ewes*, ed. Notestein, p. 433.
24 Ibid., quoting the diary of Sir John Moore, p. 433.
25 Ibid. p. 444.

to receive the money for the Scottish army. But on March 20th, the Earl reported to the House on the money he had received, and it appeared that Penington had raised only £8,000.[26] On March 6th, Arthur Capel in another attempt to expose the Alderman, proposed that twenty-five members of the House should join with the Lord Mayor and Aldermen to borrow £100,000 upon the security of the next two subsidies.[27] But on March 9th, Capel had to announce to the House that the Lord Mayor and Aldermen had refused his offer.[28]

Other attempts were made by delegations from Parliament to raise money from the City, and although the Lord Mayor and Recorder were willing enough, the ordinary merchant was very reluctant to lend. The campaign led by Alderman Penington and his supporters to ensure that no money should be forthcoming until Strafford had paid with his head, culminated in a petition to Parliament presented by his colleague, Captain Venn, on April 24th and signed, it was said, by 20,000 citizens. But agitation on this scale made it even more politically hazardous to lend. Suspicion and instability were exacerbated by the rumours that the leaders of the opposition were considering whether to accept office under Charles as the price of saving Strafford's life. The Earl of Bedford, the future Lord Treasurer in these projected schemes, was known to be turning a favourable eye on the plans of the Customs Farmer, Sir John Harrison, which aimed at making the King financially independent.[29] There seemed to be substance in these fears when the proposals of the Farmers to lend £300,000 on the security of the customs, were raised in the Commons. The City M.P.s, quick as ever to turn all political contingencies to their own advantage and exploiting the argument that no adequate security could be given by Parliament to lenders until it was secure against dissolution, suggested and drew up the Bill for the continuance of Parliament, a measure which, as Clarendon saw it, was to 'remove the landmarks and destroy the foundation

---

[26] Harl. MSS. 1601, fol. 49v.

[27] Add. MSS. 14,827, fol. 13v-14.

[28] *D'Ewes*, ed. Notestein, p. 461.

[29] Stowe MSS. 326, fol. 73. Sir John Harrison's proposition dated May 7 1641 is contained in full in the MSS. preserved in the Victoria Tower of the House of Lords, vol. April 26-May 11, 1641.

of the kingdom'.[30] Then having, according to Clarendon, passed the measure with unprecedented speed and almost universal support, the House proceeded to turn down the Customs Farmers' proposals. There was to be no financial grant without the removal of 'that great stumbling block' Strafford.

In the calmer summer days that followed Strafford's execution, this political strategy, as well as the earlier exposure of Penington's tactics by Hyde, Capel and Digby, succeeded in shaking the confidence of the moderates in the House in the Alderman's ability to act as an intermediary in negotiating City loans. Penington was not prominent as a financial go-between or Treasurer after spring 1641; when his ability to act as intermediary was challenged early in March 1641, he had been unable to raise on his own account more than £8,000, and it is unlikely that he commanded sufficient financial resources to act as Treasurer of any of the subsequent loans. In any case, the financial crisis in the City Chamber and the inability or unwillingness of the wealthiest men to lend meant that Parliament had increasingly to seek new methods and new financial circles in the City from whom to raise money.

But there was another occasion on which, at a time of Parliament's urgent need of a loan, the City M.P.s tried to use their position as intermediaries to attach political strings to the City loan. This was at the outbreak of the Irish rebellion in November 1641, when Parliament needed money to take command of the war. On this occasion, the Recorder was called to the House to express the City's view on the loan (less weight now being attached to the views of the City M.P.s since the episode in March). He told them that the failure to repay earlier loans and the question of Protections were the main obstacles in the minds of lenders.[31] Quite another view was presented by two separate reports to the House: one by the City M.P., Samuel Vassall; the other, brought back by the Puritan, Sir Thomas Barrington, and a Committee of the House from a meeting in Common Hall summoned to discuss the loan. Barrington's statement, unlike the Recorder's, was essentially radical and political: 'many good laws and many good notions had passed from this House to the Lords' House which all either were rejected or stopped

[30] Clarendon, *History*, i, p. 343.   [31] *C.J.* ii, p. 304. Harl. MSS. 6424, fol. 99.

there by the malignity of the Bishops; and therefore they desired that some speedy course might be taken for the taking
their votes away in the Lords' House'.[32] S. R. Gardiner wrote
that this declaration made public the City's support for Parliament and acted as 'a turning point in the struggle'.[33] This
was hardly the case. The declaration of Common Hall was
not the official voice of the municipality. As we have seen
earlier, the decisive point came with the advent to power in
the City government of the parliamentary puritans early in
January 1642. From that time, the City M.P.s had no need to
use financial supply to enforce their policies. Direct approach
was made by the House to the Court of Common Council
and, for the first time, radical political demands in tune with
Pym's policies accompanied their replies. When Common
Council was approached for a loan of £100,000 on January 22
1642, it replied that Parliament should hasten to take over the
power of the Militia.[34]

But even with a sympathetic City government, the traditional methods of raising money in the City would no longer
suffice. The Chamber of London had long been running into
debt, its annual expenditure considerably exceeding its income.[35] Nor could a great deal be expected from the leading
Livery Companies. They were unaffected by the political
changes in City government in 1642, and many of them were
still dominated by Wardens, and probably also Assistants, of
Royalist sympathies.[36] When money was urgently needed to

[32] *D'Ewes*, ed. Coates, p. 133.

[33] *History of England*, x, p. 71.

[34] Harl. MSS. 162, fol. 384v.

[35] See Appendix III. In spite of its growing indebtedness, considerable sums
were raised for Parliament on the bond of the City Chamber between 1641 and
1647, though the increasing pressure needed to persuade citizens to lend and the
mounting deficits on loan money greatly impaired the efficiency of this system.
The crisis in the Chamber and political hostility to the Republic temporarily
put an end to this method of raising loans in 1649.

[36] The Master Wardens of the Mercers' in 1641 and 1642 were two prominent
Royalists, Robert Gardiner, who signed Benion's Militia petition, and Alderman
John Cordell. The Master of the Skinners' in 1640 was William Cockayne, a
prominent East India Company Director and Royalist, and in 1641, Thomas
Keightley, another signatory of Benion's petition. From 1639 to 1643, the Cloth-
workers' Company elected Wardens who were probably Royalist by 1642, Roger
Drake, Thomas Burnell and Thomas Austen; one was Captain Marmaduke
Rawden, who fought in the King's army. Clement Mosse, Warden of the Mer-
chant Taylors' in 1641, was probably the controller of the City Chamber who

put down the Irish rebellion in March 1642, another method was devised for raising the money. A group of merchants who had not been leading figures in City government in the previous decade offered to raise £1,000,000 for the war, to be secured by the allocation to the Committee of confiscated lands. The promoters of this scheme included not only merchants who had been prominent in Puritan colonial enterprises, but also their aristocratic allies, Lords Saye and Sele, Brooke and the Earl of Warwick; the expedition which they financed to subdue Ireland in June 1642 was put under the command of Lord Brooke. Three of the four Treasurers[37] of the Committee were leading City parliamentary puritans, and they were soon organizing the entire financing of the Irish war. Meanwhile, Parliament made one more attempt to raise a loan from the liveries for the Irish campaign in June 1642.[38] Alderman Penington exhorted them to raise a loan of £100,000 at a specially summoned meeting of Common Hall. More than half the principal Companies objected to the calling of Common Hall for this purpose on the grounds that they were outnumbered there by the members of the lesser Companies,[39] while the Goldsmiths' agreed to raise their portion only when assurances had been given that the money was not to be used against the King.[40] The Merchant Taylors' replied that they ought first to be repaid for their share of an earlier loan granted on the Peers' security in October 1640.[41] Only the Grocers'[42] appeared to defend Gurney at his trial. The Masters of the Ironmongers' for 1642 and 1643 were Sir Hugh Windham and Sir Job Harby, both prominent Royalists. Sir Nicholas Crispe, Customs Farmer under Charles I at whose side he fought, was Master of the Salters' in 1640. Too little is known about the Assistants in these companies for a comprehensive treatment of the political attitudes of leading liverymen, or indeed of some Prime Wardens and Masters in these years.

[37] Aldermen Andrewes, Towse and Warner. See Appendix II, The New Men, pp. 309 seq.

[38] A loan of £50,000 was raised from the Livery Companies to supply the army in September 1643, but the difficulties of collecting it and its unpopularity were such that no further attempts were made during the Interregnum to raise money from the liveries.

[39] A. H. Johnson, op. cit., iii, pp. 154-5. Minutes, Court of Assistants, Merchant Taylors', vol. ix, fol. 149. J. Nicholl, Some Account of the Worshipful Company of Ironmongers, 1866, p. 257. Orders of Court, Salters', 1627-1684, Transcripts, p. 238. Court Book, Skinners', 1617-51, fol. 197. Court Book, Vintners', 1638-58, fol. 84. W. Prideaux, Memorials of the Goldsmiths' Company, 1896, i, p. 205.

[40] Prideaux, op. cit., i, pp. 204-5.

[41] C. M. Close, London during the Great Rebellion . . . , 1892, p. 21.

[42] Calendar, Court Minutes, Grocers' Company, op. cit., iv, pp. 71-72.

and to a less extent the Fishmongers'[43] showed any enthusiasm, and both these Companies were particularly subject to
pressure from highly placed parliamentary puritans among
their leading Assistants. Even Alderman Penington's persuasive
powers had failed to inspire the enthusiasm of the City's leading liverymen. There was still a large deficit six months later
when the Companies were admonished at Haberdashers' Hall
for their failure to pay the full contribution.[44]

In 1642 and 1643, it became clear that the exigencies of
war demanded new methods of raising money and, in particular, efficient and realistic forms of regular taxation. It was
typical of the part played by Alderman Penington in these
two years that he and a group of his supporters in the City
should be responsible for suggesting in a petition of June 7
1642 a measure of great political and financial importance,
a weekly voluntary collection in London.[45] When the con-
stitutionalists in the House rose to attack so unprecedented a
suggestion, Alderman Penington with sudden loss of temper,
'very rashly and against the order of the House stood up and
wished that the gentleman who last spoke [Mr. Pleydell] had
been gone out of the House before he had spoken'. This caused
a heated debate on whether the Alderman should be called
in question for infringing the privileges of Parliament by his
attempt to deny the liberty of a Member to speak his conscience
freely; but his friends came to his rescue and his misdemeanour
was overlooked.[46] His proposals, modified by a Commons'
Committee, were embodied on June 9th in an Ordinance calling on everyone to make voluntary contributions of money,
plate or horse for the country's service. The four City Members all responded enthusiastically to the proposals: Alderman
Penington promised to bring in £200 in cash; Captain Venn,
£100 in money and 'a horse ready for himself to serve always
upon'; and Alderman Soames, to bring in two horses completely furnished.[47] The Treasurers of the collection were not

---

[43] Transcripts of the Fishmongers' Records, iii, part 4, p. 1018.
[44] *C.C. for A.M.*, i, p. 114. *C.J.* ii, pp. 870, 877.
[45] *C.J.* ii, p. 610.
[46] Harl. MSS. 162, fol. 157.
[47] From a MSS. list entitled 'The names of the members of the House of
Commons who engaged to advance horses, money and plate in defence of the
Parliament'. Tanner MSS. vol. lxvi, fol. 51.

the City's Chamberlain or the senior Aldermen, but the four
men who became Parliament's leading financiers and financial
administrators between 1643 and 1645: Aldermen Sir John
Wollaston, John Warner, John Towse and Thomas Andrewes.
Their headquarters was in Haberdashers' Hall, one of the few
Livery Companies to show consistent Puritan sympathies,[48] and
a place soon to be execrated by City Royalists for its alleged
extortions and oppressions. This voluntary collection proved
to have a significance beyond that of the money immediately
raised. Nominally a loan, it was expected that all who could
would contribute, and it prepared public opinion for the next
step, the resort to regular taxation in the form of the weekly
assessment, which Pym in close collaboration with Penington,
was able to introduce in November 1642. Moreover, it is not
difficult to imagine how this voluntary levy for a popular purpose helped Alderman Penington and his allies to promote
even further agitation and organization among the middle and
lower ranks of the London citizens.

THE CITY MEMBERS, CHURCH REFORM, AND THE CITIZENS' PETITIONS

The collection of money was not the only activity nor the
only subject which filled the streets and churches with argument, tumult and exhortation during these critical years. The
City M.P.s, particularly Alderman Penington, were able to
help forward the parliamentary puritan programme in the
Commons through their support of radical measures, especially in connexion with ecclesiastical reform. Other radical
weapons were to hand: they backed Pym's policy in the Commons and helped to develop and give coherence to their support in the City through the organization of circulating
petitions and popular demonstrations.

In the early days of the Long Parliament, all four City
M.P.s were active in presenting lengthy petitions of grievances[49] from those who had suffered under Charles's government. But the close ties which existed between the City Burgesses
and the parliamentary puritan movement in the City were

---

[48] D. A. Williams, 'Some Aspects of the Puritan movement in London', Ph.D.
thesis, Washington University, U.S.A., 1951, chapter viii, *passim*.

[49] *D'Ewes*, ed. Notestein, pp. 91-92, 109, 299.

more evident when Alderman Penington on November 9 1640 presented to the House the citizens' petition, which he and his colleagues had received from Common Hall on the day of their election. It cannot have been accidental that Penington's presentation of this petition, to which he had appended additional protests against the fortification of the Tower, coincided with the excited debate of November 11th, a result of rumours that Charles and Strafford were planning to resort to military action. When Sir Thomas Roe, a member of the Privy Council, protested that the manœuvres at the Tower were only to display the soldiers' training, Alderman Penington jumped up and asked, 'Why the baskets and grenadoes were still up seeing it was only a Triumph?'[50] The debate culminated in Pym's fateful suggestion, accepted by the House, that a committee should be set up to prepare a charge against Strafford. Evidence of Penington's ability to mobilize the citizens was immediately provided, for on the following day, he offered on his account (and not on the part of the City government) to raise a citizen army to guard Parliament.[51] His offer was rejected. But on November 23rd, after the attempt to assassinate Sir Thomas Heywood, a Westminster Justice of the Peace, while he was compiling a list of recusants, the Alderman repeated his offer, informing the House, 'that there were about one hundred citizens about the door with swords to secure us, and to distinguish themselves had blue ribbons in their hats'.[52] The House again refused him, but the incident revealed the strength of Penington's following among the citizens and foreshadowed the degree of influence that he was to attain in the City in the critical days of 1641 and 1642. This organized strength of the Puritan movement was overwhelmingly revealed a few days later when William Prynne and Henry Burton made their triumphal entry into London. Their procession was timed to gather at Charing Cross at two o'clock on the afternoon of November 28th. Burton and Prynne led the procession carrying sprigs of rosemary in their hands, and they were followed, it was estimated, by more than ten thousand people on horseback or on foot, with rosemary (for remembrance) or bay (for

---

[50] Ibid. p. 24.   [51] Ibid. p. 31.
[52] Ibid. Appendix B, p. 541, transcribing Rawlinson MSS. C. 956, a diary which has now been identified as in the hand of Sir John Holland.

victory) in their hands and their hats.[53] It made a tremendous impression and again showed the widespread support that Penington would later have at his command.

Besides the financing of the armies, another great issue exercised the opposition. The part played by the City Members in the struggle for ecclesiastical reform was of crucial importance in the development of opposition to the crown and the growth of radicalism in the Long Parliament. Although religious disputes were far from being the sole cause of conflict in the Lower House in the first session, the ecclesiastical debates divided episcopalians from reformers, and helped to widen the gulf between what were shortly to become two contending parties. The religious issue also divided the moderate Puritan reformers from the supporters of Root and Branch, the radicals, and presaged some of the future divisions which were to split the Long Parliament. `

Alderman Penington, as one would expect from his earlier history, was particularly prominent on committees concerned with ecclesiastical reform, and in presenting petitions concerned with reform of the Church. By December 1640, he was already connected in the public eye with radical ecclesiastical measures; indeed, with the entire abolition of episcopacy. On December 11 1640, he presented the Root and Branch petition to the House. If Baillie is correct, his timing on this occasion was considered premature by the leaders of the opposition in the Commons. He wrote on December 2nd, 'the petition against episcopacy subscribed with some thousands of hands . . . had been given in, and pressed hard before now, had not friends in both the Houses . . . advised to spare the pressing of that conclusion till first they had put the whole Bishops and their Convocation in a *praemunire*, for their illegal canons which now they are about; also till they had brought down some of the prime Bishops . . . which they had not will to assay till they had closed the process of the Lieutenant'.[54] That it represented a more militant Puritan standpoint in the City is evident when this measure is contrasted with the mild petition of Churchwardens and Sidesmen of London on November 16th, which complained only of the Articles of Visitation and the oath of Presentment exacted from Churchwardens.

[53] Clarendon, *History*, i, p. 265.   [54] Baillie, op. cit., i, p. 275.

As Baillie had hinted, the majority of the Lower House was anxious to avoid a full debate on the petition, so they voted to send it to committee. But the more radical members of the House had done their work. The Sub-Committee on religion was stimulated into presenting its report to the House, and on December 19th it was transformed into a Select Committee to inquire into the causes of the decay of preaching and the increase of Popery and 'scandalous' ministers.[55] The lack of an adequate preaching ministry had been the chief concern of the Puritan movement since the days of Elizabeth, and the particular interest of the Feoffees of Impropriations. It is interesting that Alderman Penington headed the list of the Committee members and John White, himself one of the Feoffees and now a Member for Southwark, was made Chairman. The Root and Branch petition was followed by similar petitions from other counties, and stimulated the more moderate Puritan clergy to present the Ministers' petition of January 25 1641 which, because of its greater moderation and acceptability, was to form, during the spring, the basis for further debates on ecclesiastical reform. But the presentation of this more moderate petition, coinciding with the Alderman's financial report from the City, gave him an opportunity, as we have seen, to attack the reprieve of John Goodman the Jesuit and denounce the House of Lords' letter to the City 'countenancing innovations'.[56] This offensive spurred the House to issue an Order for the sending of a commission into the country to deface and demolish 'relics of idolatry',[57] and Penington pressed home the attack on February 5 1641, by bringing in a Bill to abolish superstition and idolatry,[58] which was given a second reading and committed on February 13th.[59]

The debate of February 8th and 9th which began on the subject of sending both the London petition and the Ministers' petition to one committee, was transformed into a full debate on Church government. A good part of the debate, however, was taken up with attacking not so much the contents of both petitions, as the startling way in which one of them had been

[55] *C.J.* ii, p. 54. W. A. Shaw, *A History of the English Church, 1640 to 1660.* 1900, ii, p. 177.
[56] *D'Ewes*, ed. Notestein, p. 277. Transcripts of the French Ambassador, P.R.O. 31/3/72.
[57] *C.J.* ii, p. 72.   [58] *D'Ewes*, ed. Notestein, p. 327.   [59] *C.J.* ii, p. 84.

circulated and delivered. For the presentation of the Londoners' Root and Branch petition had revealed a highly organized political machine among the parliamentary puritans of the City, the existence of which had been hinted at earlier in Penington's offer of a citizen army: it was clearly a movement that was operating in close contact with the City Members of Parliament, particularly with Alderman Penington. It was well known that the petition had been circulating in the City for some time before its presentation on December 11 1640 and had gained a vast number of signatures. Contemporary estimates ranged from between 10,000 and 20,000.[60] It was presented to the Commons by a delegation of respectable, well-to-do citizens, 'a world of honest men in their best apparel',[61] impressive enough in dignity and number, even if they were no more than the 300 one witness reported, although another thought that there were four times as many.[62] Lord Digby said of the petition that at first he looked upon it 'as upon a comet or blazing star, raised and kindled out of the stench of the poisonous exhalation of a corrupted Hierarchy'. But then he saw that it had a deeper significance: '. . . me thought the comet had a terrible tail with it, Sir, and pointed to the north; the same fears dwell with me still concerning it. . . . I shall desire those worthy Alderman, and the rest here of the City of London, not to take anything I shall say, in the least way of disparagement or reflection on the City; I look upon this petition not as a petition from the City of London, but from I know not what 15,000 Londoners, all that could be got to subscribe.'[63]

The Alderman did not answer this gibe; but he was quick with a rejoinder to those who were horrified that the petition

[60] Sir Henry Townshend in his diary said there were about 10,000 signatures to it. J. W. Willis Bund, ed., *Worcestershire Historical Society*, 1910, i, p. 10. D'Ewes in a letter to his wife said there were 15,000 signatures: Whitelock in his *Memorial* agreed with this estimate, while Clarendon thought there were 20,000.

[61] Baillie, op. cit., i, p. 280.

[62] Nathaniel Fiennes in the debate on February 9th asserted that it was presented by about 300–400 of the 'better' sort of citizens. *A Speech of the Hon. Nathaniel Fiennes . . . 1641*. The French Ambassador informed his government that it was presented by about 1,200 people led by two Aldermen. Transcript, Reports of the French Ambassador, P.R.O. 31/3/72.

[63] Nalson, op. cit., i, p. 749. Hamon L'Estrange later emphasizes that the petition came from the 'Citizens (not from the City) of London'. *The Reign of King Charles*, 1655, p. 201.

should have been circulated among ordinary folk. They were not 'mean rebellious' people, he said, but 'men of worth and known integrity'. Penington had no intention of apologizing for any of his followers. But he stood at a momentous threshold of history. How was he to reconcile the desires of the men of substance, his own class, with those of the poorest citizens and convey this solidarity to Parliament? His words resolved the dilemma and pointed the way forward to the radical debates of the next twenty years. It was a good petition—quiet disciplined men of worth had promoted it and signed it, but the honest, hard-working poor and their strong arms were not to be despised. 'If there were any mean men's hands to it,' he said, 'yet if they were honest men, there was no reason but these hands should be received. And for the delivery of it, himself was one of them who received it from persons of quality and worth. It was done without tumult, and then upon a word after they that came with the petition, though many in number, departed quietly. There was no course used to rake up hands, for . . . he might boldly say, if that course had been taken, instead of 15,000 they might have had fifteen times 15,000'[64]—perhaps, Penington's estimate of the whole population of London. It was inevitable that Pym's opponents should suggest that corrupt methods must have been used to get so many signatures—'strange uningenuity and mountebankry', Hyde called it—but the only evidence brought into the House, in connexion not with the Root and Branch petition, but with the Ministers' of January 25 1641, proved to be unfounded.[65] The House felt that the petition undoubtedly represented the genuine anti-episcopalian views of a vast number of citizens; it was thus sent back to the Committee

---

[64] *D'Ewes*, ed. Notestein, p. 339.

[65] In the case of the Ministers' petition, Clarendon alleged that different versions were prepared for some of the subscribers, the signatures being then detached and appended to a quite different petition. *History*, op. cit., i, pp. 271-2. But D'Ewes' diary throws a different light on the matter. On February 1st Lord Digby informed the House that some of the ministers who signed the petition now disavowed it. Further inquiry revealed that the two ministers in question were Cornelius Burges and Calybute Downing. Both men told the House that it was only the length of the document to which they objected. The procedure of the ministers who brought in the petition had been to frame the remonstrance from the several county petitions and then to cut off and append signatures to the composite petition. D'Ewes, ed. Notestein, op. cit., pp. 313-15.

of Twenty-four, though additions were now made to the Committee to weight it in favour of the supporters of radical reform in Church government.

In the spring of 1641, the religious debate was a minor issue in comparison with the political strife which revolved around Strafford's trial. The movement in the City which was capable of producing support on such a scale for the Root and Branch petition was soon at work organizing petitions in favour of Strafford's execution. On April 21 1641, a petition calling for the death of 'notorious offenders' and the reform of the Church[66] was brought down to the Commons by a great multitude of citizens, 10,000, it was said,[67] led by three City captains in the Trained Bands, one of whom was the radical John Venn,[68] soon to succeed Matthew Cradock as a Member for the City. This was another monster petition: Sir John Coke the younger described it as having about 8,000 names attached, although previously he had heard rumours that 20,000 or 30,000 names had been subscribed.[69] The King immediately forbade the City authorities to countenance this petition or any other similarly subscribed.[70] This last injunction did the crown a great disservice, for it prohibited even petitions in favour of the King and, in fact, no such petitions were circulated in the City from this time until February 1642.

The parliamentary puritan campaigners now turned from circulating petitions to organizing demonstrations outside Parliament. These were sparked off by the rumour that the King planned to use force rather than assent to the Bill of Attainder. Five thousand demonstrators, respectable merchants and tradesmen (and some of them very wealthy men, worth £30,000 or £40,000 it was said), began to line the approaches to Westminster Hall so that members of both Houses had to pass between two columns of belligerent citizens shouting for Strafford's execution.[71] While Parliament was sitting, the

---

[66] Rushworth, op. cit., v, p. 233. Nalson, op. cit., ii, p. 161. A longer version of this petition in a contemporary hand is to be found in Sloane MSS. 1467.

[67] Harl. MSS. 164, fol. 183.   [68] C.J. ii, p. 125.

[69] H.M.C. Twelfth Report, Cowper MSS., pp. 278, 280.

[70] C.S.P.D. 1640–1641, vol. 479/25. At least one petition in favour of episcopacy had previously been circulating in the City, but according to Baillie, it was given up in despair, there being so little support for it. Baillie, op. cit., i, p. 296.

[71] The Diurnall Occurrences . . . from the third of November 1640 to the third of November 1641. May 3 1641. S.P.Dom. 16/480/11.

crowd spent its time posting up placards in vilification of those 'Straffordians, betrayers of their country' who had voted against the Attainder. The author of this list was said to have been William Wheeler, Puritan member of Parliament for Westbury, a resident of Westminster and later a wealthy housing speculator in Spitalfields.[72] During the second and third readings of the Bill and before the royal assent, the crowds outside Palace Yard and Whitehall changed their composition and character, becoming more menacing and of a rougher class. Some bore swords or clubs and many were now described as ordinary 'mechanic folk' from Southwark.[73] The Lord Mayor issued precepts forbidding anyone to go down to Westminster in a 'tumultuous manner',[74] but this had no effect; only the leaders of the parliamentary puritans could control the citizens. On May 10th, Charles was finally persuaded to pass the Bill of Attainder.

Even the traditionally prudent City tradesmen familiar to us from the gibes of anti-Puritan Jacobean playwrights had been ready to buckle on their swords against the 'traitor' and his friends. Violence, happily tasted, became something of a habit with the shopkeeper and his apprentice. But of great importance is the evidence that the readiness of the City to act was directed and organized; moreover, it extended to the ranks of ordinary shopmen. Before the news of Charles' surrender over Strafford reached the City, Nehemiah Wallington, a shopkeeper of St. Leonard's Eastcheap, described the state of affairs and the call to arms. 'Most of the City', he wrote, 'made account to go again and some did, and would have all our shops shut up, and so, all to go up to Westminster with weapons, for to have justice executed upon this traitor, the Earl of Strafford, but there were some did persuade me to the contrary, so that most of us did tarry at home and did not go.'[75] Contact between Pym's party in the Commons and the parliamentary puritan party in the City was obviously direct and well organized.

[72] J. L. Sanford, *Studies and illustrations of the great rebellion*, 1858, p. 346. F. H. W. Sheppard, ed., *Survey of London*, xxvii, 1957, p. 97. E. G. Wheler, *Autobiography of Sir George Wheeler*, 1911, Birmingham, pp. 37-46.
[73] Tanner MSS. lxvi, fol. 83.
[74] J.Co.Co. 39, fol. 195v.
[75] Nehemiah Wallington, op. cit., i, pp. 244-5.

The City M.P.s were also playing a leading part in the Opposition campaign in the Commons. In the first week of May, the fear of a *coup d'état* had been greatly heightened by the news brought by Alderman Penington and Matthew Cradock, that the Tower was being fortified and Sir John Suckling was bringing armed men into the City.[76] On May 4th, the day after Pym made his controversial proposal for a 'Protestation',[77] the two City M.P.s, Matthew Cradock and Samuel Vassall, brought in a petition delivered by 'divers ministers and captains' to the effect 'that they had with great joy and gladness seen and approved our Protestation to the maintenance of the true religion and approved it'. They petitioned that they should be allowed to take the Protestation in the City. This request provided the parliamentary leaders with the opportunity to prepare a Bill for the Protestation to be taken throughout the country.[78] There is, of course, no note of this petition or any of the earlier ones in the municipal records, and it obviously had not gained the assent of the City government. Although the Court of Aldermen took the Protestation on May 11th, they were unwilling to give effect to the Order appended to the Commons' Protestation that it should be taken by all the citizens in their parish churches.[79] It was not until fresh authority had been sent down to the municipality, that the Lord Mayor finally on May 31st, issued a precept for a house-to-house visitation to induce the inhabitants to sign.[80] But the parliamentary puritans had not waited for the City government's authorization. According to *Persecutio Undecima*, they had already distributed the Order throughout the City, on the initiative of Edmund Calamy and his 'juncto of ministers': it was thrown into Churchwardens' houses 'by unknown hands'.[81]

[76] Harl. MSS. 164, fol. 197.

[77] According to a pamphlet entitled, *A Narrative of Some passages in, or relating to, the Long Parliament, By a Person of Honour*, 1670, the leaders of Parliament were at first opposed to the idea of a Protestation, but were forced into adopting it by Henry Marten, who 'moved it the next day in Parliament and found the House so disposed, as a vote was presently passed for a protestation'. *Somers Tracts*, 1811, vi, pp. 589 seq. D'Ewes, however, related that the Protestation was brought into the House by Pym, 'who plotted the whole business before'. Harl. MSS. 164, fol. 196.

[78] Harl. MSS. fol. 197v.   [79] J.Co.Co. 40, fol. 2v.

[80] J.Co.Co. 39, fol. 203v.   [81] *Persecutio Undecima*, pp. 57-58.

In June, the ecclesiastical problem rose again, this time more sharply, as a result of the Peers' rejection of the Bill for the exclusion of the Bishops from the House of Lords. This Bill, a piecemeal measure against the Bishops, was at this point a concession to moderate opinion in the Commons, but the action of the Lords gave the extreme reformers an excuse to reintroduce the proposal for the complete extirpation of episcopacy. It is strange to find, in view of Alderman Pening-ton's early part in presenting the Root and Branch petition, that he is not mentioned in D'Ewes or elsewhere as playing a part in drawing up the Root and Branch Bill or in speaking to it. We know from D'Ewes' diary that on June 10 1641, a meeting was held at the Earl of Warwick's house in Essex, attended by Pym, Hampden and Stephen Marshall, at which it was decided, contrary to earlier plans, to introduce the Bill into the Commons on the next day instead of the following week.[82] There is no evidence to connect Penington with this move. Yet we know that the main reason for introducing the Bill into the Commons in June, was the refusal of the Peers to pass the Bishops' Exclusion Bill, which had particularly dis-mayed the City. Slingsby wrote to Sir John Penington, '. . . the next day, the Lords did throw the . . . Bill quite out, and so left the Bishops in the state they were before. This bred much murmuring in the City. The discourse of all men is they must now strike at Root and Branch.'[83] It is probable that Pym and the leaders thought it wiser not to embarrass themselves with the support of the citizens on this occasion, for already Alderman Penington and Captain Venn were becoming the nucleus of a radical group which was capable of being a liability to the leaders of the House. The opposition's choice of Sir Edward Dering to introduce the Root and Branch Bill on May 27th[84] was evidence of its desire to enlist moderate support as far as possible and to avoid alienating the moderates by employing the services of the 'fiery spirits'.

Alderman Penington was soon active over another vexed ecclesiastical question. It will be recalled that in the previous

[82] J. L. Sanford, op. cit., p. 365. The reason that Pym chose June 11th for the debate was in order to exploit the disclosures of the Army plot. Notes of Parlia-ment, June 2 to June 15 1641, Sloane MSS. 1467, fols. 98-101v.

[83] C.S.P.D. 1641-1643, vol. 481/22.

[84] Clarendon, History, i, p. 314.

February, he had brought in a Bill for abolishing idolatry and superstition which was read a second time and committed a week later. On August 8th, he made his report from the Committee, and moved 'that this being the Lord's day he conceived it were fit to make some declaration that might tend to the glory of God and now that many of the weak brethren suffered very much by the innovations now crèpt into the Churches and therefore desired that an order might be made for pulling down the rails and removing of the communion tables'.[85] The House accepted his report and declared that the Churchwardens of every parish should have power within their own churches to take down the rails from the communion tables, but added a conservative rider that none should oppose the government of the Church established by law.[86] A more extreme mood prevailed in September. The House of Commons on September 8th issued an Order on the recommendation of the Committee of Preaching Ministers, of which Alderman Penington was a member, making it lawful for parishes to appoint a weekly lecturer.[87] By this means, Penington and his Puritan friends hoped to establish a Puritan ministry throughout the country. If it was accepted, the victory of Puritanism would be achieved painlessly, and even without further parliamentary action. Although these Orders were rejected by the House of Lords,[88] the House of Commons Committee for the Recess, on which all four City Members sat, took advantage of the temporary authority with which they were vested to disperse them throughout the counties. Their victory was shortlived. The attempt to enforce them was almost immediately accompanied by open disorder and violence in parishes all over the country. When Parliament met again in October, the parliamentary leaders, conscious of the dubious legality of the Orders, deliberately shelved them; after testing the feeling of the House in the debate on October 21st characteristically introduced by Captain Venn, who proposed a motion against a Churchwarden of St. Giles', Cripplegate, for attacking them, they quashed further discussion on a measure that was alienating moderate opinion and dividing the House on a minor issue.[89] Alderman

[85] Harl. MSS. 164, fol. 7v.   [86] C.J. ii, p. 246.

[87] Ibid. pp. 281-3.   [88] L.J. iv, pp. 391-2.

[89] D'Ewes, ed. Coates, pp. 19-20. Only Henry Marten and D'Ewes are mentioned as speaking in its favour.

Penington, on this occasion, was not prepared to put parliamentary tactics before what he had long believed to be one of the essential aims of the Puritan movement. On November 4th, he made a last attempt to reopen the debate, but he won no support for his motion and the matter was dropped.[90]

By the end of November 1641, events both in Parliament and in the City were reaching crisis. With the emergency created by the Irish war, Pym needed to make yet greater inroads into the King's constitutional powers, and to do this he needed once again the help of his supporters in the City. Tension was increased when Charles, remembering the earlier riots in Palace Yard, replaced the London Trained Bands who had been guarding Parliament for the last months, by a Company from Westminster under the command of the Earl of Dorset. When the citizens thronged around Parliament at the end of November with their cries of 'No Bishops' in support of the proposal that the Lords Spiritual should be removed from the Upper House, the Earl of Dorset turned his guns on them and a noisy, rough affray ensued. Captain Venn's wife, it was said, sat weeping and wringing her hands in a neighbour's shop when rumours reached the City, illfounded as it proved, that some of her friends including her husband had been slain.[91] When their supporters in the House protested, Sir John Strangeways and Edward Kirton, hurled back the gauntlet by accusing Captain Venn of having encouraged his followers in the City to put pressure on the Commons, particularly during the debate on the Grand Remonstrance. On this occasion, they alleged, a message went out to a citizen in Wood street to desire him to come away speedily armed to the House of Commons for swords were there drawn and the well-affected party was likely to be overborn by the others'.[92] Edward Kirton, who had recently joined the crown's sympathizers, having acquired a post in the royal household, told the House that as a result of Venn's message, 300 armed citizens had gone up to Westminster, 'and more still coming until the House did rise'.[93] Venn offered to clear himself of the charge, but Pym refused to allow the matter to be discussed further and all inquiries were shelved.[94]

[90] Ibid. p. 79.   [91] Clarendon MSS., xx, 1542.   [92] D'Ewes, ed. Coates, pp. 215-16.
[93] Clarendon MSS., xx, 1542.   [94] D'Ewes, ed. Coates, p. 216, n. 11.

The political crisis of the following two months was accompanied by a great organized agitation on the part of the City parliamentary puritans. In the early days of December 1641, it was widely known that another petition was circulating in the City. On December 11th, Alderman Penington announced that there were 'divers able and grave citizens of London attending without to present this House with the formidable petition we had been told of that should be brought to us by 10,000 persons: but he said that a small number were come with it, and that in peaceable and humble manner'.[95] The moderates in the House might well be antagonized if popular pressure became too blatant. According to D'Ewes, the leaders had at first appointed Monday, December 13th, as the day to deliver the petition, 'but at twelve of the clock yesternight they agreed that four only out of every ward should come down with the said petition this afternoon and kept it so secret as few had notice of it and so they avoided the coming down of multitudes'.[96] The petition, clearly organized as part of the parliamentary puritan campaign, nevertheless enjoyed widespread and spontaneous support from the citizens. A printed copy of the petition stated that it was 'subscribed with the names of above 20,000, by Aldermen, Aldermen's Deputies, Merchants, Common Councilmen and many others of great rank and fashion to the number of four hundred who were selected to deliver the petition, all riding out of the City of London in fifty coaches, or thereabouts, to the Parliament House'. The Commons, hearing of their approach, admitted 100 of the petitioners.[97] Although D'Ewes said the petition was presented to the House in the name of 'the Aldermen, Common Councilmen and Freemen of London' it was not subscribed by the City government, and the official title described it as a petition from 'the Common Councilmen, Subsidymen, and other inhabitants of London', with no mention at all of support from Aldermen. The Lord Mayor and Recorder did all in their power to obstruct it.[98] The contents were a complete expression of Pym's policy, that the Bishops' votes

[95] *D'Ewes*, ed. Coates, p. 270.   [96] Ibid. p. 271.

[97] *The Citizen of London's Humble Petition to the Right Honourable the Knights, Citizens and Burgesses* . . . 1641 (Guildhall A.5.5).

[98] *D'Ewes*, ed. Coates, op. cit., p. 319, n. 6.

in the Lords should be abolished and that Parliament should take command of the Militia—and including as a rebuff to the City magnates, who had so lavishly banqueted the King on his return from Scotland, 'that whereas it had been divulged upon the King's late entertainment in the City that the City had deserted the Parliament, they abhorred the same and should always be ready to spend their estates and lives for our safety'.[99] It was presented to the House by John Fowke, an opponent of the City magistrates and the crown in the struggles against the unparliamentary levy of tonnage and poundage and Ship Money, and soon to become a member of the Militia Committee and a leading ally in the City of Alderman Penington.

This petition was quickly followed by two others. When the House of Lords declared, on December 17th, that no religion other than the established one was to be tolerated, it called forth three days later, a petition from certain City ministers, presented by Captain Venn, asking that they might not be forced to use prayers which their consciences could not accept, and calling for a national synod.[100] On December 23rd, Alderman Penington presented a petition from some Common Councilmen and City captains, said to have been signed by 30,000 people, demanding once again the abolition of episcopacy and protesting against Charles's dismissal of Balfour from the Lieutenantship of the Tower and his replacement by that ruffian soldier, Colonel Lunsford.[101] Two petition forms appended to this last petition are still extant,[102] and are of great interest. Over 200 signatures appear beneath one of them, and over thirty beneath the other. There are no Aldermen among the signatories. Some make their mark only, but in most cases these are personal signatures which are obviously genuine. There were nine signatures on the copy that was sent to the House of Lords: only three[103] of the signatories were

---

[99] *C.S.P.D. 1641-1643*, vol. 486/42.

[100] Nalson, op. cit., ii, pp. 764-766. *D'Ewes*, ed. Coates, op. cit., p. 325.

[101] Ibid. p. 337.

[102] Egerton MSS., 1048, fols. 26, 28.

[103] Stephen Estwicke, Richard Price and Richard Turner. Of the other signatories, Maximilian Bond and Randall Mainwaring were both Captains in the Trained Bands. Mainwaring, Estwicke and another signatory, Samuel Warner, were elected Militia Commissioners in January 1642. *L.J.* iv, December 23 1641.

prominent in Common Council, but all were later active supporters of the parliamentary puritans in the City.

The tumultuous days that began on December 26th at the start of the twelve days of Christmas festivities, were partly spontaneous manifestations of popular feeling in face of rumours that Charles intended to resort to force, and went beyond the control of the Lord Mayor or even of the parliamentary puritan leaders. The stairs from the river to Palace Yard were blocked by citizens who refused to let the Bishops land to take their seats in the Lords. Some of the wilder spirits, among them the young radical John Lilburne, were involved in an affray with Colonel Lunsford and his soldiers, who were goaded on by their cries of 'No Bishops'. The leader of the rioters, Sir Richard Wiseman, was killed, and became the martyred hero of the apprentices.[104] It was all that Captain Venn could do to restrain the rioters from following it up by an attack on the Lord Mayor's house.[105] Instead, they fell back on the traditional sport of releasing the prisoners from the City prisons.

The King's attempt to seize the five Members brought the struggle to its climax. The five Members were sheltered in Coleman street, if not in the house of Alderman Penington, in that of one of his Puritan neighbours. A Grand Committee of the Commons was set up to deal with the emergency and sat nearby at Grocers' Hall in Poultry. As has already been seen, the newly elected Common Councilmen took up their seats on January 5th and carried all before them in City government. The constitutional changes which they initiated gained parliamentary sanction through the intervention of Captain John Venn and Alderman Penington. The Committee of Safety, elected by the Common Council, was given executive powers which were authorized by the Lower House and included authority to force the Lord Mayor to call a Common Council when it thought fit.[106] This Committee worked out plans of defence for the City in conjunction with a Committee of the Commons, on which sat Alderman Penington, John Venn, and Samuel Vassall. On the initiative personally of

[104] According to *Persecutio Undecima*, his funeral expenses were defrayed by a collection among the apprentices, p. 64.

[105] *A true relation of the most wise and worthy speech, made by Captain Venn . . . to the apprentices of London.* December 29 1641. [Thomason Tracts.]

[106] *C.J.* ii, p. 376.

Captain Venn, who had moved similar proposals earlier at the time of the Army plot,[107] the City was placed in a posture of defence. The Trained Bands were increased, equipped and placed under the command of Major-General Skippon. From that time, Parliament had the backing not only of the City government but of an effectively organized armed force, the City Trained Bands.

The changes in City government, however, did not mean that all the controversial petitions which had previously come unofficially from the citizens, now received the official support of the municipality. The moderately phrased petition of January 5 1642,[108] protesting at the arrest of the five Members, was drawn up by Common Council 'notwithstanding all the opposition the Lord Mayor of London, the Recorder and the gravest and most substantial Aldermen could make'.[109] The sympathies of the Lord Mayor, the Recorder, and the majority of the Aldermen were already on the side of the crown. On some occasions, therefore, to avoid open conflict in Common Council, the City M.P.s presented petitions in the name of the citizens rather than in that of the municipality, although on other issues, the Court of Aldermen, and Common Council subscribed their support.

In January 1642, Alderman Penington and Captain John Venn presented to the House a number of petitions from citizens demanding the passage of Bills that were being blocked by the House of Lords. On January 17th, Captain Venn brought into the House, a petition of 'several merchants' calling for the appointment of a Lieutenant of the Tower in whom they could trust.[110] Two days later their assertion that merchants were refusing to bring in their bullion to the Tower because of the failure to appoint a new Lieutenant was endorsed by Common Council.[111] On January 24th, as has been said earlier, the Court of Common Council was persuaded to draw up a petition of great political significance, addressed to the House of Lords, in the name of the Lord Mayor, Court of Aldermen and Common Council. It urged the Lords to pass

---

[107] Framlingham Gawdy, 'Notes on the Long Parliament', Add. MSS., 14,827. fol. 83.

[108] J.Co.Co. 40, fol. 12.   [109] Clarendon, *History*, i, p. 496.

[110] Harl. MSS. 162, fol. 334v.   [111] J.Co.Co. 40, fol. 17.

the Bill for excluding Bishops from the House of Lords, and pressed both Houses to assume the power of the sword. This victory of the parliamentary puritan party in Common Council was followed up the next day by a visit to the Commons from Alderman Atkins, on behalf of the Court of Aldermen and Common Council, informing them that the City could not make loans for suppressing the Irish rebellion, unless 'the employing of ill affected persons in places of trust and honour in the state, who were continued by means of the votes of Bishops and popish Lords in the House of Peers' was remedied.

The pressure of the Commons and the City government was not sufficient to move the House of Lords. But in the City where political uncertainty and trade depression meant idle hands, a crowd of like-minded citizens could easily be gathered together to shout their views in Palace Yard. On January 31st, some of the poorest citizens, 15,000 labourers and porters of the 'meanest rank and quality', were met by Captain Venn at Westminster, who received from them a petition calling on Parliament to suppress the 'adverse' party, to send speedy help to Ireland and cause the Cinque Ports to be fortified.[112] A very similar petition was handed in from the London seamen. On February 1st, Palace Yard was filled with women led by Ann Stagg, a brewer's wife from Southwark,[113] who warned the House of their poverty and distress brought about by the decay of trade. We have seen earlier how ready women were to join militantly in the political struggle. Faced by these vociferous, even violent housewives, Major-General Skippon was uncertain where his duty lay. He hastened to seek the advice of the Commons, explaining that he knew not how to act 'there being so many people pressing about both Houses', the women in particular having threatened him that whereas there were 100 now, in a day or so there would be 500. He desired to know 'how he might carry himself inoffensively to them and serviceably to this House'. The Commons seemed not in the least anxious. The women were given a warm welcome, and their petition was read on the suggestion, significantly, of the radical Henry Marten. Some of their friends were

[112] Harl. MSS. 162, fol. 360v.
[113] 'A true Copy of the Petition of the Gentlewomen' . . . 1642. *Harleian Miscellany*, v, p. 271.

even more highly placed, for it is recorded that five Members of the House, including Pym and Alderman Penington, then went out to Palace Yard to thank the women personally for their support.[114] Denzil Holles, a few days later, armed with another Londoners' petition, this time from the artificers, did not scruple on presenting it to the House of Peers to exploit fully their Lordships' fear of a popular uprising. He waxed lyrical on the fate of the poor. 'The cries of the poor do pierce the Heavens and make impressions in the hearts of the House of Commons,' he told them, adding that he hoped it would be the same with their Lordships. 'Want makes them cry and hunger, which breaks through walls,' he continued; 'they have not bread to put in their mouths: that cannot be but by settling of trade and restoring it; trade will not be settled till those fears and distractions be taken away: . . . that those evil Counsellors be removed who have discomposed our frame of this Commonwealth; that we may secure ourselves, and be in a posture of defence.' He ended apologetically: 'There were some things in the petition extraordinary, which at another time, the Parliament should be tender of; but now, considering the necessity of a multitude, the House of Commons thinks it not good to waken a sleepy lion; for it would pull on the mischief sooner.'[115]

This pressure persuaded the Lords to join with the Commons in sending a petition to the King, that he would entrust the fortresses and the Militia to persons in whom Parliament could confide. Within a few days the Lords had passed the Bishops' Exclusion Bill. Before a week had passed, the King had agreed to place Sir John Conyers in charge of the Tower. In spite of their successes, however, the Commons was fully aware that they were playing with a double-edged weapon, and on February 5 1642, the moderates in the House were able to secure a Committee 'to consider what way to hinder the people from gathering together to come hither . . . or to any other place, to be sent to the several ministers in and about London to be published tomorrow'.[116]

On February 11th, on the initiative of Captain Venn, the members of the City's Safety Committee were suggested to the

---

[114] Add. MSS. 14,827 fols. 25, 29v.
[115] *L.J.* iv, p. 559.   [116] Add. MSS. 14,827, fol. 30v.

House of Commons as suitable Commissioners for the Militia. The dispute which followed on this issue and which brought the conflict in City government to a head has already been described. It should be noted, however, that after Walter Long had first introduced the petition of Sir George Benion and other citizens against the appointment of the City's Safety Committee as City Militia Commissioners, Alderman Penington reintroduced the matter two days later and called for a full debate on the misdemeanours of those who had 'contrived' the petition.[117] The result of the inquiry led, as we have seen, to the impeachment of the Recorder, Sir Thomas Gardiner, and of Sir George Benion, a wealthy, influential citizen and ex-member of Common Council. Similarly, when the King's Commission of Array was distributed in the City it was on the initiative of the City Members and the City Militia Committee that the Royalist Lord Mayor, Sir Richard Gurney, was accused and impeached by Parliament.[118] Alderman Penington and Captain Venn, having played a leading role in initiating ecclesiastical reform and having helped to establish parliamentary control over the nation's militia, were now turning to the problem of consolidating parliamentary puritan control over the City government.

HOW THE CITIZENS WERE ORGANIZED

The methods used by the parliamentary opposition to win support in the City have long been of interest to the historian. The charge was frequently made in the seventeenth century by Clarendon, Nalson and others, that the parliamentary leaders engineered a party from among the City 'rabble'. Such a term is itself pejorative. The demonstrators were men of 'solid worth', shopkeepers and citizens of middle rank, although they were joined often enough by the labouring classes of the City and suburbs. Many of these deprecating assertions were made by men writing a generation later, such as John Nalson, Sir William Dugdale and Anthony à Wood, and they cannot always be corroborated by contemporary evidence. It was rumoured on more reliable authority that the relatives of some Members of the House were concerned in the rioting, such as Sir Nathaniel Barnardiston's son, Samuel, and Humphrey Salwey's brother,

[117] Harl. MSS. 162, fols. 398, 402v, 403.   [118] Ibid. fol. 544v.

Richard, a Grocer of London.[119] It is also clear that some of the parliamentary leaders, the Earl of Warwick, the young Sir Henry Vane and above all Lord Brooke, joined in a number of social and commercial activities with the City parliamentary puritans. But we have no evidence that they used their connexions to foment riots.[120] Why should they? The activities of their City colleagues, the City Burgesses, made it unnecessary for them to play the incendiary or descend to the market-place. Our evidence has shown that the City Members, particularly Alderman Penington and Captain Venn, put themselves at the head of a large parliamentary puritan organization in the City, which represented much spontaneous feeling among Puritan citizens and merchants of middle rank, and which their work helped to stimulate and direct. It is also evident that Alderman Penington and Captain Venn, and to a less extent Samuel Vassall and Matthew Cradock, used their influence with the parliamentary puritans in the City to further Pym's policy in the Commons.

The chief weapon in their armoury proved to be the circulating petition. The revival of the petition was itself a startling political development, since Charles' government had always insisted that it was illegal and seditious to arouse popular support in this way. How much more so when the petitions were subscribed by some of the lowest classes of London society. These petitions and their humble signatories were the favourite butt of Royalist scribblers:

> To Pym King of the Parliamented,
> The grievances are here presented
> Of Porters, Butchers, Broom-men, Tanners,
> That fain would fight under your banners;
> Weavers, Dyers, Tinkers, Coblers,
> And many other such like Joblers. . . .[121]

Behind this bustle of popular activity was a serious political campaign, and it is obvious that Pym and the leaders of the House depended on it in 1640 and 1641 to help win support

---

[119] *D.N.B.*

[120] A brief M.A. thesis by Alla B. Ransom, 'The Mob in the Year 1641' (Minnesota University Library), fails to prove the charges that have been made.

[121] 'A Mock Remonstrance referring to the Porters' Petition', *Rump Songs*, op. cit., i, p. 79.

for their policies in the House. Pym himself on a famous occasion declared: 'God forbid that the House of Commons should proceed in any way to dishearten people to obtain their just desires in such a way.'[122] Urgent business was laid aside when news reached the House that the citizens were on their way to Westminster with a carriage to bear their petition and its rolls of signatures. The citizens' spokesmen were invariably welcomed at the Bar of the House and encouraged to elaborate their petitions with a lengthy political speech. This procedure was no part of the City government's traditional privileges: in previous Parliaments, only the Sheriffs (or, in their absence, two Aldermen and four Common Councilmen) had enjoyed the right of presenting petitions at the Bar of the House. Nor can it be said to be part of the practice by which strangers 'avowed' private petitions in person before the House at this time.[123] The citizens of London in these years addressed the House at length on controversial political and religious topics that were under current debate. These political harangues from private citizens were, as far as is known, without precedent and showed how much Pym and the leaders of the House relied on the support of the City parliamentary puritans in the first two years of the Long Parliament. In 1642 and 1643, the leaders of the House showed less sympathy to petitions prepared by their own left wing, the radicals and the war party, and to the petitions of some of the more turbulent and less controllable citizens among the labouring population. They found it irksome when their own weapons were turned against themselves.

How did the City M.P.s and the leading parliamentary puritans mould and guide public opinion in 1640 and 1641? Their chief agents for spreading information and later for raising subscriptions, were, as one would expect, the Puritan ministers and lecturers of the City, especially in the handful of parishes which have been described earlier as Puritan strongholds, above all, St. Antholin's. The popular, if shadowy, figure of the Puritan divine as a man remote, over-pious and other-worldly, like the Banbury fanatic who 'hanged his cat

---

[122] *D'Ewes*, ed. Coates, p. xxxiv.

[123] H.S.E., *Rules and Customs which by long and constant practice have obtained the Name of Orders of the House . . .*, Dublin, 1692, ch. xii, *passim*.

for killing of a mouse on Sunday', has obscured the passionate
and practical reality of these latter-day 'saints' whose preaching on Sundays and weekdays horrified the Archbishop and
the King. The Puritan rector of St. Antholin's, Charles Offspring, as we have seen, was accustomed not only to hurl his
verbal thunderbolts from the pulpit—he also carried on the
good work in the crowded streets of his parish and even elsewhere. He and his enthusiastic vestrymen organized house-to-
house collections and canvassed support to augment the
lecturers' stipends. This was an activity that extended to
other parts of the City and included contributions from several
inhabitants of St. Stephen's, Coleman street.[124] It is reasonable to suppose that all this helped to provide much experience
of Puritan agitation. Moreover, the lists of sympathizers and
contributors arising from this activity would have been most
valuable to Penington and others in mobilizing support, collecting signatures, and raising voluntary levies in the critical
early years of the Long Parliament. After 1640, there must
also have been the closest ties between the City Puritans in
St. Antholin's and the Scottish High Commissioners. From
November 1640, the Commissioners were lodged next door to
St. Antholin's and were able to enter the church by a private
gallery. Clarendon tells us that it became a centre of 'seditious
lecturers', to hear whose sermons, 'there was so great a con-
flux and resort, by the citizens out of humour and faction . . .
that from the first appearance of the day in the morning on
every Sunday to the shutting of the light, the church was
never empty'.[125]

From early in James's reign until the days of Laudian repression, Londoners had been entertained by 'political' sermons. With Laud's downfall after 1640, many of the parishes
which had instituted Puritan lecturers, long silenced by Laud,
were able to enjoy their preaching once more. After the calling of the Long Parliament, the pulpits again vibrated with
their political harangues while the printing presses, partially
throttled by Laud before 1640, now poured forth their sermons in pamphlet form to be eagerly devoured by the public.
On November 14 1641, a sermon was preached at St. Stephen's,
Coleman street, by John Goodwin which was later printed,

---

[124] *The New Haven Colony*, op. cit., p. 10.   [125] Clarendon, *History*, i, p. 251.

bearing the title, *Ireland's Advocate: or a sermon . . . to promote the contributions by way of lending, for the present relief of the Protestant party in Ireland.*[126] Similar political sermons were preached at the Artillery Garden and before the Livery Companies.[127] Thomas Case, lecturer at St. Mary Magdalen, Milk street, from 1641, and later chaplain to Alderman Penington during his mayoralty, was renowned for his sermons inviting his congregation to communion with the words, 'you that have freely and liberally contributed to the Parliament for the defence of God's cause and the gospel, draw near'.[128] These 'political' sermons were not occasional random affairs, but were alleged by one contemporary writer to be part of an organized campaign. The author of *Persecutio Undecima* tells us that the Puritan clergy of the City used to meet in Edmund Calamy's house in Aldermanbury to discuss ways of propagating the godly cause in Parliament and among the citizens, and that it was in these meetings that the Westminster Assembly of Divines had its origin. The citizens, he says, could learn from their sermons and lectures 'not only what was done the week before [in Parliament] but also what was to be done in Parliament the week following; besides the information, which their pulpits gave the people, for coming in tumults to the House for justice'.[129] This evidence seems to corroborate the assertions of many royalist writers that the City clergy were involved in the citizens' demonstrations, and gives perhaps greater authenticity to the persistent gossip that Cornelius Burges, Calamy's colleague and friend, was directly involved in stirring up the apprentices, his 'bandogs'[130] in December 1641.

How else were petitions and political activity organized in these turbulent days? The Commons' investigation into the

---

[126] Thomason Tracts.

[127] E.g. Samuel Fawcet, *A Seasonable Sermon for these troublesome times Preached to the Right Worshipful Companie of the Haberdashers*, 1641. [Thomason Tracts.]

[128] *A Letter from Mercurius Civicus*, p. 415. Mary Penington, daughter-in-law of Alderman Penington, described to her grandson how much her first husband, Sir William Springett, had been influenced by the sermons of Thomas Case. Maria Webb, op. cit., pp. 36 seq.

[129] *Persecutio Undecima*, p. 57. According to John Vicars, the agreement between Presbyterians and Congregationalists described by Robert Baillie, to forbear from public controversy until episcopacy was abolished, had been made at Edmund Calamy's house. *The Schismatick Sifted. Or, The Picture of Independents*, 1646, pp. 15-16.

[130] *Persecutio Undecima*, p. 62.

methods used to obtain signatures to the citizens' petition of
December 11 1641 revealed that this activity was not just a
parish affair, but was organized in the wards and wardmotes
as well.[131] In one ward, the Alderman's deputy was said to
have summoned all the parish to his house to solicit their signatures.[132] From another source, we know that the parliamentary
puritans thought it worth while to get their nominees elected
to the most humble offices in the City, and no doubt these
officials played their part.[133] But the command of places of
assembly and communication is vital to any movement of this
nature. We have already seen how Isaac Penington, and before
him his wife, ran an 'ordinary', which may have served as a
reception centre for visiting Puritans. Tavern Clubs, also, appear to have been centres of political agitation at this time.
The early history of such places is a neglected study of social
and political activity in the seventeenth century. Harrington's
Rota, at the end of the Interregnum, was preceded by many
other assemblies at taverns. In Jacobean days, literary societies,
among them Ben Jonson's Apollo Club, used to meet in City
taverns. More political was the little known 'philosophical'
society later called the Robin Hood Club. This society, of
which the Puritan Sir Hugh Middleton, creator of the New
River Canal, was a member, is said to have met in a City
tavern in 1613.[134] What was more likely than that taverns
should have been used for political purposes in the turmoil of
1640 and 1641 ? Indeed, under the Commonwealth, they were
known as meeting places for Levellers. A royalist ballad of
about this time speaks of bearded roundheads who 'talk
of State and carry it at the Club'.[135] The citizens' petition of
December 11 1641 was, it seems, on display in the White Lion
Tavern.[136] Above all, there is evidence provided by the author
of *Persecutio Undecima* that the Puritan faction 'by daily Tavern
clubs in each ward', communicated 'intelligence to, and from
their Table Junto's or Subcommittees sitting in divers private
houses in London (Brown's house, a Grocer near Cheapside

---

[131] S.P.Dom. 16/486/30.
[132] Ibid.
[133] *Persecutio Undecima*, p. 58.
[134] Nicholas Hans, *New Trends in Education in the Eighteenth Century*, 1951, p. 163.
[135] 'The Round-heads Race', *Rump Songs*, op. cit., i, p. 66.
[136] S.P.Dom. 16/486/45.

Cross; also a Draper's house in Watling street . . .) to prepare
results of each day's passages in the City, to report to Mr.
Pym and his close committee when they came from the Parliament to be feasted at night in confiding citizen's houses'.[137]
Taverns were convenient meeting places partly because here
the country carriers brought their messages and took away
pamphlets and news-sheets; in particular we are told there
were special 'Bible carriers' who brought messages to and fro
from the 'brethren' in the country.[138] It was in the taverns,
also, that news-sheets, which suddenly proliferated in 1641,
were circulated and read aloud; for these early journals,
printed in London, were highly sympathetic to Parliament,
and it was some time before the Royalists learnt the need to
retaliate with their own propaganda.

City shops could also be used for political activity. As again
in the eighteenth century, City shopkeepers were accustomed
to keep petitions on their counters for customers to sign. The
information that Sir John Strangeways and Edward Kirton
brought against Captain Venn, that he urged the apprentices
to go armed to Westminster, revealed that City shops were
recognized places for discussing political affairs.[139] A few
months later, Sir George Benion's petition protesting at the
nominations for the City Militia Commissioners was said to
have been on display in Mr. Mosse's shop.[140] But for the great
number of people said to have been involved in these campaigns, much larger assembly places were also needed. According to Clarendon, the people of the City and suburbs used the
fields surrounding the City walls as places of assembly for
initiating campaigns and organizing petitions: 'all the factious
and schismatical people about the City and suburbs', he
wrote, 'would frequently . . . convene themselves, by the
sound of a bell or other token, in the fields, or some convenient
place, and receive orders from those by whom they were to
be disposed'. Such meetings, he asserted, were held in Southwark, 'in a place where the arms and magazine . . . were
kept'.[141] His reference is to St. George's Fields, where, as we
have already seen, a great meeting was held in May 1640.

[137] *Persecutio Undecima*, pp. 60-61.   [138] *Persecutio Undecima*, p. 55.
[139] Clarendon MSS., xx, 1542.   [140] *C.J.* ii, p. 452.
[141] Clarendon, *History*, i, p. 453.

Its lasting tradition as a place of assembly for the common
people is exemplified more than a century later in the famous
'massacre of St. George's Fields' in the Wilkite disorders. In
the northern suburbs, Moorfields, which had been laid out
with walks and trees some years earlier, and the newly built
piazza of Covent Garden[142] were two such convenient assembly
places, and were both used for meetings. On one occasion
when signatures were required for a petition, a Livery Company Hall was hired for the day. In August 1643, printed
notices were distributed in the City asking citizens to come to
Merchant Taylors' Hall to sign a petition. The Hall, it appears,
was to be open for this purpose on a Saturday from four in
the morning to eight o'clock at night.[143]

*   *   *

We have seen that the parliamentary puritans who won the
control of the City government in 1642 had been active previously in certain Puritan parishes; in trading companies like
those for the New England Plantations, as a powerful opposition party in the Levant Company, and even as a small
minority in the East India Company; and at the Artillery
Garden and other places where citizens met to exercise their
skill in archery and with the pike and musket. Before 1640,
they had made little headway in the City government, although a few of them were Common Councilmen. After the
calling of the Long Parliament and the election to it of four
of their leading members, they began to sweep all before them
in the City. Their campaigns in the municipality and among
the citizens were greatly strengthened now that their spokesmen in Parliament, the City Members, had the ear of the
leaders of the House and played the part of intermediary between the City and Parliament. Their challenge to the Aldermen gained parliamentary support through the prompting of
Alderman Penington and Captain Venn. In turn, the City
Members and their citizen allies helped to mobilize popular
support for Pym's policies by their petitions and demonstrations, supported by a great number of substantial citizens,

---

[142] 'An Humble Declaration of the Apprentices and other young men', 1642
[1643]. *Harleian Miscellany*, v, p. 304.
[143] See Chapter VII, p. 270n.

shopkeepers and traders as well as seamen and artisans and labourers from the City poor and the suburbs. By their activity, they partially obscured the fact that many Aldermen, Common Councilmen and wealthy citizens sympathized with the crown. The parliamentary puritans, through their circulating petitions, their demonstrations, their Puritan preaching and their secular tavern clubs, created a movement which made a considerable contribution, underestimated by historians, to Pym's victory over the crown. Their leaders, Alderman Penington and Captain Venn, had a further role to play. They became the nucleus of a radical party in the House of Commons that, strengthened by a group of supporters in the City and the suburbs, became, as we shall now see, an acute embarrassment to Pym in 1643.

CHAPTER VII

The New Course, 1642-3

IN 1640 and 1641, the Members of Parliament for the City, particularly Alderman Penington, acted as a link between Pym and the parliamentary opposition and their supporters in the City, presenting their petitions to the House of Commons and pursuing their policies in debates and committees. The municipality was not controlled by the City parliamentary puritans and did not support the policies and tactics of the radical group with which Alderman Penington, Matthew Cradock and Captain John Venn were associated. Alderman Penington gained his political ascendancy through his self-appointed role of intermediary between the City and the House of Commons, and through his influence and prestige among the Puritan clergy and the parliamentary puritan citizens of the liveries. When their supporters in the City won control over the municipality early in 1642, it was the influence of the City M.P.s especially of Alderman Penington and Captain Venn, which gained Parliament's authorization for some of the important constitutional changes that were taking place in City government.

Once these changes had taken place and the City parliamentary puritans were finally established in power, with Penington as Lord Mayor, the City M.P.s no longer had such a vital role to play. In times of acute political crisis, the intervention of Alderman Penington or Captain Venn might still be very useful,[1] and the Commons had agreed that Penington, although Lord Mayor, should be given special dispensation to continue his seat in Parliament.[2] But now that the official body

---

[1] As on the occasion of the petition against accommodation with the crown on August 7 1643. Harl. MSS. 164, fol. 145v.

[2] Clarendon, in his description of Alderman Penington's presentation of a petition against 'accommodation' with the King, on August 7th, writes that the Alderman 'from the time of his mayoralty had forborne sitting in the House as a Member'. *History*, Bk. vii, 170. D'Ewes in his diary, however, records at least one instance in which the Lord Mayor was present at a debate. Harl. MSS. 164, fol. 265v. Other instances are recorded in the Commons' Journals.

of the City supported the parliamentary cause it was obviously more effective for the City government to express its view to Parliament officially by petition and deputation. From August 1642, whenever the City government as a body agreed on important political proposals, they expressed their views to Parliament through an elected deputation, headed by one of the Aldermen, usually a member of the Militia Committee. Even this procedure was not wholly traditional. It was the custom for official City deputations to parliament to be led by one of the Sheriffs; during Penington's mayoralty, the Sheriffs to their resentment never performed this function.[3] But in any event the deputations from the City were usually more representative of the municipality than in the previous year, even though, as will be shown below, agreement could not always be reached in the City councils, and on some occasions 'the most active and godly part of the City' was obliged, as it had been in 1641, to present its views to Parliament, without the official authorization of the City government.

The real initiative in the municipality from August 1642 until October 1643, came from Alderman Penington (now Lord Mayor), on some occasions with the support of the leading members of the Militia Committee. Penington himself was more radical than this Committee and often gave his support to the 'fiery spirits' of the City or the 'war party' on occasions when the members of the Militia Committee were probably more disposed to support Pym and the 'middle group' in the House of Commons. The majority of members of the Militia Committee might perhaps be described as supporters of the 'middle group' in the Commons, but with a strong bias against the manœuvres of the 'peace party' and a sympathy with the less extreme aspects of the radical programme.

More than any other group in the City, they adhered to the policy of Pym. They were not conservative supporters of the 'middle group'; of the seven Aldermen and twelve Commoners on the Committee all but four[4] were removed by the City political presbyterians in May 1647, in their attempt to

[3] Harl. MSS. 164, fol. 309. Samuel Vassall's report from the Sheriffs to the House of Commons on February 28 1643.

[4] Aldermen Sir John Wollaston, John Langham, James Bunce and William Gibbs.

eradicate political independency from the City government.
At the same time, its members were influential merchants who
were becoming Parliament's financiers and Customs Farmers
and as such eschewed the violent policies of the radicals and
the war party.

Nevertheless, the Militia Committee remained a more radical
force than the Court of Aldermen. Although many of the new
additions to the aldermanic Bench were men moderately sympathetic to Pym and the 'middle group' of the Commons, there
was still a group of senior Aldermen on the Bench (and one
or two junior Aldermen also) who were declared Royalists,[5]
and openly opposed the policy of the City, as well as a number
who wanted immediate accommodation with the crown.[6] Four[7]
of the Royalists were, however, removed from the aldermanic
Bench during the spring of 1643, while others were absent
from the Bench for part of the year, either for political reasons
or because they had no choice as a result of their imprisonment
for refusal to contribute towards the assessments. The men
who replaced them, and the majority of those who had been
elected Aldermen between January 1642 and the summer of
1643 were conservative[8] supporters of the 'middle group' and
later, political presbyterians. Throughout his mayoralty,
Penington never relied on the Court of Aldermen as an instrument in his policy: indeed, he carried further the policy of
limiting aldermanic power in the City constitution.[9] Instead,
he worked with Common Council and the Committee of the
Militia as far as he could, but on the occasions when his radicalism outran the enthusiasm of the Committee, he was thrown
back to work with the 'fiery spirits' of the Commons, William
Strode, Sir Henry Ludlow, and Henry Marten, in conjunction
with the radicals of the City.

---

[5] Aldermen Sir Hugh Windham, Sir William Acton, Sir Henry Garway,
Sir George Whitmore and Sir John Cordell.

[6] Aldermen Sir Edmund Wright, Sir John Gayre, Thomas Adams, Sir George
Clarke and Abraham Reynardson.

[7] Aldermen Sir Hugh Windham, Sir William Acton, Sir Henry Garway and
Sir George Whitmore.

[8] I have kept to the terminology used by J. H. Hexter in his book, *The Reign
of King Pym*, in describing shades of opinion within the main political groupings.
The 'conservative' members of the 'middle group' were those who tended to ally
with the 'peace party' whenever peace negotiations were under discussion.

[9] See below, p. 246 seq.

THE NEW MEN

In view of the decisive power of the Militia Committee in the City in the crucial months between January and August 1642 and its continuing influence after that date, its personnel is of particular interest. Four of the nine Aldermen on the Committee in September 1642,[10] Aldermen John Wollaston, John Towse, John Warner and Thomas Andrewes were also Parliament's main collectors of loans and assessments. These were the men who had been appointed Treasurers for the Irish subscriptions in March 1642[11] and of the loan money in arrears, and Treasurers under the Ordinance for bringing in plate, money and horses in June 1642.[12] They had also been appointed to receive the subscriptions for raising dragoons in September 1642[13] and to receive the weekly assessments according to the parliamentary Ordinance of November 29th.[14] Aldermen John Wollaston, John Warner, and Thomas Andrewes were later made Treasurers for War.[15] Five of the eight Commissioners of Customs[16] appointed by Parliament in January 1643 were members of the Militia Committee, Alderman Thomas Andrewes, Alderman John Fowke, William Berkeley, James Russell and Stephen Estwicke. Three of the Excise Commissioners[17] were also members of the Committee, Alderman John Towse, Alderman Thomas Andrewes and John Kendricke. Alderman Thomas Andrewes, Alderman John Fowke, Alderman William Gibbs, James Russell and Stephen Estwicke were appointed Trustees for the sale of Bishops' lands.[18] Alderman Thomas Atkins, Stephen Estwicke,[19] and Francis Peck[20] were the main suppliers of clothing and provisions to the parliamentary armies.

It appears, then, that the members of the Militia Committee, apart from their military and political duties, were largely responsible for organizing money for the parliamentary army.

---

[10] Aldermen Sir John Gayre and Sir Jacob Garrard were removed from the Militia Committee early in September 1642, and were replaced by Alderman Penington and the two Sheriffs, Aldermen John Langham and Thomas Andrewes. J.Co.Co. 40, fol. 37v.

[11] *C.J.*, ii, p. 465.   [12] Ibid. p. 618.   [13] Ibid. p. 800.   [14] Ibid. p. 868.

[15] *C.S.P.D. 1644-1645*, vol. 506/84.   [16] *C.J.*, ii, p. 927.

[17] Firth and Rait, *Acts and Ordinances of the Interregnum, 1642-1660*. 1909, i, p. 203.

[18] *C.J.*, iv, p. 684.   [19] *C.S.P.D. 1641-1643*, vol. 491/124.   [20] Ibid.

What background had these men who, behind Pym and his middle group, became the financiers of the war? It is instructive to compare the Aldermen who sat on the Militia Committee with the leading Aldermen who held office in 1640. The leading Aldermen in 1643, with a few exceptions, had not held important state office previous to 1642, that is to say, they had not sat on commissions appointed by the King to examine or regulate trade or administrative policy, nor had they held commercial offices under the crown, as far as it is possible to tell. Nor were they senior Aldermen or Aldermen of long standing. On the whole, they had not held the highest offices in the City; in a few cases they were recently elected Aldermen, had held the office of Sheriff and that of Assistant in their Livery Company, but the majority had held only minor positions in City government. They were not among those who controlled the interlocking directorates of the export-import companies.[21] They did not fill the governorships or deputy-governorships of the big commercial companies, nor were they 'committees' (with one or two exceptions) of the Levant Company or the East India Company. The absence of records for the French, Eastland, Muscovy, and Guinea companies, and the Merchant Adventurers, makes it impossible to discern whether they held positions as 'committees' in these companies. But from the records of the East India and Levant Companies and chance lists that exist of the leading merchants of other companies, it appears that the 'new men' of the City were not those who had monopolized both City and company office in the period before 1640. Two of them, Alderman John Wollaston and Alderman William Gibbs, had been in receipt of a lucrative patent granted by Charles I for refining gold and silver used in the wiredrawing trade,[22] and Wollaston was exceptional among his colleagues in having, in 1642, already been a City Sheriff, Warden of the Goldsmiths' Company, and Deputy Governor of the Irish Society. Alderman Thomas Atkins had held the office of Sheriff from 1637 to 1638 and followed it as was customary by accepting the office of

[21] For pluralism in office-holding among the Directors and 'committees' in the big trading companies, see A. Friis, *Alderman Cockayne and the Cloth Trade*, Copenhagen, 1927, *passim*.

[22] See Appendix II, The New Men, pp. 320-1, 328-31.

Alderman, but no one forgot that he was a newcomer to the
City, a provincial cloth merchant from King's Lynn and Norwich, who had won a reputation as an opponent of the Laudian
practices of the Bishop of Norwich.[23] The disputatious and
acquisitive Alderman John Fowke, who quarrelled with the
East India Company and every government in turn during
his long career,[24] had previously held none of the high offices
in the City, nor was he descended from an influential City
family, though his rise to prominence was very fast after 1642.
He was a member of the Haberdashers' Company, who together with the Mercers' were the only major Livery Companies before 1640 to sponsor consistently the election of
Puritan ministers to their church livings and lectureships.[25] It
was said of Fowke, however, that he was 'not much noted for
religion', though 'a countenancer of good ministers'.[26] Alderman Thomas Andrewes, money-lender and prosperous wholesale linen draper from New Fish street,[27] preferred to pay
fines rather than accept City office prior to 1640. Connected
by marriage with Matthew Cradock, the Puritan City M.P.,
he accepted at first reluctantly, the office of Sheriff and Alderman, and more willingly that of parliamentary Treasurer in
the space of a few months after the victory of the parliamentary
puritans in 1642. Alderman John Warner and Alderman John
Towse, who became two of the greatest administrators of parliament's finances during the Civil War, took practically no
part in City government before 1639. In that year, the Puritan
John Warner, who with his younger brother Samuel, had a
druggist business in Bucklersbury, accepted office as Sheriff at
a time when no one could be prevailed upon to take office;
not one of the wealthiest men of the City, although a substantial citizen, it was rumoured that the City was to allow
him half the charges if he accepted office.[28] Perhaps his election was already a move in the campaign of the City parliamentary puritans, for it was followed in June 1640, by the

---

[23] See Appendix II, The New Men, pp. 311-13.   [24] Ibid. pp. 316-20.
[25] D. A. Williams, 'Some Aspects of the Puritan movement in London, 1610-
1640.' Unpublished Ph.D. thesis, Washington Univ., U.S.A., 1951. chapter viii,
passim.
[26] *C.S.P.D. 1660-1661,* vol. 32/105.
[27] See Appendix II, The New Men, pp. 309-11.
[28] Add. MSS. 11,054, fol. 54.

election of John Towse as the popular candidate for the shrievalty. Previously, Towse had not even served as an Assistant
in the Livery of his company, the Grocers'.[29] Both men enjoyed
a meteoric rise to power in the City after 1642. Alderman
John Langham eschewed City office prior to 1640, though he
enjoyed the traditional trading connexions with the East India
and Levant Companies during that period and accepted office
reluctantly in 1642. Of these eight Aldermen who sat on the
Militia Committee, six became political independents,[30] while
only two were staunch political presbyterians;[31] but with
many of these Aldermen expediency rather than principle
motivated their political life, as with Alderman Wollaston, who, though known to be an ally of the political presbyterians in 1646, threw in his lot with the winning side in the
following year. These men were clearly not among the great
merchant princes who monopolized office and enjoyed the
greatest fortunes before 1640. They were wealthy, but not the
wealthiest men in the City, merchants of middle and occasionally upper middle rank, unwilling to take office in the City
in the sixteen-thirties for political or conscientious reasons, or
because they felt that their business interests and income did
not merit the expenditure of time and money involved in holding office.

On the whole the Common Councilmen on the Militia Committee reveal similar patterns. With a few exceptions, they had
not held the highest offices in the municipal government or in
the East India and Levant Companies; nor had they held commercial or administrative offices under Charles I and in many
cases they were actively engaged in disputes with the crown.
Stephen Estwicke, a trader in small haberdashery who had
clashed with the new incorporation of silk men[32] and had been
imprisoned by the crown for refusing to pay Ship Money, had
sat on Common Council committees for less than a year; so
had Nathaniel Wright, an interloper in the Eastland and East
India trades, and James Bunce, a Captain in the Trained

---

[29] Calendar of the Court Minutes, Grocers' Company, iv, p. 11.

[30] Aldermen Towse, Warner, Fowke, Andrewes, Atkins, and Wollaston. See
Appendix II, pp. 309 seq.

[31] Aldermen Gibbs and Langham. See Appendix II, pp. 320-2.

[32] C.S.P.D. 1635-1636, vol. 314/89. See Appendix II for biographies of these
Common Councilmen.

Bands. Another member of the Militia Committee, Francis Peck, a draper from Watling street, had sat on Common Council committees since 1637, and Captain Randall Mainwaring, ex-Treasurer of the Honourable Artillery Company, from 1640. Samuel Warner, a brother of Alderman John Warner, James Russell, one of the less wealthy traders of Coleman street, and William Berkeley did not sit on any of the leading Common Council committees prior to 1642, and may not have been members of the Court. Two of the committee, the republican silk merchant, Owen Rowe, and Alexander Normington were among those 'upstarts' whom Royalist writers so bitterly accused of seizing power in the City in 1642, though Rowe had at some time previously sat on Common Council.

Neither had the men elected to the aldermanic Bench between January 1642 and the summer of 1643, held important commercial or municipal office. The careers of four of the twelve men who were elected in this period have already been touched upon as aldermanic members of the Militia Committee. The careers of the other eight,[33] (three of whom had been Common Councillor members of the Militia Committee) show some similarities. None of them, with the exception of William Ashwell (who was discharged within a year possibly for 'delinquency')[34] and Richard Chambers[35] had held office in the East India Company or Levant Company, and none of them had been prominent on Common Council committees before 1640. Richard Chambers was famed in the City for his opposition to Charles I and his refusal to pay tonnage and poundage and Ship Money. A member of one of the minor Livery Companies, he accepted the office of Alderman in September 1642 at the importunity of certain members of Parliament, who, as he alleged some years later, wished to see him 'in a place of trust'. But the financial burdens of City office depleted still further his fortune, impaired by his earlier imprisonment, and he died in 1658 in debt but still asserting his claim to £13,680 from the government, which had been promised him in compensation for his losses during Charles'

[33] Aldermen Richard Chambers, Samuel Warner, William Berkeley, William Ashwell, John Kendricke, Thomas Cullum, James Bunce, Thomas Foot. See Appendix II for their biographies. Samuel Warner, William Berkeley, and James Bunce were previously members of the Militia Committee, as already mentioned.
[34] See Appendix II, p. 311.   [35] Ibid. p. 314.

personal rule. Samuel Warner had been engaged in a dispute
with the government of the East India Company for conniving
at private trade. Like Aldermen Andrewes and Langham, he
at first declined to hold the office of Alderman and suffered
imprisonment before accepting his election in January 1643;
and in the following year, he was discharged from the Bench
for his 'miscarriage and offences',[36] probably a reference to his
refusal to submit his accounts of the General Rising Committee
to public audit. Five[37] of the eight Aldermen became moderate
or conservative supporters of political presbyterianism, but at
least one of these (Alderman Foot) accommodated himself to
the political changes of the Commonwealth and Protectorate.
The other three, William Berkeley, Samuel Warner and John
Kendricke,[38] seem to have been political independents; the
last two were to play a radical role in 1643 on the Committee
for the General Rising.[39]

It has been shown that the members of the Militia Committee and the new Aldermen who took office during 1642
and 1643, were not the men who had held the leading positions
in municipal government or, in the East India and Levant
Companies before 1640. Nor, on the whole, had they held
important commercial and administrative appointments under
the crown. These differences, however, were not of a fundamental character as far as commercial and financial interests
were concerned, and it is not surprising to find that the new
Aldermen and members of the Militia Committee frequently
adopted commercial policies, and what is of more concern
to us here, policies in regard to municipal affairs, which were
very similar to those of their predecessors. In their attitude to
national politics, the majority of the Aldermen were moderate
by inclination and politically presbyterian. This was not so
with the members of the Militia Committee, many of whom
became political independents. But their political independency was of a conservative character dictated by business interests and the advantages of accepting the *status quo*, as is
clearly apparent in the careers of two of its most prominent

---

[36] Ibid. p. 327.
[37] Aldermen Ashwell, Cullum, Bunce, Foot and Chambers.
[38] See Appendix II, pp. 313, 321, 327.
[39] *C.S.P.D. 1625-1649*, vol. Dxxxix. no. 150.

members, Alderman Fowke and Alderman Wollaston; it certainly did not imply a preference for radical policies in the City or in national politics.

THE MUNICIPALITY AND CONSTITUTIONAL REFORM, 1642-3

Whatever the attitude of the leading members of the Militia Committee and the new Aldermen to later political changes, Alderman Penington now Lord Mayor, was assured of their support for the parliamentary cause in September 1642. Under his leadership, further minor reforms were made in the City government and constitution, and the minor character of these reforms and the absence of any movement to give permanent legislative embodiment to the revolutionary expedients of the spring and summer of 1642 provide an indication of the moderate tone of the dominant group in the City government.

Within a month of Alderman Penington's accession to the mayoralty, the Court of Aldermen re-established the procedure of the ballot box in the Court, the use of which had been forbidden by Charles I in 1637.[40] Penington was clearly concerned to prevent the City government from falling into the hands of a small clique. Similarly, on September 23rd, Penington introduced into the Court of Common Council long overdue proposals to reduce the excessive charges for feasting and ceremonial which had previously been borne by the Lord Mayor and Sheriffs, suggesting that a review should be made of the sources of revenue by which they supported their expenses.[41] Although some of the traditional ceremonial of office was reduced as a result of these proposals, no fundamental change in the method by which these officers recouped their expenses, occurred until the days of the Commonwealth.[42] Constitutional changes were accompanied also by changes in the personnel of City offices, and in the methods of appointment. John Weld, a

[40] Rep. 56, fol. 15.

[41] J.Co.Co. 40, fols. 39-39v.

[42] In December 1649, the expenses of the Lord Mayor and Sheriffs were not only further reduced, but it was decided that they should no longer recoup themselves by the sale of offices. Instead, they were to be paid a monthly allowance of £208. 6s. 8d. for the Lord Mayor and £150 each for the Sheriffs. J.Co.Co. 41, fols. 12v, 13.

Royalist, was removed from the Town Clerkship and Robert Mitchell appointed in his place.[43] Thomas Wiseman, the Royalist Remembrancer, was dismissed and his office abolished, as an unnecessary charge to the City. The City Marshals, William Davies and Henry Fitch,[44] were discharged for negligence and because their office was unnecessary. As for minor offices, it was decided on June 1 1643 to limit the operation of reversions. The Court of Aldermen declared that 'they are not bound in point of right to admit any person into any office or place notwithstanding that he hath a grant in reversions of the same or a nomination or designation to it'.[45] According to a petition to the House of Commons in 1661, from three holders of reversions,[46] this measure was instigated by Penington in order to elect John Bradshaw (later one of the Regicides) into the office of Undersheriff of the Sheriff's Court. Whatever the truth of this, his election was at the time also part of a dispute between the Court of Aldermen and the Court of Common Council; on September 20, 1643, Common Council claimed the right as against the Court of Aldermen to elect to this office, and chose John Bradshaw in preference to the aldermanic candidate Richard Proctor.[47]

Of greater constitutional importance was the decision of the Court of Common Council on April 28 1643, that 'all the Alderman's deputies which now be [deputies], and are not members of this Court shall be from henceforth removed from their several places of deputies. And henceforth, the Alderman shall choose no deputy but such as are members of the Court.'[48] This limited the Alderman's choice of an officer who played an important part in ward elections and in administration, and had an immediate practical significance in restricting the power of those Royalists still on the aldermanic Bench. The most important constitutional measure, however, was the repeal in June 1643 of two Acts of Common Council of Henry VII, which confined the final choice of the City Chamberlain and Bridgemasters to the Court of Aldermen. Instead, Common Council asserted that Common Hall should both nominate and elect these officers.[49] The election of a new City Chamberlain,

[43] J.Co.Co. 40, fol. 38v.   [44] Ibid. fol. 48.   [45] Rep. 56, fol. 186.
[46] H.M.C. Seventh Report, House of Lords MSS., p. 152.
[47] J.Co.Co. 40, fol. 74v.   [48] Ibid. fol. 59.   [49] Ibid. fol. 65v.

Gilbert Harrison, a Goldsmith and Alderman from 1638-41,[50] in place of Robert Bateman, who had held the office since 1625, was the immediate outcome of this measure. The concentration of certain loan and assessment moneys into the hands of particular treasurers usually appointed by Parliament, reduced the importance of the Chamberlain in Parliament's financial arrangements. Nevertheless, the City Chamber still raised substantial sums, and the change in the method of election was no doubt intended to increase the speed and facility with which loans could be made available to Parliament. Moreover, the system of indirect election to the leading City offices was now abolished (except in the case of Lord Mayor), the right of Common Hall to elect both Sheriffs having been conceded by the Lords in the disputed shrieval election of 1641. But leading citizens in the seventeenth century were not preoccupied with constitutional forms for their own sake; in the election of Sheriffs for 1643 to 1644, it is interesting that Penington showed no zeal for constitutional rights when they stood in the way of the election of his candidate, Alderman John Fowke, whom Common Hall seemed prepared to accept, but not before making it plain that it enjoyed the sole right of election.[51] In general, however, Penington supported the claims of Common Council, as a body more likely to support a vigorous prosecution of the war; and it was agreed by contemporaries,[52] that it was from the time of Penington's mayoralty that the aldermanic veto on Common Council, hitherto the greatest limitation on the power of that Court, had been dropped, although it was not officially altered by Ordinance.

A further constitutional innovation introduced during Penington's mayoralty was also designed to solve an immediate problem—recruitment to the aldermanic Bench. The reconstitution of the membership of the aldermanic Bench took place gradually. Between January 1642 and May 1643 twelve changes took place on the Bench. Seven[53] of the Aldermen who had held office before 1640 were discharged either for delinquency or neglect

[50] Rep. 56, fol. 199.

[51] *A modest enquiry concerning the Election of the Sheriffs of London*, op. cit., p. 42.

[52] J.Co.Co. 40, fols. 126 seq.

[53] Aldermen William Abell, Sir Edward Bromfield, Sir Richard Gurney, Sir Hugh Windham, Sir William Acton, Sir Henry Garway and Sir George Whitmore.

of duties; two[54] died, and three[55] asked to be relieved of their offices. During this period, there was thus twelve vacancies to fill with men who were both sympathetic to Parliament and eligible for office. This meant a considerable recruitment problem, exacerbated by the tradition that not more than six Aldermen of one Livery Company should hold aldermanic office at the same time.[56] In the election to Vintry Ward[57] in March 1642, the proceedings had been declared invalid since the only eligible candidate, Samuel Warner, was a Grocer, and there were already six Grocers on the aldermanic Bench. This ruling was abolished in December 1642, 'after much debate' in Common Council, and Samuel Warner was thereupon elected to the Bench on January 13 1643.[58]

The constitutional changes in the City government during Penington's mayoralty were designed to achieve practical and immediate ends—to limit the power of Royalists in municipal government—rather than to alter the balance of popular representation. Although Common Council's claim to disregard the aldermanic veto over its proceedings was never openly challenged during Penington's mayoralty, no ordinance was passed which would secure its power beyond legal dispute. It seems that after the initial revolutionary fervour of the spring of 1642, there was no great movement in the City government to make further fundamental changes. The Committee of the Militia which assumed the leadership of the City councils early in 1642, for the purpose of securing the City's support for Parliament, did not as a body in the following year, take the initiative in formulating municipal policy. Probably the Militia Committee was too involved in organizational and military matters to monopolize the politics of Common Council. A few of its members, notably Alderman John Fowke, played some part on nearly every Common Council committee, but on the whole the committees of Aldermen and Common Councilmen who drew up proposals and policy were drawn from other members of the Court. The addition of eleven members to the Committee in July 1643,[59] making thirty members in all,

---

[54] Aldermen Sir Morris Abbot and Sir James Cambell.
[55] Aldermen Sir Henry Pratt, Gilbert Harrison and Sir Hugh Windham.
[56] Beaven, op. cit., ii, p. xlvi.   [57] Rep. 55, fol. 380.
[58] J.Co.Co. 40, fol. 45v, 93v.   [59] Ibid. fol. 67v.

decreased its political effectiveness as a policy-making body. The failure of this Committee to take a more leading part in the City under Penington may have been the cause, or the reflection, of the growing strength of moderate elements in the City government. By vacating the position it had held early in 1642, it left open to view, the warring factions within the City councils and increased Penington's isolation in the municipal government by forcing him openly to fall back on the support of the 'fiery spirits' in Parliament and the City radicals.

THE MUNICIPALITY AND PARLIAMENT, 1642-3

Penington's period of greatest influence in the City extended from August 1642, when he succeeded Alderman Gurney as Lord Mayor, until October 1643, at the end of his second term of office. During this time, when it was a question of practical measures to organize and finance the war, Penington worked in close conjunction with Pym, helping him to introduce both regular taxation to provide for his armies, and the taking of the Oath of Association and the religious Covenant. The King, with some justification, saw him as the chief instrument in capturing the City government. But it was Penington's extreme radicalism, his sympathy with the war party in the House of Commons and amongst the citizens, which made him the subject of political vituperation by Royalist pamphleteers, and gave an appearance of plausibility to the Royalist allegation that the City was being governed by Brownists and sectaries. The history of Penington's mayoralty makes it abundantly plain that divisions, both amongst the citizens and in the City government, were always operating beneath the surface of events, although they might be hidden at certain times of crisis. The Royalist party in the City was far from negligible, drawing much of its strength from some of the wealthiest citizens in the City and in Westminster. The peace party and the moderates were increasingly powerful on the aldermanic Bench and by August 1643 were beginning to win support even from a few members of the Militia Committee. Penington's radical associates included a number of the Militia Committee, a handful of Common Councilmen, a few Captains of the Trained Bands and some prominent City clergymen; at

first they expressed their policy in petitions to Parliament, purporting to come from the 'godly' part of the City, but later
through organizations, such as the Sub-committee of Volunteers sitting at Salters' Hall and, in July 1643, the Committee
for the General Rising, both of which came into conflict with
the official municipality and with the Committee for the
Militia. J. H. Hexter in his admirable pioneering study of this
year, *The Reign of King Pym*, implies that the leading groups
in the municipality were all of one opinion in their attitude
to the war, though they suffered from 'an outward tendency'
on occasions 'to hearken to the hasty counsels of hot-headed
puritan preachers'.[60] But it is now evident that within the City
government, there was more than one opinion, and that there
were moderate as well as radical pressure groups; it is in
the light of these conflicts that the period from the summer
of 1642 to the August of 1643 must be viewed.

In the late summer and autumn of 1642, the City of London
provided the backbone of the Parliamentary forces, both in
men and finance. Earlier in 1642, the City's Trained Bands
had been enlarged and re-equipped; in all there were now six
regiments for the City and three for the suburbs, numbering
around 10,000 men. In their first flush of enthusiasm for the
cause, the Court of Common Council was also raising voluntary
levies for service outside the City; on July 6th, a levy of 10,000
volunteers was raised for active service under the Earl of Essex,
and on September 2nd, two regiments of foot (with 1,200 in
each) and four of horse were being raised in addition. When
the King was known to be marching on London in October,
the Captains of the City Trained Bands and the majority of
their men came to the fateful decision to follow their leaders
for service outside the City.[61]

The opening of peace negotiations with the King, however,
was sufficient to break down the City's apparent unity. Two
days after the proposal for the reopening of peace negotiations
had been made in the Lords, the Lord Mayor and 'divers citizens of the City of London out of their good affections for the
safety of the City and Commonwealth' informed the House
that they were raising volunteers to block the King's approach

[60] J. H. Hexter, op. cit., p. 95.
[61] *England's Memorable Accidents*, October 17 1642. [Thomason Tracts.]

to London.[62] This offer had not come from Common Council. On November 13th, the King seemed to be about to turn down Parliament's peace offer; his troops were on the outskirts of London pillaging and raiding as far as Brentford, whose gallant defence 'to save th' Athenian walls from ruin bare', was undertaken by Denzil Holles and his City apprentices. Even then Common Council was no more prepared to support proposals for a speedier prosecution of the war, so the City radicals were galvanized into action again; on that day 'the most godly and active part of the City' led by Richard Shute[63] (who had been involved in organizing citizens' petitions in 1641) sent a deputation to the House of Commons deploring the movement on foot to make an accommodation with Charles and offering to raise at once 1,000 light horse and 3,000 dragoons for service under Philip Skippon, now promoted to the rank of Sergeant-Major-General in Essex's army. The 'divers ministers and citizens' responsible for the petition also made an attack on the conduct of the war, the opening shot in what was to become a barrage of complaint by the radicals on the state of the army of the Earl of Essex. Not only was it badly paid and equipped, they said, but the leadership was weak, the officers being 'not so careful and diligent as they ought, nor all so trustworthy'.[64]

The same group of citizens were also putting forward radical proposals on financial policy. Previously, Parliament had mobilized loans from the City, both through the Chamber and through private treasurers. Four leading members of the Militia Committee, as has been seen, were acting as Treasurers for the voluntary loans and subscriptions that were being raised to fight the Irish rebellion and provide a parliamentary army. On September 15th, a loan of £100,000 was undertaken by the municipality. But the proposals for a more permanent system of financing the war came not from the City government, but from Richard Shute's 'active and godly citizens'. On November 13th, they suggested that a Sub-Committee

---

[62] *C.J.*, ii, p. 847.

[63] Shute was one of the recently appointed Commissioners for the Sea Adventure to Ireland in June 1642. Firth and Rait, op. cit., i, p. 9. In October 1643, Parliament conferred on him a post in the Customs' House that had previously been held by Sir John Wolstenholme. *C.J.*, iii, p. 284.

[64] *C.J.*, ii, p. 847.

should be set up in London to collect subscriptions, and followed up their proposal a week later with the suggestion that compulsory weekly assessments should be levied on London and Westminster. This was all that Pym needed to seize on the opportunity of obtaining regular taxation. On November 26th, an Ordinance imposing a weekly assessment on London was pushed through Parliament.[65] A Committee was established at Haberdashers' Hall, which included Lord Brooke, Lord Saye and Sele, Pym, Vassall and Soames, to work out methods of collecting the assessment. They empowered the Lord Mayor and Sheriffs to set up a City Committee, which sat at Weavers' Hall, to appoint collectors in each parish.[66] This Committee, which consisted according to Clarendon, of 'such persons whose inclinations' the parliamentary puritans 'well knew',[67] was given powers to fix individual assessments,[68] levy distresses and call in the assistance of the Trained Bands to deal with recalcitrants. Such a Committee, though it soon antagonized the wealthier citizens, must have given the City parliamentary puritans new organizational strength. Moreover, further financial demands could now be made on the citizens. On the security of this tax, Pennington suggested that a loan of £30,000 be raised from London—and once more clergymen were called on to exhort people from the pulpits to give generously to the cause, while Churchwardens were ordered to keep accounts of the sums raised.

Although Parliament's negotiations with the King had already collapsed by the end of November, another petition denouncing 'counsels of accommodation' and calling for a speedy prosecution of the war was delivered to the Commons on December 1st by a group of 'active and godly citizens', Sir David Watkins, Richard Shute and three City clergy, Jeremiah Burroughs, preacher in the radical parish of Stepney,

[65] Ibid. p. 858. Firth and Rait, op. cit., i, p. 38.

[66] C.C. for A.M., i, pp. 1-2.

[67] Clarendon, History, ii, p. 400. Three of the Committee, John Dethick, John Kendricke and Thomas Foot, were later Aldermen and political independents; one was Christopher Nicholson, probably the lowly chandler satirized by Royalist writers; another was William Walwyn, perhaps the Leveller and pamphleteer; and one was John Bellamy, a parliamentary puritan member of Common Council. C.C. for A.M., i, pp. 1-2. For Bellamy see also p. 274 n. below.

[68] The rate of assessment was one-twentieth of real property and one-fifth of personal estate.

Hugh Peter and John Goodwin, in company with ninety-five of their supporters.[69] The petition not only asked that an end might be put to the treaty with the King and that no accommodation might be made except on 'honourable and safe conditions', but also put forward demands that became an essential part of the radical programme in 1643. They wanted reparation to be made out of delinquents' estates for the vast sums expended by the City: 'that life may be given to such Ordinances as concern the seizing and securing of the malignant persons and estates, both in city and country'. They demanded that Essex should march forth immediately against the King and offered to raise 6,000 dragoons to go to his aid. They ended with the request that malignant ministers should be sequestered and 'godly ministers' appointed to their places. The Court of Common Council, however, had not given its assent to these proposals. Whittaker records that the petition was presented by forty or fifty citizens 'but no Aldermen with them'.[70] The House of Commons, so a contemporary pamphlet tells us, was inclined to be critical; it inquired from the petitioners if it was the 'whole City's Act' and sent the petitioners back to win the support of the Aldermen and Common Council for their proposals.[71] Penington summoned a Common Council to consider the petition, but after much debate it was rejected. It seems that radical policies, far from enjoying an easy passage in the City government, were, at this stage, entirely unacceptable. Nevertheless, the petition influenced Parliament to pass the Orders of December 14th and 16th, authorizing the assessors and collectors to execute without delay the Ordinance for extending the assessments throughout the kingdom.[72]

The strength of the moderates and the 'accommodation' party in the City is evident in the widespread resistance to assessments which was immediately apparent amongst the senior Aldermen and some of the wealthiest citizens. One report claimed that there were at least eight hundred names

---

[69] *The True and Original Copy of the First Petition which was delivered by Sir David Watkins . . .* 1642. [Guildhall Pamphlets.]

[70] Add. MSS. 31,116, fol. 24.

[71] *The True and Original Copy.* Common Council probably disapproved of these radical activities, as no record of the debate was made in its Journal.

[72] *C.J.*, ii, p. 892.

on the City government's list of malignants.[73] Many of the senior Aldermen still held their positions on the Bench. Some of them had already been imprisoned in Gresham College and Crosby House for refusal to contribute to the scheme for advancing money and plate;[74] others, like Alderman Wright,[75] suspected of harbouring arms, had had their houses searched by the Lord Mayor and Sheriffs. The organized activity of the City Royalists drove Common Council on December 12th to forbid the wearing of 'favours' or party colours since, as they said, 'divers ill-affected persons within this City and the liberties . . . have of late time been disturbers of the common peace of this City by raising of dissentious debates, and . . . the better to effect their ill designs, have combined together and . . . do wear divers colours and ribbons and the badges to their hats . . . whereby the better to know each other'.[76]

Royalist sympathies and support for 'accommodation' were given a greater impetus by reason of the antipathy that was aroused by the organized activities of the radicals. The 'peace' petition which was circulated in the City early in December was said to have originated as an answer to Richard Shute's petition and it mobilized behind it too significant a following to be ignored. Penington was compelled by the petitioners at a meeting in Haberdashers' Hall to agree to bring their petition to the notice of Parliament.[77] To offset its influence, he organized an official petition from the municipality to be presented to Parliament with the proposal that it should be sent to the King, stating that the City was prepared to accept peace on certain safe conditions. Richard Shute, meanwhile, in denouncing Royalist 'peace' petitions, dismayed the House of Commons by his abusive tone and was out of favour.[78] It

---

[73] D. Gardiner, *The Oxinden and Peyton Letters, 1642-1670*, 1937, p. 11.

[74] *Catalogue of Knights, Aldermen, . . . denying to contribute money to public safety . . .* 1642. [Guildhall Broadsides]. The Aldermen mentioned are Sir Henry Garway, Sir George Whitmore and Sir John Cordell. Other wealthy citizens included Sir John Jacob, William Garway, Roger Gardiner, Robert Alden and Mr. Langhorne.

[75] But nothing was found, and the House of Commons ordered 'that the person of Sir Edmund Wright shall be freed from any restraint or imputation of disaffection'. *C.J.*, ii, p. 814.

[76] J.Co.Co. 40, fol. 44.

[77] *The Lord Wharton's Speech, To the Petitioners for Peace, on 8th December at Haberdashers' Hall*, 1642. Pages unnumbered. [Thomason Tracts.]

[78] *C.J.*, ii, p. 887.

was clear to the leaders of the Commons that radicalism could be a political liability. This was particularly felt in the City where political divisions were so marked that one pamphleteer considered 'if these factions are suffered to grow to a head, London will become a second Jerusalem, and be destroyed by her own children'.[79] Penington, as a Member of Parliament, attended the House during the hearing of the City's petition. Afterwards, he asked the Commons to order that bail should be refused to the instigators of the Royalist 'peace' petition whom he had imprisoned, and that they should be removed with the Aldermen and wealthy citizens in Crosby House, to Lambeth, presumably a place less likely to become a venue of protest demonstrations. The feeling in the City was such, however, that Penington begged the House 'that the odium of the business might not lie upon him, that Captain Mainwaring might be appointed to take the said several persons and carry them to Lambeth House'.[80]

As on previous occasions, the King's obstinacy and refusal to compromise reunited a divided City. His answer to the conciliatory petition of the municipality, and his insulting reception of the City's delegation to Oxford, provoked and dismayed the citizens.[81] The Lord Mayor, Alderman John Fowke, Captain John Venn and Captain Randall Mainwaring, Deputy to the Lord Mayor, were to be surrendered and tried for high treason. Was there any guarantee that other leading citizens who had supported the changes in City government in 1642 would not suffer a similar fate? Especially since Charles prefaced his demands with the observation that 'the wholesome government of that City . . . is now submitted to the arbitrary power of a few desperate persons of no reputation but for malice and disloyalty to him'.[82] Pym had little difficulty in convincing Common Hall that Charles was laying a trap for them. The attempt of City Royalists to create a disturbance at the meeting failed,[83] and Clarendon felt bound to admit

[79] *The Lord Wharton's Speech*, op. cit.

[80] Harl. MSS. 164, fols. 265-265v.

[81] *H.M.C. Portland MSS.*, i, p. 85, ed. A. Clark, *The life and times of Anthony Wood* . . . 1891, i, p. 80.

[82] Clarendon, *History*, Bk. vi, 216.

[83] A tract entitled, *A Speech made by Alderman Garroway, at a Common Hall, on Tuesday the 17th of January* . . . 1643, alleges that a great disturbance took place at this meeting which so unnerved Penington that he could hardly find his voice

in his history that the speeches of Pym and the other parliamentarians were 'received and entertained with all imaginable applause and (that meeting) was concluded with a general acclamation that "they would live and die with the House" and other expressions of that nature'.[84] The radicals in the City took advantage of the peace party's defeat to present their petition of December 1st once more to Parliament, but they again failed to win support.[85]

The uncompromising reply of Charles to Parliament's peace proposals early in February 1643 helped further to consolidate the parliamentary ranks in the City. It could not influence, however, the senior Aldermen who were now open and avowed Royalists. On December 24th the Undersharers and officers of the Customs' House, including Aldermen Whitmore, Cordell, Windham, Acton and Gayre, refused outright Parliament's request for a loan.[86] It was rumoured in January and February that seven Aldermen were committed to prison (most of them outside the City in 'safe' Puritan areas) for refusal to pay their assessments.[87]

It may have been the absence of these influential partisans of the King, the obdurate demands of Charles himself, or more tactful strategy on the part of the City radicals, which caused the Court of Common Council between February 18 and February 21 1643 to discuss and agree to submit proposals to

amidst the loud cries of 'No money, No money' and 'Peace, Peace'. *Harleian Miscellany*, v, p. 231. But all other accounts of the meeting say that it gave overwhelming support to Pym and the Lord Mayor. This seems insufficient reason, however, to dismiss the tract altogether as an obvious forgery, as did Professor C. H. Firth. Garway may have made such a speech, though in its published form, a masterly piece of Royalist pleading, it was obviously much embellished.

[84] Clarendon, *History*, Bk. vi, 228.

[85] *The humble Petition of divers of the best affected Ministers of the citie of London* . . . *Also the humble Petition of many grave citizens of London.; being both delivered on the 21st day of this instant January.* 1642 (1643) [Thomason Tracts.]

[86] *C.J.*, ii, p. 900.

[87] *Mercurius Aulicus*, January 25 and February 5 1643. 'Aulicus' mentions by name Sir George Whitmore, Sir Henry Windham (presumably Sir Hugh Windham), Sir William Acton, Sir John Cordell, Sir George Clarke, and Sir John Garrett (presumably Sir Jacob Garrard). On February 7th, he reported that they had been joined by Alderman Backhouse, who had been committed to the Tower. On February 21st, Alderman Garway, it was said, had been sent to Rochester jail for refusing 'to contribute at the command of the House'. Also, *A Perfect Diurnall of some Passages in Parliament*, January 23 1643, and *Certaine Informations*, January 23-30, 1643, p. 10. [Thomason Tracts.]

Parliament similar in content to those submitted by the radicals in November and December. These proposals, purged of radical phrases, were designed to achieve the broadest possible support. They were closely attuned to Pym's political strategy. He had agreed to the Peers' wish to continue negotiations with the King provided the Upper House passed the Assessment Bill, and two of the sets of propositions put before Common Council were designed to strengthen his hand. At the same time the peace party and moderates in Common Council were strong enough to produce their own list of proposals. The three sets of proposals were considered by Common Council on February 18th. The first two bore the imprint of radical demands, but were moderately phrased, and agreed perfectly with the policies of Pym and the middle group. They demanded, not the breaking-off of the negotiations with the King (which had been one of their main demands in the previous November) but practical measures that would increase the efficiency of the parliamentary fighting machine and the means of financing it; that the rents, revenues and estates of delinquents should be seized; that the Ordinance for the weekly assessment should be distributed throughout the kingdom; and that a religious covenant should be entered into to bind together the 'well-affected' of the kingdom.[88] The third list of propositions was much more distinctly the proposals of the moderates and gave support to the policy of the peace party in the House of Commons. It contained no reference to a religious covenant, to the imposition of the weekly assessment, or to the seizing of delinquents' estates; instead, it appealed for a reduction in the City's assessment quota with an extra allowance towards the cost of guarding the City. They asked that Members of Parliament should help to promote subscriptions by subscribing themselves and, as an indication of their opposition to the petition of the City radicals, that no 'private informations' should be considered as the 'sense' of the City unless they came from the Court of Common Council or the Court of Aldermen.[89]

A Committee of Common Council was elected to decide which of these propositions should be presented to Parliament. The Committee, although probably equally divided between

88 J.Co.Co. 40, fols. 47v-48.   89 Ibid. fol. 48.

men who were later political presbyterians and political independents,[90] presented to Parliament on February 20th, a
petition which contained no reference to delinquents' estates
or to a religious covenant, but was almost identical with the
third list of moderate propositions. On February 21st, however, when Common Council met again, dissatisfaction was
expressed with the Committee's selection and it was in-
structed to present further demands to Parliament—concerning the reformation of abuses in the army (which was another
way of attacking Essex), the entering into a religious covenant
and the seizing of the rents and revenues of those who refused
to enter into the Association.[91] These demands were well received by the middle group of the House of Commons, though
the omission of support for the weekly assessment showed that
Pym was by no means assured of Common Council's whole-
hearted support for his policies. But the City radicals were
even more dissatisfied. On February 23rd, when Alderman
Fowke reported to Common Council on his second deputation
to Parliament, some members for the Court arose to say that
they thought it necessary 'to express in the last of those general
heads (i.e., concerning a religious Covenant) their desire for
a thorough reformation.' A discussion followed, but according
to the Journal, 'albeit this Court did declare their unanimous
desire thereof, nevertheless being put in mind that the Lords
and Commons had provided for the same in the propositions
last sent to his Majesty, it was thought fit, that instead of petitioning for it, the said Committee should from this Court,
render all humble thanksgiving into both Houses of Parliament for this great wisdom and provident care manifested in
the said propositions to obtain that thorough reformation so
much desired'.[92]

The radicals were not at all convinced, however, that such
a 'thorough reformation' was in fact intended, and were by
no means prepared to drop their proposals. Meanwhile,
moderate and conservative opinion in the City government
was reflected in a deputation of Aldermen to the House of

[90] Alderman William Gibbs, Theophilus Riley (who was later concerned in
Sir Basil Brooke's plot to win over the City to the crown) and Abraham Chamberlain (possibly a political presbyterian), Alderman John Fowke, James Russell
and John Kendricke, who were political independents.
[91] J.Co.Co. 40, fols. 49-50.   [92] Ibid. fol. 50v.

Commons on February 28th, led by Alderman Wright, asking
for an abatement of £10,000 a week in their assessments.[93] On
March 11th, when Pym and a Committee of the House of
Commons asked for a further supply of men and money from
the City, Penington was forced to tell them that only a third
of the £60,000 had been levied, 'that men of ability did refuse
to lend and they had no means to enforce them', and that the
£30,000 previously lent was not repaid. Nor could they supply
more troops. Two of their regiments were on active service
and the third was at the outguards, 'which they must keep
here (for that there are discontents about the town)'. But the
City radicals, in a petition originally presented to Common
Council by Alderman Fowke, made up for the lack of response
by offering to raise at their own charge three regiments of
horse and seven of foot.[94] Parliament and the municipality
accepted their offer and by an Ordinance of April 12th, a
Sub-Committee, subordinate to the Militia Committee, was
established at Salters' Hall for this purpose.[95]

Now the radicals had an organization of their own, with
an official status in the City. This was a major political achievement. In the previous autumn, when the City radicals had
undertaken to raise volunteers and had set up a Committee
with that energetic citizen, Richard Shute, as Treasurer,[96] it
was not given official status by the City authorities. Encouraged by their success, the radicals turned to propagating their
political and religious policy in Common Council. On March
30, 1643, a group of citizens presented a petition to Common
Council, together with a Remonstrance directed to Parliament.[97] The Remonstrance and petition were the work of the
men who had drawn up the radical petitions of the previous
November and December: Sir David Watkins, Richard Shute
and Randall Mainwaring, Deputy Lord Mayor to Penington.
The contents of the Remonstrance[98] throw considerable light

[93] C.J., ii, p. 984. Mercurius Aulicus, March 7 1643.
[94] J.Co.Co. 40, fol. 55v.
[95] Firth and Rait, op. cit., i, pp. 130-1.
[96] C.C. for A. of M., i, p. 3.
[97] J.Co.Co. 40, fol. 57.
[98] Remonstrans redivivus: or An Accompt of the Remonstrance and Petition, formerly
presented by divers Citizens of London, to the view of many; and since honoured by the late
Conspirators, to be placed under their Title of Extreame ill Designes with the Remonstrance
itselfe. July 25 1643. [Thomason Tracts.]

on the political ideas of the City radicals. By far the greatest part of the document was directed to proving the supremacy of Parliament, and clearly reveals the intimate alliance that existed between the Republicans and the war party of the House of Commons and the City radicals. It made the funda-mental claim that supreme power lay in the people and in Parliament to whom power was delegated. The power of call-ing and dissolving Parliament and of passing Bills was 'but matter of form annexed' to the office of King, and 'not left to his will'; his absence from Parliament, therefore, was no hindrance to the making of laws. It concluded by stating the usual radical demands, that only those who were 'trustworthy' should be given public office, that no conditions with the King should be accepted which would 'involve us and our posteri-ties in perpetual thraldom', and that a national covenant should be drawn up. Randall Mainwaring's support for it suggests very strongly that Penington had also much to do with its preparation. 'Mercurius Aulicus', often surprisingly well-informed on City affairs, informed his readers, that when the petition came before Common Council, 'Penington pressed hard to have it voted and so did others of the Aldermen, who came prepared for the business'. Others in the Court opposed it as strongly, but the radicals must have won the day, be-cause it was committed to four Aldermen, John Towse, John Warner, John Fowke and Thomas Andrewes, who were 'four of the most seditious in the whole pack', according to 'Aulicus,' 'and likely to have had the greatest hand in promoting it'. When Robert Steele, the deputy City Recorder, was asked who drew up the petition, he replied, so 'Aulicus' said, 'it was drawn by the advice of the best lawyers and divines in the City; and that Peter, one of the Amsterdamians, that now rules the roost, and passeth in the number of their best divines, stood at the hall door and earnestly pressed every man as he went in to have a care of that petition'.[99]

No one was in doubt about the Lord Mayor's radicalism, or about the austere and militant way in which he dedicated himself to the cause. Least of all the Royalist press. The Oxford newsletters bore a heavy crop of rumours about him in the war of propaganda that was being fiercely waged while the

[99] *Mercurius Aulicus*, April 2 1643.

two sides cumbersomely prepared themselves for military action. He had begun his mayoralty, it was said, by making a speech against the Book of Common Prayer and had never subsequently allowed it to be read before him.[100] The burning of the Book of Sports and Penington's suggestion, adopted by Parliament, that the Lord Mayor and Aldermen should appoint the preachers at St. Paul's Cross, were denounced fiercely enough by Royalist newswriters. But when facts failed them, they resorted to fiction. Wild and exaggerated stories were spread, such as that he had refused to take action against someone who had declared in public that he hoped shortly to wash his hands in the King's blood.[101] There was mounting resistance to his militancy in the City; when Common Council ordered that Cheapside Cross, with its 'idolatrous' and superstitious figures thereabout set', should be demolished, a fight broke out between a group of citizens and the City officers entrusted with the work.[102] Above all there was the burden of increasing taxes and charges. Even a moderate supporter of Parliament found them a heavy burden. How much more so the Royalist supporters and ballad-mongers, as they showed in their jingle, 'London's Farewell to the Parliament':

> Farewell little Isaac, with hey, with hey,
> Farewell little Isaac, with hoe,
> Thou hast made us all like Asses,
> Part with our Plate, and drink in Glasses,
> Whilst thou growest rich with 2s. Passes,
> With hey trolly, lolly, loe. . . .[103]

The right to pass in and out of London, a security precaution, had now to be bought too—for two shillings from the Lord Mayor.

But not all Penington's schemes as Lord Mayor aroused such widespread antagonism. The great work on which the City government under Penington's lead embarked in the spring of 1643 to fortify the City and suburbs, was not merely a radical policy: it received widespread support from the

---

[100] 'A speech made by Alderman Garway', op. cit., *Harleian Misc.*, v, p. 228.

[101] *Mercurius Aulicus*, January 22 1643.

[102] *V.S.P. 1642-1643*, p. 272. *Cheapside Cross censured and condemned*, 1643.

[103] *Rump: or an exact collection of the choycest poems and songs relating to the late Times*, 1662 [Reprinted 1874], i. p. 94. But worse was said of others. See p. 182.

City government and the citizens. For the moderates and those who wanted a negotiated peace with the crown, it was a way of strengthening the City as an independent force capable of bargaining with either side. It also strengthened the power of the municipality against the less well-organized and sometimes more radical suburban areas. The radicals saw it as a way of strengthening the City against the plots of its own Royalist citizens, while providing a vast military magazine from which the parliamentary army could draw on at its need. The idea of building armed defence posts around the City was first mooted in Common Council in September 1642. In October orders were given to strengthen the portcullis, chains and turnpike gates in case of street fighting in London.[104] The City government lost no time in gaining parliamentary sanction for its general plan of fortification, and when the Royalists were known to be planning a threefold attack on London early in 1643, a comprehensive scheme of fortification was evolved enclosing not only the City and the liberties but the entire outparishes and suburbs. The work aroused tremendous enthusiasm among ordinary citizens. This was their defence against the marauding terrors of Prince Rupert and his cavaliers. The pillaging of Brentford in the previous November was a bitter memory, to be compared by some Puritans with the Catholic atrocities at Magdeburg in the Thirty Years War.

Two distinct fortifications were undertaken in 1642 and 1643 which, when completed, ringed London with a line of trenches dominated by forts placed within sight of one another so as to leave no place unguarded. Open streets leading out into the suburbs were barricaded and armed, and batteries of ordnance were mounted at strategic points. This gigantic work was made possible by unprecedented popular support, ably marshalled, which temporarily united the citizens around one predominant, if limited, rallying cry—the defence of London. Already in October 1642, when the first earthworks had gone up, the Venetian Ambassador had written of the great number of people employed including 'women and little children'.[105] Soon, as the main fortifications arose, the movement took on the widest possible character. Now was the triumph of the primitive organization built up in church and vestry, ward

---

[104] J.Co.Co. 40, fol. 40v.   [105] V.S.P. 1642-1643, p. 192.

and precinct, shop and workplace; the humble collections of
St. Antholin's now bore compound interest. At the order of
Common Council, pulpits were to resound with the call to de-
fend the City. Ministers were to 'stir up the parishioners' to
complete the fortifications with the aid of their children and
servants.[106] The Venetian Ambassador, often amazed in this
Puritan city, marvelled that the work continued even on Sundays.[107] Even more remarkable was the prominent part played
by women. It is not surprising that Penington's wife, the Lady
Mayoress, was there (armed with an entrenching tool, said a
Royalist ballad)[108]—we have already encountered her staunch
Puritanism. But ladies of rank were also present, as well as
fish wives who had marched from Billingsgate in martial order
headed by a symbolic goddess of war.[109] Well might Butler in
his *Hudibras* deplore the women who—

> March'd rank and file with drum and ensign,
> T'entrench the City for defence in.
> Rais'd rampiers with their own soft hands,
> To put the enemy to stands;
> From ladies down to oyster wenches
> Labour'd like pioneers in trenches,
> Fell to their pick-axes and tools,
> And help'd the men to dig like moles.[110]

Some of the paraphernalia of pageantry and military organization were borrowed. Columns with drums beating and flags
flying were sent through the City to recruit more volunteers
until 20,000 persons, it was said, were working without pay,
drawing only their rations.[111] An observer reported that 'the
daily musters and shows of all sorts of Londoners . . . were
wondrous and commendable'. The work was allocated by
whole parishes, and different trades and Livery Companies,
who marched out with 'roaring drums, flying colours and

---

[106] *A Perfect Diurnall of Some Passages in Parliament.* April 29 1643. [Thomason
Tracts.]

[107] *V.S.P. 1642-1643*, p. 256.

[108] 'On the demolishing the forts' in *Rump: or an Exact Collection of the Choycest
Poems and Songs*, op. cit., pp. 245-7.

[109] William Lithgow, *The present Surveigh of London and England's State*, 1643,
reprinted in *Somers Tracts*, op. cit., iv, p. 538.

[110] Samuel Butler, *Hudibras*, ed. by Z. Grey 1774, Part ii, canto ii, lines 805 seq.

[111] *V.S.P. 1642-1643*, p. 273.

girded swords'; over fifty trades were said to have competed in friendly emulation: one day it was 5,000 Feltmakers and Cappers with their families; the next almost the entire Company of Vintners with their wives, servants and wine-porters; on another, all the 2,000 City Porters 'in their white frocks', followed by 4,000 or 5,000 Shoemakers, a like number from St. Giles-in-the-Fields and thereabouts, and the entire inhabitants of St. Clement Dane.[112] In this astonishing manifestation of unity, even the 'clerks and gentlemen' participated as a profession. Those belonging to Parliament, the Inns of Court, and other public offices, were mustered in the Piazza in Covent Garden at seven o'clock in the morning with 'spades, shovels, pickaxes and other necessaries'.[113]

Popular enthusiasm for the fortifications could reach no higher pitch. Whatever the military value of the defences, the successful mobilization of a great mass of the ordinary people proved the power of parliamentary puritan organization and leadership. But the universality of their support should not be exaggerated. The City had been united in one desire—London should not become a battlefield. The achievements of the parliamentarians in harnessing this fear were very great and of marked effect. They had led a popular movement for a limited demand, but this could not hide the growing strength of the royalist minority.

The Venetian Ambassador shrewdly observed that the chief purpose of the fortifications would prove to be that of keeping under control the City's political minorities.[114] The strength of the Royalist minority was not fully demonstrated in the conspiracy led by Edward Waller in May 1643, for his plot was unearthed by Parliament's Committee of Safety before it had time to mature. But the Committee investigating it revealed that some of the wealthiest citizens had been involved, including ex-Common Councilmen Sir George Benion, Robert Alden and Captain Marmaduke Rawden,[115] together with three of

---

[112] *A Perfect Diurnall*, nos. 47, 48, 50, 51.

[113] Broadsheet issued by Clerks and Gentlemen of Parliament, dated June 6 1643. [Thomason Tracts.]

[114] *V.S.P. 1642-1643*, p. 252.

[115] A prominent Common Councilman, Clothworker and member of the Hon. Artillery Company, who was among the largest traders in wine with France. *Life of Marmaduke Rawden*, ed. Robert Davies. Camden Society, 1863. Introduction, *passim*.

the wealthiest men in the City, Sir Edward Carleton,[116] and two of the greatest Customs Farmers, Sir Paul Pindar and Sir Nicholas Crispe. They would undoubtedly have enjoyed the support of other wealthy Aldermen, had not Parliament already placed some of the notorious Royalists under restraint. On May 2nd, the Court of Aldermen discharged Sir Henry Garway and Sir George Whitmore from the Bench since they 'stand committed' by Parliament;[117] Sir Hugh Windham and Sir William Acton were also discharged for neglecting their duties as Aldermen,[118] and so was Sir Thomas Gardiner, the former Recorder, for having fled to the King.[119] Five other Aldermen[120] were still languishing in gaol for refusing to pay their assessments, as well as many other well-established and wealthy citizens and merchants.[121] Two of the Aldermen, John Gayre and William Ashwell, complained bitterly of the rough treatment they suffered from members of the Trained Bands who came to arrest them at the most awkward hours, and asked the Court to be more considerate in future.[122] There was a general feeling that the senior magistrates were being held in little respect, while new men who a year or so ago were far removed from high office now held absolute sway. 'I have no more authority in the City than a Porter, not so much as an Aldermanbury Porter,' Alderman Garway was reported to have said, perhaps fictitiously, though no doubt the words were a faithful expression of his sentiments.[123]

The East India Company, whose leading directors and committee members were nearly all Royalist in sympathy, refused any co-operation with Parliament. It was obstructive when approached by the Committees at Haberdashers' Hall and

[116] David Lloyd in *Memoires of the Lives*, says that he was 'blessed with a vast trade and estate', p. 634.

[117] Rep. 56, fol. 166v.   [118] Ibid. fol. 164v.   [119] Ibid. fols. 166v-167.

[120] Aldermen Henry Pratt, Sir Edward Bromfield, Sir Richard Gurney, William Abell and Sir Hugh Windham. *C.C. for A. of M.*, op. cit., i, pp. 120, 128, 158, 159, 235, 329, 382, 383.

[121] Sir Nicholas Crispe; Marmaduke Rawdon; Lawrence Halstead, a wealthy Merchant Adventurer and pin-making monopolist; Thomas Nevill, Goldsmith and money-lender; Robert Abdy, son of Alderman Abdy; Daniel and Elias Abdy, East India merchants who in the sixteen-thirties had petitioned Laud against the exactions of Sir Abraham Dawes, the Customs Farmer; Sir John Gore; and many others.

[122] Rep. 56, fols. 98-98v, 224v.

[123] *Harleian Miscellany*, op. cit., v, p. 226.

Goldsmiths' Hall to sequester delinquents' stocks,[124] and refused outright to lend its ordnance to the City Militia Committee,[125] though ordered to do so by Parliament. It ignored Parliament's order dismissing Alderman Garway from all his offices in the City and made no preparations for the election of another Governor in his place until the traditional day of election early in July.[126] The Levant Company also made no attempt to depose Garway from the governorship of the Company, and he continued in office until February 1644, when Alderman Penington was elected in his place.[127] As we have seen, the City government showed a certain coolness towards Parliament's incessant demands for money; although in February it had agreed to raise a loan of £60,000, it was careful to demand securities and accompanied its answer by the complaint that the City was too highly rated towards the weekly assessment. Parliament's request for a further loan of £40,000 from the Court of Aldermen in April met[128] with more enthusiasm, no doubt encouraged by Penington and his supporters. But again the collection was tardy; even Alderman Soames, who had refused to be bullied by Charles in May 1640 and had gone to prison, refused to pay in his share of £2,000, in spite of frequent prompting by the Commons.[129]

Alarmed at the way in which Royalist and neutralist opinion was gaining ground in the City, and at the dilatory proceedings of the parliamentary army, the City radicals were spurred into a new frenzy of activity. This activity brought them into conflict not only with Common Council (with whom they had had differences previously) but with the Committee of the Militia, a body that could hardly be accused of wavering in its support of Pym and the middle group of the Commons. The radicals, through their Sub-committee of Volunteers, formalized since April 12 1643 by parliamentary Ordinance, fell into dispute with the Militia Committee over their proposal to establish in the City and suburbs a voluntary collection of the value of one weekly meal from every inhabitant. They

[124] *Court Minutes, E.I.C., 1640-1643*, pp. 329-30.
[125] Ibid. pp. 309, 310.
[126] Ibid. p. 331.
[127] Court Minutes of the Levant Company. S.P. 105/150, fol. 103.
[128] Ibid. p. 29.
[129] *C.J.*, iii, p. 64. *Mercurius Aulicus*, April 10 1643.

intended to devote the proceeds of the levy to raising regiments
of, as they said, 'honest and well-affected persons . . . under
command of known and trusted officers', to be appointed by
themselves. They not only impugned the management of the
war, but claimed powers to levy men to fight on their sole
authority, without reference to the Committee of the Militia.[130]

The radicals were, in fact, about to obtain their own independent military force. The Militia Committee, alive to this
danger, denied that the Sub-Committee had the power to
organize a levy independently or even to levy volunteers on
their sole authority.[131] The dispute was taken to Common
Council, where it was referred to a committee almost entirely
composed of moderates. As one would expect, they came
down heavily on the side of the Militia Committee and suggested that an Ordinance should be presented to Parliament
conferring sole power over all forces raised in the City on the
Militia Committee, subject to Parliament. As a sop to the
Sub-Committee, they suggested that Common Council should
elect seven of their number to sit on the Militia Committee;
in this way, it was hoped to weaken, if not destroy, this centre
of radical activity. When their demands were finally presented
to Parliament in a petition from Common Council presented
by Alderman Adams, a supporter of the peace party, no reference was made to the appointment of 'trusty' officers or to
army reform.[132] It is clear that the moderates and peace
party in the City government had joined forces with the
Militia Committee to defeat the policies of the radicals. It
should also be said, that as far as the City government was
concerned, this was not only a political issue between the
middle group and the radicals. The Sub-Committee wanted
to extend its operation beyond the City to the suburbs. The
City government, even before Charles I's New Incorporation,
had been jealous of any separate organization or jurisdiction
established in the radical suburbs and liberties. It was not impossible that, from some of the poorest and most desperate

---

[130] *A Declaration and Motive of the Persons trusted usually meeting at Salters Hall in
Bread Street, to all well affected persons in the severall Parishes within London, and the
Parts adjacent, for Contributing the value of a Meale Weekly, towards the forming of some
Regiments of Voluntiers, to be payd during these times of Danger.* May 6 1643. [Thomason
Tracts.]

[131] J.Co.Co. 40 fol. 62v.   [132] Ibid. fol. 68. *C.J.*, iii, p. 171.

slum-dwellers, active and organized leaders might recruit a force which would menace the social and political fabric of City government, and perhaps of the State. The municipality, therefore, stood now, as previously, on its traditional policy of excluding rival jurisdictions in these areas: and in the twenty-eight Propositions which it demanded of Parliament in 1644 to strengthen City government, a prominent place was given to its desire to control the militias of the suburban areas within the weekly Bills of Mortality.[133]

The limited character of Common Council's petition, and the subordination of the Sub-Committee for Volunteers to the Militia Committee, gave rise, therefore, to a new move on the part of the radicals. For several months they had been campaigning against the inefficiency and over-cautiousness of Essex and his army. Now they combined a demand for a new and independent Committee of Volunteers with the proposal that it should be commanded by a Commander-in-Chief independent of the Earl of Essex. These were the proposals which were embodied in the suggested 'Committee for the General Rising'. A similar proposal for arousing the whole people had been made in May by the Lord Mayor and 'divers citizens' (but not the municipality, it should be noted), suggesting that every inhabitant in the City should be enrolled for active offensive against the Royalist army, either by personal service or contributions, under the leadership of Members of Parliament, Aldermen and Common Councilmen of the City.[134] On this occasion, the City radicals suggested that the entire population of London should be enrolled on the basis of their trades, and anticipating later developments in the New Model Army, that six or eight 'godly' men should be chosen from each trade (an interesting precursor of the 'agitators') to keep a check on Royalist suspects. Again, early in July, propositions were drawn up by 'divers well-affected persons in the City' offering to finance an additional army to that

[133] Ibid. fols. 108, 115.

[134] *An Humble Proposal of Safety to the Parliament and Citie, In this time of present danger, viz. In case the Parliament should go forth into the Field, as was lately moved by the honourable House of Commons, and as we hope will be speedily and unanimously resolved on* . . . 1643. [Thomason Tracts.] This pamphlet bears a MS. note by Thomason: 'this was presented to the House the day my Lord Mayor and citizens went to oppose the accommodation that the Lords would have made about May 25th'.

of Essex, consisting of 10,000 men, with a separate Commander-in-Chief and with officers who were 'godly men of honest life and conversation'.[135] The suggestion was next heard on July 20th, two days after Alderman Adams had presented Common Council's moderate proposals on the organization of the Militia to Parliament. On that day, 'thousands of well-affected inhabitants of the Cities of London and Westminster and the suburbs', asked the House of Commons in a petition that had been circulating in the City for some days previously, to establish a parliamentary committee for raising the whole population of the City and organizing them into regiments under a new Commander-in-Chief, by authority derived from the Earl of Essex. The Committee suggested by the petitioners was to be composed of some of the most prominent radicals of the House of Commons, including Henry Marten, Dennis Bond, and William Strode, together with the Lord Mayor, Isaac Penington.[136] The petition was said to have been subscribed by 20,000 people and was brought into the House by Lord Brooke's younger son, Fulke Greville, Sir Giles Overbury, Mr. Norbury and John Hat, a Guildhall attorney.[137]

It was clear from the petition that its proposals aimed at rehabilitating a radical committee with its own independent forces. The parliamentary Committee was to have power to appoint its own Commander-in-Chief and all other officers, and to appoint sub-committees 'of such persons as themselves shall approve of, and to put in execution whatsoever shall be necessary for this service; that so the fullness of their Commission may encourage the whole nation as one man (according to the true intent of the late Covenant) with all cheerfulness and vigour to join themselves with us for the speedy ending of this destructive war'.[138] The proposal to set up radical

---

[135] *Instructions and Propositions containing incouragements to all good men to subscribe for the raising of an Army of ten thousand men. . . .* July 8 1643. [Thomason Tracts.]

[136] *C.J.*, iii, p. 176.

[137] Whittaker's Diary, Add. MSS. 31,116, fol. 128.

[138] *The humble Petition of thousands of well-affected Inhabitants of the Cities of London and Westminster and the Suburbes thereof . . .* 1643. [Guildhall Broadsides]. The petition in which these proposals were included had been circulating in the City previously. There is a printed notice in the Thomason Tracts headed: 'All sorts of well-affected persons who desire a speedy end of this destructive war, are entreated to meet at Merchantaylors' Hall tomorrow, being Wednesday the 19th of July 1643 at any hour of the day, from 4 of the clock in the morning till 8 in

sub-committees was a prominent part of their programme, and if it had been carried out, might have formed an interesting parallel with the revolutionary 'sections' established in Paris in the French Revolution in 1792. Some extremists among the citizens differed from the Committee on the 'voluntary' principle, insisting that the forces and money should be raised by compulsion, if their work was to succeed.[139] The proposal for a new Commander-in-Chief was, as we have seen, an attempt to create a rival force to that of Essex, who had for a long time been the subject of radical attack. It seemed that in this respect at least the petition was to have an effect; on July 27th at a meeting organized by the Lord Mayor at Merchant Taylors' Hall, in which Henry Marten took a prominent part, Sir William Waller was voted Commander-in-Chief of all the forces to be raised by the new committee. Two days later, however, they found that the Militia Committee had once more stolen a march on them. Parliament ordered Sir William Waller to be put in command of 'all forces to be raised within the City of London, and all other forces, that are or shall be under the command of the militia of London', and thus ensured that the Committee of the General Rising should not enjoy a separate command from that of the Militia Committee.[140] By appointing Sir William Waller Commander-in-Chief over all the City forces, Parliament skilfully prevented the formation of that independent army for which the radicals were working. This no doubt accounts for the rumours that soon began to spread around the City, that the radicals intended to put their forces under the command of Henry Marten[141] instead of Waller, another example of the close co-operation between the City radicals and the war party in the House of Commons.

Both Parliament and the City government were suspicious

the evening there to hear and subscribe a petition to Parliament, (to which thousands have already subscribed) for raising the whole people of the land as one man, against those Popish blood-thirsty forces raised, to enslave and destroy us, and our posterity.'

[139] 'A declaration of the Honourable Committee of the House of Commons at Merchant-Taylors' Hall, August 3, 1643'. E. Husbands, *A Collection of all the publicke orders, ordinances and declarations of both houses of parliament* . . . 1646, p. 281.

[140] *C.J.*, iii, pp. 187, 281-2.

[141] *Mercurius Aulicus*, September 11 1643.

of a Committee so largely composed of 'fiery spirits' and radicals. The *Parliament Scout*, which in the main voiced the
opinions of the middle group of the House of Commons, had
denounced the General Rising Committee from the start on
the grounds that it was 'not good to adventure all at once'
and that 'trading would wholly cease'.[142] At the end of July,
they were of the opinion that the two City Committees should
be joined.[143] The Committee for the Militia had in any case
forestalled the radicals by securing control over all forces to
be raised in the City by the Ordinance of July 20th. On
August 1st, the Court of Common Council officially denied
the rumours that it had cast aspersions on the Earl of Essex.
It elected a Committee composed both of moderates and
men who were, later, political independents, to visit the Earl
and assure him of their support and loyalty.[144] On August 7th,
the City government, nevertheless, at Penington's instigation
and with Pym's connivance it was said, petitioned the Commons urging them to turn down the 'accommodation' proposals of the Lords.[145] But during the following days, as if to
anticipate the change of fortune and the loss of revolutionary
initiative by the radicals, violent demonstrations by women,
this time demanding peace, took place outside Parliament, to
the encouragement of Royalist hopes. With some embarrassment, and not without bloodshed, they were dispersed by
Waller's troop of horse. After this turn in the radical tide,
the Committee for the General Rising soon faded out from
lack of recruits and lack of compulsive powers; but not before
a final dispute with the Militia Committee. Henry Marten
wanted Sir William Waller to march out with the City forces
against the Royalists; Glynne, the City Recorder, and the
Militia Committee preferred the City forces to stay at home and
defend London.[146] By the middle of September, however, the

---

[142] *The Parliament Scout*, no. 4, July 13-20 1643, p. 30.

[143] Ibid. no. 5.

[144] J.Co.Co. 40, fol. 69.

[145] Both D'Ewes and *Mercurius Aulicus*, August 11 1643, attributed the authorship of this petition to Pym. Whether this was so or not, it was clear that this was
an occasion on which the City radicals worked in alliance with the middle
group and the leaders of the House of Commons. The petition was presented
to the Commons by Alderman Thomas Atkins, a member of the Militia Committee and later a political independent.

[146] J. H. Hexter, op. cit., p. 128.

Committee for the General Rising was ordered by the Commons to pay over its funds to the Committee for Subscriptions at Grocers' Hall,[147] and Henry Marten had been sent to the Tower (ostensibly for insulting the King). The Committee was as good as dead.

City radicalism never again (before the victory of the army in 1647) brought pressure to bear on Parliament and the City government with as much success as during the summer months of 1643. The failure of the Sub-Committee to achieve independent status and the election of Alderman Wollaston as Lord Mayor in the place of Penington removed the main props of the radical party. A Sub-Committee at Salters' Hall, Bread street, was still sitting in 1644, and still organizing radical petitions to Parliament, but the radicals were not able to make it independent of the Militia Committee; nor were they able to secure any foothold in the City government. Their most likely allies were probably to be found on the Militia Committee, but this body, subject to an increasingly moderate Common Council and with its political effectiveness impaired by its increased membership and its absorption in military organization, could not assume again the initiative it had seized in the spring and summer of 1642. The members of this Committee promoted to the offices of Customs and Excise Farmers and collectors of assessments would be likely to oppose at all costs a restitution of the *ancien régime*, for their personal fortunes were involved with those of Parliament; but they were unlikely to be the initiators of social revolution.

*   *   *

Although the parliamentary puritans won control of the municipality in January 1642, this achievement of political organization, astonishing though it was, was not evidence of a unity of ideas or policies. After the outbreak of hostilities, proposals for prosecuting the war and furthering constitutional or religious reform, immediately divided them into groups which, though they might unite on a limited programme, were always liable to splinter into a welter of small parties. There was a large Royalist minority in the City who continued to exercise influence on the Bench until May 1643 and drew

[147] *C.J.*, iii, pp. 240, 241.

support from the wealthy oligarchies who controlled the major
Livery Companies and the trading companies. The City
government as a whole inclined towards moderate policies,
but could when necessary be gingered into support of Pym
and the middle group by members of the Militia Committee.
More vociferous than either was the small but highly organized
group of radicals, drawing support from one or two highly
placed individuals on the Militia Committee, some City clergymen, and more humble followers in the City and the suburbs.
When it was a matter of the defence of London, these groups
could still unite to create again the overwhelming display of
strength that had brought them victory in 1642. But when
constructive proposals were needed on ways of fighting the
war, unity disappeared, and an organized minority, like the
radicals, backed by some influential supporters, including
Penington, could seize the initiative. In the event, political
isolation quickly caused their support to dwindle. From October 1643, when Penington gave up the mayoralty to be succeeded by the moderate Sir John Wollaston, there was a shift
in power in the City government. The radicals, however,
could not be dismissed so easily; a new position of strength
was created in the City in July 1643 by Penington's assumption of the Lieutenantship of the Tower, and he held this
powerful office until 1645, when he surrendered it under the
terms of the Self-denying Ordinance.[148] But in the City government, the moderates slowly consolidated their strength. One
feature of this rightward movement was the attempt to revive
the aldermanic veto over Common Council early in 1645, a
measure which was supported by all the Aldermen except
five,[149] and on this occasion, it appears, even by Alderman
Penington. The proposal unleashed a war of pamphlets, and
an irreconcilable dispute between the Court of Aldermen and
Common Council.[150] The matter was therefore referred to

[148] *C.J.*, iv, p. 154. The *D.N.B.* antedates his appointment by a year.

[149] Aldermen John Warner, Thomas Andrewes, James Bunce, Samuel Warner
and William Berkeley. Rep. 57, fol. 45v.

[150] J.Co.Co. 40, fols. 121v, 123, John Bellamy, *A Plea for the Commonalty of
London*, 1645, *passim*. Anon., *Bellamius Enervatus; or, A Full Answer to a Book entitled
A Plea for the Commonalty of London . . . 2 May 1645*. John Bellamy, *Lysimachus
enervatus, Bellamius reparatus: Or, a reply to a Book, intitled, full answer to a plea for the
commonalty of London: . . . 1645*. [Thomason Tracts.] See p. 253 n. above.

Parliament and conveniently shelved for the time. Meanwhile, political presbyterianism strengthened by the failure of the radicals and by the Militia Committee's rejection of radical policies, had captured the City government, and the defeat of the radicals left the way clear for the alliance between political presbyterians and Royalists in the City which almost succeeded in bringing back the King in the spring of 1647.

Conclusion

OUR evidence has shown that the municipality of London was more sympathetic to the crown than to Parliament in the national crisis of 1641. Between 1625 and 1638, the City government, far from leading the opposition to Charles I, was prepared to raise loans if good securities could be obtained, as in 1627; to negotiate with the crown on matters in dispute; and even, at the beginning of the crisis of the Scottish war, when popular discontent was at its height, to make a formal agreement with the King over its disputes, as signified by the charter of 1638. Even in the political and financial crisis of 1639 and 1640, when the municipality would not risk raising money for the crown, some of the Aldermen were found willing to lend either directly or indirectly as Undersharers of the Customs Farmers.

The Court of Common Council, often referred to by modern historians as a more democratic body than the Court of Aldermen, the 'Commons' of the City, showed no consistent signs of opposition to the Aldermen or to the crown until 1639, when it drew up a petition of grievances to be presented to the King; even then, the aldermanic veto over its proceedings and the sympathies of leading Common Councilmen prevented the petition from being passed. Nor in 1640 or in 1641 did the Court of Common Council as a body show any sign of support for Pym and the parliamentary opposition. None of the citizens' petitions to Parliament gained the authorization of the municipality. The committees of Common Council were composed of at least as many men who were later Royalists as parliamentarians; thus Common Council agreed to support the aldermanic proposal to banquet the King in 1641, even though one of their members, Captain John Venn, did his best to dissuade them.

The aldermanic Bench appears to have been predisposed to sympathize with Charles I from the time of the calling of the Long Parliament. Only five of the twenty-six Aldermen who held office in September 1640 were later to become active parliamentarians. A small group were neutralist or lukewarm sympathizers of Parliament, but the majority of the Aldermen were too bound to the crown through their activities as City magistrates or as office-holders in the City or in the State to throw in their lot with Parliament. Ironically, the crown was unable to derive advantage in the crisis of 1641 and 1642 from its highly placed sympathizers in the City. The financial insolvency of the City Chamber, the political risks involved in financing the King, and above all, Parliament's speed in attacking the fortunes of the Customs Farmers and monopolists who had helped to finance Charles during 'the tyranny', greatly diminished the possibility of a concerted attempt in the City to free Charles of Parliament. The capture by the parliamentary puritans of the City government and the Trained Bands, so giving Parliament its earliest soldiers, followed by the King's early departure from Whitehall in January 1642, forestalled a successful counter-revolution in London.

From the beginning of the Long Parliament in November 1640, the relations of the City government with Parliament were far from cordial. The House of Commons did not devote as much attention to the petitions of the municipality, as it did to those of the citizens, even though the citizens' petitions should never have been presented to Parliament without the authorization of the municipality. Not only did the Commons rebuke the Lord Mayor and Aldermen for their slowness in collecting loans, but they led the attack on the fortunes and reputations of many Aldermen and leading Common Councilmen for their part in carrying out the policies of Charles's government. Parliament countenanced the demonstrations of the parliamentary puritans in the City and supported their constitutional claims in the disputed shrievalty elections in August 1641. It therefore not only increased the turbulence in the City and placed heavier administrative burdens on the City magistrates, but strengthened the popular party and helped them to challenge successfully the leaders of the municipality early in 1642. When the parliamentary puritans took power in the City, Parliament gave official authorization to the constitutional changes which they had brought about and impeached the Lord Mayor and Recorder, so confirming in authority their supporters among the citizens.

It is of absorbing interest to see how the City parliamentary puritans were organized before the existence of political parties and party organization in our modern sense. But although their movement anticipated many later forms of political struggle, it would be a mistake to see it as part of a clearly worked-out political programme or platform of the type to which we are accustomed. Indeed, the diversity of the parliamentary puritans and the tactical alliance which they formed for limited ends was at once their strength and their weakness. Their strength because of the tremendous weight of opinion which they represented. Their weakness because, having won power, this revolutionary alliance would eventually fall asunder without a solid programme which united all its constituents. The diversity of their origins, the disparities in status, and the wide variety of political and religious thought, made their unity remarkable enough, and for a time all was subordinated to the winning of power. A sprinkling of Puritan lords and sons of the nobility, sometimes expressing a predilection for aristocratic government,[1] headed the movement and rubbed shoulders with substantial middle-rank merchants of the trading companies, often the victims of oligarchic privilege and financial extortion. Joining them came humbler shopkeepers and traders with their apprentices: of inferior social position, the butt of Royalist writers, many of them would soon display their talents as soldiers, organizers, and business men in the upheavals of the Civil War. Below the respectable classes, the anonymous labouring poor, swayed violently, as among the seamen, by religious, political or economic pressures, were ready to lend a hand in their own fashion. In a position apart were the many divines and preachers, inspiring the alliance with a fervent faith and yet, in the many-sided nature of their Puritanism, reflecting the different tendencies within their congregations. In other less exalted ways, a common activity helped to unite the movement. The Artillery Garden with its

---

[1] See the proposals for government that Lords Saye and Brooke and other 'persons of quality' placed before the government of Massachusetts in 1635 as a condition of their emigrating to the colony. Their demand that their heirs should inherit the title and position of 'gentlemen' was rejected by the leaders of the colony who opposed 'hereditary power' as a matter of principle. Their proposals and the answers to them also revealed religious differences: the colonists asserting that civil rights could only be obtained through membership of the Church, whereas the Puritan lords favoured a property qualification. R. E. L. Strider, *Robert Greville Lord Brooke*, Cambridge, Mass., 1958, pp. 22-25.

'manly' and martial exercises, and, perhaps not far off in kind, the crowded Tavern Clubs, loud with the din of drinking and debate, were favourite haunts of the more proselytizing of the parliamentary puritans. Ardent propagandist and pleasure-seeking citizen alike—few had the kill-joy qualities given to all the Puritans by later legend.

The alliance of the parliamentary puritans, loosely knit and without formal ties, was a movement of great *élan*. It enjoyed the overwhelming support of the middle and lower ranks of the London citizens, men by no means to be dismissed as a mere 'rabble' or 'mob': although there was a large element of spontaneous protest and social revolt, it was not the upsurge of a desperate population. Its day to day tactics (but not its long-term strategy) bore all the signs of careful planning and resolute leadership, and the stages of the campaign followed with powerful and logical precision: the timing and organiza-tion of the petitions, the capture of the Artillery Company and the Trained Bands, the shift in control in Common Council, and the setting up of the Militia Committee with new and, in the circumstances, revolutionary powers. All these events de-monstrated the existence of able directing forces. The revolu-tion never really got out of hand. Even in the tumultuous days of Christmas 1641, Captain Venn was able to restrain the rioters from any violent excesses. The French Ambassador, M. La Ferté Imbaut, an intelligent and keen observer of these events, remarked on the discipline and orderliness of the re-spectable shopkeepers and merchants who barricaded the streets in the 'revolutionary' days at the end of December, and was astonished at the lack of bloodshed: blood would certainly have flowed, he said, had similar events occurred in Paris. One contemporary thought that the organization of the parlia-mentary puritans was so developed that even the most humble ward and parish offices were contested. In the minutely di-vided parishes of the City, where even a populous ward like St. Stephen's, Coleman street, had only 400 householders,[2] canvassing support either for elections or petitions would have presented no difficulties among neighbours and acquaintances. Greater organization would have been required to win sub-urban support, though here social problems and trade depression

[2] J.Co.Co. 40, fol. 45v.

combined to provide fertile ground for popular agitation. Leaders were provided for the movement in the persons of Alderman Penington and Captain Venn who by their connexions in Parliament and with the City Puritans, put themselves at the head of the parliamentary puritan party. By means of the circulating petitions and popular demonstrations, they helped to mobilize the citizens and suburban dwellers into a highly effective campaign. If Penington and Venn acted as the parliamentary wing of the party and as organizers of support in the City, its clerical wing must also be remembered. Men like Edmund Calamy and Cornelius Burges were in many ways the counterparts of their lay brethren, actively campaigning for the parliamentary puritan cause in pulpit and vestry.

The City Members of Parliament not only organized the citizens, but brought great pressure to bear on the House of Commons to support the policy of Pym and the political opposition. Alderman Penington and Captain Venn went further. They were radicals who as early as the Root and Branch debates of 1641 and the financial negotiations with the City government, became a liability to Pym and the opposition by their extreme views which alienated the moderates. The radicalism of Penington and Venn, and with them a significant group of citizens, became an even more obvious embarrassment to Pym in 1643 when they worked in close conjunction with the war party of the Commons led by Henry Marten. Their radicalism did not only divide the Commons: it also divided the municipality and helped to throw the moderates into the arms of the peace party and later the political presbyterians.

Apart from the municipality's support for Parliament in 1642, what changes of policy, it will be asked, occurred as the result of the constitutional changes in the City? The policies of the 'new men' who took office in the City in 1642 did not initiate startlingly new trends in municipal policy. Even the constitutional changes of the early months of 1642 remained in some degree nebulous, since those who planned them were as much concerned to remove Royalist office-holders and facilitate the passage of measures designed to support Parliament's preparations for war, as to create revolutionary changes in the City's constitutional machinery. The suspension of the aldermanic veto over the proceedings of Common Council, the most important single constitutional development of 1642 in the City, since it gave much greater freedom to the populous assembly of Common Council, was not formalized in a City Ordinance, and therefore, in a different situation in 1645, could be attacked with some degree of success. It was not until 1649 that the City passed ordinances limiting the powers of the Lord Mayor and the aldermanic Bench. In the same way, no fundamental reform of the City Chamber was undertaken until 1649, or proposals made to throw open elections in Common Hall to the commonalty, in place of the Livery Companies. Nevertheless, many of these later developments were rehearsed in 1642 and 1643 in the enlarging of the activities of Common Council and Common Hall, and the diminishing of the powers of the Lord Mayor and Aldermen.

The administrative history of London in these years suggests that the changes occurring in the City government in 1642 were far from revolutionary in their effect on the internal development of the municipality. In 1644, the City government placed before Parliament twenty-eight Propositions,[3] suggesting ways of strengthening its government and its administrative powers, and the proposals bear a very close relation to the articles, 'Things desired', drawn up for the King's approval in 1637. Both documents uphold their claims to the same traditional chartered privileges and ancient feudal rights, the Propositions of 1644 being no more predisposed to allow unfettered commercial dealings in the City than the earlier proposals. The City magistrates before 1640 and after 1642 had similar views on the governmental problem of the suburbs and liberties. Neither group of magistrates wished to see unfettered industrial development in the suburbs, yet they did not want to interfere too much in the administrative problems of these areas or undertake the burden of enforcing apprenticeship regulations there too rigidly. Both groups faintly recognized the grave lack of policing in the suburbs and both, inevitably at that time, sought *ad hoc* and inadequate remedies rather than a far-reaching cure. Their failure, although shown up in the political turmoil of 1641, did not become disastrous until 1647 in the contest between Parliament and the Army for the control of London.

[3] J.Co.Co. 40, fols. 108 seq.

But the changes in the personnel of City government were significant in the history of the municipality in ways perhaps less immediately apparent. The 'new men' who came to power in 1642 differed, as we have seen, in some respects from those who had held office previously. On the whole, they were neither Customs Farmers, patentees nor directors of the chartered trading companies. They appear to have represented a combination of interests in the City. There were a few very wealthy merchants, like Alderman Sir John Wollaston, who foresaw that the parliamentary era might be at least as lucrative to the merchant as the reign of Charles I had been, and who managed to consolidate and increase their fortunes. There were cynical fortune hunters, of little religion and less principle, like Alderman John Fowke, who saw in Parliament opportunities of feathering their own nests. But there were other more significant groups. There were a few merchant-manufacturers among the leading parliamentary puritans of the City. Their leader, Alderman Penington, ran a brewery (already a highly capitalized industry employing a large number of workers); Matthew Cradock was, besides his other trading interests, active in shipbuilding, also an industry employing much capital; Samuel Vassall, an exporter of new draperies, was closely concerned with the interests of merchant-manufacturers. But it is not the interests of manufacturers or industrialists which find obvious expression in national policy after 1642. The most significant group to be found among the 'new men' were the middle rank merchants, important traders but not directors of the chartered companies, like Richard Chambers, Samuel Vassall and John Langham, who objected to the excessive influence exercised by the directorates of the companies and the heavy taxation imposed by the crown. A more radical wing were those merchants, like Maurice Thompson and Thomas Andrewes,[4] who in the sixteen-forties were interlopers in the trade of the chartered companies and who desired more extensive changes in national commercial policy and in company organization.

The extent to which these men stood for a policy of economic

---

[4] Andrewes, however, gave up his interloping activities after 1650 when he became Lord Mayor, and he was subsequently made Governor of the East India Company. See Appendix II, p. 310-11.

reform can be discovered from a pamphlet of Lewes Roberts, one of the general committee of the East India Company and a Captain of the Honourable Artillery Company. Roberts published in 1641 and dedicated to the House of Commons his work entitled *The Treasure of Traffike, or A Discourse of forraign Trade*. The main points made by the author can be summed up as the demand for the reduction of customs duties and less interference from the crown in the affairs of the chartered companies. In particular, he suggested that all customs on re-exports should be abolished, that the privileges of the trading companies should be firmly upheld and that a merchants' council should be established to advise the crown on all matters in which commerce was concerned. The merchant-manufacturer was slightly accommodated in that it was stated that protection for home manufacturers should be encouraged as long as the exporter and importer were compensated by the reduction of customs. It is plain, however, that these were not primarily the views of industrialists or traders outside the chartered trading companies. They represent the standpoint of City merchants of the middle rank, the men in fact who as parliamentary taxation increased and the years of war dislocated trade, soon showed apathy and eventual hostility to the parliamentary cause. By that time, some of them were too deeply committed to abandon Parliament, while other merchants who held office in the City (amongst whom were some notable interlopers such as Maurice Thompson and Thomas Andrewes) stayed on and played their part in the events of 1649. But it must be said that the contribution of these middle-rank merchants in advancing commerce was by no means meagre; it was the lesser merchants of the trading companies and the interlopers who besides attacking the monopolistic structure of the companies, were pioneers in search of new markets abroad and cheaper products.

But although these middle-rank merchants of the chartered companies wished to exercise greater control over State policy in economic affairs, and therefore at some stage found themselves opposed to Charles I's government, they did not want changes in the commercial world or in the City government that would threaten their own highly privileged position. The clamour of the outports and the interlopers, and the radicalism of some of the citizens and the suburbs, quickly drove them to defend their own highly privileged status in the commercial world and in the government of London. The conservatism of these merchants when faced with the growth of radical policies became speedily apparent in the development of political presbyterianism in the City after 1643. This attitude may help to explain why reluctance to oppose Charles' government before 1640 was not confined only to the Customs Farmers and holders of monopoly patents in the City, but affected, as we have seen, a wider circle in the chartered trading companies, as reflected in some of the larger Livery Companies and in a powerful group in Common Council. The subsequent political standpoint of the leading groups in the chartered trading companies strengthens the thesis of this work (although it cannot, of course, be said to confirm it) that their sympathies in the crisis of 1641 and 1642 lay primarily with the crown and that the eventual alignment of London with Parliament was the result of *force majeure*, that is to say, of the seizing of power in the City by the parliamentary puritans.

The Aldermen, October 1640–December 1641

SOME biographical information about the Aldermen who held office between October 1640 and December 1641, mainly relating to their political sympathies and the offices which they held.[1]

* indicates the subject of a *D.N.B.* article.

*ABBOT, Sir Morris (1565-1642). Alderman of Bridge Without from 1626 to 1631, and of Coleman street from 1631 to 1642, Abbot came of an influential family with ecclesiastical, commercial, and gentry connexions. He was the son of a City Clothworker and the son-in-law of the wealthy Alderman Bartholomew Barnes. His brother George was Archbishop of Canterbury, and another brother, Robert, was Bishop of Salisbury.[2] His trading connexions were ubiquitous: he was free of the Turkey, Italian, French, Spanish, and Muscovy Companies.[3] In at least four Companies, he had held some of the highest positions. An Incorporator of the East India Company, he was Deputy Governor from 1615 to 1624, and Governor from 1624 to 1637; he was an Incorporator and Director of the North-West Passage Company in 1612, Treasurer of the Levant Company from 1614 to 1616 and then, one of the Court of Assistants to 1624. He was an opponent of the Sandys group in the Virginia Company and was therefore proposed for the post of Treasurer by the crown in 1620 and 1622 in opposition to the ruling party. In 1624, he was appointed one of the royal Council set up to discuss the future of Virginia.

[1] I have excluded the following six Aldermen who were elected (in some instances not sworn) between 1640 and 1641 but chose to fine after a very brief interval rather than hold office: George Benson, Robert Hudson, Peter Blore, Thomas Lawley, Isaac Jones, and Thomas Keightley. Beaven, op. cit., ii, p. 65. These short accounts are not intended as exhaustive biographies, but as brief summaries of the basic information relating to the position of these men in City government and mercantile circles, and to their attitude to the court and Parliament. I have therefore included material from such biographies as are given in the *D.N.B.* only where it is relevant to their status in the City and to their political sympathies. Some of the *D.N.B.* articles contain numerous errors. These have been corrected by A. B. Beaven in *The Aldermen of the City of London*, 1908, 2 vols., which remains the standard work on the City offices held by the Aldermen. For the sake of completeness and a logical narrative, I have included briefly here information about the Aldermen which is given elsewhere in the present work.

[2] *The Genesis of the U.S.*, p. 811.

[3] T. Heywood, *Porta Pietatis, or the Port or Harbour of Piety*, 1638, *passim*.

Abbot sat as M.P. for Hull from 1620 to 1622 and in 1624 and 1625, and for the City of London in 1626, but he is not recorded as having played any part in the controversial discussions of those Parliaments. He was one of the Farmers of the Great Customs from 1621 to 1627, and of the Petty Farms until 1632.[4] For his services to the crown in helping to raise a loan from the City, he received the first knighthood granted by Charles.[5] Nevertheless, in 1628, he was named amongst those merchants who refused to pay the increased imposition on currants. It has been suggested that this was a consequence of his exclusion from the main Customs Farm by Sir Paul Pindar and his associates.[6] A more likely explanation can be found in the fact that Abbot conducted considerable trade with the Levant and was therefore particularly affected by the new imposition.[7] In December 1638, when he was Lord Mayor, he and his son Robert were made collectors of impositions on lawns, cambrics and silks at the Port of London.[8]

As Governor of the East India Company, Abbot came in for the full blast of unpopularity from the opposition party in the Company, led by the lesser City merchants and supported by Lord Saye and Sele, Lord Brooke, and the Earl of Warwick, who were fighting to limit the power of the Directorate. Some of the leaders of this opposition later became leaders of the parliamentary cause. Abbot was accused of refusing the ballot-box for voting, of allowing committees to take exorbitant brokerage, and of attempting to engross the whole trade into the hands of a few.[9] Examples were produced in the Courts of the Company to show that committees were buying up imported wares much below their real value. In 1628, the opposition party petitioned the Privy Council with a statement of their grievances, only to be rebuffed. The crown staunchly supported Abbot and the Directors, and wrote to the Company emphasizing its displeasure and asking for the names and objects of the opposition party.[10] By 1635, Abbot was being attacked so fiercely by his opponents that he and the other Directors evolved a plan to falsify the Company's accounts rather than reveal the extent of their liabilities to the General Court.[11] Although

[4] Dietz, op. cit., p. 348.   [5] *The Letters of John Chamberlain*, ii, p. 612.

[6] Abbot was still one of the Petty Farmers, and it is not therefore likely that he would have connived at the refusal of Parliament to pass the Tonnage and Poundage Act, as Dietz suggests. Dietz, op. cit., pp. 333 seq.

[7] Ledger of the Levant Company, vol. 1627-35. S.P. 105, 158.

[8] Patent Roll, c.66.2824. S.P.Dom. 16/404/35.

[9] *C.S.P. East Indies, 1625-1629*, pp. 522 seq., pp. 506, 635; *vol. 1630-1634*, pp. 264-266.

[10] Ibid. *vol. 1630-1634*, p. 298.   [11] Ibid. *vol. 1635-1639*, pp. 62 seq.

the crown supported Abbot and the other Directors against the opposition, this did not prevent Charles from damaging the interests of the Company by raising the Book of Rates on luxury imports and licensing the rival Association of Sir William Courteen.

Abbot resigned the governorship of the Company in 1637 and was elected Lord Mayor in the following year, when he was also elected Master of the Drapers' Company for the second time. Although as Lord Mayor he was unable to persuade the City to lend to the King, he proved more successful over the matter of Ship Money. When the Aldermen refused to hire a ship as they had previously done, 'only because they would not engage the Chamber of London in the charge', Abbot hired the ship himself, and assessed the cost on the twelve Livery Companies on his own security.[12] He was active in collecting Ship Money in the City, not sparing to send the citizens to Newgate if they refused.[13] He was also active in keeping order at a time when the lawlessness of the citizens was becoming a serious problem. Secretary Windebank congratulated him on his vigilance in foiling John Lilburne's seditious activities, and wrote to Charles that the Lord Mayor had taken 'great pains and done a very considerable service in preventing such a mischief' and that 'my Lords thought fit to take notice of it to himself and to his brethren'.[14] Despite this, Abbot was independent enough to join with fourteen other Aldermen in refusing to lend to the crown in June 1639,[15] and although this may well have been due to the lack of security, he appears in unusual company as a member of the Puritan vestry of St. Stephen's, Coleman street, and even of the vestry meeting which elected the Puritan leader, John Davenport, as vicar in 1624.[16]

Abbot retired from political life after his mayoralty. He attended the Court of Aldermen in June 1640 for the last time and he may have surrendered his lease of the customs, since he was not amongst the list of Customs Farmers who were fined as delinquents by the House of Commons. Although he took no part in political affairs in 1641, his fortunes were affected by the general instability of trade, for his son Edward went bankrupt.[17] The Alderman died early in December 1642, leaving his entire personal estate to his son-in-law, Thomas Marshe.[18] Advanced in years in 1641, he was unlikely to have been a partisan in the political conflict, but he might well have been prejudiced in favour of the King, in view of his earlier opposition as a crown nominee to the Sandys group and his struggle in the East India Company, much of it conducted on

[12] S.P.Dom. 16/417/110.   [13] C.S.P. ii, p. 53.   [14] Ibid.
[15] See Chapter III, p. 97.   [16] Letters of John Davenport, p. 21.
[17] H.M.C. Fourth Report, Part I, House of Lords MSS., p. 73.   [18] P.C.C. Rivers 5.

a bitter personal level with the Puritan Lords Saye and Sele, Brooke, and the Earl of Warwick.

ABDY, Anthony (d. 1640). A close colleague of Sir Morris Abbot, Abdy had direct dealings with the crown in many capacities. Descended from a small landowning family of Yorkshire, he was the third son of Robert, a citizen and Merchant Taylor of London, and he married into the aldermanic family of the Cambells.[19] He held the office of Sheriff in 1630-1 and was Master of the Clothworkers' Company in 1632. He had previously held important commercial offices in the City; with Abbot he was one of the opponents of the Sandys group in the Virginia Company and he was a member of the Royal Commission which finally terminated the Joint Stock Company in 1624. Even earlier, he had been a member of the Court of Assistants of the Levant Company in 1614 and between 1616 and 1623, and Deputy-Governor of the Company from 1627 to 1629; in this position he tried to prevent the General Court from presenting a petition to Parliament against the increased imposition on currants, suggesting instead further private negotiations with the crown.[20] His proposal was rejected, and his replacement as Deputy-Governor in 1629 may have been due to the unpopularity he incurred as a result of making it. At this time, he conducted considerable trade with the Levant, although he was not amongst the greatest traders.[21]

His most important commercial connexions were probably with the East India Company. He served as a 'committee' from 1619 to 1640 and exercised very great influence. He was a firm supporter of Sir Morris Abbot and Sir Christopher Clitherow as Governors of the Company in their struggle with the opposition. Abdy was, indeed, one of the men who had held official position for many years in succession, a practice against which the opposition was striving.[22] He was frequently sent with the Governor and Deputy to remonstrate with the crown over the Company's grievances. In August 1640, he supported Lord Cottington's proposal to buy up £60,000 worth of pepper as a method of raising a royal loan, and he agreed to buy £3,000 of the total himself.[23] He had also served the crown on commissions and was one of the Underwriters of the Customs Farmers at the time when they were raising royal loans in 1639 and 1640.[24]

[19] Rev. J. Hunter, *History of South Yorkshire*, 1831, ii, p. 75.
[20] Court Book of the Levant Company, vol. 1617-31, fol. 194v.
[21] Ledger of the Levant Company, 1627-1635, S.P. 105:158.
[22] *C.S.P. East Indies, 1630-1634*, pp. 264-6.
[23] Ibid. *vol. 1640-1643*, p. 88.   [24] Stowe MSS. 326, fol. 108.

A copy of a letter which was purported to have been written by Abdy to a Scottish nobleman in 1639, expresses his view that the Scottish 'rebels' were not likely to triumph.[25] This view accords well with what is known of the Alderman's outlook. His death on September 11 1640 came too soon to prove his loyalty to the King, but Windebank, on hearing the news, wrote in dismay to Charles lamenting the passing of 'a great servant to his Majesty'.[26] Abdy's descendants in the eighteenth century were so Tory that their name was adopted in Essex as an election cry.[27] His eldest son, Thomas, was knighted and created a baronet within a year of his father's death, and two other sons later received baronetcies.[28]

* ABELL, William (fl. 1614-52). The most notorious of the Aldermen who held office under Charles I was William Abell, the wine monopolist. The spate of pamphlets which appeared in 1641 held him up to ridicule and abuse, and said that he came of humble origin, had enjoyed a meteoric rise in the world, and had acquired the Ship Tavern in Fish street and a fortune in the region of £10,000.[29] The records of the Vintners' Company, however, show him to have been of sufficient standing in the Company to be elected to the Livery in 1614 and Assistant in 1628.[30] He rose to honour in the City, being Alderman's deputy for Queenhithe Ward in 1634,[31] Sheriff in the summer of 1636, and Warden in 1637-8. During the course of his year as Sheriff, he assisted the Judges of the Court of High Commission by helping to execute the sentence against Henry Burton. Abell forcibly entered Burton's house with great violence and carried him off to prison.[32] His part in this episode was mentioned in the Committee of Grievances. Unpopular as his treatment of Burton had made him amongst some Londoners, his conduct of the wine monopoly made him universally execrated.[33] The wine monopoly was taken up by Abell with the connivance of

25 Rawlinson MSS. D.11, fol. 3v.

26 C.S.P., ii, p. 116.

27 Defoe in *New Discovery of an Old Intreague* refers to an election cry of 'Abdy, Harvey', which has been taken to refer to the political activities of these two Essex Tory families. See *Notes and Queries*, vol. 197, pp. 232, 305, 328. P. Morant, *History of Essex*, i, pp. 166-7.

28 *Complete Baronetage*, ed. G.E.C., 1902, Exeter, ii, p. 98.

29 *An Exact Legendary, compendiously containing the whole life of Alderman Abel, the main Projector and Patentee for the raising of wines.* 1641. [Thomason Tracts.]

30 Court Book of the Vintners' Company, vol. 1610-29, fol. 450. vol. 1638-58, fol. 1.

31 *The Visitation of London, 1633-1635*, op. cit., i, p. 2.

32 Rushworth, op. cit., iii, p. 301.

33 *An Exact Legendary*, op. cit.

the Marquis of Hamilton[34] and, through an intermediary, Richard Kilvert, a Proctor in the Prerogative Court of Canterbury.[35] This alliance of a Laudian ecclesiastical laywer, a courtier, and an Alderman who was a monopolist presented City wits and popular pamphleteers with an unholy trinity whose potentialities they were quick to exploit.[36] Many parables were exchanged including one on Cain and Abel. On the threat of a second Star Chamber prosecution, Kilvert suggested to the Wardens and Assistants of the Vintners' Company that in return for permission to dress meat and sell beer they should pay an annual rent to the crown of £30,000 to be raised by a tax of 40s. on every tun of wine.[37] Abell and the officers of the Company after some opposition from the 'generality of the retailers' to the obligation that was also involved of buying fixed quantities of wine from the Spanish and French merchants,[38] managed to secure the Company's authority for their project. The severity with which the contractors of the patent exercised their monopolistic powers made them hated by vintners all over the country. Recalcitrants who refused to obey the monopoly found themselves rebuked by the Privy Council, while Abell as an officer of the Vintners' Company used his powers to remove licences from those who refused their payments.[39]

When the Short Parliament met, complaints against Abell came in thick and fast, and it was rumoured that fearing action against him, he had made over his estate to 'feoffees in trust, to preserve it to his posterity'.[40] He was saved for a while by Parliament's sudden dissolution. Opposition to his patent, however, culminated in November 1640, when the Long Parliament arraigned him as a delinquent. So hateful had he become in the City that every bookshop carried some pamphlet or broadside in which he was held up to contempt. On November 11 1640, he was ordered to appear before the Committee of Grievances. On November 27th,

[34] Doquet Book, Signet Office, vol. 6811 (11). The payment of £8,000 by the Farmers to the Marquis Hamilton was deducted by the crown out of their rent.

[35] S. R. Gardiner says of Kilvert that he was the 'wretch who had been the main agent in the ruin' of Bishop Williams. *History*, VIII, p. 287.

[36] For instance, a pamphlet entitled *Reader, Here you'll plainly see Judgement perverted by these three: A Priest, A Judge, A Patentee*. 1641. [Thomason Tracts.]

[37] Patent Roll, c.66.2813. Court Book, Vintners' Company, vol. 1629-38, fol. 143. Bankes Papers 52/12. S.P.Dom. 16/472/63.

[38] Court Book, Vintners' Company, vol. 1629-38, fols. 157, 159. This was the only point on which the Company opposed the patent as far as can be seen from its records, though they were not prepared to invest £1,000 of the Company's funds in the Farm. Ibid. fol. 173.

[39] S.P.Dom. 16/420/24, 80, 174, 175. S.P.Dom. 16/421/5, 40, 41, 82. S.P.Dom. 16/422/97. S.P.Dom. 16/414/159.

[40] Add. MSS. 11,045, fols. 105-105v.

a petition was presented to the Commons by some of the Vintners' Company in which he was accused of making them take an oath not to petition or 'to complain elsewhere, till they had first complained in their own Hall'.[41] On January 19th, Abell, who had already been taken into custody, was refused bail. The Commons declared the wine patent illegal on May 26th and named Abell and Kilvert as the principal projectors. During the debate Penington spoke 'somewhat in mitigation' of Abell and 'shewed that Kilvert was the principal'.[42] From the evidence, Kilvert does indeed appear as the chief promoter of the scheme, although the main punishment fell upon Abell. He was ultimately bailed on September 1 1641, and in the following April bought his pardon on payment of £2,000.[43] He was discharged from the aldermanic Bench on June 7 1642 because of his long absence and the neglect of his duty of which his '. . . Ward hath much complained . . .' and the charge of delinquency levied against him by Parliament.[44] From 1644 to 1645 he was taken into custody for neglecting to pay his assessments,[45] and again in 1652 for 'uttering dangerous words' against the Commonwealth.[46]

ACTON, Sir William, Bart. (1593-1651). Acton was born on September 7 1593, the son of Richard, a Mercer. He was apprenticed to Thomas Henshawe of Cheapside, and soon became a prominent member of the Merchant Taylors' Company. He was elected Alderman of Aldersgate Ward on February 12 1628 and Sheriff in the following summer. It was as City Sheriff that he first became an ally of the court. He was imprisoned in 1629 on the order of the House of Commons for his refusal to grant a *replevin* to the merchants who had been detained by the crown for their refusal to pay customs duties.[47] Charles rewarded him with the first baronetcy conferred on a City dignitary during his reign.[48] In 1639-40, he was an Undersharer of the Customs and lent large sums to the King.[49] So unpopular was he that the citizens refused to elect him Lord Mayor in spite of the customary rules of precedency. His defeat was considered a repulse for the royal cause in the City and an embarrassment to his colleagues in his Livery

---

[41] *C.J.*, ii, p. 37. Court Book, Vintners' Company, vol. 1638-58, fol. 43.
[42] Harl. MSS. 163, fol. 231.
[43] *C.J.*, ii, p. 159.
[44] Rep. 55, fol. 438.
[45] *C.C. for A. of M.*, i, p. 382.
[46] *C.S.P.D.*, *1651-1652*, vol. 24/9.
[47] Rushworth, op. cit., i, pp. 419-20. See Chapter III, p. 78.
[48] *Complete Baronetage*, ii, p. 72.   [49] *C.S.P.D. 1640*, vol. 468/69.

Company, and on the aldermanic Bench. On October 9th, the
Merchant Taylors sent a delegation to him bearing a sympathetic
message and entreating him to show 'his accustomed favour unto
them'.[50] The Aldermen, to settle the difficult matter of his pre-
cedence, agreed on January 20 1642, that Acton, who should have
become Lord Mayor before Edmund Wright, would rank as senior
to all the Aldermen who had as yet not held the office.[51]

On July 21 1642, he was amongst those senior Aldermen who
refused to elect a *locum tenens* in place of Sir Richard Gurney, who
had been impeached by the House of Commons. By October, he
had become a delinquent lodged in Crosby House.[52] He refused
to accede to the request for a loan of £1,000 on the security of the
'Public Faith' in December (he had, however, been prepared to
lend towards the relief of Ireland earlier in the year), and in March
1643, his houses in Wood street, Cripplegate Within, and in Milk
street, were seized.[53] On May 2 1643, he was discharged from the
aldermanic Bench for non-attendance.[54] Until March 11 1644, he
was under the surveillance of both the Committee for Compounding and the Committee for Advance of Money, during which time
another house at Richmond was seized and dividends in the East
India Company were detained towards his assessments.[55] He was
finally discharged and died in 1651.

* ADAMS, Sir Thomas, Bart. (1586-1668). One of the newest
recruits to the aldermanic Bench at the beginning of the Long
Parliament, Adams was Sheriff in 1639-40, Master of the Drapers'
Company in the same year, and Alderman from October 1639.[56]
He did not belong to one of the great merchant families of the City,
but was descended from a yeoman family of Shropshire. He was
a substantial woollen draper by trade and employed twenty-one
apprentices in his shop in Gracious street.[57] Adams was not made
free of the East India Company until October 1641.[58] As far as
can be seen, he stood aside from the constitutional disputes in the
City in 1641 and 1642, and after the outbreak of the Civil War he
became one of the moderates on the aldermanic Bench. He was
one of the leading Aldermen responsible for dissolving the radical
sub-committee at Salters' Hall in the summer of 1643, and he
personally presented the petition to the Commons asking that all
troops raised in the City might be put under the command of the

[50] Court of Assistants, Merchant Taylors' Company, vol. 9, fol. 118.
[51] Rep. 55, fol. 354.   [52] S.P.Dom. 16/492/45.   [53] *C.J.*, ii, p. 989.
[54] Rep. 56, fol. 164.   [55] *C.C. for A. of M.*, i, pp. 235-6.   [56] Beaven, op. cit., ii, p. 64.
[57] A. H. Johnson, op. cit., iv, p. 140.   [58] *Court Minutes, E.I.C., 1640-1643*, p. 198.

Committee of Militia.[59] He soon became known as a political presbyterian or neo-Royalist. As Lord Mayor in 1646, he was suspected of having hidden the King in his house after his escape from the hands of Parliament. He was impeached in September 1647 for his opposition to the Army, but the impeachment was dropped in June 1648. He was elected an M.P. for London in 1654 and 1656, and he survived to welcome the Restoration and receive a baronetcy from Charles II.

ATKINS, Thomas. As a leading City parliamentary puritan, Atkins is described in Appendix II.

AUSTEN, Thomas (d. 1658). Elected Sheriff in 1639, Austen declined to serve. He was Master of the Clothworkers' Company in 1641, and elected Alderman for Vintry Ward on October 5 1641, but he chose to fine and on January 25 1642, three and a half months later, he paid £1,000 for his discharge from the Bench. Nothing is known with certainty about his political views, but he was probably the 'Mr Austen of Broad street Ward' named by Lloyd as a Royalist who refused to pay his assessments.[60] Austen died in 1658.

BROMFIELD, Sir Edward (fl. 1625-46). Master of the Leathersellers' Company in 1625-6, and Sheriff in 1626-7, Bromfield became identified with the court as a result of the strong measures he took as Lord Mayor in 1636-7 against those citizens who opposed royal policy. He had been elected Alderman for Dowgate Ward in 1626 as a Leatherseller, but in 1636, when he was next in succession to the mayoralty,[61] he secured his transference to the Fishmongers' Company, one of the twelve large Companies, and from 1637 to 1642, when he was discharged, he was Alderman for Walbrook Ward. On his transference to the Fishmongers' in 1636, he was promptly made Prime Warden of the Company, being 'placed before the Assistants'. He was knighted on June 4 1637 and became a Governor of the Irish Society in 1637-8. David Lloyd wrote of him that he was made '. . . a prey by the factious after his mayoralty [in] 1636 for keeping a strict hand over them during it, being troubled . . . for what he levied of the Soap Money, Ship Money and Customs in his office and immediately after it . . .'.[62] His proceedings, indeed, became notorious in the Long Parliament. Richard Chambers, the Levant merchant and later Alderman, and Robert Oake, a Collector of Ship Money,

---

[59] See Chapter VII, p. 268.
[60] *Memoires of the Lives*, p. 634.
[61] Beaven, op. cit., ii, p. 59.
[62] *Memoires of the Lives*, p. 633.

petitioned against him for their imprisonment for neglecting to pay their share of the tax.[63] Chambers claimed in a petition of 1646 that Bromfield, by his persecution, forced him to go bankrupt; whereupon the Alderman seized his house and held his mayoralty there.[64] Bromfield had also imprisoned John Bartlett, a bookseller and printer of Puritan sermons, together with other citizens who refused, in spite of the injunctions of the Privy Council, to remove their shops from Cheapside.[65] In the year of his mayoralty, Bromfield and his business partners were reinstated into the Soap Monopoly, buying out the Westminster Company with £43,000 and promising to raise the sum paid to the King on every ton of soap from £4 to £8. The new Company was given the same monopolistic rights as the old: powers to test all manufactured soap and suppress any of unauthorized manufacture.[66] Although this was mentioned as a grievance in the Long Parliament, it was the Westminster Company which was singled out for attack, and the London soap-boilers[67] maintained their position until after the Restoration.

Bromfield did not sign the refusal to lend to the crown in June 1639, and after much persuasion he agreed to lend £1,000 in the spring of 1640.[68] After the calling of the Long Parliament, he was once more summoned before the Committee of Grievances. After January 1642, he stopped attending the Court of Aldermen, and on August 26th, the Court discharged him from the Bench because of absence and non-residence in the City[69] (he lived in Southwark). In 1642, also, he ceased to be a Colonel in the Trained Bands, a position he had held since 1638. By 1644, he was imprisoned for refusing to pay his assessments, and his estates were sequestered for delinquency in 1646.[70]

CAMBELL, Sir James (1570-1642). Related by marriage to Alderman Sir John Gore, Alderman Sir Christopher Clitherow, and Alderman Anthony Abdy, Cambell came of a well-established City family. His father had been Lord Mayor and he himself had held the highest City offices, being Master of the Ironmongers'

---

[63] *D'Ewes*, ed. Notestein, p. 218.

[64] *Humble Petition of Richard Chambers* . . . , and broadsheet beginning *Now Right Honourable*, 1646 [Thomason Tracts].

[65] *C.S.P.D. 1644*, vol. DI, no. 18.

[66] Patent Rolls, 13 Charles I, Part 39, no. 10.

[67] A complaint was sent to the Committee for Trade about Sir Edward Bromfield's conduct of the soap monopoly, but no action appears to have been taken against the London Company, probably because it incorporated the main producers of the commodity and because it was a legal corporation under the terms of the Monopoly Act of 1624.

[68] See Chapter III, p. 100.   [69] Rep. 56, fol. 7.   [70] *C.C. for A. of M.*, i, p. 142.

Company in 1615, 1623, and 1641, Sheriff in 1619-20, and Alderman since 1620, being elected for Billingsgate Ward, and transferring to Lime street Ward in 1625 until his death. He was President of St. Thomas's Hospital from 1626 to his death, and Lord Mayor in 1629.[71] In 1631, he was made a Colonel of the Trained Bands. Cambell had also held some of the most important commercial positions as Governor of the French Company for over twenty years, and Governor of the Merchants of the Staple.[72] He was a 'committee' of the East India Company from 1622 to his death (except for a few years), and he supported the Governors of the Company against the opposition party. In 1639, he was one of the Aldermen with whom the crown hoped to negotiate a private financial deal.[73] He lent £500 towards the loan for suppressing the Irish rebellion in 1641, but on his death, to the evident disappointment of Parliament, he left nothing of his enormous fortune of £50,000 to the same cause, although £10,000 went to the executors to dispose of in two years, at their sole discretion, for any charitable and pious uses.[74] The Commons tried to persuade two of the executors, his nephew Sir James Cambell and Sir Thomas Abdy, to give £1,000 which had been left for the rebuilding of St. Paul's to the fund for the suppression of the Irish rebels,[75] but they resolutely refused. By his will and a curious eulogy written by his clerk, Cambell is revealed as a deeply religious man of strong Puritan faith who lived his life according to the severest code. He is said to have drunk in the theological writings of William Perkins and Richard Grenham, the sixteenth-century Puritan divines, and his household was nourished upon prayers. He had a reputation for being 'near, austere, and hard', his servant admitted, and sometimes this, with his frugality, might be taken for covetousness and even miserliness, but he hated throwing debtors into prison, and in his will he left large legacies for good works, including the relief of poor prisoners. Other bequests were associated with Puritanism, such as the relief of a 'silenced minister' and donations to French and Dutch congregations, although in strange conjunction was the gift towards the rebuilding of St. Paul's.[76]

CLARKE, Sir George (d. 1649). Before his election as Alderman for Bridge Ward on August 5 1641, Clarke, a Grocer, was highly

[71] Beaven, op. cit., ii, p. 54.
[72] Edward Browne, *A rare Paterne of Justice and Mercy*, 1642, p. 39. [Bodleian.]
[73] See Chapter III, p. 97.
[74] Strype, op. cit., Bk. I, pp. 274-5.
[75] *C.J.*, ii, p. 381.
[76] Edward Browne, op. cit., pp. 37, 43 seq.

placed in City circles. He was a son-in-law of Alderman Robert Palmer; a member of Common Council in 1641,[77] and a 'committee' of the East India Company from 1640 to 1644.[78] He was Sheriff in 1641-2, and was responsible for the election of Sir Richard Gurney as Lord Mayor in October 1641.[79] He was knighted on December 3 1641. In 1643, he was in trouble with the Committee for the Advance of Money for refusal to pay his assessments and was said to have been committed to prison.[80] He was discharged from the aldermanic Bench in September 1648 because of ill-health,[81] and died in the following year.

* CLITHEROW, Sir Christopher (d. 1641). Son of a wealthy citizen, an Ironmonger, Clitherow married twice, on both occasions into other wealthy aldermanic families—the Rowlands and the Cambells.[82] From 1601 onwards, he was a highly influential member of the chartered trading companies. He was an Incorporator of the East India Company in 1601, the Virginia Company in 1612, and the Bermuda Island Company in 1615. Clitherow was an Assistant of the Levant Company in 1616-17; from 1614 he served on the Committee of the East India Company, where he was Deputy-Governor from 1624 to 1635 and Governor from 1638 to 1641. He was also Governor of the Eastland Company from at least 1638. The King recommended him as a suitable person for office in the Virginia Company in 1622. He held important City offices, as Master of the Ironmongers' Company in 1618 and 1624, Sheriff from 1625 to 1626, M.P. for London in 1628-9, and Lord Mayor in 1635-6. He had been Alderman of Aldersgate Ward from 1626 to 1628 and of Billingsgate from 1628 to 1641.[83] In 1633, he had been appointed to a Royal Commission to examine the accounts of the fund that was being raised to suppress the pirates of Algiers and Tunis.

As Deputy-Governor and Governor of the East India Company, Clitherow was an opponent of the reforming party. At the same time he was active in petitioning the King against the newly licensed associations trading to the East Indies.[84] In April 1640, however,

[77] J.Co.Co. 40, fol. 8.   [78] Beaven, op. cit., ii, p. 65.   [79] See Chapter IV, p. 124.

[80] *Mercurius Aulicus*, Oxford, February 5 1643.   [81] Rep. 59, fol. 283v.

[82] *The Visitation of London, 1664*, Harleian Society, 1940, p. 42.

[83] A. Brown, op. cit., ii, p. 855. Beaven, op. cit., ii, p. 59.

[84] As Governor of the Eastland Company, Clitherow was said to have refused a nominee of the King free admittance to the Company because the Company's finances would suffer. When the King said he would do the Company a good turn, Clitherow is said to have replied, 'they all knew well enough what the King's good turns were when they came to seek them'. S.P.Dom. 16/395/2.

when the General Court proposed to petition Parliament on their grievances, he reported to the Company the view of the Recorder that they should not proceed with this course, but should 'consider how the King will take the application to Parliament, which will make his proceedings notorious'.[85] The petition was therefore not dispatched. Moreover, although he was 'fearful at first', as he said, he supported Lord Cottington's proposal to take up £60,000 worth of pepper from the Company in August 1640, and managed, despite opposition, to get the proposal accepted by the generality by forcing it through without putting it to the vote.[86] After the calling of the Long Parliament, the General Court again decided to petition the Houses. The King persuaded Clitherow against such action and the Alderman agreed to withdraw the petition.[87] Instead, direct negotiations were once more opened with the crown. In the autumn of 1641, as part of a conciliatory policy, the crown granted the Company permission to petition Parliament on the confirmation of its charter and the granting of rebates on re-exports.[88] By that time, Parliament was investigating a number of complaints against the Company, which thereupon prepared a defence against ill-government explaining the reason for the fall in profit.[89]

Clitherow died in November 1641, before the Company had openly revealed its opposition to Parliament, and before the Alderman had had occasion to declare himself an open supporter of one side or the other. A Royalist writer, however, describing those who had suffered for the royal cause, said of him that he was an adherent of the King and 'a great stickler for the Church, and a great benefactor to it; a great honorer of clergymen in the best times'.[90]

CORDELL, Sir John (d. 1649). Sheriff in 1634-5, and Alderman from 1635 to 1647, Cordell was the son of a wealthy Alderman who had been Master of the Mercers' Company three times and an Incorporator of the East India and Virginia Companies. Like his father, he enjoyed a prominent commercial career; he was on the Committee of the East India Company from 1625 to 1648 except for a few interruptions, Treasurer of the Levant Company from 1626 to 1628, and Deputy-Governor of the Irish Society from 1631 to 1632. He was Master of the Mercers' Company in 1632, 1643 and 1648.[91] A petition was presented to the Commons in January 1641 by a Mr. Singleton, accusing Cordell while Sheriff of unlawfully imprisoning the plaintiff, but the investigation proved

85 *Court Minutes, E.I.C., 1640-1643*, pp. 34-35.   86 Ibid. p. 82.   87 Ibid. pp. 130-1.
88 Ibid. p. 180.   89 Ibid. p. 109.   90 *Memoires of the Lives*, p. 632.
91 A. Brown, op. cit., ii, p. 862. Beaven, op. cit., ii, p. 63.

that the real responsibility lay with the Lord Mayor, and that the Sheriffs had stood by and done nothing.[92] Cordell, therefore, unlike some of his colleagues, was not brought up for questioning. Nevertheless, he seems to have been drawing near to the crown towards the end of 1641. He was a member of the aldermanic deputation to the crown after the City banquet and was knighted by the King on December 3 1641.[93] When Parliament asked the Court of Aldermen to call a Common Council to appoint a *locum tenens* in place of the Lord Mayor, who was now in the Tower, Cordell was among those Aldermen who upheld the power of the Lord Mayor to make the appointment.[94] According to the customary rule of precedency, he was due to hold the mayoralty in 1642, but he was defeated at Common Hall by Alderman Penington.[95] In November 1642, he was imprisoned for 'denying to contribute to[wards the] public safety',[96] and in December, in his capacity as a previous Undersharer of the Customs, he refused Parliament's demand to lend £1,000.[97] It was rumoured that he was again imprisoned in 1643 for his refusal to pay assessments,[98] but was again elected Master of the Mercers' Company in spite of his opposition to Parliament. He died early in 1649.

CRANMER, Samuel (d. 1640). Alderman for Cripplegate Ward between 1632 and 1640 and a great London brewer, Cranmer had distinguished connexions with the Church. He was the last male heir of the eldest of Archbishop Cranmer's sons, and his wife was the sister of the Bishop of Lichfield. Sheriff in 1631, and Master of the Brewers' Company in 1631-2 and 1638-9, he died on October 5 1640 before the Long Parliament met.[99]

GARRARD, Sir Jacob, Bart. (d. 1666). Sheriff in 1636-7 and Alderman for Bishopsgate Ward from 1637 to 1640 and then for Candlewick Ward to 1648, Garrard, a Salter, was a 'committee' of the East India Company from 1641 to 1656. He was knighted on December 3 1641. In January 1642, he was elected to the Militia Committee, but was removed in the following September for having 'deserted the service'.[100] He was imprisoned for refusing to pay

[92] *D'Ewes*, ed. Notestein, pp. 218-19.
[93] See Chapter IV, p. 129.
[94] *L.J.*, iv, p. 229.
[95] See Chapter IV, p. 157.
[96] *Catalogue of Knights, Aldermen . . . denying to contribute money to the public safety.* November 1642. [Guildhall, Broadsides].
[97] *C.J.*, ii, p. 901.
[98] *Mercurius Aulicus*, January 25 1643.
[99] Beaven, op. cit., ii, pp. 62, 180.   [100] See Chapter IV, p. 140n.

his assessments, and after the Restoration he was created a baronet in 1662. He died in 1666.[101]

GARRETT, Sir George (d. 1648). Sheriff in 1641-2, Master of the Drapers' Company in the same year, and Alderman for Castle Baynard from 1641 to 1648,[102] Garrett was a supporter of the parliamentary opposition in these years. He was probably not the George Garratt who sat as M.P. for Hindon in the Short Parliament.[103] By 1643, he seems to have been a 'moderate' and a member of the peace party. He was chosen to present the City's peace petition to the King in January of that year.[104] He died on November 30 1648.

* GARWAY, Sir Henry (1575-1646). One of the wealthiest merchant princes of the City, Garway's family had been settled in the City for a century, but it was his father, Sir William, the Customs Farmer, who played the greatest part in establishing the family fortunes.[105] Henry Garway was said to have been educated both as a scholar and as a merchant. As a young man he travelled widely on the Continent and in the Levant.[106]

He held the highest municipal offices from 1627, when he was elected Sheriff, Alderman for Vintry Ward, and Master of the Drapers' Company, culminating in his election to the mayoralty in 1639, a year when he became Master again and also Alderman (for Broad street Ward until 1643). In the commercial world, he held office over many years, serving on the Committee of the East India Company from 1614 to 1643, where he was Deputy-Governor from 1636 to 1639 and Governor from 1641 to 1643. In this position, he was, with Alderman Abdy, under attack by the opposition party, who objected strongly to the undue influence exercised by the two Aldermen as a result of their uninterrupted tenure of office. Garway became Governor of three other leading chartered trading companies: the Levant from 1635 to 1643 (he was on their Court of Assistants from 1614 to 1628), and the Greenland and Russia Companies from at least 1639 to 1643.[107]

---

[101] Beaven, op. cit., ii, p. 64.   [102] Beaven, op. cit., ii, p. 65.

[103] Beaven thought that he was probably the George Garratt who sat for Hindon, but the Member was a nominee of Lord Cottington, the Roman Catholic Master of the Wards and later Royalist. It does not seem likely, therefore, that he was Alderman Garrett. *V.C.H. Wiltshire*, v, 1957, p. 135.

[104] J.Co.Co. 40, fol. 45v.

[105] T. Heywood, ed. *Norris Papers*, Chetham Society, 1846, vol. 12, Introduction, *passim*.

[106] T. Heywood, *Londini Status Pacatus*, 1639, *passim*.

[107] Beaven, op. cit., ii, p. 60. *Londini Status Pacatus*, op. cit. Court Book, Levant Company, vol. 1635-44, *passim*.

He continued his father's interest in the Customs Farms, although he was excluded from the main Farm after 1627. He does not appear to have been involved personally in the demonstrations against the increased impositions on currants, as was his brother, William Garway, and his business partner, Alderman Sir Morris Abbot. His early re-accommodation into the Customs as a Petty Farmer may have been his reward.

His connexions with the court must have been strengthened by his nomination to a sub-committee to advance the rebuilding of St. Paul's,[108] a favourite project of Laud and Charles, as well as by his nomination to the Commission for New Buildings,[109] whose activities were included in the grievances of the Grand Remonstrance. In his office as Lord Mayor in 1639-40, he attempted to overrule Common Council by dissuading it from petitioning the King on its grievances and by pushing through the proposal to levy two hundred men for the Scottish garrisons without putting it to a vote.[110] He was active in distraining on those who refused to pay Ship Money, and he was responsible for taking severe action against the attackers of Lambeth Palace in May 1640. A Royalist writer applauded him for 'executing the ring leaders and imprisoning the promoters . . . , clearing the streets with his presence, and aweing the combination with his orders'.[111] In July 1640, before Charles had agreed to call Parliament, he was busy trying to levy £120,000 from the reluctant Livery Companies. He did his best to secure the election of Sir William Acton to the mayoralty in September 1640, in spite of the overwhelming hostility of Common Hall, which finally rejected him.

Although Garway gave evidence against Strafford at his trial,[112] he can have had little sympathy with the parliamentary opposition after their attack on the Farmers of the Customs. On June 1 1641, he was included amongst the seven leading Farmers who were declared 'delinquents', and was condemned to pay £15,000 of the £150,000 imposed on them.[113] He and his brother petitioned against the penalty, claiming that they had only farmed the Petty Farms under James I and had been 'but sharers' since. Whereupon Denzil Holles retorted that 'they were not questioned for any money taken in King James' time but since'. The House rejected their petition.[114] In spite of his financial reverses and the condemnation by Parliament, he was elected Governor of the East India Company a month later. In August, a contemporary noted, '. . . though

[108] C.S.P.D. 1634-1635, vol. 267/66.   [109] C.S.P.D. 1637, vol. 367/88.
[110] See Chapter III, p. 99.   [111] Memoires of the Lives, op. cit., p. 633.
[112] Rushworth, op. cit., iv, pp. 584 seq.   [113] C.J., ii, p. 163.
[114] Harl. MSS. 163, fol. 279.

Sir Henry Garway be cracked, yet the Turkey Company comes to his house, and gives him still the due respect of Governor'.[115]

According to rumour, Garway and the Lord Mayor, Sir Richard Gurney, attempted to prevent the King committing the blunder of leaving Whitehall in January 1642.[116] In the following months Garway refused to obey the orders of Parliament and in November 1642 he was imprisoned for refusal to pay his assessments. In January 1643, at Common Hall he was said to have supported the royal demand for the surrender of the Lord Mayor and other leading citizens as the price of a treaty with Parliament.[117] On April 10th, Parliament discharged him as a delinquent from the governorship of his Companies, and in May he was discharged from the aldermanic Bench.[118] David Lloyd, the Royalist writer, said, 'he was tossed as long as he lived from prison to prison and his estate conveyed from one rebel to another . . .'.[119] He died in 1646, but his son lived to reap the reward of his father's sufferings. At the Restoration, he became a Farmer of the Customs and a Member of Parliament, at first belonging to the 'country' party, but ultimately going over to the King.

* GAYRE, Sir John (d. 1649). Gayre was Sheriff in 1635-6, Alderman of Aldgate Ward from October 1636, Prime Warden of the Fishmongers' Company in 1638, and Colonel of the Trained Bands from 1638 to 1642.[120] Treasurer of the Levant Company from 1630 to 1632, he was also on the Committee of the East India Company from 1626 to 1649, except for the interruption of a few years, and he was elected Deputy-Governor in 1639, but declined to serve, pleading his unfitness 'to undertake so great a charge'.[121] Before the opening of the Long Parliament, Gayre was looked upon as one of the popular party. He was imprisoned in May 1640 for his refusal to submit a list of the wealthy inhabitants of his ward to the King.[122] In the following September, he was one of the 'popular' candidates for the mayoralty. He was knighted at Whitehall in December 1641, when he visited the King as a member of the City delegation, but he seems to have allied himself with the supporters of Parliament by January 1642 and was elected to the City's Committee of Safety, later to become the Militia Committee. By September 1642, however, his sympathies had changed and he was removed from the Committee for having 'wholly deserted the said service'.[123] Thereafter he was imprisoned for refusing

[115] S.P.Dom. 16/483/74.   [116] Roger Coke, op. cit., p. 134.
[117] See Chapter VII, p. 256 n.   [118] Ibid. p. 266.   [119] *Memoires of the Lives*, p. 633.
[120] Beaven, op. cit., ii, p. 63.   [121] *Court Minutes, E.I.C., 1635-1639*, p. 308.
[122] See Chapter III, p. 100.   [123] See Chapter IV, p. 140 n.

to pay his assessments, and he complained of the rough treatment he had suffered at the hands of the Trained Bands when they had dragged him off to answer before 'the Close Committee'.[124] Together with Alderman Cordell and the other Undersharers of the Customs, he refused to make a loan of £1,000 to Parliament in December 1642.[125] He soon became a political presbyterian or neo-Royalist. His election as Lord Mayor in September 1646 was a disappointment to Robert Baillie and the Scottish Presbyterians, who called Gayre 'a greater malignant than sectary'.[126] After the victory of the Army in 1647, Gayre was one of the five Aldermen impeached ostensibly for abetting tumults; he was removed from the office of Alderman in 1649 and died soon afterwards. Lloyd, in his memoirs of those who suffered for the King, described him as 'a gentleman of very discerning judgment, impartial integrity, pressing the Parliament to do what they fought for, that is, bring home the King'.[127]

* GURNEY, Sir Richard (1577-1647). Descended from a Westmorland family, Gurney was born at Croydon in Surrey in 1577 and was apprenticed to a silkman in Cheapside. His fortune, in true City tradition, was said to have originated in industrious service to his master (who left him a business worth £6,000) and by a successful marriage into the wealthy Sandford family.[128] He held important City offices in 1633, serving as Sheriff and as Master of the Clothworkers' Company.[129] In June 1639, he was amongst those Aldermen who refused to lend to the crown.[130] In 1641, he was responsible for prosecuting the case against Protections on behalf of the City before the Committees of the House of Commons; the slowness of Parliament to enact reforms of the abuse may have turned his sympathies towards the King. He was certainly known to be a sympathizer of the crown in the autumn of 1641, when his election as Lord Mayor was hailed as a Royalist victory. Gurney welcomed Secretary Nicholas's proposal that the City should greet the King on his return from Scotland, and he expensively entertained him at his own cost.[131] It was rumoured that he tried to prevent the King leaving Whitehall in January 1642.[132] Until his impeachment in July 1642 by Parliament, Gurney strove to maintain the *status quo* in the constitution of the City government and obstructed as far as he was able the policies of Parliament and the

[124] Rep. 56, fols. 98-98v.   [125] See Chapter VII, p. 257.
[126] Baillie, op. cit., ii, p. 400.   [127] *Memoires of the Lives*, p. 631.
[128] Daniel Gurnay, *The Record of the House of Gournay*, 1848, pp. 533-5.
[129] Beaven, op. cit., ii, p. 63.   [130] See Chapter III, p. 98.
[131] See Chapter IV, p. 126.   [132] Ibid. p. 145.

parliamentary puritans in the City. He was found guilty of these and similar charges in July 1642, imprisoned in the Tower, heavily fined, and his estate was sequestered. In 1645, he was allowed to compound for the sum of £5,000. A petition of his executors, summing up his punishment, asserted that Parliament had taken £7,500 of his estate, besides Gurney House and his house in Wiltshire, which was made a garrison; and that he suffered five years' imprisonment, dying in prison, and the loss of credit and trade.[133]

HARRISON, Gilbert (d. 1651). No evidence of the sympathies of Harrison has been found before 1640. He was Sheriff in 1633 and Alderman between 1634 and 1641. In 1634, he was elected Prime Warden of the Goldsmiths' Company. On September 16 1641, at his own request, he was discharged from the aldermanic Bench, but he was elected Chamberlain, after the office was declared to be entirely vested in Common Hall in 1643, and remained in the office until his death in 1651.[134]

HIGHLORD, John (d. 1641). Master of the Skinners' Company in 1632, and one of the Trustees of the Royal Contract Estates,[135] Highlord was a Committee member of the East India Company from 1630 to 1641 (except for one year). He was Sheriff in 1634-5, and Alderman from 1635 to his death in December 1641.[136] No evidence has been found of his attitude to the breach between the King and Parliament.

*PENINGTON, Isaac (1587?-1661). As a City M.P. and a central figure in these events, Penington has already been described at length elsewhere in this book. (See especially Chapter V, pp. 176-84.)

PRATT, Sir Henry, Bart. (d. 1647). Master of the Merchant Taylors' Company from 1630 to 1631, Pratt served as Sheriff in 1631, but could not secure the customary election as Alderman until 1633, after he had been three times rejected by the wards; his election was the result of the intervention of the Lord Mayor and Aldermen, who rejected all the other nominations for the vacant aldermanry as 'unfit' and used their prerogative power to elect him.[137] Pratt had previously been a Common Councilman and was elected to the Committee of Sales for the Royal Contract estates.[138] He was one of those from whom the King expected to

[133] C.C.C., ii, pp. 858-60.   [134] Beaven, op. cit., ii, p. 63.
[135] C.S.P.D. 1629-1629, vol. 144/46.   [136] Beaven, op. cit., ii, p. 63.
[137] L.Bk. LL. fol. 225. L.Bk. K.K. fol. 57.   [138] L.Bk. K.K. fol. 212.

raise a loan in May 1639. At first, according to Windebank, he
held out no hopes, but he was not amongst those Aldermen who
signed a refusal to lend to the crown in the following month:[139]
in May 1640, he agreed to lend £500. Pratt was mentioned as a
likely supporter for Windebank in his intended candidature for a
parliamentary seat in Berkshire, where the Alderman possessed an
estate.[140] He was an Undersharer of the Customs,[141] and was
therefore probably affected by Parliament's attack on the Farmers.
On July 26 1641, he was knighted by the King and made a baronet
a few days later.[142] He secured his discharge from the aldermanic
Bench in the same month, probably to avoid the political crisis so
obviously looming ahead.[143] Although he was slow to pay his
assessments, he did not at first show open defiance of Parliament.
It was not until March 1647 that he was accused of 'delinquency',[144]
but he died a month later. Information came to light in the following year that he had lent over £1,000 to the Royalists in January
1643 to carry on the war against Parliament, and the sum was
forfeited to the State.[145]

* RAINTON, Sir Nicholas (1569-1646). Sprung from a Lincolnshire family, Rainton was the only senior Alderman to show any
real sympathies with the parliamentary puritans before 1642: from
1642, he was less sympathetic to Parliament. He was a Mercer by
trade and imported satin and taffeta from Florence, and velvet
from Genoa.[146] He enjoyed considerable wealth and was the owner
of a fashionable mansion built for him by Inigo Jones, called Forty
Hall, in Enfield.[147] He was Sheriff in 1621-2, Alderman from 1621,
twice Master of the Haberdashers' Company, and Lord Mayor
from 1632 to 1633. He was knighted in May 1633.[148] Rainton was
known to be of Puritan sympathies, and in 1632 he was elected
by the City Feoffees of Impropriations as chairman of their meetings to give a casting vote.[149] The organization was dissolved by
Archbishop Laud in the following year. At the same time, as Lord

[139] *Miscellanea Genealogica et Heraldica*, op. cit., p. 51.
[140] S.P.Dom. 16/435/72.
[141] Stowe MSS. 326, fol. 108.
[142] Beaven, op. cit., ii, p. 62.
[143] Rep. 55, fol. 177v. He paid £100 to the Chamber to secure his discharge.
[144] *C.C. A. of M.*, i, p. 128.
[145] Ibid. iii, p. 999.
[146] T. Heywood, *Londini Artium and Scientiarum Scaturigo*, 1632, *passim*.
[147] Lysons, op. cit., ii, p. 196.
[148] Beaven, op. cit., ii, p. 55.
[149] I. M. Calder, *Activities of the Puritan Faction of the Church of England, 1625-1633*, 1957, p. xii.

Mayor, Rainton was involved in a quarrel with the Bishop of London over his right to carry the ceremonial sword into St. Paul's Cathedral.[150] In 1639, he was one of the Aldermen who refused to lend to Charles I. In May 1640, he was imprisoned for his refusal to name the wealthiest men of his ward, information demanded from him as the preparation for a forced loan.[151] Rainton in January 1642 was the only senior Alderman to be elected to the Committee of Safety (later to become the Militia Committee), but, perhaps becoming more prudent, he begged to be excused, plead-ing 'many other employments'.[152] When Parliament, in July 1642, asked the Court of Aldermen to appoint a *locum tenens* in place of Gurney, the Lord Mayor held in the Tower, Rainton was amongst those Aldermen who upheld the power of the Lord Mayor alone to make the appointment. After the conclusion of Gurney's im-peachment, however, Rainton obeyed the order of Parliament and called Common Hall to elect a new Lord Mayor.[153] Previously in July he had acted as one of the witnesses for the defence during Gurney's trial.[154] From 1642 until his death in 1646, Rainton played little part in municipal or national affairs, but he was now over seventy years of age, and his attendance at the aldermanic Bench and at Common Council naturally became intermittent. Until his death, he appears to have been a close friend of Alderman Richard Chambers, a prominent supporter of Parliament in the City, to whom he left £20 in his will for the purchase of a memorial ring. He also left a bequest to Thomas Foxley, Clerk to the Feoffees.[156]

*REYNARDSON, Sir Abraham (1590-1661). Sheriff in 1639-40, and Master of the Merchant Taylors' Company in 1640-1, Reynardson was elected Alderman on November 12 1640. He was a prominent East India Company merchant, and was elected a 'committee' in 1636. He was also active in the Levant Company, where he was elected Assistant in 1634, and Treasurer from 1639 to 1641.[156] His wife was a daughter of the Royalist Customs Farmer, Sir Nicholas Crispe, and although at first his attitude to the conflict was undeclared, by 1643 he was strongly rumoured to be a Royalist. He is said to have destroyed in 1648 a list naming his 'fellow citi-zens' in the City government who had evinced support for the King,[157] and in 1649 he was deposed from the mayoralty for his refusal to make public the Act abolishing the monarchy, imprisoned in the Tower, and fined £2,000. He was knighted by Charles II

[150] *C.S.P.D. 1641-1643*, vol. 499/78.   [151] See Chapter III, p. 100.
[152] J.Co.Co. 40, fol. 16.   [153] See Chapter IV, p. 157.   [154] *L.J.*, v, p. 247.
[155] P.C.C. Twisse 129.   [156] Beaven, op. cit., ii, p. 65.
[157] Lysons, op. cit., iv, Part II, p. 763.

in July 1660, when he declined the mayoralty because of his ill-health, and he died in the following year on his Tottenham estate.[158]

SOAMES, Sir Thomas (1584?-1671). As a City M.P., Soames has already been described in Chapter V.

TOWSE, John. As a newly elected Alderman and a leading parliamentary puritan in the City, Towse is described in Appendix II.

WARNER, John. As a newly elected Alderman and a leading parliamentary puritan in the City, Warner is described in Appendix II.

*WHITMORE, Sir George (d. 1654). Whitmore came of a Shropshire gentry family with important London connexions, his grandfather being a City Alderman and Sheriff in 1567, and his brother-in-law a Lord Mayor in 1610. One of the greatest money lenders in the City, Whitmore rose to eminence in the municipality, becoming a member of the Virginia Company in 1609, Sheriff in 1621-2, Alderman for Farringdon Within from 1621 to 1626 and for Langbourne Ward from 1626 to 1643, Master of the Haberdashers' from 1621-2 and again in 1631-2, Lord Mayor in 1631-2, and President of Bethlem and Bridewell from 1632 to 1642. He was knighted on May 27 1632.[159] With his brother, Sir William, he was one of the main creditors of the Earl of Strafford,[160] and he was amongst those Aldermen who did not sign a refusal to lend to the crown in June 1639. When the King returned from Scotland in November 1641, Whitmore made a new road through his Hoxton estate to ease the progress of the royal party. It was rumoured that when the intention of Charles to leave London was known in January 1642, Whitmore waited on him and offered to raise 10,000 men to guard him in London.[161] As an officer of the Customs and an Undersharer, the House of Commons approached him for a loan in December 1642, but he refused, saying, 'he had no money; he could receive no rents'.[162] He was imprisoned first in Crosby House, then at Yarmouth, Winchester House, and Lambeth Palace for his refusal to pay assessments.[163] He was discharged from the aldermanic Bench on May 2 1643 on the ground that his imprisonment prevented him from performing his duties as a Justice of the Peace.[164] His estate was finally sequestered, but he received

---

[158] *D.N.B.*   [159] Beaven, op. cit., ii, p. 55.
[160] *H.M.C. Fourth Report, Part I, House of Lords MSS.*, pp. 57-58.
[161] See Chapter IV, p. 145.   [162] *C.J.*, ii, p. 901.
[163] *C.C. A. of M.*, i, pp. 120-1.   [164] Rep. 56, fol. 166v.

his discharge in 1651.[165] Lloyd described him as one who until his death was a great supporter and 'sufferer for his Majesty's government'.[166] Whitmore died in 1654 and left considerable estates to his sons in Yorkshire, Northumberland, Berkshire, Somerset and Dorset.[167] His relations formed alliances with other powerful Royalist families in the City, a sister married Sir William Craven (Lord Mayor in 1610-11), a daughter married another Lord Mayor (Sir John Robinson, who took office in 1662), and a nephew married the daughter and sole heiress of Sir William Acton.[168]

WOLLASTON, Sir John. As an Alderman who had sat a short time and a leading parliamentary puritan in the City, Wollaston is described in Appendix II.

WRIGHT, Sir Edmund (d. 1643). Sheriff in 1629-60, Alderman for Cordwainer Ward from 1629 to 1643, and Lord Mayor in 1640-1, Wright, a member of the Grocers' Company, was like Acton committed to the crown to some extent by his action as a City magistrate in opposing a popular movement. As Sheriff, he was accused of having used force to break open Dr. Alexander Leighton's study and seize his papers. When told in March 1641 while he was Lord Mayor that this action eleven years before was against the law declared in Parliament, Wright replied deploring Parliament's intervention in matters of law and liberty.[169] A later dispute with some City Puritans brought him into direct antagonism with Alderman Penington. According to Lloyd, Robert Chestlin, rector of St. Matthew's, Friday street, was 'molested by a combination in the parish' who planned to pay no tithes as a protest against the imprisonment of his predecessor, Henry Burton. Chestlin appealed to Wright, who found him, says Lloyd, 'so resolvedly honest' that when Penington (probably as Sheriff) 'threatened to stave him off from doing justice', Wright retorted, 'What! Shall I be afraid to do justice!'[170] and committed those who refused to pay the tithes to gaol, where they remained until the House of Commons freed them in 1641. Chestlin paid for this affair by being imprisoned in Colchester in 1642, when Penington informed the House that he had denounced Parliament in his sermons. As Lord Mayor in 1640-1, Wright, knighted on June 20 1641, incurred Parliament's displeasure[171] in July and August by the tardiness with which he collected the Poll Money, urgently required to pay off the northern

[165] C.C.C., op. cit., iv, p. 2890.   [166] Memoires of the Lives, op. cit., p. 631.
[167] P.C.C. Alchin 407.   [168] Beaven, op. cit., ii, pp. 178, 179.
[169] D'Ewes, ed. Notestein, p. 517.   [170] Memoires of the Lives, p. 630.
[171] C.J., ii, pp. 224, 226, 236.

and Scottish armies. The King's projected journey to Scotland had
made the Commons fear that he might win over the undisbanded
armies. Thereafter, Wright showed increasing reluctance to obey
the commands of Parliament. He was amongst the senior Aldermen who refused to elect a *locum tenens* to call a Common Hall on
the deposition of Sir Richard Gurney. On October 14 1642, an
order was made in Parliament authorizing a search of his house
in Coleman street for arms.[172] In the same year, he added to his
non-political honours the presidency of St. Thomas's Hospital.[173]
He was repeatedly rebuked for his failure to pay in his assessments,
although a charge of 'delinquency' was never brought against him,
in spite of many threats; he was reported by 'Mercurius Aulicus'
on February 7 1643 to have offered £1,300 as a composition for
the assessment of one-twentieth of his income, but to have failed
to satisfy his examiners in the House of Commons.[174] On February
28 1643 he led the deputation to the House asking for a reduction
of the monthly assessment imposed on the City.[175] He died in July
of the same year. Two of Wright's daughters married into influential Royalist families, but another daughter became the wife of
Sir James Harrington, the Regicide and Republican, while his wife
was connected by marriage with another parliamentary notability,
Rowland Wilson.[176]

[172] *C.J.*, ii, p. 808.   [173] Beaven, op. cit., ii, p. 62.
[174] *Mercurius Aulicus*, February 7 1643.   [175] *C.J.*, ii, p. 984.
[176] Beaven, op. cit., ii, pp. 180, 234.

APPENDIX II

The New Men

SOME biographical information about the Aldermen and Common Councilmen who were members of the Militia Committee in 1642 and 1643, and about those newly elected as Aldermen in the same period.[1]

* indicates the subject of a *D.N.B.* article.

ANDREWES, Thomas (d. 1659). Alderman. Andrewes was probably the son of Robert, of Feltham in Middlesex, one of the Plymouth Adventurers who sold out his interests in 1626 and subsequently subscribed £25 to the Massachusetts Bay Company.[2] One of the original quartet of parliamentary financial administrators, he appears to have avoided high municipal office before 1640, although he had been a member of Common Council.from at least 1638. The author of *The Mystery of the Good Old Cause* asserted that before 1640 he was 'a great dealer in projects',[3] but no evidence of this has been discovered. From 1631 to 1659, he ran a wholesale linen-drapery in the parish of St. Margaret's, New Fish street.[4] That he was a prosperous merchant with money to lend is evident in his position as one of the Undersharers of Charles I's Farmers of the Customs;[5] in this, he differed from his other newly

---

[1] As in Appendix I, these accounts are intended to provide the essential information about the offices held by these men and their political sympathies. In the main, only material relevant to these themes is given. I have included Common Councilmen where they were elected members of the Militia Committee in 1642, because, as explained in Chapter VII, this Committee dominated City government in 1642 and, in a less degree, in 1643. This appendix is thus intended as a more detailed description of the new men mentioned in that chapter. One method used in these biographies to discover whether a leading City Alderman or Common Councilman was a political presbyterian or political independent has been to see whether he was included in Parliament's remodelled Militia Committee of May 1647, in which case he would be a political presbyterian, or whether he belonged to the Committee that was reinstated after the triumph of the Army in July 1647, in this instance, a political independent. *C.J.*, v, pp. 181, 256.

[2] Rose-Troup, op. cit., p. 133.

[3] *The Mystery of the Good Old Cause Briefly Unfolded . . . 1660*, p. 45. [Bodleian.]

[4] J. C. Whitebrook, 'Sir Thomas Andrewes, Lord Mayor and Regicide', *Transactions of the Congregational Historical Society*, xiii, 1937-9, p. 151.

[5] Stowe MSS., 326, fol. 108.

elected colleagues, none of whom, as far as it is possible to tell, had such close financial dealings with the Farmers. Andrewes was chosen Master of the Leathersellers' Company from 1638 to 1639, but he preferred to fine rather than serve the office of Sheriff at this time.[6] In 1642, his eldest son[7] married the daughter of Matthew Cradock, well-known Puritan M.P. for the City from 1640 to his death on May 27 1641. In January 1642, at the height of the political crisis in the City, Andrewes was nominated an Alderman. At first, he refused to take the usual Oath of Allegiance and Supremacy before the Court of Aldermen, pleading conscientious reasons, and he was committed to Newgate. But soon he decided to submit and on February 15th, he was sworn a member of the aldermanic Bench.[8] His election was of great service to the parliamentary cause. Within a month, he had been chosen one of the four parliamentary Treasurers for Irish subscriptions, and in June, a Treasurer for raising plate and money. Subsequently, he was a Treasurer for other activities: the arrears of subsidies and poll-money, raising dragoons, the weekly assessments and, in 1645, a Treasurer for War. He was elected to the Militia Committee in January 1642, and Sheriff for the year 1642-3.[9] From an inauspicious start, he had risen to become one of the greatest financiers of the day—perhaps the greatest, since, in January 1643, he was also elected a Commissioner for the Customs, and in this office he advanced large sums to Parliament on the security of the receipts.[10] Later, he spent nearly £10,000 in the purchase of Bishops' lands, being among the largest buyers in the City, and over £1,000 on Dean and Chapter lands.[11]

Like the other parliamentary financiers, Andrewes was not sprung from one of the princely merchant families who tended to dominate the Joint Stock Companies and City government in the first half of the seventeenth century. He was one of the group of 'outsiders', who, in the sixteen-forties, were involved in disputes with the most powerful of the Joint Stock Companies, the East India Company. He was not elected a 'committee' until 1643.[12] In the sixteen-forties he was a business partner of Maurice Thompson, Samuel Moyer, Nathaniel Wright and others (Thompson and Wright were also members of the Militia Committee) in a scheme to settle a plantation

---

[6] Chamb. Acc. 1/5, fol. 222.   [7] J. C. Whitebrook, op. cit., p. 159.

[8] Rep. 55, fols. 367, 373.   [9] Beaven, op. cit., ii, p. 66.

[10] With two other merchants, he offered to advance £30,000 to Parliament in October 1647. *C.J.*, v, p. 331. Between 1641 and 1657, he lent in addition £7,450 to the government.

[11] Rawlinson MSS. B.239, nos. 232, 239, 252, 387, 484, and 603.

[12] *Court Minutes, E.I.C., 1640-1643*, p. 331.

on the West Coast of Africa in Assada, and to operate a separate stock of £80,000 in connexion with their trading scheme to the Malabar coast. Their competition was so keen that the East India Company was forced to buy two of their ships that were operating on this coast. In 1650, however, when Andrewes was Lord Mayor and at the height of his career, he seems to have broken with his earlier partners and to have relinquished his share in the Assada scheme.[13] He did not sign the petition sponsored by his old colleagues for a 'regulated' trade,[14] and soon rose to a high position in the Company, becoming Deputy-Governor in 1657 and Governor in 1650.[15]

Like many other members of the Militia Committee, he weathered most of the political storms of the Interregnum, although he carried his religious Independency and republicanism with more conviction than some of his fellow Aldermen. He did not sign the King's death warrent, but was present at the execution. He became the first Lord Mayor to hold office under the Commonwealth and was one of the first members of a minor Livery Company to hold that position. Noble said that he fell under Cromwell's displeasure, adding: 'his sentiments were, no doubt, entirely for a commonwealth: so that a single person was odious to him whether he bore the title of King or Protector'.[16] Nevertheless, he was still in favour in the early years of the Protectorate (he was 'knighted' in December 1654), but he may have disapproved of Cromwell's growing conservatism; he died in 1659.[17]

ASHWELL, William (d. 1675). Alderman. A member of the Grocers' Company, he served as an Alderman of Aldersgate Ward from 1643 to 1644, when he was discharged,[18] perhaps for delinquency, since he had already been in trouble with the Committee for Advance of Money. An important East India Company merchant, he was a Committee member from 1639 to 1655, and although nominated for the Deputy-Governorship of the East India Company in 1642, and the Governorship in 1643, he was not elected to either post.[19] In 1641, he was appointed to a committee to submit the grievances of the Company to the King. In 1643, he was Treasurer of St. Bartholomew's Hospital. Ashwell died in 1675.[20]

ATKINS, Thomas (fl. 1635-61). Alderman. A cloth merchant of King's Lynn and Norwich, Atkins was elected Sheriff by the

---

[13] Ibid. *1650-1654*, p. 96.   [14] Ibid. p. 340.   [15] Ibid. *1655-1659*, pp. 197, 333.
[16] M. Noble, *The Lives of the English Regicides*, 1798, i, p. 82.   [17] Ibid.
[18] Rep. 56, fol. 224v.   [19] *Court Minutes, E.I.C., 1640-1643*, pp. 135, 262, 331.
[20] Beaven, op. cit., ii, p. 66.

City of London while still an Alderman of Norwich. Although the
Corporation of Norwich challenged the right of the Lord Mayor
of London to make such a nomination,[21] Atkins was not unwilling
to leave his own city. He was a well-known Puritan, and it was
rumoured that he objected to the orders suppressing preaching and
silencing lecturers that had been issued by the Bishop of Norwich
for his diocese.[22] He had been concerned in 1635, in a dispute
with Lord Maltravers, Lord Lieutenant of Norfolk, and with the
crown, for refusing to serve on the musters of the county, and he
claimed that the City of Norwich had traditionally enjoyed its
own Commission of Lieutenancy.[23] He served as Sheriff in London
in 1637-8 and as an Alderman from September 1638 until February
1661.[24] He was not elected to the livery of the Mercers' Company
until he was nominated Sheriff,[25] nor was he elected Master Warden
of the Company until he was a prospective candidate for the mayoralty.[26] In May 1640, he was one of the four Aldermen who were
imprisoned for refusing to supply a list of men in his ward as a
preparation for a forced loan.[27] He was elected to the Militia Committee in 1642, and was made a Colonel of the Red Regiment of
the Trained Bands, where his alleged lack of courage gave rise to
many ribald comments.[28] Like other colleagues on the Militia Committee, he survived with some success the political vicissitudes of
the Civil War, the Commonwealth and the Protectorate.

Throughout his career, he was associated with the more radical
City petitions and with political as well as religious independency.
But the politics of his world interested him less than the business
pickings. As Lord Mayor in 1644-5 he did little to prevent the
political presbyterians from increasing their influence in City
government. Like Alderman Fowke, he weathered all the political
storms of the Interregnum; and he was 'knighted' for his services to the
Protectorate by Cromwell in 1657.[29] He was reputed to have feathered
his own nest as a supplier of cloths and provisions to the Army, as a
Treasurer for War,[30] and as a purchaser of Bishops' lands, from
which he was amply repaid for his frequent loans to Parliament.[31]

[21] P.C.R. 2/48, fol. 75.   [22] C.S.P.D. 1637, vol. 361/92.
[23] Bankes MSS., 42/63, 18/30.   [24] Beaven, op. cit., ii, p. 64.
[25] The Repertories of the Livery of the Mercers' Company, vol. 1631-1637,
fol. 254v.
[26] Beaven, op. cit., ii, p. 64.   [27] See Chapter III, p. 100.
[28] Rump Songs, op. cit., i, p. 136, ii, pp. 54, 58, 72, 103.
[29] Beaven, op. cit., ii, p. 64.
[30] C.S.P.D. 1644-1645, vol. 506/84. The Mystery of the Good Old Cause, op. cit., p. 2.
[31] He lent over £2,000 to Parliament between 1642 and 1649. W. P. Harper,
'Public Borrowing . . . 1640-1660', unpublished thesis, London M.Sc., Econ., 1927,
Appendix B.

Norwich returned him as a Member in the Short Parliament of 1640, also from 1645 to 1653, and from 1659 to 1660; he served his constituency efficiently. To his sorrow, however, as a result of the Self-Denying Ordinance, he could not accept 'places of profit', and he wrote to the Lord Mayor of Norwich on November 23 1645, complaining that under the ordinance for the sale of Bishops' lands, several of his fellow Aldermen and citizens had obtained profitable positions, and adding regretfully, 'were I at liberty, I doubt not, but I had been partakers with them'.[32] Atkins was nominated one of the court for the trial of Charles, but he declined to serve. He remained as Alderman for some months after the Restoration, obtaining his discharge on February 12 1661, but his subsequent career is not known.

BERKELEY, William (d. 1653). Alderman. One of the four Wardens of the Haberdashers' Company from 1634 to 1635,[33] Berkeley had not held other important municipal offices before 1642. He was elected a member of the Militia Committee and Master of the Haberdashers' Company from 1643 to 1644. He was elected an Alderman in 1643 and a Commissioner for Customs from 1643 to 1645. On June 20 1645, he was discharged from his aldermanry on payment of £520.[34] He may have been dismayed at the growing political presbyterianism of the municipality, for he appears to have been a political independent.[35] He died in 1653.

BUNCE, Sir James, Bart. (d. 1673). Alderman. Bunce was the son of James, who had sat as Member for the City in the Parliament of 1628, his fellow commoner Member being the Puritan Henry Waller. A Captain of the Trained Bands and for some years a member of the Honourable Artillery Company, Bunce was not a prominent office-holder in the City before 1642. In that year he was elected to the Militia Committee and to the aldermanic Bench. In 1643-4 he was Sheriff and also Master of the Leathersellers' Company. In 1645, on Alderman Soames' resignation, he was elected President of the Honourable Artillery Company. By 1647, he had become a right-wing political presbyterian[36] and was imprisoned in the Tower with four other Aldermen for his opposition to the Army. On the order of the House of Commons, he was discharged from the aldermanic Bench in April 1649.[37] The Council

[32] G. W. Johnson, ed., *Fairfax Correspondence*, 1848, ii, pp. 323 seq.

[33] Haberdashers' Minute Book, Court of Assistants, fol. 282v.

[34] Beaven, op. cit., ii, p. 66.

[35] He was reinstated to the Militia Committee by the Army in July 1647.

[36] *C.S.P.D. 1645-1647*, vol. Dxiii, no. 28.   [37] Rep. 59, fol. 371.

of State in 1651 declared him guilty of high treason and published
a proclamation inflicting penalties on any who had correspondence
with him.[38] Bunce was a brother-in-law of Alderman Sir John
Langham. He was knighted and created a baronet in 1660, and
died in 1673.

* CHAMBERS, Richard (1588?-1658). Alderman. A member
of a London family,[39] Chambers was a leading City parliamentary
puritan who opposed the crown's demands for tonnage and poundage in 1629, and for Ship Money in 1637. He also helped to cir-
culate the citizens' petition of grievances presented to Charles I
in the summer of 1640. For his part in these various activities, he
was imprisoned for nearly seven years and lost a considerable fortune. A member of the Girdlers' Company, he was elected an
Alderman in September 1642;[40] in November, he led a troop of
horse against the King's forces at Brentford.[41] In 1643 he was appointed a Customs Commissioner, and in 1644 a Sheriff. Chambers
was one of the smaller traders in the East India and Levant Companies, and held office in the Levant Company as Assistant from
1628 to 1630, and 1638 to 1641.[42] He was an unfortunate man with
strong convictions, infrequently in favour. His sufferings over Ship
Money, exacted by Alderman Bromfield, caused the loss of his
house and fortune. The compensation of £13,680 awarded to him
by the Long Parliament in 1640 for his sufferings under the crown
was not paid and went by default; the shrievalty which he had
taken, he claimed, at the promptings of Members of the House, cost
him £4,000 in a year; the post of Surveyor in the London Customs
House, an office worth £600 a year to which he was appointed in
1648, was taken from him, together with his aldermanry, when he
refused to proclaim the Commonwealth in 1649; he now suffered
yet another term of imprisonment, finally being released from the
Gatehouse in 1651, with a pathetic gift of 20 nobles for his relief.[43]
Chambers died in 'low estate and condition' in 1658 at Hornsey,
aged about seventy years.[44]

* CULLUM, Sir Thomas, Bart. (1587?-1664). Alderman. A
younger son, descended from a well-to-do family of Suffolk, Cullum

[38] Sharpe, op. cit., ii, p. 308.
[39] *Visitation of London, 1633-1635*, op. cit., i, p. 149.
[40] Beaven, op. cit., ii, p. 66.
[41] Rushworth, op. cit., i, p. 687.
[42] Court Book, Levant Company, S.P. 105:148, fols. 181, 195v. S.P. 105:149, fols. 289, 341. S.P. 105:150, fol. 3.
[43] Rushworth, op. cit., i, p. 687. [44] Ibid.

rose by his industry to a partnership with his master, a Draper of Gracechurch street. He was admitted to the Livery of the Drapers' Company in 1627, and in 1633, he married a cousin of Sir Nicholas Crispe. His rise to political office was swift after 1642. In 1643, he was made Assistant of the Drapers' Company, Alderman of Cordwainer Ward, and a Commissioner for Excise. In spite of his high office in the City, he lent money to two Royalist relatives—Sir Nicholas Crispe and Sir George Strode.[45] A political presbyterian, Cullum opposed the Army and was imprisoned in the Tower between September 1647 and March 1648. He was made free of the East India Company in 1647, and he gave up his office as excise Commissioner in 1650 and his aldermanry in 1652. Cullum began to invest on a large scale in real estate after 1649, and in 1656, he retired to live at his newly purchased estate of Hardwick House in Suffolk.[46] He was created a baronet in 1660, though he fell temporarily into disfavour with the crown in 1662. He died on April 6 1664.

ESTWICKE, Stephen (d. 1657). Alderman. A 'haberdasher of small wares' and a member of the Girdlers' Company, Estwicke was an active parliamentary puritan who had come into conflict with the crown over the new incorporation of silkmen in 1635,[47] and had been imprisoned for his refusal to pay Ship Money.[48] He sat on Common Council Committees from 1641.[49] He signed the petition of December 23 1641, calling for the abolition of episcopacy and protesting against the dismissal of Balfour from the Tower.[50] In January 1642, he was elected to the Militia Committee, and in April he was enrolled into the Honourable Artillery Company.[51] After the outbreak of the Civil War he was one of the main suppliers of cloths to the parliamentary forces, and Parliament appointed him a Commissioner of Customs, a post which he held between 1643 and 1645 and again to the year of his death in 1657. Estwicke was Alderman from 1652 to 1657 and Sheriff in 1652-3.[52] He was chosen one of the Trustees for Bishops' lands and was one of the largest City purchasers himself.[53] He died on December 15 1657.

FOOT, Sir Thomas, Bart. (d. 1687). Alderman. A leading political independent, Foot was an Alderman from 1643 until 1660, when he was disqualified by a clause in the Act of Oblivion (12 Car. II, c. 11, sect. 44) debarring from public office all who had

45 A. Simpson, 'Thomas Cullum . . .', *Ec.H.R.*, xi, 1958-9, pp. 19 seq.
46 Ibid.   47 *C.S.P.D. 1635-1636*, vol. 314/89.   48 See Chapter IV, p. 109n.
49 J.Co.Co. 40, fol. 6.   50 See Chapter VI, p. 223n.   51 Raikes, op. cit., p. 64.
52 Beaven, op. cit., ii, p. 73.   53 Rawlinson MSS., B, fol. 239.

passed sentence of death after December 5 1648.[54] A member of the Grocers' Company, he was appointed one of the Treasurers to the Irish Adventurers in 1643,[55] and a Commissioner for Excise from 1643 to 1655. He was elected Sheriff in 1645-6, and Lord Mayor under the Republic in 1649-50. From 1649 to 1661 he was President of St. Bartholomew's Hospital. Foot was elected a Member of Parliament for the City from 1654 to 1655, and again from 1656 to 1658. He served on the Committee of the East India Company from 1657 to 1659, and as Governor of the Irish Society from 1657 to 1660. On December 5 1657, he was 'knighted' by the Protector; he was a Councillor of State in 1660, and in the same year in November he completed his political circumnavigation by being created one of Charles II's baronets.[56] Foot's wife was the daughter of a London Alderman, and two of his daughters married into influential aldermanic families; a third daughter married Arthur Onslow (to whom the baronetcy descended), progenitor of a line of celebrated Speakers of the House of Commons and ancestor of the Earls of Onslow.[57] Foot died on October 12 1687.

*FOWKE, John (d. 1662). Alderman. Fowke was one of the crown's most persistent opponents amongst the merchants of the City. Descended from a minor armigerous family of Gloucestershire,[58] he soon rose to prominence in London trading circles. He made many enemies, for his litigiousness, his ambition, and his love of profit brought him into conflict with his business associates, and even with the City government and Parliament. But his career is of interest, not merely for his personal idiosyncrasies, but because throughout the Interregnum he played a leading and sometimes a decisive part in City government and in its relations with Parliament.

Fowke was amongst those merchants who refused to pay Charles's unparliamentary levy of tonnage and poundage in 1627, and he was imprisoned at the order of the Privy Council, while his goods to the value of £5,827 were seized by the officers of the customs. He was one of the Levant merchants who refused to pay increased impositions on currants, and his stubborn refusal to submit caused the Council to accuse him ('upon false pretences', he asserted) 'of clipping of money and piracies'. For these alleged offences his ship and goods with a prize of sugar were seized, he was imprisoned, and a huge bail of £40,000 was demanded in the Admiralty for the prize.[59] In December 1630, another information charged him

---

[54] Beaven, op. cit., ii, p. lvi.　　　[55] Firth and Rait, op. cit., i, p. 192.

[56] Beaven, op. cit., ii, p. 67.　　　[57] Ibid. ii, p. 181.

[58] *Visitation of London, 1633-1635,* i, p. 288.　　　[59] *C.J.,* vii, pp. 99-100.

with dishonouring the government in a letter to his factor at Leg-horn, in which he had written, 'the Parliament is broken up with discontent; which fills us with sorrow and fear. The Lord in mercy look upon us, for we decline in honour, wealth, and safety!' In 1652, a Committee of the House of Commons considered two of his claims and adjudged his total 'damages and losses' to be worth £27,615. They had generously added interest from 1628 for two separate periods of twenty-one years and twelve years.[60]

In this early period, he was also involved in a dispute with the governing body of the East India Company. Fowke had stood security for a sum of £2,000 owed to the Company by Daniel Bonneale for saltpetre. On Bonneale's failure to pay the debt, the Company gained a decree in Chancery ordering Fowke to dis-charge his liability.[61] He refused, and the Company retaliated by seizing his 'adventure'. The affair dragged on from 1629 to 1658 with the greatest acrimony on both sides. In 1647, Fowke took the case to the House of Lords and managed to secure an award of £7,000 against the Company,[62] which, however, rallied enough support in the Commons to put a stop to the proceedings.[63] Eventu-ally, Fowke was compensated by Parliament from the sale of forest lands. This did not end the matter: he found an excuse to continue the case against the Company, and in 1658 the matter was still not settled.[64] Throughout the proceedings, particularly before Par-liament, Fowke attacked the East India Company for its support of Charles during his unparliamentary rule, for having paid tonnage and poundage, and for having 'in other ways supplied the late King'.[65] Moreover, he used the opportunity to attack the joint-stock organization of the Company, and at a General Court in 1647, he was the only member to vote against the continuance of that form of organization.[66]

After 1640, his stock in the East India and Levant Companies was very small and finally dwindled to nothing. Like some of his colleagues,[67] he preferred to lend his capital to Parliament and to undertake contracts with the State rather than invest in trade. Before 1640, he had done a considerable amount of business with the Levant Company,[68] and in 1629, at the time of his opposition

<hr>

[60] Ibid.   [61] *C.S.P. Col. East Indies, 1630-1634*, p. 68.   [62] *L.J.*, ix, p. 178.
[63] *Court Minutes, E.I.C., 1650-1654*, p. 288.   [64] Ibid. *1655-1659*, p. 269.
[65] Ibid. *1650-1654*, p. 288.   [66] Ibid. *1644-1649*, p. 197.
[67] When, as a Commissioner for Customs, Fowke was bargaining with Parlia-ment over the terms on which they were to hold their offices, he told the Com-mons that 'they had most of them left their trading and wholly applied themselves to this service, about which they spent the greatest part of their time'. Harl. MSS. 165, fol. 155.
[68] Levant Company Ledger, S.P. 105:158, fol. 48.

to the increased impositions, he was elected an Assistant.[69] This Company, less oligarchic than the East India Company, and less under the influence of wealthy Customs Farmers, was more critical of Charles's government. In 1638, he was elected to the Committee set up by the Levant Company to consider the regulation of the trade in currants,[70] and in 1641 to the Committee to lay the Company's grievances before the parliamentary Committee of Trade.[71] By 1644, however, his relations with the Company had deteriorated. He refused to pay his share of the parliamentary assessment levied on the Company, although he was ultimately compelled to pay.[72] Ten years later, he was involved in a fresh dispute over the method of repayment of a sum which he claimed to have lent the Company as far back as 1629.[73]

Until 1641, apart from his position in the Levant Company, Fowke had held few positions of importance in the City, and he held no office in his Livery Company, the Haberdashers', until November 1642, when he was elected Master as a consequence of his election to an aldermanry; he had not held any of the junior offices which were the usual prerequisite to the Mastership.[74] He was Master again in 1652-3 and in 1655. With the calling of the Long Parliament, he became prominent in the City as a supporter of the policies of the parliamentary puritans. In June 1641, he was chosen by Common Hall as one of the City's delegation to Scotland to confer on matters of trade.[75] He played a leading part in organizing petitions to Parliament and presented the petition for the removal of the Bishops from the House of Lords on December 11 1641. Within a few weeks he was elected to Common Council probably for the first time, and in the following month to the Militia Committee. Contemporaries named him as instrumental in effecting the changes in City government which ensured its adherence to Parliament, and the King cited him as one of the four citizens who would be excluded from pardon, under the terms of a pacification.

Fowke was Sheriff in 1643-4 and Alderman from 1642 to 1662. He acted as leader of some of the most important City deputations to Parliament throughout the Civil War, and on many occasions he was associated with measures urging an active prosecution of the war, as in May 1644 when he presented the petition to the

[69] Levant Company Court Bk., vol. 1617-1631, fol. 195v.

[70] Ibid. vol. 1631-1641. S.P. 105:149, fol. 288.

[71] Ibid. fol. 397v.

[72] Ibid. vol. 1641-1648. S.P. 105:150, fol. 125.

[73] Ibid. S.P. 105:151, fol. 249.

[74] Haberdashers' Court Book, vol. 1583-1652, fol. 314.   [75] *L.J.*, iv, p. 268.

Commons for the re-establishment of the Committee for both Kingdoms.[76] From 1643 to 1645, he acted as one of the Commissioners for the Customs, and drove hard bargains with Parliament. In 1645, he was sent to the Fleet by the Committee for Accounts, for his refusal to submit an account of his disbursements while farming the Customs. On the petition of Common Council, he was released after a few months, although he had to promise that he would account for the sums in question.[77] In the following year, the House of Lords, where his influence was evident in the damages awarded to him against the East India Company, recommended him to the position of Controller for the sale of Bishops' lands. Fowke considered that the salary was too small and persuaded the Court of Common Council to petition Parliament for an increase, which he thereby secured.[78] He was said to have been one of those responsible for evolving the scheme of 'doubling' (by which those who doubled the sum they had already lent to Parliament had the total sum secured on Bishops' lands). He spent £4,000 on such purchases.[79] Later he was appointed Controller for the sale of Dean and Chapter lands.

Again in 1647, he sided with those who refused to accept the King's terms for an accommodation, and he took a leading part in causing the City to surrender to the victorious Army.[80] Until after the Restoration, when he made his peace with Charles II and became a Member of Parliament, he generally managed to appear on the winning side throughout the various changes of government of the time. Together with Aldermen Andrewes, Penington, and Atkins, he was named a member of the Commission chosen to try Charles I, but, like them, refused to sign the death warrant. As Lord Mayor in 1652-3, he spent his year of office in fierce wrangling with Common Council and Common Hall, who then indicted him for misgovernment.[81] He also became so notorious in his attempts to influence Parliament against the East India Company during his mayoralty, that Henry Marten, while attempting to justify the work of the Rump in a letter to Cromwell, was forced to admit that Fowke's case was an unfortunate example of private interests absorbing the attention of Parliament.[82] Perhaps it can be said of him that he was for ever

---

[76] C.J., iii, pp. 494-5. [77] C.J., iv, p. 215.
[78] Ibid. p. 723. [79] Rawlinson MS., B.239, no. 254.
[80] C. Walker, The Compleat History of Independency . . . , reprinted 1848, p. 43.
[81] J.Co.Co. 41, fol. 91v.
[82] Marten-Loder MSS. [Brotherton Library, Univ. of Leeds], fol. 1 of 4 fols. loosely inserted in volume 'Henry Marten Papers, Political and Miscellaneous, vol. 2, 1651-1658'. I am indebted to Professor C. M. Williams for this reference.

recouping himself for the losses he suffered under Charles. His enemies indulged in sarcastic invective, mocking at his hard bargaining and love of gain. To royalist writers, he was the archetype of those self-seeking Puritans whom they loved to caricature. Fowke was certainly an easy man to ridicule; there were many unpleasant sides to his character, and some of his nepotist activity sailed close to the wind, yet his business enterprise, although not mainly of an entrepreneurial or merchant adventuring character, his stubbornness, and even his early political conviction and purpose, must also be put into the balance in assessing his character. As to his part in bringing the City over to Parliament in 1642, all observers were agreed upon its importance. Fowke died in 1662; by a curious error, his biographer in the *D.N.B.* made him a benefactor of Christ's Hospital. He was, however, its President in 1651-2.[83]

GIBBS, William (d. 1689). Alderman. A member of the Goldsmiths' Company, Gibbs was a self-made business-man, and a colleague of Alderman Wollaston, with whom he had worked from 1636 under the monopoly for the manufacture of gold and silver thread.[84] He and Wollaston had also been fellow-members of the Court of Common Council from at least 1634.[85] From 1639, Gibbs was elected to the most prominent committees of the Common Council.[86] His rise to high office in the City and his adherence to the parliamentary cause began by his election to the Militia Committee in January 1642. A succession of City honours was quick to follow. He was elected Alderman in the following August, Prime Warden of the Goldsmiths' Company in 1643-4, and Sheriff in the following year.[87] The business world, nevertheless, remained his chief concern. When war and taxation began to have adverse effects on City trade, he strongly supported the efforts for a negotiated peace with the crown. A few weeks after Wollaston had become Lord Mayor, Gibbs led a deputation to the House of Commons, to petition for the recall of the City regiments from Essex's army, claiming that there was no money left in the City to pay them. He asked the House to ease the financial burden on the City, which he alleged 'was drawn dry by taxes'. He denied that they were 'all for war', and continued, 'it is peace we pray for or fight for; but such a peace as is for the glory of God and safety of religion'.[88] In December 1643, he was almost certainly

---

[83] Beaven, op. cit., ii, p. 66.   [84] *C.S.P.D., 1635*, vol. 305/32.
[85] *Visitation of London, 1633-1635*, op. cit., i, p. 313.
[86] J.Co.Co. 39, fol. 36; 40, fol. 5.   [87] Beaven, op. cit., ii, p. 66.
[88] *C.J.*, iii, p. 315.

implicated in the movement set afoot by Royalists in the City for an immediate settlement with the King.[89] He further revealed his opposition to the growth of political independency and the policy of a radical prosecution of the war, by attempting in 1644 to resign from the aldermanry at the time of the renewal of the Ordinance for the Committee of both Kingdoms. The Court of Common Council, however, refused to accept his resignation.[90] In 1647, he was a prominent right-wing political presbyterian, but he became very unpopular with his associates by reason of the speed with which he settled his differences with the Army once it was clear where victory lay.[91] He soon fell out of favour, however, with the new régime, and he was finally discharged from the aldermanic Bench in the first days of the Republic in 1649.[92] Gibbs became a Member of Parliament for Suffolk in 1654-5 and again from 1656 to 1658. He died in 1689.

KENDRICKE, John (d. 1661). Alderman. A Commissioner for Excise from 1643 to 1650, Kendricke, a member of the Grocers' Company, was an Alderman from 1643 to 1661, Sheriff in 1645-6, and Lord Mayor in 1651-2. He was a leading political independent and a member of the Committee for the General Rising. He died in 1661.[93]

LANGHAM, Sir John, Bart. (d. 1671). Alderman. The eldest son of Edward, of Northamptonshire, Langham was not descended from one of the wealthiest and long established City families.[94] Unlike some of his fellow Aldermen on the Militia Committee, he was a prominent City trader in the East India and Levant Companies. Nevertheless, in company with Alderman Andrewes, he avoided municipal office at first. He was made an Assistant of the Grocers' Company in July 1632, but he fined for the office of Warden of the Company in 1638,[95] and also for the office of Sheriff.[96] He held office for many years in the Levant Company, being on the Court of Assistants from 1621 to 1622, and from 1634 to 1638;[97] he was nominated Governor of the Company in 1644,

[89] B. M. Gardiner, 'A secret negotiation with Charles I, 1643-1644'. *Cam. Misc.*, vol. 8, 1883, p. v.
[90] J.Co.Co. 40, fol. 99v.
[91] *The Compleat History of Independency*, p. 43.
[92] Rep. 59, fol. 425v.
[93] Beaven, op. cit., ii, p. 67.
[94] *Visitation of London, 1633-1635*, ii, p. 44.
[95] Calendar Court Minutes, Grocers' Company, iii, p. 999.
[96] Chamb. Acc. 1/5, fol. 222.
[97] Court Bk. Levant Company, vol. 1631-1640, S.P. 105:149, fols. 117 seq.

but was not chosen, and he was finally elected to the office in
1654.[98] Unlike some of his aldermanic colleagues, he did not exchange his trading activities for financial and administrative office
under Parliament. He successfully defied the Levant Company's
prohibition on the import of currants in 1643,[99] and his trade with
the Levant increased throughout the Interregnum.[100] He was also
an influential East India Company merchant, being elected a
'committee' from 1626 to 1627, and from 1618 to 1642; throughout this period he was one of the largest purchasers of cloves, silks
and indigo.[101]

It appears that he would have preferred not to take an active
part in politics during the crisis of 1642. When he was nominated
to the aldermanry of Portsoken Ward in January, together with
Andrewes, he declined to serve, and changed his mind only after
a spell in Newgate.[102] He was added to the Militia Committee *ex
officio* as the result of his election to the shrievalty for the year
1642-3. In February 1643, he told the Commons that he had received many commands to join the King, but he preferred to obey
Parliament's orders 'and be harmless'.[103] In the spring, he seems
to have been more active in support of Parliament, since he accepted
the office of Commander-in-Chief of the regiments that were being
raised to guard the City's newly built fortifications.[104] In 1645,
however, he resigned the office, by which time he was known to
have strong political presbyterian views. Robert Baillie and the
Scots had hoped that he would be elected Lord Mayor in 1646:
they thought him a more reliable candidate than the neo-royalist
Gayre, the Alderman finally chosen. Langham, with four other
Aldermen, including his brother-in-law, Bunce, opposed the policy
of the Army in 1647; they were imprisoned in the Tower on September 24th, and Langham later said that this was done 'chiefly . . .
to prevent my being chosen Lord Mayor the Michaelmas following'.[105] He was deprived of his aldermanry on April 7 1649, but
was elected a City Burgess to the first Protectorate Parliament in
1654. He was probably amongst those merchants who wished to
bring back the King, since at the Restoration he was knighted and

[98] Beaven, op. cit., ii, p. 66.

[99] *C.J.*, iii, p. 92.

[100] Ledger Bk., Levant Company, S.P. 105:159, fols. 73, 116, 184.

[101] *C.S.P. Col. East Indies, 1630-1634*, p. 414; *1635-1639*, p. 175.

[102] Rev. 55, fol. 354.

[103] *C.J.*, ii, p. 974.

[104] *A Continuation of Certaine Speciall and Remarkable Passages from both Houses of
Parliament*, 1643, no. 45, p. 5.

[105] Rem. vol. ix, fol. 8.

created a baronet. In 1660-1, he was elected a Member of Parliament for Southwark. He was also restored to his aldermanry, but was allowed to decline it because of 'his great age and infirmity'. He died on May 13 1671.[106]

MAINWARING, Randall (b. 1588). Common Councilman. Captain Randall Mainwaring (or Randolph Manwaring) was a Mercer of Cheap Ward. He came of a gentry family of ancient lineage.[107] He was Treasurer of the Honourable Artillery Company from 1631 to 1635[108] and a prominent Common Councilman from 1639. In 1641, he was associated with many of the citizen's petitions and in January 1642, he was elected to the Militia Committee. He was Lieutenant-Colonel of the Red Regiment of the Trained Bands in 1642. In August 1642, he was elected Deputy to the Lord Mayor, Isaac Penington, and he was closely connected with him and others of the war party in the City, in the presentation of radical petitions to the House of Commons in 1643.[109] In 1647, he was a political independent.

NORMINGTON, Alexander (fl. 1630-1647). Common Councilman. Treasurer of the Honourable Artillery Company in 1630-1, Normington had held a number of minor offices in his precinct of St. Dunstan's in the West[110] before being elected to Common Council in 1641 and to the Militia Committee in January 1642. He is mentioned deprecatingly in *A Letter from Mercurius Civicus* as a Cutler of inferior social status who was prominent in winning over the Common Council to Parliament. He appears to have been a supporter of the political independents in the City in 1647.

PECK, Francis (fl. 1612-1651). Common Councilman. A Draper of Watling street, and one of the biggest contractors for the supply of cloth to the parliamentary forces,[111] Peck had sat on Common Council Committees since 1637. In 1637-8, he was elected to the most important Committee—that for letting the City Lands.[112] As far as is known, he did not hold any other important City offices, but in January 1642, he was elected to the Militia Committee, and he seems to have given his support to the political independents in 1647. He had been enrolled in the Honourable Artillery Company since 1612.[113] Peck was elected Senior Warden of the Drapers' Company for the year 1650-1.[114]

[106] Beaven, op. cit., ii, p. 66.   [107] Burke, op. cit., ii, p. 1214.
[108] G. A. Raikes, op. cit., p. 4.   [109] See Chapter VII, p. 261.
[110] M. Wren, *E.H.R.*, vol. lxiv, pp. 37 seq.   [111] S.P.Dom. 16/491/124.
[112] J.Co.Co. 38, fol. 107.   [113] *The Ancient Vellum Book*, p. 18.
[114] A. J. Johnson, op. cit., iv, p. 136.

* ROWE, Owen (1593?-1661). Common Councilman. A member of the Haberdashers' Company, Rowe was a silk merchant by trade, and a prominent Puritan vestryman of St. Stephen's, Coleman street. He was the son of John, of Bickley in Cheshire, and was related to a famous and wealthy family which had given three Lord Mayors of the same name to the City since 1568. He took an active part in the affairs of the Massachusetts Bay Company and the Bermudas, sent out his son to New Haven, and bought land there in 1635 with the intention, unfulfilled, of emigrating himself.[115] At some time prior to 1638, he had sat as Common Councilman for a City precinct; his return to Common Council for St. Stephen's, Coleman street, in December 1641, was one of the disputed elections that came before the Committee of Safety in January 1642. In July, he gave evidence against the Lord Mayor, Sir Richard Gurney, at his trial. Rowe had a long association with military matters. In 1619, he enrolled in the Honourable Artillery Company;[116] in 1642, he became a Captain, and in 1643, first, a Serjeant-Major of the Green Regiment of the London Trained Bands, and then a Lieutenant-Colonel authorized by the Lords to contract for arms for Essex's army. He was a Colonel in 1646, and on July 23 1647, he was appointed to the Militia Committee. He signed Charles's death warrant and was a staunch Republican who, according to Noble, was 'greatly dissatisfied at Oliver's getting into the saddle'.[117] His main activity was now the management of the Bermuda Company, although his appointment to the Deputy-Governorship in England in 1653 was not recognized in the islands. In 1659, Rowe, reappointed a Colonel of the Green Regiment, opposed Monk. He was imprisoned in the Tower at the Restoration, and died there on December 25 1661. He was buried in the family chapel in St. John's, the parish church at Hackney, where the London branch of the family had lived in the hamlet of Shacklewell for some generations.[118]

RUSSELL, James (fl. 1640-7). Common Councilman. A member of the Drapers' Company who lived in Coleman street in 1641,[119] Russell does not appear to have been prominent in City office before 1642, when, as a member of Common Council, he was elected to the Militia Committee. In May 1640, he was described as amongst the 'fourth class' of well-to-do citizens in Coleman street

[115] I. M. Calder, *The New Haven Colony*, New Haven, 1934, p. 207.
[116] *The Ancient Vellum Book*, p. 31.
[117] Noble, op. cit., ii, pp. 150-5.
[118] Lysons, op. cit., ii, p. 318. *Middlesex Pedigrees*, Harleian Society, 1914, p. 8.
[119] A. H. Johnson, op. cit., iv, p. 132.

Ward.[120] He gave evidence against the Lord Mayor at his trial in July 1642. In 1643, Parliament appointed him a Commissioner of Customs, and later a Trustee for the sale of Bishops' lands. In 1647, he appears to have supported the political independents.

TOWSE, John (d. 1645). Alderman. A member of the Grocers' Company from at least 1627,[121] Towse was not chosen an Assistant[122] of the Company until he had been elected Sheriff for the City as the candidate of Common Hall in June 1640. In the previous year, he was a member of Common Council and its committees. From November 1640 until his death in 1645, he was Alderman for Cripplegate Ward. At the time of his election, he was living near Mercers' Chapel in Cheap Ward, and he was estimated to be one of the wealthiest citizens of his ward;[123] in view of this report, his failure to take municipal or Livery Company office is striking. He was obviously strongly in sympathy with the parliamentary opposition for, after January 1642, his rise to pre-eminence in the City was rapid. He was elected to the Militia Committee and made Colonel of the Orange Regiment of the Trained Bands (he had been enrolled as a member of the Honourable Artillery Company since 1615).[124] He was one of the four Collectors of taxes and loans appointed by Parliament, being a Treasurer of the Irish Loan,[125] Treasurer under the ordinance for bringing in plate and money,[126] and Treasurer for the weekly assessments.[127] Later, he was one of the original Excise Commissioners.[128] Until his death, he advanced large sums to Parliament and, together with the other Excise Commissioners, raised over £14,000 for the Army in 1643 and 1644.[129] He died before he could be repaid, and in his will left only £4,250.[130] On matters of national politics, as far as it is possible to judge, he was radical and sympathetic to the advocates of political independency. He died on May 28 1645 at Hampstead.

WARNER, John (d. 1648). Alderman. The early career and fortunes of Warner are obscure. He did not spring from an old City family and, in spite of his later financial pre-eminence, he did not hold any leading position either in City government or Company

[120] *Miscellanea Genealogica et Heraldica*, 1886-7, Ser. ii, vol. ii, p. 87.
[121] Calendar Court Minutes, Grocers Company, op. cit., ii, p. 565.
[122] Ibid. iv, p. 11.   [123] *Miscellanea Genealogica et Heraldica*, p. 86.
[124] *The Ancient Vellum Book*, p. 28.   [125] *C.J.*, ii, p. 465.   [126] Ibid. p. 618.
[127] Ibid. p. 868.   [128] Firth and Rait, op. cit., i, p. 203.
[129] Between August 1641 and September 1643, he lent over £2,000 to Parliament. W. P. Harper, op. cit., App. B. *C.J.*, iii, pp. 330, 362, 442.
[130] P.C.C. 74, Rivers.

before 1639. The second son of John, of Bucknell in Oxford-shire,[131] he became a member of the Livery of the Grocers' Company in 1627,[132] and conducted, in partnership with his younger brother Samuel, a druggist business in Bucklersbury, a street long famous for its drug and herb-sellers. The partnership involved him in 1628 in an accusation made against Samuel of private trading with the East Indies. John Warner was elected Sheriff in 1639-40, at a time when political uncertainty had deterred many City merchants from accepting the office. In his year, forty-one men fined for office, and there were many rumours about the conditions on which he had accepted. Rossingham wrote: 'The City does allow this new Sheriff one of the City halls for one month after Michaelmas, that he may in the meantime fit himself of a good house; this is all the City does extraordinary for this Sheriff, but the talk is otherwise, [namely], that he is allowed half his charges.'[133] This rumour must have been based on the fact that Warner was not amongst the wealthiest merchants of the City, although he was a well-to-do citizen. His acceptance of the office may well have been the result of a shrewd forecast of coming political and religious changes, which as a Puritan, he would have wished to hasten. While Sheriff, he brought into his house as chaplain, the Welsh Puritan preacher, Christopher Love.

He was elected to the aldermanic Bench in 1640, but he did not submit a list of the wealthiest men of his ward when required to do so by the Crown in May. Well known for his Puritanism, he was rumoured to have been a signatory of the Root and Branch petition in December.[134] It must have been this reputation which secured his election to the Militia Committee in January 1642. Although he had not been enrolled in the Honourable Artillery Company, the usual recruiting agency for officers of the Trained Bands, he was elected Colonel of the Green Regiment in the spring of 1642. His rise to prominence as a Collector of parliamentary loans and taxes was even more rapid. He was appointed one of the parliamentary Treasurers for the Irish subscriptions,[135] a Treasurer for receiving subscriptions of plate and money,[136] a Treasurer for collecting the weekly assessments,[137] and one of the Treasurers for War.[138] As a parliamentary Treasurer, it is very probable that his work was more that of an administrator than of a financier raising money on his own credit. He was not one of the richest merchants,

[131] *Visitation of London, 1633-1635*, ii, p. 325.
[132] Calendar Court Minutes, Grocers Company, ii, p. 565.
[133] Add. MSS. 11,054, fol. 54.   [134] S.P.Dom. 16/473/48.
[135] *C.J.*, ii, p. 465.   [136] Ibid. p. 618.   [137] Ibid. p. 868.
[138] *C.S.P.D. 1644-1645*, vol. 506/84.

and in his will he left only a small sum, his sole philanthropic bequest being £100 to be distributed amongst ten poor 'godly' ministers, their wives, and children.[139] As far as it is possible to tell, he had no prominent connexions with the export and import companies, although, like Maurice Thompson and others, he may have conducted a prosperous private trade with the East Indies. He was one of the firmest adherents of political independency among his colleagues on the Militia Committee. Warner died in 1648 as Lord Mayor, to which office he had been instituted by the victorious Army in 1647, and in which he played a noted part in suppressing Presbyterian and neo-Royalist riots.

WARNER, Samuel (fl. 1628-47). Alderman. A younger brother of Alderman John Warner, and a business partner in a druggist business which they conducted together, Samuel was accused in 1628 by the East India Company of undertaking private trade with the East Indies.[140] He was condemned by the Court of Exchequer and imprisoned. He refused at first to become a member of his Livery Company, the Grocers', claiming in 1631 that his brother was already a member (he had taken up the livery in 1627) and 'their business will not permit both of them to be absent from their engagements'.[141] He was elected to the Militia Committee in January 1642; he may have been elected to Common Council for the first time in the disputed elections of December 1641, as there is no previous record of his being a member of the Court. He refused at first to accept his election to the office of Alderman in January 1643, but changed his mind after one day in Newgate.[142] In 1645, he was elected Sheriff, but did not serve, and in November of that year he was discharged from the aldermanic Bench for 'his miscarriage and offences',[143] probably because of his refusal to submit the accounts of the Committee of the General Rising, of which he was Treasurer, to public audit.[144] He appears to have been a political independent in 1647. His daughter married Sir William Thomson, an Alderman who was a London M.P. in 1659 and from 1661 to 1679.[145]

WINDHAM, Sir Hugh, Bart. (d. 1663). Alderman. Master of the Ironmongers' Company in 1638 and 1642, as his grandfather, Alderman Richard Chamberlain, had been in 1610, Windham had

---

[139] P.C.C. 178, Essex.
[140] *C.S.P. Col. East Indies, 1625-1629*, pp. 49, 491; *1630-1634*, p. 156.
[141] Calendar Court Minutes, Grocers' Company, iii, p. 765.
[142] Rep. 56, fol. 91.   [143] Rep. 58, fol. 14.
[144] *C.S.P.D. 1625-1649*, vol. dxxxix, no. 150.   [145] Beaven, op. cit., ii, p. 82.

been created a baronet on August 4 1641. He was descended from an armigerous family of ancient lineage.[146] He had been elected Sheriff in 1637 and in 1640, but did not serve. He was Alderman for Vintry Ward from May 1642 to March 1643, when he was discharged in consequence of 'being in prison and so disabled to perform his duty as an Alderman'.[147] This imprisonment was a result of his having refused to lend £2,000, as the House of Commons had requested him to do as an Undersharer of the Customs Farms.[148] In December 1643, he was in trouble again, this time with the Committee for the Advance of Money, and his goods and house, and his shares in the East India Company, were seized.[149] By then he was in arms for the King, for whom he fought until 1645.[150] In December 1651, he was once more mentioned as a delinquent.[151] In the previous September, his cousin, Colonel Francis Windham, later a baronet, had helped to conduct Charles II to safety after the battle of Worcester.[152] Sir Hugh Windham compounded for his delinquency in 1653; he died in 1663.

WOLLASTON, Sir John (d. 1658). Alderman. A member of the Goldsmiths' Company, Wollaston was not descended from one of the greatest merchant families of the City, although his father, brother, and brother-in-law were all Aldermen. His ancestors were an armigerous family of Staffordshire,[153] and he probably began his career as a working goldsmith. By 1630, he had acquired a profitable position as Melter in the Royal Mint and, according to Thomas Violet, amassed a considerable fortune.[154] He became involved in the patent for refining all gold and silver used by the wire-drawers in their trade, under a monopoly which had been granted in 1635 to a group of merchants headed by Sir Peter Ricaut and including Wollaston.[155] They proposed that the thread should be manufactured from imported gold and silver, and that in return for the monopoly, the refiners should pay 6d. an ounce to the King, who would derive, it was estimated, a total of £8,000 a year.[156] On the opening of the Long Parliament, the refiners presented a petition to the House of Commons complaining that 'the prices allowed to them to sell their silver, and their position

[146] B. Burke, *History of the Landed Gentry*, 1886, ii, pp. 2051-2.
[147] See Chapter VII, p. 266.   [148] *C.J.*, ii, p. 900.   [149] *C.C. A. of M.*, i, p. 238.
[150] *C.C.C.*, ii, p. 964.   [151] Burke, op. cit., ii, p. 2052.   [152] Ibid. p. 2024.
[153] *Visitation of London, 1633-1635*, op. cit., ii, p. 362.
[154] *C.S.P.D., 1651*, vol. 15/85.
[155] *Rymer Foedera*, vol. xix, 718, 735.
[156] *C.S.P.D., 1635*, vol. 305/32. H. Stewart, *History of the Worshipful Company of Gold and Silver Wire-drawers*, 1891, p. 38.

as agents had been forcibly put upon them'.[157] There may have been some truth in this claim since, according to Violet, the gold and silver wire-drawers would otherwise have managed to exclude them altogether from the business of refining.

Wollaston was appointed to the Militia Committee on its formation in January 1642; his status in the City had been more eminent than that of his colleagues on the Committee. He was Deputy-Governor of the Irish Society in 1633-4 and again in 1636-7[158] before its estates were confiscated by the crown (later, he became Governor of the Society from 1654 to 1657). He had been a Common Councilman from at least 1630,[158] Sheriff with Isaac Penington in 1638-9, Prime Warden of the Goldsmiths' Company in the following year, and from February 1639 Alderman of Farringdon Without (although in 1642, 1644, and 1657, he transferred to other wards, he remained an Alderman until his death). At the time of their shrievalties, Wollaston and Penington were engaged in a dispute with the Court of Aldermen, eventually taken to the Privy Council,[160] concerning their claim to the disposal of the Keepership of Newgate. Their candidate was Wollaston's brother, Henry. The Privy Council decided in favour of the Aldermen. Wollaston's honours from 1642 included the Presidency of Bethlem and Bridewell (1642-9), and of Christ's Hospital (1649-58).

Despite his monopoly patent, Wollaston was not compliant with the crown's demand for loans. In July 1639, he was among those Aldermen who refused to lend to the crown, and in May 1640, despite repeated requests from the Privy Council, he failed to send in the names of the men in his ward from whom the crown was hoping to extract a forced loan. He was a Puritan,[161] and was rumoured to have signed the Root and Branch petition presented to the House of Commons in December 1640.[162] In 1641, he and some of his associates at the Mint were attacked in the Committee of Trade for their share in the refiners' monopoly.[163] An inquiry was instituted into the patent, but no action was taken against the holders,[164] presumably because Wollaston and his colleague, William Gibbs, later an Alderman, who was also involved, were known to be sympathetic to Parliament. Wollaston was one of the seven Aldermen who presented the municipality's petition to Charles I

---

[157] H. Stewart, op. cit., p. 41.   [158] Beaven, op. cit., ii, p. 64.   [159] L.Bk. LL. fol. 54.
[160] P.C.R. 2/16, fol. 129. Rep. 53, fol. 196.

[161] In his will, he left an annuity of £100 to the Puritan College, Emmanuel at Cambridge. He also left £10 to Joseph Caryll, a Puritan minister. P.C.C. 248, Wootton.

[162] S.P.Dom. 16/473/48.   [163] Harl. MSS. 4277, fol. 2.
[164] D'Ewes, ed. Coates, p. 126.

on December 3 1641, asking him to continue to reside at Whitehall, and condemning the demonstrations and riots of the citizens. He and the six other Aldermen were knighted. But royal favour and Royalist influence were not strong enough to deflect him from decisively throwing in his lot with Parliament. In January 1642, he was elected to the Militia Committee, and from that time his allegiance did not waver. On March 18th, he presented a petition from the City government to the House of Lords dissociating the City from Sir George Benion's petition condemning Parliament's Militia Ordinance.[165] As Colonel of the Yellow Regiment of the Trained Bands, he shut London Bridge against Royalist petitioners from Kent in April, and reported the episode to the Commons.[166] In June, he received a letter from Charles commanding him to join him in the north, but he ignored it.[167] In accordance with a parliamentary Ordinance of June 10th, he was now chosen one of the Treasurers for the advance of plate and money. Later, he became one of the Treasurers for raising the weekly assessments, a Treasurer for War, a Treasurer for Irish subscriptions, and a Trustee for the sale of Bishops' lands. He was among the largest City purchasers of Bishops' estates, buying lands at Highgate, Hornsey and Finchley, near London, and expending nearly £8,000,[168] an activity for which he and others were satirized in a booth play in 1649.[169]

Wollaston acted as a financier as well as an administrator of finances for Parliament, lending to the government in advance of the collection of loans and taxes. From 1642 to his death in 1658, he weathered every political storm, emerging with each change in government ready and willing to lend to those who controlled the State. While his enterprise and business acumen, unlike those of some contemporary entrepreneurs and traders, brought few lasting economic or commercial advantages, his genius for financial organization played no small part in the financing of the Long Parliament. His own political attitude tended to moderation or even conservatism. His moderation as Lord Mayor in 1643-4 was in marked contrast to the conduct of his predecessor, Penington. Wollaston was known to be an ally of those political presbyterians in Parliament in 1646 who were trying to bring back the King,[170] yet he made his peace with the Army once it had proved itself

---

[165] *L.J.*, iv, p. 651.   [166] Harl. MSS. 163, fol. 98v.   [167] *C.J.*, ii, p. 615.
[168] Rawlinson MSS. B.239, nos. 7,223, 435, 437, 497.
[169] *A Bartholomew Fairing*, 1649, quoted by H. Morley, *Memoirs of St. Bartholomew Fair*, 1859, pp. 196-221.
[170] He was one of the four Aldermen who were not purged from the Committee of the Militia by the political presbyterians in the spring of 1647.

triumphant. He died on April 26 1658 and was buried in the parish church at Highgate, where he owned estates and had some reputation as a benefactor.[171]

WRIGHT, Nathaniel (or Nathan) (d. 1658). Common Councilman. In 1632, Wright, a member of the Skinners' Company, was involved in a dispute with the Eastland and Greenland Companies for interloping in their trade.[172] He was first elected to a Common Council committee on January 7 1641.[173] From 1641 to 1643, he sat on the Committee for letting the City Lands, and in January 1642, he was elected to the Militia Committee. In the sixteen-forties, he was a business partner of Maurice Thompson, Samuel Moyer, and others engaged in private trade in the East Indies. In 1642, however, he was elected a 'committee' by the East India Company.[174] He preferred to fine rather than serve the office of Alderman in 1649. In the same year he was elected Master of the Skinners' Company. Wright claimed descent from an armigerous family of Essex. His half-brother was John Wright, Clerk to Parliament,[175] his son was created a baronet, and an uncle was Lord Keeper of the Great Seal under William III. Wright died on March 11 1658.[176]

171 Lysons, op. cit., iv, Part II, p. 440.
172 *C.S.P.D. 1631-1633*, vol. 191/21, 192/37.
173 J.Co.Co. 39, fol. 161.
174 *Court Minutes, E.I.C., 1640-1643*, p. 261.
175 *Visitation of London, 1633-1635*, op. cit., ii, p. 371.
176 Beaven, op. cit., pp. 182, 70.

APPENDIX III

The Chamber of London

THE Chamber of London in the seventeenth century was far more than a City treasury involved in collecting the rents of the municipality and paying out its fees and charges. It was also a banking institution, concerning itself as much with private loans, repayments and interest, as with ordinary revenue.[1] It provided a fund of capital for merchants and trading companies, as well as a source of loans to the crown. It borrowed from merchants and government officials when it required ready cash to discharge its liabilities. Its chief liquid capital resource, on which loans were transacted, was the Orphans' Fund. This fund was built up from money deposited in the Chamber by the executors of deceased citizens who left their estates to minors.[2] The minor became the ward of the Aldermen (in their capacity as a Court of Orphans), who acted as trustees of his estate and paid to him at regular intervals 'finding money' for the upkeep of the estate and for his own use. When he came of age, the estate was paid over to him, together with accrued interest which was allowed at the rate of 6 per cent. In 1633, the City was holding in trust for orphans approximately £180,000.[3] Apart from this fund, the Chamber received its income from City rents and fines for leases, from fees for enrolments of apprentices and freemen, and from leases of market rights and rent farms. These items, however, produced only about £6,000 annually, whereas an average of about £16,000 was paid annually into the Orphans' Fund. In addition there was an irregular income derived from fines imposed on citizens for refusal to serve the offices of Alderman and Sheriff. Occasionally these fines produced an imposing sum, as in 1639, when they totalled £15,600,[4] but they were unpopular and difficult to collect and gave rise to innumerable disputes.

[1] I. Benbrigge, *Usura Accomodata*, 1646, p. 5.

[2] It is sometimes stated that Orphans' executors were compelled to pay over their portions into the Chamber. But the author of *Lex Londiniensis* (1680) writes, 'if the executor shall not think fit to pay the money into the Chamber, he must become bound with three sureties to the Chamberlain of London . . . or else by bond to pay the money due to Orphans', pp. 60-61.

[3] Orphans' Ledgers, vol. 1627-1647, fol. 184.

[4] M. C. Wren, 'The Chamber of the City of London, 1635-1642', *Accounting Review*, 1948, vol. 24, p. 194, n. 2.

The yearly accounts of the City, 'the City Cash', although prepared from a much earlier period, are extant from 1633,[5] from
which date they exist in an unbroken series. Each year they were
drawn up by the City Chamberlain, who was elected in Common
Hall on June 24th, in theory for a year but in practice for life or
until his resignation. They were audited every Michaelmas by the
Lord Mayor and by a committee of the Court of Aldermen and
Common Council elected in Common Hall. Although the accounts
were prepared in great detail, their arrangement is confusing and
defies the modern accountant. A serious difficulty arises from the
fact that there was no attempt to distinguish between capital and
current account, sums of both kinds being sometimes lumped together in one item. A rearrangement and subdivision of the items
of the account is necessary before a balance sheet even for a year
could be produced. As many of the City's capital items, such as
its orphans' deposits and its loans, spread well over a decade, a
balance sheet extending over at least two decades would be required to discover whether the City's budget was in balance during
this period. But since there are only seven years of extant accounts
over which to strike a balance for our purpose, a satisfactory and
detailed balance sheet cannot be achieved: after 1640 and particularly after 1642, special economies and war expenditure distort
the picture, and these years cannot be included in a table designed
to show the state of the Chamber in 1640.

Nevertheless, a rough table has been attempted to show in very
general terms, the total liabilities and assets of the City as they
existed in Michaelmas, 1640. It suffers from many imperfections
which are difficult to eradicate. Whereas an exact figure can be
obtained for the total of the Orphans' Fund in 1640, other figures
such as the value of the City lands can only be estimated in the
most general terms. Some of the items such as money lent out of
the Chamber and fines for Aldermen and Sheriff, varied so greatly
from year to year,[6] that it was necessary to estimate them on a ten

---

[5] There is internal evidence of these records having been prepared from an
earlier date, but it is not known for certain how the earlier records perished.
They may have been burnt in the Bridgehouse fire of 1633.

[6] The total sum owed to the City by sundry creditors, and by failure to pay
fines for refusal to serve as Alderman and Sheriff, amounted in Michaelmas,
1640, to approximately £131,000, of which £23,166 consisted of arrears of fines.
Approximately £22,000 represented arrears from the levies for 'martial causes'
and for Ship Money between 1624 and 1640, which continued to appear in the
City Accounts, although they were never collected. The greatest portion of the
debt consisted of loans made to the individual citizens who raised the sum of
£60,000 in 1624 and 1625 and £100,000 in 1627 as loans for the crown, and by
expenses connected with the Royal Contract estates which the King passed over

years' average. But in spite of these difficulties, it has been felt that such an analysis provides a more informative picture of the City's financial position in 1640, than for instance, an average yearly comparison of expenditure and receipts, from 1633 to 1642.[7] In the financial crisis of 1648 and 1649, a very rough table of the City's liabilities and assets was drawn up by an unknown hand, for the year 1648,[8] and it was from such an account that the Common Council Committee in 1650 drew up its analysis of the City's deficit.

A ROUGH GUIDE TO THE FINANCIAL STATE OF THE CHAMBER
IN MICHAELMAS, 1640

Liabilities	£	s.	d.
(1) The Orphans' Fund,[9] together with interest .	170,648	5	5
(2) Approx. capital value of Trust Funds[10] .	21,000	0	0
(3). Money owed by the City plus interest[11] .	12,837	17	10
Total	204,486	3	3

to the City in repayment of these loans. Since the crown later denied that it had passed over the lands in full ownership, the City Chamber gained no real benefit from the estates during the sixteen-thirties. After 1641, as a result of an inquiry into the debts owed to the Chamber when it was discovered that the City treasury was owed over £27,000 by the funds of the Contract estates, Common Council decided that lands should be immediately sold to cover the debt and to discharge the bonds of the original lenders. I have chosen to estimate a yearly average for this item, i.e. money owed to the City and arrears of fines, rather than include the total debt to the City, since the greatest part of the debt secured on the Contract estates was eventually repaid, while the arrears of Ship Money and 'martial causes' can be described as desperate debts, as well as some items which stretch back to 1608 and were never repaid.

[7] M. C. Wren in his article, 'The Chamber of the City of London, 1633-1642', op. cit., pp. 194-6, drew up a table analysing average yearly Receipts and Expenditure as they are set out in the Accounts. The main weakness of this table is that the capital items of the City's Accounts, which are the greatest part of them, extended well over a decade and sometimes into three decades. His conclusion was that the City Chamber was running into debt at a rate of just over £3,200 a year. The Committee of Common Council in 1650, however, estimated that between 1630 and 1649, the debt had increased on a yearly average by over £9,000.

[8] 'The State of the Chamber at Michaelmas 1648', Guildhall Record Office, Misc. MSS. 166.2.

[9] Orphans' Ledger, 1627-1647, fol. 297.

[10] The amount owing by the City in 1640 has been multiplied by ten, thus estimating its approximate capital value at ten years' purchase.

[11] Chamb. Acc. 1639-1640.

Assets	£	s.	d.
(1) Money lent out with interest, plus fines for discharge of Aldermen and Sheriffs[12] .	20,966	0	0
(2) Approx. capital value of lands and tenements belonging to the City, less charges (excluding Bridgehouse properties and Royal Contract lands)[13]	101,730	0	0
(3) Rent Farms[14]	13,000	0	0
(4) Chamberlain's balance for year 1639-40 .	4,131	6	8
(5) Fees and Receipts from the enrolment of apprentices, freemen, etc.[15] . . .	11,490	0	0
Total	151,317	6	8

This table does not claim to be more than a very rough guide to the financial condition of the Chamber. It suggests that in 1640, the City's liabilities well exceeded their assets, even if some allowance is made for the value of the Bridgehouse estates, the proceeds of which were entirely devoted to the upkeep of the Bridge and were accounted for separately.[16] The Committee appointed to examine the state of the Chamber in 1650 estimated that in 1630 it was in debt to the amount of £50,000 which by 1649 had increased to approximately £264,067.[17] Many reasons were suggested for this enormous deficit, but it was agreed by the author of a description of the Chamber's debts in 1626, by the author of *Newes from Guildhall* and by the Common Council Committee of 1650, that 'the greatest cause of exceeding in expence hath been occasioned by the extraordinary payments made from time to time by order of Court and Acts of Common Council (out of the Orphans'

---

[12] An average figure for the period 1633-1642.

[13] The annual rental for the year 1639-1640 was multiplied by three to arrive at the rack rent, as was done by the valuers in 1650, and then by ten, estimating them at ten years' purchase.

[14] Estimated at ten years' purchase.

[15] Estimated at ten years' purchase.

[16] The annual fines from the Bridgehouse properties were around £1,800 for the period 1633-42. Their capital value might have been around £54,000 but if this were added to the City's assets, then of course the upkeep of the Bridge and the properties would need to be deducted. So much was spent on their upkeep, that in the sixteen-thirties, the Bridgemasters frequently found it necessary to borrow from the Chamber in order to meet expenses. Bridgehouse Accounts, 1630-1640, *passim*. The account of the City's finances drawn up in 1648 excludes from the calculation the Bridgehouse estates. Misc. MSS. 166.2.

[17] *Newes from Guildhall, or a Premonition to the Citizens of London* (title page missing), [Guildhall Library].

money) when the revenues of the Chamber would not suffice'.[18]
The yearly revenue of the City, excluding Orphans' money and
borrowings, averaged between 1633 and 1642, approximately
£14,000, while its average expenditure reached over £18,000. The
increasing yearly deficit was therefore being met, for immediate
purposes, from the Orphans' fund. The Common Council Committee of 1650 suggested that two separate and distinct accounts
should be kept for the Orphans' and for the City's revenue, but
the suggestion was never carried into operation.

Many detailed criticisms of the City's financial policy were made
by contemporaries. First, whereas the City had to borrow money
for its needs at seven per cent interest and sometimes as much as
ten per cent, and pay out six per cent interest on Orphans' estates,
the Chamber itself usually made loans to merchants at six or seven
per cent and occasionally at five per cent. Moreover, the Chamberlain and legal officers of the City were dilatory in insisting on
securities and calling in bonds. In 1633, there was about £130,000
on loan, of which £38,000 only was secured by mortgages on land.
Money owed to the Chamber plus accrued interest amounted to:[19]

1633:	£146,744	1638:	£116,678
1634:	£142,877	1639:	£92,473
1635:	£132,383	1640:	£80,332
1636:	£124,090	1641:	£70,523
1637:	£117,607	1642:	£70,019

Secondly, whenever the King floated a loan in the City it was
usual, as we have seen, for the Chamber to give its bond for the
sum raised, with the result that if the crown did not honour its
obligations, or the citizens refused to pay their assessments, the
Chamber bore the loss. £44,000 of the £146,744 due to the City
from loans in 1633 was money borrowed from the Chamber by
those citizens who lent the sum of £60,000 to the crown in 1625.[20]

Thirdly, the City undertook many charges of a public nature
which were financed from the Chamber, such as entertaining the
royal family, beautifying the City, making and paving the City
streets. These sums, according to the anonymous author of 1626,
'were fit to be raised by some public general contributions, as in
former times have been used'.[21] The City Chamber also made up
the arrears of government assessments, such as those levied for coat
and conduct money, for 'martial causes', for providing the twenty

---

[18] 'A Briefe declaration touching the State of the Chamber . . .', 1626, [Guild-
hall Record Office, Misc. MSS. 166.1.]

[19] M. C. Wren, op. cit., p. 197.   [20] Ibid.   [21] 'A Briefe declaration', op. cit.

ships in 1627, and for Ship Money. In 1640, a sum of over £22,000 was owed to the City in arrears from these assessments.

The City did not benefit financially from the sale of offices or to any great extent from judicial fees. In an essay attached to Stow's *Survay*, the author described the City's revenue as hardly sufficing 'to maintain their bridge and conduits, and to pay their officers and servants. Their toll doth not any more than pay their fee farm, that they pay to the Prince. Their Issues for default of Appearances be never levied, and the profits of their Courts of Justice do go to particular men's hands'.[22] The system of reversion of offices, by which the holder of a post sold it to the highest bidder, meant that the profits accrued to private citizens.[23] The profits of the City's rents and farms went partly to the Chamber, but partly to the merchants who leased them. Some of the rent farms, such as garbling,[24] were particularly reserved to the Lord Mayor or Sheriffs, as financial plums accruing to their office.[25]

On the debit side, large sums were paid out yearly in gratuities to highly placed courtiers, Privy Councillors and to City officials. In 1639, over £2,355 was spent by the City Chamberlain in gratuities to royal officials and City officers for their part in furthering the passage of the City's Charter.[26] The author of *Newes from Guildhall* stated that the Committee of 1650 discovered during its investigations 'that great sums of money and annuities [were] given to divers officers of the City by way of gifts and rewards over and above their ancient salaries and allowances, which in time of the Chamber's stock declining are most fit to be spared'.[27] The same author complained also of the excessive number of workmen hired by the City and the financial burden this placed on the Chamber. He also complained of the 'presents, gifts and superfluous entertainments' granted by the City treasury to the magistrates, and of the survival of antiquated customs which brought in little profit and entailed great expense of ceremonial, such as 'an annual charge of

[22] Stow, *Survay*, ii, p. 209.

[23] The report of Common Council in 1650, on the sale of offices, states that this practice was partly responsible for the crisis in the Chamber. J.Co.Co. 41, fols. 10v, 12v, 13.

[24] The Garbler was a City official whose business it was to inspect the quality of all drugs and spices sold within the City. The profitability of the office is shown by the long contest between the City government and the Grocers' Company for the right of appointment.

[25] Common Council, in 1650, decided to put an end to this system and to make yearly allowances instead to the Lord Mayor and Sheriffs. But future holders of these offices refused to accept the responsibility unless the perquisites were restored, and in 1652, they reverted to the Lord Mayor and Sheriffs.

[26] Chamb. Acc. 1638-1639, fol. 49v.   [27] *Newes from Guildhall*, p. 6.

£600 or £700 per annum expended in keeping courts in Kent, Essex, Surrey and about the . . . Thames, for conservation of the river . . . and yet small or no fines or other profit ariseth thereby to the City, whereby the said charge may be defrayed'.[28]

Finally, although the Lord Mayor and Court of Aldermen and Common Council frequently declared that no money should be paid out of the Chamber except with the consent of the Court of Aldermen, a report made for the aldermanic Bench in spring 1641 revealed that money was in fact paid out without the required authorization.[29] This state of affairs caused the author of *Newes from Guildhall* to suggest that in future if 'the Chamberlain shall issue out any monies other than by Act of Common Council . . . unless for finding money, or upon satisfaction to be made to Orphans for their portions, that then the Chamberlain shall answer and make good the same and forfeit his place'.[30]

The City's mounting deficit meant that by 1640 it was increasingly difficult for loans to be made out of the Chamber, or for the City seal to be pledged for repayment, before outstanding debts were collected and before serious modifications were made in the City's loan policy. When the Long Parliament decided to raise immediate loans from London, the City government was faced with a dilemma. All hope of securing its debts from the King and the Exchequer had already vanished. If ready money was to be obtained it could only be done by calling in loans to merchants. Such a measure would particularly affect the Aldermen. When an investigation into the debts owed to the Chamber was made by the Court of Aldermen in December 1640, it was discovered that at least one large debt dated back to 1609, and that the chief debtors were the Aldermen themselves, the Customs Farmers and a few wealthy Common Councilmen: Alderman Sir Edward Bromfield, Alderman Sir Henry Garway and his brother William, Alderman Sir Robert Parkhurst and Common Councilman and Customs Farmer Sir Nicholas Crispe. The Garway brothers alone owed more than £4,500 plus interest, of which more than £3,500 had been loaned at 7 per cent and £1,000 at 6 per cent.[31] The result of this investigation was a decision to call in the money owed to the Chamber, which must have struck a financial blow at many of the leading Aldermen at a time when trade, through political insecurity, was at a low ebb. The blow was greater for those merchants and Aldermen, such as Aldermen Garway and Abell, who also became involved in compounding for delinquency as a result of their activities as Farmers of the Customs, and as monopolists.

[28] *News from Guildhall.*   [29] Rep. 55, fols. 75-77v.
[30] *Newes from Guildhall*, p. 6.   [31] Rep. 55, fols. 29v-30.

BIBLIOGRAPHICAL NOTE I

Manuscript Sources

A COMPLETE record of the sources used in this work is contained in the footnotes. The primary printed material, the pamphlets, diurnals and newsbooks, contained in the Thomason Tracts, in the Guildhall Library and in the Bodleian provided much information, and the locations of these sources are given in the footnotes. For the sake of the readers' convenience, a separate list of the MSS. sources is given here, since much of the MSS. material, in the Guildhall Library and Record Office, has not been widely known to or used by historians. The principal Livery Companies, with the exception of the Fishmongers', preserve their records in their own Halls. I was not able to gain access to the records of the Clothworkers' and Ironmongers' Companies.

(1) City of London, Guildhall Record Office
Common Hall Book, vol. 1.
Journals of Common Council, vols. 33-40.
Letter Books, vols. KK-PP.
Liber Fleetwood.
Liber Legum.
Lists of Common Councilmen for Aldersgate Within (from 1585).
Aldersgate Without (from 1624).
Bishopsgate Without (from 1618).
Bridge Without (from 1635).
Cornhill (from 1572).
Precinct Book of Aldgate Ward.
Remembrancia.
Repertories of the aldermanic Bench, vols. 39-57.
Miscellaneous MSS. relating to the constitutional powers of the Court of Aldermen and Common Council.

Small MS., Box 36, no. 12.

MSS. 112-19.

Small MS., Box 55, no. 17.

Small MS., Box 47, H.2.

Small MS., Box 4, nos. 3 and 4.

MS. 169.9.

MS. 128.3.

P.A.R. Book 9, no. C.12.

Misc. MSS. 149.17.

MS. 101. 8 and 9.

MS. 107.6.

Financial Records

Chamberlain's Cash Accounts; 1633-1643.

Depositions in connexion with the Great Contract.

Informations and Answers concerning sale of royal contract estates. Shelf 185/6, no. 79.

Misc. MSS. 166.1. The State of the Chamber, 1626.

Misc. MSS. 166.2. The State of the Chamber at Michaelmas, 1648.

MS. Shelf 150.

MS. Shelf 185/6, no. 19.

Orphans' Ledgers, vol. 1627-1647.

Rentals of the Bridgehouse Estates, 1627-1633; 1634-1642.

Royal Contract Estate Returns. C.R. 185/6.

Royal Loans Ledger, vol. 1, 1616-1629.

(2) City of London, Guildhall Library

Court Minute Books of the Worshipful Company of Fishmongers.

Inventory of the goods and chattels of Anthony Abdy, November 18 1640.

Vestry Minute Books.

Wardmote Books.

Ward Inquest Presentments.

(see also Bibliographical Note II.)

(3) Public Record Office

Court Minutes and Ledgers of Levant Company.

Dispatches of the French Ambassador.

Doquet Books of the Signet Office.
Patent Rolls.
Privy Council Registers. p.c.r.2/, vols. 39-53.
State Papers (including letters from Alderman Isaac
  Penington to Sir John Penington).

(4) British Museum
  Memoirs of the Earl of Manchester, Add. MSS. 15,567.
  Rossingham's Newsletters, Add. MSS. 11,045.
  Whitelocke MSS. Add. MSS. 37,341-7.

  Parliamentary diaries.
  D'Ewes, Harl. MSS., vols. 162-165.
  Gawdy, Add. MSS. 14,827.
  Moore, Harl. MSS. 478-479.
  Whittaker, Add. MSS. 31,116.
  Young, Add. MSS. 18,777-8.
  Harl. MSS. 1601, March 1-April 10 1641.
  Harl. MSS. 6,424.
  Sloane MSS. 1,467, unsigned notes of Parliament, June
    1641.

  Miscellaneous MSS.
  Egerton 2533.
  Egerton 1048.
  Harg. 179
  Harg. 153
  Harl. 4277
  Harl. 6363
  Lansdowne 160
  Lansdowne 169
  Lansdowne 1075
  Sloane 3945
  Stowe 326
  Stowe 397
  Stowe 796

(5) Bodleian Library
  Bankes MSS.
  Clarendon MSS.
  Tanner MSS.
  Rawlinson MSS.

Parliamentary diaries
>Rawlinson MS. D.1099
> ̄Rawlinson MS.C.956
>Rawlinson MS.D.932
>Tanner MSS.lxiv.
>Microfilm of the diary of Sir Thomas Peyton, 1640-1642.
>(Original, Minnesota University Library, U.S.A.)

(6) Somerset House, Probate, Divorce and Admiràlty Division
>Wills. P.C.C. Rivers 5. Alderman Sir Morris Abbot.
>> Coventry 120. Alderman Anthony Abdy.
>> Grey 44. Alderman Sir William Acton.
>> Hene 39. Alderman Thomas Adams.
>> Rivers 100. Sir Robert Bateman.
>> Bunce 33. Alderman James Bunce.
>> Cambell 1. Alderman Sir James Cambell.
>> Wootton 417. Alderman Richard Chambers.
>> Evelyn 81. Matthew Cradock.
>> Wootton 520. Alderman Stephen Estwicke.
>> Twisse 107. Alderman Sir Henry Garway.
>> Fairfax 133. Alderman Sir John Gayre.
>> Ent 80. Alderman William Gibbs.
>> Fines 201. Alderman Sir Richard Gurney, Bart.
>> Evelyn 150. Alderman John Highlord.
>> Duke 79. Alderman Sir John Langham.
>> Coventry 161. Robert Penington.
>> Fairfax 41. Alderman Sir Henry Pratt, Bart.
>> Twisse 129. Alderman Sir Nicholas Rainton.
>> Rivers 74. Alderman John Towse.
>> Pembroke 123. Captain John Venn.
>> Essex 178. Alderman John Warner.
>> Alchin 407. Alderman Sir George Whitmore.
>> Wootton 248. Alderman Sir John Wollaston.

(7) MSS. Collection, Friends' House. John Penington's Collection of his father's manuscripts. 4 vols. Letters from Isaac Penington junior to Alderman Isaac Penington, vol. 1, fols. 120-127.

(8) House of Lords MSS., Victoria Tower, House of Lords.

(9) Chartae Miscellanae, Lambeth Palace Library.

(10) Livery Company Records
  (i) *Goldsmiths*, Court Minutes.
     Vol. R, pt. 2 (1631-1634)
     Vol. S, pt. 1 (1634-1635)
     Vol. S, pt. 2 (1635-1637)
     Vol. T (1637-1639)
     Vol. V (1639-1642)
  (ii) *Grocers*. Orders of the Court of Assistants. Typescript Calendar.
     Vol. ii (1616-1634)
     Vol. iii (1634-1640)
     Vol. iv (1640—)
  (iii) *Haberdashers*, Court Minutes.
     Vol. i (1583-1652)
  (iv) *Mercers*, Repertories of the Acts of Court.
     Vol. 1631-1637
     Vol. 1637-1641
  (v) *Merchant Taylors*, Court Books.
     Vol. ix (1636-1654)
  (vi) *Salters*, Orders of Court, Transcripts.
     Vol. 1627-1684
  (vii) *Skinners*, Court Book.
     Vol. 1617-1651
  (viii) *Vintners*, Court Books.
     Vol. iii (1629-1638)
     Vol. iv (1638-1658)

Manuscript references giving returns of Common Council members which illustrate the changes in personnel at the elections of 1641.

A list of wards and precincts for which information on
Common Council returns is extant

Ward or precinct	Common Council Members for whom returns are extant for 1640 and earlier years and 1641	Common Council Members included in previous column, but newly elected in 1641
(*Vestry Minute Books—Guildhall Library*)		
St. Stephen's, Coleman street		
MS. 4458:1	2	2
St. Dunstan's in the West		
MS. 3018	3	3
St. Benet, Paul's Wharf		
MS. 877:1	2	2
St. Bartholomew, Exchange		
MS. 4384:1	2	1
*St. Augustine's, Watling street		
MS. 635:1	2	1
*St. Andrew Hubbard, Eastcheap		
MS. 1278:1	1	—
St. Botolph, Billingsgate		
MS. 943:1	3	1
St. Nicholas Acons		
MS. 4060:1	1	—
St. Botolph without Bishopsgate		
MS. 4526:1	4	—
St. Margaret, New Fish street		
MS. 1175:2	2	—
St. George, Botolph Lane		
MS. 952:1	1	1

Ward or precinct	Common Council Members for whom returns are extant for 1640 and earlier years and 1641	Common Council Members included in previous column, but newly elected in 1641
(Vestry Minute Books—Guildhall Library)		
St. Olave Jewry		
MS. 4415:1	1	—
*St. Mary Aldermanbury		
MS. 3571:1	4	3
(Wardmote Books—Guildhall Library)		
Cornhill		
MS. 4069:1	6	1
Aldersgate Within		
MS. 2050:1	4	2
Aldersgate Without		
MS. 2050:1	4	2
(Journal of Common Council—Guildhall Record Office)		
J.Co.Co. 40, fols. 21 seq.		
Cripplegate Without . . .	3	3
St. Benet Fink	1	1
Farringdon Within . . .	11	2

* M. Wren in his article in *E.H.R.*, vol. xliv, 1949, pp. 34-51 investigated the elections of 1641, but he does not appear to have used these three Vestry Minute Books. See Chapter IV, pp. 134 seq.

Index

Abbot, Edward, 287
— M. P., George, 194n
— Alderman Sir Morris, 63, 77n, 91n, 92n, 97, 99, 114n, 149n, 158, 177, 249n, **285-8**, 300
— Robert, 285
Abdy, Alderman Anthony, 92n, 93, 98, 101, 101n, 104, 114n, 158n, 170, 266n, **288-9**, 294, 299
— Daniel, 266n
— Elias, 266n
— Robert, 121, 150, 266n
— Sir Thomas, 289, 295
Abell, Alderman William, 41, 91, 93, 98, 114n, 118, 119, 158, 188, 248n, 266n, **289-91**, 338
Acton, Alderman Sir William, 78, 92n, 96, 97, 101n, 104, 110-11, 114n, 119, 149n, 159n, 192, 239n, 248n, 257, 257n, 266, **291-2**, 300, 307
Adams, Alderman Sir Thomas, 114n, 126n, 142, 144, 149n, 154n, 157, 169, 239n, 268, 270, **292-3**
Agitators, 269
Alden, Robert, 126n, 147, 148n, 255n, 265
Aldermen, see London (Constitutional): *Aldermen and Court of Aldermen*
Aleconners, 51
Aliens, 14, 15, 25, 26, 107
Alum works, 15
Andler, Emil, 2, 4
Andrewes, Alderman Thomas, 169, 185, 208n, 210, 240, 240n, 242, 243n, 245, 261, 274n, 282, 282n, 283, **309-11**, 319, 321
Apollo Club, 233
Apprentices, 35, 35n, 107, 174, 181, 281
Archer, John, 108
Archer, John (minister), 165
Artillery Garden, see Honourable Artillery Company
Arundel, Earl of, see Howard, Thomas
Ashe, Edward, 194n

Ashe, Simeon, 168n
Ashwell, Mr., 126n
— Alderman William, 244, 244n, 245n, 266, **311**
Assada scheme, 311
Atkins, Alderman Thomas, 97, 100, 108, 114n, 140n, 144, 154n, 156, 157, 173, 196n, 226, 240, 241-2, 243n, 272n, 293, **311-13**, 319
Auditors of Accounts, 51, 120
Austen, Alderman Thomas, 207n, **293**

Backhouse, Nicholas, 121
Bagg, Sir James, 111
Bagshaw, Edward, 195
Baillie, Robert, 184, 198, 199, 212-13, 232n, 302, 322
Balfour, Sir John, 143, 223
Banbury, 160, 230
Bancroft, Archbishop, 160
Bankes, Sir John, 21
Barber Surgeons' Company, 102
Barbon, Dr. Nicholas, 42n
Barbour, Gabriel, 165
Barnardiston, M.P., Sir Nathaniel, 192, 228
— Samuel, 228
— Thomas, 168
Barnes, Alderman Bartholomew, 285
Barrington, M.P., Sir Thomas, 206-7
Bartlett, John, 294
Bateman family, 150
— Richard, 121
— Robert, 66, 92, 248
Bedford family, 42
— fourth Earl of, see Russell, Francis
Bedingfield, Anthony, 194n
Bedlam, see Bethlem
Bell founding, 16
— William, 194n
Bellamy, Captain Edward, 144
— John, 137, 152, 253n
Bence, M.P., Alexander, 194n
Benion, Sir George, 117n, 150, 151, 207n, 228, 234, 265, 330
Bennett, Alderman Thomas, 73n

Benson, George, 285n
Berkeley, Alderman William, 140n, 155, 240, 244, 244n, 245, 274, **313**
Bermuda Island Company, 296, 324
Bethlehem, see Bethlem
Birkenhead, Sir John, 133n
Blore, Peter, 285n
Bludder, Sir Thomas, 194n
Bohun, William, 45, 49, 64
Bond, M.P., Dennis, 270
— Maximilian, 223
— Mr., 180
Bonneale, Daniel, 317
Book of Rates, 88, 92, 287
Booker, Captain John, 144
Bradley, Captain, 120
Bradshaw, James, 181
— John, 247
Brass mills, 16
Brentford, 252, 263, 314
Brewers' Company, 298
Brewing, 16, 40, 176, 179-80, 282
Brickmaking, 16
Bridewell, 16
Bridgehouse properties, 335, 335n
Bridgemasters, 51, 120, 136, 247, 335n
Bridges, Francis, 165
Bristol, 14
Bromfield, Alderman Sir Edward, 29n, 91, 93, 98, 100, 114n, 118-19, 126n, 158, 248n, 266n, **293-4,** 294n, 314, 338
Brooke, Edward, 22
Brooke, first Lord, see Greville, Fulke
— second Lord, see Greville, Robert
— Sir Basil, 259n
Buckingham, first Duke of, George Villiers, 73, 74, 77
Building, poor quality, 17-18, 38; on new foundations, 13, 18-20, 116; proclamations and legislation concerning, 19-23, 23n, 86n, Commission for new buildings, 20-21, 91, 300; profits from, 18
Bunce, M.P., James, 313
— Alderman Sir James, 126n, 140n, 159n, 171, 238n, 243, 244n, 245n, 274n, **313-14**
Burges, Cornelius, 109, 166, 174, 195, 215n, 232, 280
Burghley, Lord, William Cecil, 19, 25, 28, 30, 43
Burnell, Thomas, 207n

Burroughs, Jeremiah, 40, 253
Burton, Henry, 118, 166, 211, 289, 307
Bushell, William, 90
Butchers' Company, 87
Butler, Samuel, 264
Button-makers, 25
Byron, Sir John, 141

Calamy, Edmund, 166, 166n, 195, 218, 232, 232n, 280
Calthrop, Sir Henry, 47, 48
Cambell, Alderman Sir James, 91n, 93, 96, 97, 114n, 158, 249n, **294-5**
Camden, William, 9
Capel, M.P., Arthur, 202, 205, 206
Carleton, Sir Dudley, Viscount Dorchester, 78
— Sir Edward, 266
Carolina, colony of, 189
Carpenter, John, 47
Carrall, Sampson, 189
Carriers, country, 234
Cartwright, Abraham, 189
— Mr., 137
Caryll, Joseph, 329n
Case, Thomas, 232, 232n
Catharine Hall, Cambridge, 167
Catholics, 39
Chamber, City, see London (Constitutional): *City Chamber*
Chamberlain, Abraham, 259n
Chamberlain of the City, see London (Constitutional): *City Chamberlain*
Chambers, Alderman Richard, 5, 64n, 78, 108, 118, 170, 171, 180n, 193, 244, 244n, 245, 245n, 282, 293-4, 305, **314**
Chapman, a scrivener, 76
Charles I and Privy Council, see also crown and, under London (Constitutional): *Aldermen and Court of Aldermen, Common Councilmen and Court of Common Council;* Parliament, *House of Lords;* City Aldermen and, Ch. III *passim,* 110-12, 122, 123, 126-30, 177n, 192, 241, 276-7, 286-7, 291-2, 295, 297, 298, 301, 302, 304, 305, 306, 307, 312, 319, 320-1, 326, 329; City government and, 1-4, 19-23, 26-27, 29, 32-37, 43-44, 67, Ch. III *passim,* 107, 126-30, 155-6, 155n, 228, 246, 276, 287, 329, 336-7; City parliamentary

Charles I—*cont.*
 puritans and, Ch. IV *passim*, 175-6,
  186, 189, 190, 192, 193-4, 211,
  250, 262, 318, 330; flight from
  Whitehall of, 129, 144-5, 301, 306;
  Honourable Artillery Company
  and, 170-2, 188; Patents and, 93,
  241, 320, 328-9; peace negotiations and, 251-2, 253-4, 256-7,
  319, 320, 321; petitions and, 95-96,
  120-1, 122-3, 166, 174, 175, 216,
  227, 229, 256, 286; Trading and
  Livery Companies, 91-92, 92n, 94,
  189, 207-8, 208n, 283-4, 286-7,
  290, 296, 296n, 297; Trial and
  death warrant, 184n, 189n, 311,
  313, 319, 324
Charlton, Robert, 122n
Charterhouse, 11, 20
Charters, see London (constitutional):
  Charters
Chestlin, Robert, 307
Chettle, Henry, 38
Christ's Hospital, 16
Churches, see individual churches
  under London and suburbs (topo-
  graphical): *Churches, parishes and
  precincts*; Lectures and Lecturers;
  church reform and, under Parlia-
  ment, *House of Commons*; also
  Church, Lecturers and, under
  Parliament, *House of Lords*
City Marshal, 16
Clarendon, Earl of, see Hyde, Edward
Clarke, Alderman Sir George, 114n,
  124, 149n, 154n, 156, 239n, 257n,
  295-6
— Roger, 126n, 136, 196n
Clegate, Nicholas, 75, 118
Clerkenwell Priory, 11
Clerks, 265
Clitherow, Alderman Sir Christopher,
  91n, 93, 94n, 101, 114n, 158n,
  195n, 288, **296-7**
Clockmaking, 16
Clothworkers', 16, 38, 107; tenteryards,
  11n.
— Company, 207n, 288, 293, 302
Coat and Conduct Money, 336
Cockayne, William, 121, 150, 196n, 207
Coke, Sir Edward, 76
— Sir John, 80, 80n, 81, 83, 147
Combmakers' Company, 87

Committee for Advance of Money, 253,
  266, 292, 296, 311, 328
— for Compounding, 7, 267, 292
— of Safety, see Militia, Militia Com-
  mittee
Common Council, see London (con-
  stitutional): *Common Councilmen and
  Court of Common Council*,
— Hall, see London (constitutional):
  Common Hall
— Hunt, 70n
— Packer, 70n
— Sergeant, 51, 62n, 64
Coningsby, Fitzwilliam, 194n
Conyers, Sir John, 227
Copper mills, 16
Cordell, Alderman Sir John, 91n, 92n,
  98, 101n, 114n, 119, 148n, 149n,
  157, 207n, 239n, 255n, 257, 257n,
  297-8, 302
Cordwainers' Company, 25
Cornish, Henry, 167, 167n
Cottington, Lord Francis, 101, 288,
  297, 299n
Coulson, Christopher, 169
Court of Hustings, 49n, 60
Courteen, Sir William, 88, 92, 287
Cradock, Damaris, 185, 310
— Matthew, 113, 169, 170, 172, 173,
  175, 176, **185-7**, 189, 216, 218, 229,
  237, 242, 282, 310
Cranfield, Lionel, Earl of Middlesex, 93
Cranmer, Alderman Samuel, 298
Craven, Alderman Sir William, 307
Crispe, Sir Nicholas, 7, 119, 121, 148n,
  194, 194n, 207n, 266, 266n, 305,
  315, 338
Cromwell, M.P., Oliver, 41, 191n, 311,
  312, 316, 324
Cropley, Edward, 96, 96n
Cullum, Alderman Sir Thomas, 64n,
  244n, 245n, **314-15**
Customs Farms, Farmers and Commissioners of, 72, 78-79, 91, 92, 93,
  96, 97, 99, 100, 101, 101n, 106,
  110, 119, 122, 239, 240, 257, 266,
  277, 283, 286-7, 288, 300, 309-10,
  313, 314, 315, 316-19, 325, 338
Cutlers' Company, 26

Dalton, James, 46
Davenport, John, 161, 163, 165, 179,
  183, 287

Dawes, Sir Abraham, 78, 266n
Delane, Mr., 96
Dering, Sir Edward, 219
Dethick, Alderman John, 253n
Devereux, Robert, third Earl of Essex,
    251, 252, 254, 269, 271-2, 320, 324
D'Ewes, Sir Simonds, 150, 199, 202,
    203, 204, 214n, 215n, 219, 222
Digby, George, second Earl of Bristol,
    204, 206, 214, 215n
Distillers' Company, 87
Dockworkers, 107, 178
Dorchester Company, 169, 185
Doughtie, Thomas, 84n
Downham, John, 166
Downing, Calybute, 42, 109, 168, 174,
    195, 215n
Drake, Roger, 126n, 137, 150, 196n,
    207n
Drapers' Company, 75, 102, 190, 190n,
    287, 292, 299, 315, 324
Dugdale, Sir William 7, 228
Dye works and dyers, 15-16, 16n
Dyson, Humphrey, 9-10, 46

Earle, M.P., Sir Walter, 203
East India Company, 12, 66, 77n, 88,
    92, 92n, 97, 99, 101, 119, 121,
    122-3, 150, 170, 174n, 176, 186-7,
    192, 207n, 235, 241-5, 266-7, 282n,
    283, 285-8, 300-1, 303, 305, 310,
    311, 314, 316-18, 321-2, 327, 328,
    331
Eastland Company, 92, 241, 296, 296n,
    331
Edwards, David, 126
Elections, see elections and, under
    London (constitutional): Aldermen
    and Court of Aldermen, Common
    Councilmen and Court of Common
    Council, and election of, under
    London (constitutional): Lord
    Mayor, Sheriffs and Sheriffs' Court
Eliot, M.P., Sir John, 75, 171, 175
Emmanuel College, Cambridge, 167,
    329n
Estwicke, Alderman Stephen, 109n,
    120, 140, 156, 223n, 240, 243, 315
Excise Commissioners, 240, 315, 316,
    321, 325

Fairfax, Thomas, third Baron Fairfax
    of Cameron, 28
Faithorne, William, 9

Feltmakers and Cappers, 15, 265
Feoffees of Impropriations, 79, 109, 161,
    162, 164-5, 169, 183, 189, 195,
    213, 304
Ferté Imbaüd, La, French Ambassador,
    143, 214n, 279
Fiennes, Nathaniel, 203, 214n
— William, first Viscount Saye and
    Sele, 1, 42, 92, 97, 137, 148n, 155,
    160, 163, 170, 208, 253, 278n, 286,
    287-8
Firth, Professor C. H., 3, 4
Fishmongers' Company, 137n, 177,
    179, 209, 293, 301
Fitzstephen, William, 46
Fleet river, 12, 13, 17n, 40
Fleetwood, William, 30, 43, 47
Foot, Alderman Sir Thomas, 244n, 245,
    245n, 315-16
Forster, J., 1
— Captain Matthew, 173, 173n
Founders' Company, 75
Fowke, Alderman John, 5, 78, 120,
    130, 138, 140, 140n, 146, 155,
    158n, 170, 172, 182, 223, 240, 242,
    243n, 246, 248, 256, 259, 259n,
    260, 261, 282, 316-20
Foxley, Thomas, 109, 305
French Company, and merchants trad-
    ing to France, 78, 92, 97, 285, 290,
    295
French Revolution, 143, 271

Gardiner, Robert, 150, 207
— Roger, 126n, 137, 255n
— Sir Thomas, 66-67, 71n, 90, 94, 95,
    103, 104, 112, 119, 125, 127, 128,
    129, 130, 131, 149, 150, 151, 175,
    193, 195, 200, 206, 228, 266, 277,
    297
— S. R., 2, 207
Garrard, Alderman Sir Jacob, 91n, 98,
    114n, 126n, 129, 140n, 141, 149n,
    154n, 157, 159, 240n, 257n, 298-9
— George, 20, 21, 37, 83, 89
Garrett, Alderman George, 129, 141,
    149n, 158n, 299
Garway, Alderman Sir Henry, 63-64,
    91, 91n, 92n, 93, 99, 100, 102, 103,
    104, 112, 114n, 119, 123, 145,
    149n, 156, 157, 159n, 195n, 239n,
    248n, 255n, 256n, 257n, 266, 267,
    299-301, 338

Garway, John, 64
— Sir William, 99
— Thomas, 64
— William, 77n, 121, 255n, 300, 338
Gataker, Thomas, 168
Gayre, Alderman Sir John, 91n, 92n, 98, 100, 111, 114n, 126n, 129, 140n, 141, 149n, 154n, 156, 157, 159, 196n, 239n, 240n, 257, 266, **301-2**, 322
General Rising Committee, 251, 269, 270, 271, 272, 273, 321, 327
Gibbs, Alderman William, 126n, 140n, 173, 238n, 240, 241, 243n, 259n, **320-1**, 329
Girdlers' Company, 314, 315
Glassmaking, 15, 24
Glaziers' Company, 75
Glovers, 40, 107
Glynne, John, 195, 272
Goldsmith, Mr., 126n
Goldsmiths, 25
— Company, 208, 241, 303, 320, 328, 329
Goodman, John, 119, 200, 201, 213
Goodwin, Sir Arthur, 184
— John, 163, 177, 183, 184, 184n, 231-2, 254
Gore, Alderman Sir John, 266n, 294
— Joan, 80n
— William, 80n
Gorges, Sir Francis, 186
Goring, George, Baron Goring, 194n
Gouge, William, 162, 165, 179
Grand Remonstrance of 1641, 23, 91, 126, 129, 192, 221, 300
Greenhill, William, 40
Greenland Company, 99, 299, 331
Greenwax, 21, 80, 84, 84n
Greville, Fulke, 172, 270
— — first Lord Brooke, 41, 160
— Robert, second Lord Brooke, 92, 97, 165, 169, 170, 172, 208, 229, 253, 278n, 286, 288.
Grocers' Company, 94n, 161n, 174, 208, 243, 307, 311, 316, 321, 325, 326, 327, 337n
Guinea Company, 241
Guines (France), 14
Gunfounders, 11n
Gutstring makers, 87
Gurney, Alderman Sir Richard, 93, 98, 114n, 117, 124-5, 126, 128, 130,

131, 145, 146, 148, 149, 153, 154-8, 159, 161, 207-8, 228, 248n, 250, 266n, 292, 296, 298, 301, **302-3**, 305, 308, 324

Haberdashers' Company, 94n, 209, 210, 232n, 242, 304, 306, 313, 318
Halstead, Lawrence, 266n
Hames (France), 14
Hamilton, James, third Marquis of Hamilton, 290
Hampden, Mrs Elizabeth, 42, 183
— M.P., John, 42, 171, 175, 183, 184, 203, 219
Harby, Sir Job, 93, 187, 208n
Harrington, Sir James, 233, 308
Harrison, Alderman Gilbert, 98, 114n, 158n, 247-8, 249n, **303**
— Sir John, 101, 194, 194n, 205
Harvey, Daniel, 78, 121, 150
— Eliab, 150
Harwood, George, 165
Hat-band makers, 87
Hat, John, 270
Heath, Sir Robert, 73
Henrietta Maria, Queen, 27, 145
Herne, Mr., 156
Hexter, Professor J. H., 3-4, 251
Heylin, Alderman Rowland, 164
— Peter, 7, 133n, 164
Heywood, Peter, 34
— Sir Thomas, 211
Hickes, Sir Baptist, 17n, 93
Hicks' Hall, 17, 29, 74
Highlord, Alderman John, 91n, 114n, 158n, **303**
Holborn, 10, 12, 16, 39, 41
Holland, Earl of, see Rich, Sir Henry
— Sir John, 211n
Hollar, Wenceslaus, 9
Holles, Denzil, 203, 227, 300
Honourable Artillery Company, and Artillery Garden, 42, 87, 162, **170-173**, 175, 188, 191, 244, 278-9, 283, 313, 315, 323, 324, 325, 326
Horners' Company, 87
Hough, Ralph, 75
Howard, Henry Frederick, Lord Maltravers, 180, 312
— Thomas, second Earl of Arundel and Surrey, 108, 180
Howell, James, 63

Howes, Edmund, 10, 12
Hudson, Robert, 285n
Hughes, George, 163, 165, 189
Huguenots, 178, 189
Hyde, Edward, first Earl of Clarendon,
    1, 39, 40, 50, 71, 79, 113, 125, 132,
    135, 151, 158, 184, 199, 199n,
    202-4, 206, 215, 228, 231, 234,
    253, 256

Incorporation of the suburbs, **31-37,** 43,
    87, 116, 128-9, 268-9, 281, see also
    under London (constitutional):
    Aldermen and Court of Aldermen,
    suburbs
Ingram, Sir Arthur, 194n
Inns of Court, 166, 265, and individual
    inns under London, (topogra-
    phical): *Residences and Buildings*
Irish Rebellion, 53, 206, 208, 221;
    loans for suppression of, 125, 207-8,
    226, 252, 295; petition of Common
    Council, 143; Irish Adventurers,
    208, 316
— Society, and City's Irish estates, 22,
    81-87, 91, 94, 106, 127, 128, 241,
    293, 297, 316, 329
Ironmongers' Company, 26, 294-5,
    296, 327
Isaacson, Mr., 126n
Italian Company, 285

Jacob, Sir John, 194, 194n, 255n
James, Margaret, 45
Jannsen, Cornelius, 182n
Jenner, M.P., Robert, 194n
Jermyn, M.P., Sir Thomas, 204
Joiners' Company, 75
Jones, Inigo, 12, 304
— Isaac, 285n
Jonson, Ben, 233
Journals and Repertories of the City
    government, see London (con-
    stitutional): *Aldermen and Court of*
    Aldermen, Common Councilmen and
    Court of Common Council, Common Hall
Justices of the Peace, 17, 19-20, 28-31,
    35, 60 (see also under Middlesex
    and Surrey)

Keepers of the Compters, 64, 329
Keightley, Mr., 196n, 207-8n, 285n

Kendricke, Alderman John, 240, 244n,
    245, 253n, 259n, **321**
Kilvert, Richard, 290, 291
King, Gregory, 14
King's Lynn, 242, 311
Kirke, Mr., 88n
Kirton, M.P., Edward, 221, 234
Knightley, Sir Richard, 160

Lambarde, William, 9
Lambe, Sir John, 189
Lancaster Castle, 166
Langham, Alderman Sir John, 126n,
    158n, 173, 238n, 240n, 243, 243n,
    245, 282, 314, **321-2**
Langhorne, Mr., 255n
La Rochelle, 178
Laud, Archbishop William, 40, 79, 91,
    94, 107, 109, 163, 164, 165, ·166,
    167, 180, 181, 181n, 184, 195, 231,
    266n, 300, 304
Law and order, see law and order and,
    under London (constitutional):
    Aldermen and Court of Aldermen,
    Common Councilmen and Court of
    Common Council, Lord Mayor (and
    office and functions of, under)
    Sheriffs and Sheriffs' Court; Riots and
    disturbances; Justices of the Peace;
    Trained Bands)
Lawley, Thomas, 285n
Leathersellers' Company, 293, 310, 313
Leatherworkers, 15, 40, 107, 229
Lectures and Lecturers (see also Puri-
    tans and Puritanism), 161, 163-7,
    220-1, 230-2; St. Anne's, Black-
    friars, 162-3; St. Antholin's, 79
    163-5, 167, 230-1; St. Sepulchre's,
    Holborn, 165; St. Martin-in-the-
    Fields, 165; All Hallows, Lombard
    street, 165; St. Matthew, Friday
    street, 166; St. Bartholomew Ex-
    change, 166; All Hallows', Bread
    street, 189; St. Mary Magdalen,
    Milk street, 232; Commons' Order
    for appointment of lecturers, 220
Leicester, Earl of, see Sidney, Robert
Leighton, Dr. Alexander, 118, 307
Levant Company, 92, 99, 122, 150, 162,
    169, 176, 187, 190, 191, 235, 241,
    243, 244, 245, 267, 285, 288, 296,
    297, 299, 301, 314, 317-8, 321-2
Levellers, 233, 253n

Lewkenor, Christopher, 34

Liberties and outparishes, 19-20, 23-29, 36, 37, 38, 43, 281-2, see also individual places under London and suburbs (topographical): *Liberties, suburbs and environs*; Incorporation of the suburbs

Lilburne, John, 107, 224, 287

Limeburners, 16n

Littleton, Sir Edward, 71n

Livery Companies and Liverymen, 15, 17, 34, 35, 36, 38, 50, 53, 55, 58, 59, 60, 60n, 63, 67, 69, 75, 80, 80n, 86, 86n, 87, 90, 94, 102, 116, 120, 126, 207-9, 242, 264-5, 274, 284, 287, 311 (see also individual Companies)

Lloyd, David, 297, 301, 307

Loans and requests for loans, see also loans and, under London (constitutional): *Aldermen and Court of Aldermen, City Chamber, Common Councilmen and Court of Common Council, Common Hall, Lord Mayor*, and under Parliament, *House of Commons*, City government and (1625), 72-73; (1626), 73, 286; (1639-40), 94-104, 287, 300; (1640-41), 198-207; (1642-3), 252-3, 259-60, 267; City Chamber and (1626-43), 73, 89, 96, 103-4, 151, 198, 206, 207, 248, 252, 336, 338; City finances and (1626-50), 332-8; 'Royal Contract' (1627), 73-75; Livery Companies and (1628-43), 75, 102-3, 207-9, 210; Customs Farmers and (1639-42), 96, 100-101, 101n, 106, 205-6, 257, 291, 302, 306, 328; Common Council and, (1639-42), 94-95, 98-99, 103-4, 207; Acton, Alderman, and (1639-40), 111, 291; Aldermen and, (1639-43), 74-76, 94-104, 177n, 192, 205, 267, 303-5, 306, 312, 326, 328, 329; Merchant Adventurers (1640), 101; 'Pepper', East India Company (1640), 101, 288, 297; Common Hall and (1641), 132, 206-7, 208; Penington, Alderman, and (1641), 198-206, 208, 253, 260, 267; Commons and, (1641), 197-8, 202-5, 260; Strafford's execution and (1641), 201, 205-6;

City M.P.s and (1641), 198-9, 206; Irish Rebellion (1642), 208, 226, 252; weekly assessments and (1642), 252-3; 'voluntary collections' and (1642), 209-10;

London, aliens in, 14-15, 25-26, 39, 107; fortification of, 183, **262-5,** 322; growth of, Ch. I *passim*, 69n; historians and, 1-4, 7, 45-49, 134-6; maps of, 9, 9n; plague in, 13, 17, 17n, 43, 123; predominance of, 13-14, 69, 69n; Tower, Lieutenant of, 27, 27n, 143, 223, 224, 225, 274 (see also, Balfour, Conyers, Lunsford and Penington); Tower, The, see under London (topographical): *Residences and buildings*

— and suburbs (topographical): *Churches, parishes and precincts,* All Hallows, Bread street, 162, 163, 164, 189; All Hallows, Lombard street, 165; All Hallows the Great 166; St. Alphege, Cripplegate, 55n; St. Andrew Hubbard, 55n, 344; St. Andrew's, Holborn, 13; St. Anne's, Blackfriars, 162; St. Antholin's, 79, 163, 167, 231, 264; St. Augustine's, Watling street, 55n, 344; St. Bartholomew Exchange, 55n, 166, 344; St. Benet Fink, 135n, 344; St. Benet, Paul's Wharf, 55n, 135n, 344; St. Botolph, Aldgate, 36; St. Botolph, Billingsgate, 55n, 344; St. Botolph Without Bishopsgate, 344; St. Bride's, 13; St. Clement Dane, 265; St. Dunstan's in the West, 135n, 137, 344; St. George, Botolph lane, 55n, 344; St. Giles', Cripplegate, 13, 16, 220; St. Giles-in-the-Fields, 265; St. John's, Hackney, 324; St. Leonard's, Eastcheap, 133, 217; St. Magnus, London Bridge, 166; St. Margaret, Lothbury, 183; St. Margaret, New Fish street, 55n, 309, 344; St. Martin-in-the-Fields, 13, 40; St. Mary Aldermanbury, 55n, 74, 166, 166n, 345; St. Mary Magdalen, Milk street, 232; St. Mary Newington, 31; St. Matthew, Friday street, 166, 307; St.

London—*cont.*
Nicholas Acons, 55n, 344; St.
Olave Jewry, 183, 345; St. Paul's,
79, 91, 94, 180, 262, 295; St.
Sepulchre's, Holborn, 13, 40, 165;
St. Stephen's, Coleman street, 75,
97, 135n, 137, 140, 163, 169, 183,
184, 231, 279, 287, 324, 344; St.
Swithin's, London Stone, 185
—— *Liberties, suburbs and environs,*
19-20, 23-29, 36, 37, 38, 43, 281-2;
Alsatia, 38; Bermondsey, 15, 29,
40, 107; Blackfriars, 14, 23, 32, 36,
37, 40-41; Blackwall, 12; Brentford,
252, 263, 314; Chelsea, 42;
Clerkenwell, 13, 14, 16, 23;
Deptford, 12, 16; Duchy of Lancaster, 14, 24, 27, 30n; Duke's
Place, 36, 37; Finchley, 330;
Hackney, 12n, 31, 41, 168, 324;
Hampstead, 325; Highgate, 136n,
330; Holborn, 10, 12, 16, 39, 40,
41; Holywell, 14; Hornsey, 314,
330; Houndsditch, 11n; Hoxton,
14; Isleworth, 16; Islington, 16, 31;
Kensington, 42; Lambeth, 15, 29,
31, 256; Liberty of the Rolls, 24;
Limehouse, 11-12, 12n; Mile End,
38; Minories, 23, 24, 26; Norton
Folgate, 14, 24; Paris Garden, 29,
29n; Poplar, 12, 12n; Ratcliffe,
11-12, 12n; Richmond, 292;
Rotherhithe, 16, 31, 168; St.
Katherine's, 10, 14, 23; St. Martin's le Grand, 14, 23, 25, 36;
Shadwell, 11; Shoreditch, 14;
Southwark, 13, 13n, 14, 15, 23,
28-29, 30, 40, 43, 107, 116, 234,
294; 323; Spitalfields, 15, 42n,
217; Stepney, 12, 12n, 15, 29, 31,
32, 40, 253; Tower Liberties, 26,
27; Wapping, 11, 12n, 13, 14, 40;
Westminister, 11, 13, 15, 16, 25,
28, 28n, 33, 34, 37, 39, 40, 42, 69,
74, 129, 145, 151, 180; Whitechapel,
11, 14, 16; Whitefriars, 23, 24, 32,
36, 38, 40-41, 176, 179-80
—— *Residences and buildings,* Apollo
Club, 233; Arundel House, 108,
180; Austin Friars, 24; Balmes
House, Hoxton, 126, 306; Bethlem,
17, 24n, 329; Blackfriars, monastery of, 23, 24; Bridewell, 17; 329;
Brooke House, Hackney, 41;
Brooke House, Holborn, 41;
Charing Cross, 211; Cheapside
Cross, 233-4, 262; Christ's Hospi-
tal, 17, 320, 329; Clink, the, 29;
Crosby House, 255, 256, 292, 306;
Crutched Friars, 24, 24n; Dorset
House, 180; Elsing Spital, priory
of, 24; Ely House, 24; Fleet Prison,
180, 319; Flushing Inn, Wapping,
40; Forty Hall, Enfield, 304;
Goldsmiths' Hall, 202; Gresham
College, 255; Grey Friars, 24;
Grocers' Hall, 147, 224; Haber-
dashers' Hall, 209, 210, 255;
Hampden House, 42; Hampton
Court, 129; Holland House, 42;
Holy Trinity, monastery of, 23,
24n; Inner Temple, 180; Lambeth
Palace, 108, 144, 256, 300; Leaden-
hall, 144; Lincoln's Inn, 166, 168,
London Bridge, 330; Mercers'
Chapel, 325; Merchant Taylors'
Hall, 235, 270n; Middle Temple,
195; Mint, the, 29, 29n, 328, 329;
Newgate Prison, 109, 287, 310, 322,
327; Northumberland House, 18;
Oxford Place, 18; Red Bull
Theatre, 41; Robin Hood Club,
233; St. Bartholomew's, Hospital
and priory of, 16, 23, 24, 26, 32,
316; St. John's, Clerkenwell, priory
of, 24; St. Katherine's, Hospital
of, 23, 26; St. Martin's le Grand,
24n; St. Mary Graces, 24, 24n; St.
Mary Spital, 18, 24n; St. Thomas'
Hospital, 16, 308; Salters' Hall,
251, 260, 273; Serjeant's Inn, 180;
Ship Tavern, Fish street, 289; Star
Inn, Coleman street, 184; Temple
Bar, 142; Tower of London, 101,
105, 131, 141, 143, 145, 150, 211,
218, 223, 225, 227, 274, 298, 305,
322, 324; Warwick House, 41;
Weavers' Hall, 253; Whitefriars,
monastery of, 23, 24, 24n; Whitehall, 62, 129, 132, 141, 143, 144,
277, 330; White Lion Tavern, 233;
Worcester Place, 18
—— *Streets and public places and areas,*
Aldermanbury, 232; Aldgate, 32,
36; Artillery Garden, 164, 168,
170-3, 232, 235; Artillery Yard,

London—*cont.*

142; Billingsgate, 264; Bread
street, 187, 273; Brick lane (earlier
Hog lane), 11; Broken Wharf, 177;
Bucklersbury, 242, 326; Candlewick street, 188n; Chancery lane,
10, 12; Cheapside, 143, 156; Coldharbour, 26, 32; Coleman street,
77, 140, 145, **183-4,** 224, 244,
308, 324; Covent Garden, 12, 39,
40, 42, 265; Drury lane, 11, 12, 13;
Gracechurch street, 315; Gray's
Inn lane, 41, 160, 169; Great
Queen street, 12; Hangman's
Gains, 15; Hog lane, see Brick
lane; Holywell street, 15; Houndsditch, 10, 11; Lincoln's Inn Fields,
12, 22, 42n; Long Acre, 12, 13;
Long lane, 10; Mark lane, 84, 130;
Milk street, 292; Moorfields, 107,
235; New Fish street, 242, 309;
Nicholas lane, 188n; Palace Yard,
221, 224, 226; Port of London,
145; Poultry, 224; Russell's Row,
Shoreditch, 18; St. George's Fields,
107-8, 181, 234-5; St. John's street,
14, 41, 71; St. Martin's lane, 11,
12; St. Swithin's lane, 169;
Strand, 11, 12; Turnmill street,
14; Vauxhall, 144; Watling street,
234, 244, 323; Wood street, 221,
292

—— *Wards*, Aldersgate, 11, 25-26,
135, 291, 296, 311, 345; Aldgate,
291; Basinghall, 148n; Billingsgate, 295, 296; Bishopsgate, 13, 15,
32, 298; Bread street, 188; Bridge,
295; Bridge Without, 28, 285;
Broad street, 139, 299; Candlewick, 298; Castle Baynard, 299;
Cheap, 325; Coleman street, **183-4,**
285, 324-5; Cordwainer, 307, 315;
Cornhill, 137, 139, 345; Cripplegate, 32, 150, 298, 325, 345;
Dowgate, 293; Farringdon Within,
135, 136-7, 306, 345; Farringdon
Without, 32, 329; Langbourne,
135, 139, 306; Lime street, 295;
Portsoken, 32, 322; Queenhithe,
289; Vintry, 147, 249, 299, 328;
Walbrook, 293

— (constitutional): *Aldermen and Court
of Aldermen*, City Chamber and,

56, 62, 76, 287, 338; Committees'
33, 56, 115n, 117, 120-1, 125, 128,
149n, 149-50, 227-8, 238-9, 240-1,
243; Common Council and, 54-58,
83-84, 95, 109-10, 114-16, 117, 121,
125, 135, 138, 146-59, 225-6,
247-8, 274-5, 276, 281, 338;
Common Hall and, 51-53, 110,
113, 120-2; composition of, 91-93,
113-14, 158-9, 238-9, 240-6, 248-9,
265-7, 276-7, 282-4, App. I and II
passim; constitution of, 48n, 59-62,
110-12, 125, 146-59, 246-50, 274,
280-1, 291, 298; crown and, Ch. III
passim, 110-12, 122, 123, 126-30,
177n, 192, 241, 276-7, 286-7, 291-2,
295, 297-8, 301, 302, 304, 205, 306,
307, 312, 319, 320-1, 326, 329;
elections and, 110-12, 120-2, 124-5,
171-2, 188, 191, 298, 303, 308;
law and order and, 16-17, 29-31,
37-44, 76-77, 104, 108, 110, 119-20,
125, 128-9, 131-2, 141-3, 156-7,
214-17, 224; loans and, 74-76, 94-
104, 177n, 192, 205, 267, 303-5, 306,
312, 326, 328, 329; Parliament
and, 1-3, 22-23, 115n, 116n, 117-19,
128, 193-6, 205, 230, 259-60,
268-9, 276, 277, 281; parliamentary puritans and, 74-75, 104-6, 120,
128, 130-1, 147-59, 174-84, 191-3,
196, 239-51, 255, 261, 266, App.
II *passim*; petitions of, 82-83,
116-17, 128-9, 130-1, 151-5, 174,
196, 222-6; political attitude of,
1-5; 91-93, 109-10, 113-14, 116-19,
123-31, 142, 144, 148n, 149-50,
158-9, 196, 218, 250-1, 255-7,
261-2, 266-7, 274, 276-7, 280, 281,
284, 292, 294-5, 302, 310, 312, 313,
314, 315, 326; privileges and
powers of, 16-17, 30-31, 59-62, 64,
66, 86, 146, 152, 152n, 170-1, 188,
329, 332, 333n, 338; puritanism
and, 79, 161, 179-81, 183-4, 212-
14, 262, 295, 312, 326, 329, 329n;
Repertories, 4-5, 32, 45-46, 49, 118,
339-40; suburbs and, 23-37, 43-44,
268-9, 281

—— *Charters*, 22, 45-49, 80-88; (1227)
47-48; (1406) 28; (1443) 28;
(1445) 21-22, 84n; (1462) 28;
(1505) 84n; (1507) 22; (1608) 27,

London—*cont.*

30, 31-32, 36; (1638) 22, 30-31, 36, 86-87, 276; (1640) 87-88, 128-9

—— *City Chamber*, Aldermen and, 56 62, 76, 287, 338; Common Council and, 56; financial state of, 73, 83, 87, 206, 207, 207n, 277, 332-8; loans and, 73, 89, 96, 103-4, 151, 198, 206, 207, 248, 252, 336, 338; Orphans and, 332, 332n; reform of, 281, 336-8; Ship Money and, 118

—— *City Chamberlain*, 76, 92, 136, 335; election of, 52, 120, 303, 333; duties of, 65-66, 336, 337

—— *City government, privileges, powers and revenues*, 17, 21-22, 27n, 34, 35n, 36-37, 65n, 76, 80, 84-86, 88n, 115n, 128-9, 149n, 268-9, 274, 276, 281, 336-7, 337n, 338

—— *Common Councilmen and Court of Common Council*, Aldermen and, 54-58, 83-84, 95, 109-10, 114-16, 117,121,125,135,138,146-59, 225-6, 247-8, 274-5, 276, 281, 338; Committees, 56, 75, 115-16, 117, 125, 128, 134, 135, 136, 136n, 137, 138-9, 140-1, 143-4, 146-9, 149n, 151, 187, 188, 224, 228, 243-6, 258-9, 267-8, 276, 315, 324, 325, 331, 334, 336, 337; crown and, 81-86, 88-91, 94-95, 98-99, 102, 103, 103n, 126n, 127, 132-3, 141, 143-4, 148n, 151, 225, 255, 276, 300; defence of the City and, 139-41, 144-5, 146, 148-51, 251-2, 258, 262-5; elections and, 132-40, (returns on elections, wards and precincts) 345; Irish Estates and, 81-84, 94, 128; Journals of, 4-5, 32, 53, 96n, 115-16, 134, 137, 147, 173, 339-40; law and order and, 125, 131-2, 225, 251; loans and, 94-95, 98-99, 103-4, 207; Parliament and, 1-3, 114-17, 118, 126-7, 128, 132-59, 224-5, 230, 239, 258-9, 281; parliamentary puritans and, 95-96, 114-16, 126, 132-59, 243-4, 247-9, 262-5, 276, 277-9; Penington and, 177n, 239, 247-9, 250-74; petitions and, 95-96, 96n, 115-16, 129, 143-4, 148n, 151-5, 222-3, 225, 230, 254-5, 258-9, 260, 269, 276,

330-1; political attitude of, 1-3, 25, 88, 90, 95-96, 102, 114-17, 132-41, 143-4, 250-1, 252, 254, 255, 257-9, 261, 262, 272, 274, 276, 280, 281 284; privileges and powers of, 17, 53-58, 146-9, 154-5, 338; Puritanism and, 262; radicals and, 250-1, 259, 260-1, 267-9, 272, 280, 284; suburbs and, 32-33, 268-9

—— *Common Hall*, City Chamberlain and, 303, 333; City M.P.s and, 101-2, 112-13, 175; constitution of, 50-53, 67, 281; Fowke and, 318, 319; Journal of, 53, 147; loans and, 132, 206-7, 208; Lord Mayors and, 104, 110-12, 124-5, 298; meeting at (January 1643), 256, 301; petitions and, 113, 211; Sheriffs and, 120-2, 131, 248, 325

—— "*Corporation*", 2n

—— *Lord Mayor*, aliens and, 15, 107; Common Council and, 58, 102, 103, 110, 146-7, 148-58, 224, 300; crown and, 17n, 89-91, 123, 126-30, 131, 144, 155, 287; election of, 51, 110-12, 124-5, 157-8, 192; functions, privileges and powers of, 17n, 25, 59, 60, 62-64, 246n, 281, 333, 337, 337n; Gurney, 125, 126, 127, 128, 129, 130, 144, 146-58, 277, 324, 325; Honourable Artillery Company and, 171, 191; law and order and, 119-20, 125, 130-1, 174, 217; loans and, 97-103, 205, 260, 267; Militia and, 148-51; new buildings and, 13, 18-19, 300; Penington, 157-8, 183, 237, 246 seq.; petitions and, 17n, 112, 113, 130, 174, 222-3, 225, 226; Protestation and, 218; Remembrancer and, 67, 71, 123; Sheriffs and, 48, 52, 120-2, 122n. (See also Abbot, Andrewes, Foot, Fowke, Garway, Rainton, Reynardson, Warner, Whitmore, Wollaston, Wright.)

—— *Minor City Officers* (City Marshals, Common Sergeant, Hunt and Packer, "Seacolemeators", Secondary and Keepers of City Compters), 16, 51, 62n, 64, 70n, 329

—— *Recorder*, 30, 51, 60, 66-67, 71, (see also Gardiner, Sir Thomas; Littleton, Sir Edward; Glynne, John)

London—*cont.*

—— *Remembrancer*, 67, 71, 247 (see also Wiseman, Thomas)

—— *Sheriffs and Sheriffs' Court*, 13n, 83, 118, 129, 130, 253, 255, 297-8, 314, 326; election of, 47-48, 48n, 52-53, 63, 110, 120-2; Clarke, George, 124-5; Commission of Array and, 155, 155n; office and functions of, 64-65, 99n, 230, 238, 246-8, 337; Ship Money and, 88-90; Under-sheriff, 64, 247

—— *Town Clerk*, 52, 62n, 64, 246-7

—— *Wardmote*, 54, 55, 59, 138-9

Long, M.P., Walter, 149, 228

Lord Mayor, see London (constitutional): *Lord Mayor*

Love, Christopher, 167, 167n, 189n, 326

Lowe, M.P., George, 194n

— Alderman Sir Thomas, 48n

Ludlow, M.P., Sir Henry, 239

Lunsford, Colonel, Sir Thomas, 131, 141, 143, 224

Lusher, Thomas, 137, 139, 150

Magdalen College, Oxford, 167

Mainwaring, Randall, 120, 140, 144, 154-5, 156, 171, 173, 196n, 223n, 244, 256, 260, **323**

Maitland, William, 26, 45

Maltravers, Lord, see Howard, Frederick Henry

Manly, Sir Richard, 42

Marshall, Sir George, 84n, 86n

— Stephen, 219

Marten, M.P., Henry, 218, 220n, 226, 239, 270, 271, 272, 280, 319

— Sir Henry, 85n

Mason, Robert, 71n

Massachusetts Bay Company, 148n, 162, 165, 169, 185, 186, 187, 189, 309, 324

Medford, river, 185

Mercers' Company, 94n, 207n, 242, 297, 312

Merchant Adventurers' Company, 77, 101, 241

— Taylors' Company, 187, 188, 207-8, 208n, 235, 288, 291, 292, 303, 305

Mercurius Aulicus, 133n, 261, 308

'Mercurius Civicus', *A Letter from Mercurius Civicus to Mercurius Rusticus*,

Oxford, 1643, 133, **133n**, 137, 139, 140, 142, 146, 148, 152, 155, 160, 162, 164, 167, 170

Merian, Matthew, 9

Middlesex, 15, 16, 17, 30, 31, 37, 74

— Justices of the Peace, 17, 19-20, 28n, 29, 30n (see also Justices of the Peace)

Middleton, Alderman Sir Hugh, 233

Militia, Militia Committee, and Committee of Safety, see also Militia and, under London (constitutional): *Lord Mayor*; 120, 152, 159; Committee of Safety as Militia Commissioners, 147, 148-50; composition of Committee of Safety, 140-1; composition of Militia Committee, 169, 238-46, 298, 301, 305, 309n, 310, 311, 312, 313, 313n, 315, 318, 320, 321, 323, 324, 326, 329, 330, 330n, 331; functions, powers, and political attitude of Militia Committee, 238-9, 249-50, 251, 252, 267-8, 271-2, 272n, 279; Militia Committee and impeachment of Gurney, 228; Parliament and Militia, 223; political attitude and powers of Safety Committee, 145-7; opposition of Lord Mayor and Aldermen to, 148-51

Milton, John, 168, 172

Mitchell, Mr., 156

— Robert, 247

Monastic sites, 11, 13, 18, 23-24, 26-27

Monk, George, first Duke of Albemarle, 324

Monopolies, 93, 94, 95, 117, 119, 175, 241, 289-91, 293-4, 320, 328-30

Montague, Edward, Lord Kimbolton and Viscount Mandeville, 42

Mosse, Clement, 156, 207-8n

— Mr., 139

Mosse's shop, 234

Moyer, Samuel, 310, 331

Mun, Thomas, 16

Munday, Anthony, 9, 46, 85n

Muscovy Company, 92, 241

Nalson, John, 1, 7, 228

Nevill, Thomas, 266n

Newcourt, Richard, 9

New England, Council for, 169

New England Plantations Companies, 161, 162, 164-5, 185, 186, 191, 235
'Newes from Guildhall', 335-6, 337, 338
Newhaven, colony of, 169, 183
New Inn Hall, Oxford, 167
Newitt, William, 118
New Model Army, 269
News-sheets, 234, 261
Newton, William, 42n
Nicholas, Sir Edward, 122, 123, 124, 126, 128, 131, 302
Nicholson, Christopher, 148, 155, 253n
Norbury, Mr., 270
Norden, John, 9
Normington, Alexander, 137, 140, 140n, 171, 244, **323**
Northcote, Sir John, 190
North-West Passage Company, 285
Norton, George, 45

Oake, Robert, 118, 293-4
Offspring, Charles, 163, 165, 231
Ordinaries, 179, 233
Orphans, Orphans' Court and Fund, 60, 62, 66, 73, 76, **332-4**, 336, 338, see also under London (constitutional): *City Chamber*
Overbury, Sir Giles, 270

Parkhurst, Alderman Sir Robert, 118n, 194n, 338
Parliament, see below, also Parliament and, under Parliamentary puritans, and under London (constitutional): *Aldermen and Court of Aldermen, Common Councilmen and Court of Common Council*
— *Acts and Bills* (see also Parliament, *Ordinances and Orders*), 20-21, 21-22, 81, 84n, 201-2, 205-6, 213, 216-17, 219-20, 227, 315
— *House of Commons*, see also General Rising Committee; Parliament and, under London (constitutional): *Aldermen and Court of Aldermen;* Parliamentary puritans; Petitions; Petitioning; Radicals; Acton, Alderman, and, 78; Army and (1647), 282; Church reform and, 212-16; City government and, 1-3, Ch. IV *passim*, 193-6, 205, 224-5, 230, 238, 239, 250-73, 276, 277, 338; City M.P.s and, 191,

193-6, Ch. IV *passim*, 237-9, 279-80; City parliamentary puritans and, 125, 127-8, 130, 132-3, 140 seq., 314, 316-17, 317n; City radicals and, 252, 260-1, 270-3; Committees of, 76, 118-19, 181, 194n, 224, 253, 265-7, 270-3, 289, 290, 294, 294n, 318, 319, 321, 329; East India Company and, 122-3, 296-7; Five Members and, 141, 143, 145, 224-5; Grand Remonstrance and, 126, 221; Langham, Alderman, and, 322; loans and, 72-76, 197-210, 248, 252-3, 257, 259-60, 267, 306, 325, 326, 328, 330, 338; London connections of Members, 193-4; 'middle group' of, 238-9, 239n, 241, 258-9, 267, 274; Ordinances and Orders of, 123-4, 136, 209-10, 220, 253; 'peace party' and, 239n, 250, 255-8, 272, 320; Penington, Alderman, and, 113, 129, 158, 178, 179, 184, Ch. VI *passim*, 237-9, 250-75, 280; petitions and, 131, 149, 196, 212-16, 221-3, 225-7, 228, 229-30, 232-3, 268, 270, 272, 280, 288, 296-7; Roberts' pamphlet, and, 283
— *House of Lords*, Bishops, exclusion of, 128, 130-1, 145, 206, 219, 221, 224, 225-6, 227; Church, Lecturers, and, 200, 213, 220, 223; City constitution and, 120-2, 154, 157; crown and, 144, 258, 259, 272; Fowke, Alderman, and, 317, 319; 'Mercurius Civicus' on, 152; Militia and, 145, 149, 227; Protections and, 117, 128, 150-1
— *Ordinances and Orders* (see also Parliament, *Acts and Bills*), 209-10, 218, 220-1, 240, 252-3, 267, 272, 310, 313
Parliamentary puritans, see also City parliamentary puritans and, under Charles I and Privy Council; Parliamentary puritans and, under London (constitutional): *Aldermen and Court of Aldermen, Common Councilmen and Court of Common Council;* City parliamentary puritans and, under Parliament, *House of Commons;* Petitioning; City

Parliamentary puritans—*cont.*
  government and, 68, 73-75, 91, 104,
    105, 110-13, 115, 125, 128, 131-
    59, 207; Common Council and,
    95-96, 114-16, 126, 132-59, 173,
    243-4, 247-9, 262-5, 276, 277-9;
    composition of, 5, 120, Ch. V
    passim, 223-4, 237-46, 282, App. II
    passim; diversity of opinion among,
    273-5, 277-9, 283-4; organization
    of, 6, 214, 217, 218, 222-4, 226,
    230-5, 253, 263-5, 277-80; Parlia-
    ment and, 75-76, 105, 144, 218,
    222-4, 226, 253; Privy Council
    and, 103, 108, 109; Pym and,
    228-230; the term, 5-6
Peard, M.P., George, 131
Penington, Abigail, 176n
— Judith, 176
— junior, Isaac, 176n, 182, 184
— Mary, 176n, 179, 233, 264
— Mary (daughter-in-law of Alder-
    man Penington), 232n
— M.P., Alderman Isaac, 65, 97, 100,
    113, 114n, 129, 140, 140n, 143,
    144, 146, 150, 158, 159, 163, 170,
    171, 172, 175, **176-84**, 188, 191,
    193, **198-206**, 209, **210-16, 218-21,**
    223, 224, 225, 227, 228, 229, 232,
    232n, 233, 235-40, 246-51, 253-6,
    256n, **260-5,** 267, 269, 270, 273,
    274, 280, 282, 298, 307, 319, 323,
    329
— Robert, 176n
— Sir John, 65, 129, 176n, 178, 219
Peck, Francis, 120, 171, 173, 196n,
    240, 244, **323**
Perkins, William, 137, 148, 148n, 155,
    169
Persecutio Undecima, 1648, 41n, 134, 172,
    173, 179, 218, 232, 233-4
Peter, Hugh, 40, 42, 165, 169, 184, 254,
    261
Petitioning, see also Petitions; and
    petitions of, under London (con-
    stitutional): *Aldermen and Court of
    Aldermen, Common Councilmen and
    Court of Common Council,* and *Com-
    mon Hall;* and petitions, under
    Parliament, *House of Commons;* and
    petitions and, under Charles I and
    Privy Council; Bar of House of
    Commons and, 196, 229-30; City

  government approval and, 115,
    117, 196; Committee of Safety and,
    146; Commons' investigation of,
    131, 232-3; Lord Mayor (Garway)
    and, 300; obstructions against,
    131; parliamentary puritan cam-
    paign and, 119, 140, 147-55, 173-5,
    210, 213-16, 222-3, 229-30, 232-4,
    315, 319-20, 323; royalist, 330;
    royal prohibition of, 95, 216, 229;
    Shute, Richard, and, 252, 253;
    tactical presentation of, 212; tav-
    erns and, 233
Petitions (see also Petitioning), from
    East India Company (1628), 286,
    (1640-41), 122, 297; from Burton's
    parishioners (1636), 166; from
    Grocers' Company apprentices
    (1639), 174; from City government
    against new buildings (1639), 22;
    for 'redress of grievances' (1639,
    1640), 39, 95, 102, 108, 111, 113,
    174-5, 210-11, 314; against Lau-
    dian Canons (1640), 109, 166, 174;
    'Root and Branch' (1640), 116,
    129, 140, 201, 213, 214-16; from
    Churchwardens and Sidesmen
    (1640), 212; from City govern-
    ment on Incorporation, Southwark
    and the poor (1640-41), 37, 116;
    from Livery Companies (1640-41),
    37, 116; for execution of Strafford
    (1641), 116, 205, 216; for the
    Protestation (1641), 218; for ex-
    clusion of Bishops and other de-
    mands (1641), 116, 128, 130, 222-3,
    226, 318; Singleton against Cordell
    (1641), 297; against Protections
    (1641), 117, 128; 'The Ministers',
    for Church reform (1641), 213-14,
    215-16; disputed election of Sheriff
    (1641), 120-1; for 'abatement of
    duty' on re-exports (1641), 122-3;
    from City government against dis-
    orders (1641), 129, 329-30; for
    abolition of Episcopacy and other
    demands (1641), 223, 315; for
    Episcopacy and Book of Common
    Prayer (1641), 133, 216n; for a
    National Synod (1641), 223;
    against royal policy and removal
    of Balfour (1642), 143-4, 145; for
    exclusion of Bishops, control of

Petitions—*cont.*
  Militia, and other demands (1642),
    145, 225-6; Benion's, against
    Militia Committee (1642), 149-50,
    207n, 234, 330; from Common
    Council against Lord Mayor
    (1642), 154; against arrest of Five
    Members (1642), 225; against
    obstruction by Lords (1642),
    225-6; from eastern suburbs
    (1642), 40; labourers and porters,
    seamen, and artificers (1642), 226;
    for control of fortresses and the
    Militia (1642), 227; against peace
    and for army reform (1642), 252;
    against peace negotiations (1642),
    253-4, 257; 'Kentish' (1642), 330;
    for peace (1642), 255-6; from City
    government for peace (1643),
    255-6, 299; from Common Council
    to Parliament (1643), 258-9; Re-
    monstrance for supremacy of
    Parliament and other demands
    (1643), 260-1; on powers of
    Militia Committee (1643), 268-70;
    for the General Rising (1643), 270;
    against 'accommodation' (1643),
    237n, 272; for re-establishment of
    Committee of Both Kingdoms
    (1644), 318-19; from City govern-
    ment for appointment of Lieuten-
    ant of Tower (1644), 27n; for
    Fowke (1645, 1646), 319
Philips, Thomas, 115
Phillippes, Sir Thomas, 81
Pierrepont, M.P., William, 125
Pindar, Sir Paul, 93, 96, 266, 286
Player, Thomas, 144
Plays and playhouses, 41, 330
Pleydell, M.P., William, 209
Plumbers' Company, 75
Political independents, 6, **238-9**, 243,
    259, **309n**, 312, 313, 315, 323, 325,
    327
— presbyterians, 6, **238-9**, **243**, **258-9**,
    293, **309n**, 312, 313, 315, 330, 330n
Porter, Endymion, 194n
Porters, 226, 229, 265
Pouchmakers, 25
Pratt, Alderman Sir Henry, 92n, 96, 98,
    101n, 109-10, 114n, 158n, 249n,
    266n, **303-4**
Preston, John, 6, 160-1, 163, 166-7, 184

Price, Richard, 223n
Printing trades, 16
Privy Council, see Charles I and Privy
    Council
Proby, Sir Peter, 70
Protections, 115, 117, 128, 132, 136,
    150-1, 206, 302 (see also Protec-
    tions and, under Parliament,
    House of Lords)
Protestation, 115, 145, 148, 148n, **218**
Providence Island Company, 41, 165,
    168-9, 178
Prynne, William, 166, 211
Pulling, Alexander, 45
Puritans and Puritanism, see also Par-
    liamentary puritans; Lectures and
    Lecturers; Political independents;
    Political presbyterians; and under
    London (constitutional): *Aldermen*
    and *Common Councilmen*; 79, 161,
    295, 304-5; attempt to establish
    Puritan ministry, 220; Church
    practises, 124; City Puritan move-
    ment, Ch. V *passim*, 211; collec-
    tions, 231, 264; disorder in London
    and, 107-9, 123-4; diversity of
    opinion within Puritan movement,
    278-80; exhortations from pulpit,
    231-2, 253, 264; opposition to
    Laud's policy, 107-8, 161, 166,
    167, 174, 181, 183, 189; puritan
    ministers, 242, 278, 280; suburbs
    and, 40-42; the term puritan, 5-6,
    124, 160-2
Purprestures, 21, 22, 84, 84n, 86 (see
    also Wastes)
Pym, M.P., John, 1, 41-42, 113-14, 117,
    126, 132, 145, 158-9, 160, 162, 166,
    182, 183, 184, 195, 196, 198-9,
    201-3, 207, 210-11, 217-19, 221,
    227, **228-30**, 234, 237, 239, 241,
    250, 253, 256-7, 258-9, 260, 267,
    272, 272n, 274, 276, 280

Quakers, 184

Radicals, City, and radicalism (war
    party and 'fierie spirits'), 201, 203,
    238, 239, **250-62**, **267-75**, 280, 284
    see also radicals and, under
    London (constitutional): *Common
    Councilmen and Court of Common*

Radicals—*cont.*
  Council; City radicals and, under
  Parliament, *House of Commons*
Rainton, Alderman Sir Nicholas, 100,
  114n, 118, 139, 140, 149n, 156,
  157, 161, **304-5**
Ranke, Leopold von, 2
Rawden, Marmaduke, 121, 172, 188,
  207n, 265, 266n
Recorder, see London (constitutional):
  Recorder; Gardiner, Sir Thomas;
  Littleton, Sir Edward; Glynne,
  John
Reading, John, 34, 37
Refiners of Gold and Silver used by
  wiredrawers, 328-9
Remembrancer, 67, 71, 247 (see also
  Wiseman, Thomas)
Repertories of Court of Aldermen, 4-5,
  32, 45-6, 49, 118, 339-40
Revenues, see Customs Farms; Excise
  Commissioners; loans and requests
  for loans; London (constitutional):
  *City government, privileges, powers and
  revenues* and *City Chamber*; Ship
  Money; Tonnage and Poundage;
  Weekly assessment; Weekly volun-
  tary collection
Reynardson, Alderman Sir Abraham,
  149n, 154n, 239n, **305-6**
Ricaut, Sir Peter, 328
Riccard, Andrew, 121, 150
Rich family, the, 26-27
— Robert, first Earl of Warwick, 26, 42n
— Robert, second Earl of Warwick, 41,
  92, 115, 166, 168, 170, 204-5, 208,
  219, 229, 286, 288
— Sir Henry, Earl of Holland, 27, 42
Riley, Theophilus, 259n
'Rily the Bodice maker', 148
Riots and disturbances, see also law and
  order and, under London (con-
  stitional): *Aldermen and Court of
  Aldermen, Common Councilmen and
  Court of Common Council, Lord Mayor*;
  City government, law and order,
  and Trained Bands (1570-1641),
  16, 17, 37-41; (1641-2), 40, 119-20,
  125, 131-2, 141-3, 156-7, 181,
  216-17, 221, 224, 226; seamen and
  (1626-42), 76-7, 107-8, 145, 178,
  278; clothworkers, apprentices and
  artisans (1639-41), 107-8, 180-1,

217, 224, 227, 234, 235; Garway,
  Alderman, and (1640), 300; Puritanism and (1641), 40-41, 107-9,
  123-4, 161; Catholics and (1641),
  39; citizens against Bishops (1641),
  130-1, 222-4; citizens against
  Strafford (1641), 216-17; Gurney,
  Alderman, and (1641-2), 156-7;
  citizens at Westminster (1641-2),
  39, 181, 216-17, 221, 224, 226-7,
  235; labourers and porters
  (1641-3), 226-7, 228, 236, 278;
  Gayre, Alderman, and (1647), 302;
  Warner, Alderman, and (1647),
  327; St. George's Fields, 107-8,
  181, 235
Roberts, Captain Lewes, 283
Robin Hood Society, 233
Robinson, Alderman Sir John, 307
Roe, M.P., Sir Thomas, 211
Rogers, Christopher, 167, 167n
Rolle, M.P., John, 78, 194n
Rossingham, Edward, 95, 96, 98, 99,
  102, 112, 174
Rowe, Francis, 144
— Owen, 41, 137, 140, 144, 155, 156,
  169, 171, 244, **324**
Royal Contract Estates, 81-82, 84, 85,
  86, 93-94, 98, 118, 303, 333n
Rudge, Edward, 114n
Russell, Francis, fourth Earl of Bedford,
  42, 205
— James, 140n, 156, 240, 244, 259n,
  324-5
— Sir William, 77
Russia Company, 99, 192, 299

Sackville, Sir Edward, fourth Earl of
  Dorset, 180, 221
Saddlers' Company, 75
Sailors, 12, 76-77, 107-8, 145, 178, 226,
  278
St. Antholin's, 79, 163, 167, 231, 264
  (see also Lectures and Lecturers)
— Bartholomew's Fair, 26
— Bartholomew's Hospital, 11, 16, 23,
  311
— Bartholomew the Great, Priory of,
  11, 26-27, 42n
St. John's Priory, 11
— Mary Spittle, Priory of, 11, 18
— Paul's, scheme for rebuilding, 71, 79,
  91, 94, 180, 295

St. Thomas' Hospital, 16, 295
Salters' Company, 94n, 102, 161n, 185, 207-8n
Salwey, M.P., Humphrey, 228
— M.P., Richard, 228
Sandys, Sir Edwin, 285, 288
Saye and Sele, Lord, see Fiennes, William
Scots Army and War, 91, 103, 104, 107, 175, 197, 202-3, 289, 307-8
Scots Commissioners, 131, 199-200, 231
Seamen, see Sailors
Secondary of City Compter, 64
Sharpe, R. R., 2, 46
Sheriffs, see London (constitutional): *Sheriffs and Sheriffs' Court*
Sherland, Christopher, 165
Shetterden, Isaac, 176
Shipbuilding, 12, 185-6, 189, 282
Ship Money, 21, 62, **88-91,** 106, 109, 117, 118, 118n, 175, 190, 192, 223, 243, 244, 287, 293, 314-15, 33n, 337
Shoemakers, 25, 229, 265
Shops, 217, 221, 234
Shute, Richard, 174, 252, 252n, 253, 255, 260-1
Sibbes, Richard, 166, 179
Sidney, Robert, second Earl of Leicester, 200
Silk industry, 15, 16, 25
Silkmen, Incorporation of, 243, 315
Singleton, Mr., 297-8
Skinners' Company, 94n, 117, 161n, 187, 207n, 303, 331
Skippon, Philip, 144, 173, 226, 252
Smethwicke, Thomas, 123
Smith, Thomas, 65
Soames, Alderman Sir Thomas, 89, 97, 100, 111, 112, 114n, 124, 129-30, 157, 172, 175, 188, **191-2,** 198, 204, 209, 253, 267
Soapboilers, London Company of, 93, 119, 294
Southwark, 13, 13n, 14, 15, 23, **28-29,** 30, 40, 43, 107, 116, 234, 294, 323
Spanish Company and merchants trading to Spain, 285, 290
Spectaclemakers' Company, 87
Speed, John, 9
Spurstow, M.P., William, 75, 169, 194n
Stagg, Mrs. Ann, 226

Staple, merchants, of, 97, 295
Star Chamber, Court of, 37, 86, 111, 178, 186, 187, 192
Stationers, 25
Steele, Robert, 261
Stock, Richard, 163, 164, 165, 189
Stone, Mary, 167, 167n
Stoughton, John, 166
Stow, John, 9, 10, 11, 12, 18, 24, 25, 38, 46-47, 48, 337
Strode, M.P., William, 150, 201, 203, 239, 270
Strangeways, M.P., Sir John, 202, 221, 234
Strype, John, 10, 14, 45, 48, 59, 66
Sub-committee concerning weekly assessment, Weavers' Hall, 253
Sub-committee of Volunteers, Salters' Hall, 251, 260, **267-9,** 292
Suckling, Sir John, 218
Sugar-refining, 15
Surrey, Justices of the Peace, 17, 28, 29, 30, 31 (see also Justices of the Peace)

Tailors, 15, 25
Tanners, 107
Tavern clubs, 233-4, 279
Taylor, Thomas, 74, 166, 179
Thompson, Maurice, 172, 174, 282-3, 310, 327, 331
Thomson, Alderman Sir William, 327
Tile-making, 16
Tobacco-pipe-makers, 87
Tonnage and Poundage, 72, 118, 122, 123, 171, 175, 190, 223, 244, 314, 316
Tower, Lieutenant of, see London
Town Clerk, 52, 62n, 64, 246-7
Towse, Alderman John, 140n, 144, 151n, 154n, 158n, 171, 173, 208n, 210, 240, 242-3, 243n, 261, **325**
Trading Companies (see also individual companies), 241n, 274, 278, 282-4
Trained Bands, 17, 70, 77, 95, 105, 108, 119, 127, 131-2, 142, 144-5, 149n, 159, 162, 173, 181, 191, 216, 221, 223n, 225, 251, 253, 266, 277, 279, 294, 301, 312, 323, 324, 325, 326, 330
Trevor-Roper, Professor H. R., 133n
Turner, Richard, 223n

Undersheriff, 64, 247

Vane, M.P., junior, Sir Henry, 42, 186, 203, 229
— M.P., senior, Sir Henry, 103
Vassall, John, 189
— M.P., Samuel, 75, 78, 87, 108, 113, 118n, 146, 169, 170, 172, 175, 176, 187-8, **189-91,** 193, 206, 218, 224, 229, 253
Venetian Ambassador, 98, 107, 152n, 190-1, 263, 265
Venn, M.P., Captain John, 115, 126, 131, 146, 151n, 155, 156, 163, 167, 169, 172-3, 175, **187-9,** 196n, 205, 209, 216, 219, 220, 221, 223, 224, 225, 226, 227, 228, 229, 234, 236, 237, 256, 276, 280
Venner's rising, 184
Vere, Lady Mary, 41
— Sir Horace, 173
Vernon, Christopher, 21, 84n
Vicars, John, 232n
Vintners' Company, 75, 76, 94n, 265, 289, 290, 291
Violet, Thomas, 328-9
Virginia, colony of, 189
— Company, 285, 288, 296, 297, 306
Visscher, C. J., 9

Waller, Edmund, 136n, 148n, 204, 265
— M.P., Captain Henry, 75, 171, 175, 313
— Sir William, 271, 272
Wallington, Nehemiah, 133, 141, 142, 217
Walwyn, William, 253n
Wardmote, see London (constitutional): *Wardmote*
Wardour, Sir Edward, 85n
Warner, Alderman John, 100, 114n, 140, 144, 149, 156, 167, 167n, 208n, 210, 240, 242, 243n, 244, 261, 274n, **325-7**
— Alderman Samuel, 140n, 151n, 223n, 242, 244, 244n, 245, 249, 274n, 326, **327**
Warwick Castle, 165
Wastes, 21, 22 (see also Purprestures)
Watermen, Company of, 120
Watkins, Sir David, 253, 254n, 260

Watkins, William, 194n
Weaving trade, 15, 16, 38, 107, 229
Webb, Thomas, 194n
Weekly assessment, 210, 253, 257, 258, 260
— voluntary collection, 209-10
Weld, John, 246-7
Wentworth, Sir Thomas, first Earl of Strafford, 20, 80, 83, 85, 100, 115, 151, 201, 205, 211, 216, 217, 300, 306
West, Francis, 144
Westminster, 11, 13, 15, 16, 25, 28, 28n, 33, 34, 37, 39, 40, 42, 69, 74, 129, 145, 151, 180
— Assembly of Divines, 232
— Company of Soapboilers, 119, 294
Weston, Richard, first Earl of Portland, 79
Wheeler, M.P., William, 42n, 217
White, John, 169, 194-5, 213
Whitmore, Alderman Sir George, 92n, 93, 96, 97, 98, 101n, 114n, 118, 119, 126, 126n, 129, 145, 149n, 153, 154n, 157, 159n, 195n, 239n, 248n, 255n, 257, 257n, 266, **306-7**
Wilde, Serjeant, 151, 156
Williams, Thomas, 37
Wilson, Alderman Rowland, 144, 308
Windebank, Sir Francis, 97, 103, 104, 109, 110, 111, 112, 200, 287, 289, 304
Windham, Alderman Sir Hugh, 158n, 207n, 239n, 248n, 249n, 257, 257n, 266n, **327-8**
— Edmund, 194n
— Colonel Francis, 328
Winthrop, John, 188, 192, 194-5
Wiseman, Sir Richard, 224
— Thomas, see also London, (constitutional): *Remembrancer*; 67, 110, 121, 123, 129, 129n, 149, 156, 247
Withers, John, 137, 196n
Wollaston, Alderman Sir John, 97, 100, 114n, 126n, 129, 140n, 144, 154n, 157, 171, 210, 238n, 240, 241, 243, 274, 282, 320, **328-31**
Wolstenholme, Sir John, 93, 252n
Women, 143, 226, 264, 272
Wood, Anthony à, 7, 167n, 228
Wren, Matthew, Bishop of Norwich, 242, 312
Wren, Melvin, 3, 4, 134-5, 137

Wright, Alderman Sir Edmund, 91, 98, 111, 112, 114n, 118-9, 120-2, 149n, 156, 159, 239n, 255, 259-60, **307-8**
— John, 331
— Nathaniel, 140n, 169, 171, 196n, 243, 310, **331**

Wroth, M.P., Sir Peter, 124
Wyngaerde, Anthony van, 9

Young, Lewis, 176, 179
— Matthew 179
— Thomas, 168